COMMUNICATION DESIGN 2000

A handbook
from
Heinz Kroehl

Ein Handbuch
von
Heinz Kroehl

Un manuel
de
Heinz Kroehl

For all who
are concerned
with
communication,
advertising
and design.

Für alle,
die mit
Kommunikation,
Werbung
und Design
zu tun haben.

Pour toutes les
personnes qui
travaillent dans le monde
de la communication,
de la publicité
et du design.

ABC Edition
Zurich

ABC Verlag
Zürich

Editions ABC
Zurich

1

Nowadays, communication must be regarded as the central function of design. By derivation, the literal meaning of "to communicate" is "to make communal". Communication is always based on an exchange of signs and can operate only when communicator and recipient give these signs the same meaning. In this context it is necessary to define design as "planning" rather than "execution". That is to say that planning must precede action. The designer is no longer simply the executant, putting external ideas into effect within the framework of a scheme, but one who takes the attitude of the public as the object of his creative work, in which he makes use of science, technology and aesthetics.

Kommunikation muss heute als die zentrale Aufgabe des Designs angesehen werden. Wörtlich übersetzt heisst Kommunikation «Herstellung von Gemeinsamkeit». Sie beruht immer auf dem Austausch von Zeichen, und sie kann nur funktionieren, wenn Sender und Empfänger die gleiche Bedeutung damit verbinden. In diesem Zusammenhang ist es notwendig, dass Design als «Planen» definiert wird und weniger als «Ausführen». Das analytische Denken muss also dem Tun vorausgehen. Der Designer ist nicht mehr nur Ausführender, der innerhalb eines Schemas von aussen kommende Ideen materialisiert, sondern er nimmt mit Hilfe von Wissenschaft, Technologie und Ästhetik das Rezipientenverhalten selbst zum Gegenstand seiner Kreationen.

L'on doit considérer aujourd'hui la communication comme étant la mission centrale du design. Etymologiquement, communication signifie «mise en commun». Elle est toujours fondée sur l'échange de signes et ne peut fonctionner que si l'émetteur et le récepteur leur confèrent la même signification, ce qui revient à dire que le répertoire de signes doit être commun. A ce propos, le design doit être défini comme «planification» plutôt que comme «exécution». Ainsi, la planification réfléchie doit précéder l'action. Le designer n'est plus seulement un exécutant qui matérialise dans un certain cadre des idées venant de l'extérieur; au contraire, avec l'aide de la science, de la technologie et de l'esthétique, il fait du comportement du récepteur lui-même l'objet de ses créations.

2

Looking at mankind's communicative relationships and our communicative environment leads to the question: "Do we have too much or too little communication today?" Our answer will not in any way agree with the widespread notion that we are overwhelmed by an avalanche of information. To some researchers it seems almost unbelievable that ever larger groups of people declare: "We want more information!" Up to 60 per cent of the population would be glad to have more information on countless political and economic matters. Our thesis is that we are suffering neither from a lack nor from an excess of information, but from the present level of competence of verbal and visual communication in a chanching world.

Der Blick auf die kommunikativen Beziehungen der Menschen zueinander und ihrer Kommunikationsumwelt führt zu der Frage: «Haben wir heute zuviel oder zuwenig Kommunikation?» Die nachfolgende Antwort passt überhaupt nicht zu der weitverbreiteten Vorstellung, wir kämpften mit einer Informationslawine. So klingt es für die Forschung geradezu unglaublich, wenn immer wieder grössere Bevölkerungsgruppen erklären: Wir wollen mehr Information. Zu unzähligen Themen aus Politik und Wirtschaft hätten gerne bis zu 60 Prozent der Bevölkerung mehr Informationen. Unsere These: Wir leiden weder unter einer Flut noch unter einem Mangel an Information, sondern am Niveau der verbalen und visuellen Kommunikation unserer Zeit.

Une observation des rapports entre les hommes et le milieu de communication dans lequel ils vivent suscite la question de savoir si nous avons aujourd'hui trop ou trop peu de communication. La réponse que nous apportons ci-dessous s'oppose à l'idée largement répandue selon laquelle nous nous débattons contre une avalanche d'informations. Ainsi, les chercheurs n'en croient pas toujours leurs oreilles quand des secteurs de plus en plus larges de la population réclament davantage d'information. Jusqu'à 60% des gens souhaiteraient être plus informés sur d'innombrables sujets politiques et économiques. Notre thèse est la suivante: nous ne souffrons ni d'un déluge ni d'une pénurie d'information: c'est plutôt du niveau de la communication verbale et visuelle que nous pâtissons.

3

The development of visual and audiovisual media has utterly changed communication behaviour. The omnipresence of the picture plays the principal role in the formation of a pictorial sign system as an independent form of communication. It is not only that technical development has led the picture to take an ever greater share in communication. This purely quantitative aspect is joined by a decisive qualitative factor, namely the development of an independent "pictorial language". Films, television, illustrated magazines and comics have all made a contribution to this development, which undoubtedly finds its most systematic use in the field of advertising. Questions of creativity are becoming more and more urgent at the same time as the material of pictorial communication becomes increasingly important.

Die Entwicklung der visuellen und audiovisuellen Medien hat das Kommunikationsverhalten entscheidend verändert. Die Allgegenwart des Bildes spielt vor allem bei der Herausbildung eines bildlichen Zeichensystems als eigenständige Kommunikationsform eine wichtige Rolle. Nicht nur, dass die technische Entwicklung zu einem immer grösseren Anteil des Bildes an der Kommunikation führte, zu diesem zunächst rein quantitativen Aspekt tritt eine entscheidende qualitative Komponente: die Entwicklung einer eigenständigen «Sprache des Bildes». Film, Fernsehen, Illustrierte und Comics haben zu dieser Entwicklung beigetragen, die wohl am systematischsten im Bereich der Werbung genutzt wird. Gerade weil bildliches Kommunikationsmaterial eine ständig wachsende Bedeutung erlangt.

Le développement des médias visuels et audiovisuels a considérablement modifié les comportements en matière de communication. L'omniprésence de l'image joue un rôle particulièrement important dans la formation d'un système de signes figuratif en tant que forme autonome de communication. Certes, l'évolution technique a donné à l'image une part de plus en plus grande dans la communication; mais outre cet aspect purement quantitatif, une composante qualitative décisive apparaît: le développement d'un «langage de l'image» indépendant. Le cinéma, la télévision, les illustrés et la bande dessinée ont contribué à ce phénomène, qui est sans doute exploité de la manière la plus systématique dans la publicité. C'est précisément parce que le matériel de communication figuratif qui acquiért une importance croissante.

4

Neglect of basic research in this special area has so far stood in crass contrast with the scientific and economic findings mentioned here. It is astonishing to observe that so far there is no general theory of visual communication, despite the fact that, in the future, the optimization of communicative processes will become essential. The designer of communication, as the "sign maker" for nearly all areas of life, must become aware of this problem and try to work it out. Design now covers the planning of our material environment, a challenge which calls for interdisciplinary collaboration.

Im krassen Gegensatz zu der hier skizzierten Bedeutung von wissenschaftlichen und ökonomischen Erkenntnissen steht die bisherige Vernachlässigung von eigener Grundlagenforschung. Man ist mehr als verwundert über die Tatsache, dass wir bis heute über keine Theorie der visuellen Kommunikation verfügen. Und dies trotz der Tatsache, dass in Zukunft die Optimierung kommunikativer Prozesse unabdingbar wird. Der Kommunikationsdesigner als «Zeichenproduzent» nahezu aller Lebensbereiche muss sich dieser Problematik bewusst werden und sich intellektuell mit ihr auseinandersetzen. Design umfasst letztlich die Planung unserer materialen Umwelt und braucht die interdisziplinäre Zusammenarbeit bei dieser Herausforderung.

L'importance évoquée ici des connaissances économiques et scientifiques contraste violemment avec l'absence observée jusqu'à présent de toute recherche fondamentale propre. On ne laisse de s'étonner qu'il n'existe pas aujourd'hui de théorie de la communication visuelle, alors qu'à l'avenir l'optimisation des processus de communication sera indispensable. Le designer de communication, en tant que «producteur de dessins» pour presque tous les domaines de la vie, doit prendre conscience de ces problèmes et prendre la peine d'y réfléchir. Le design englobe la planification de notre environnement matériel; pour relever ce défi, une collaboration interdisciplinaire est essentielle.

5

Consideration of the development of communications research brings us to the subject of modern semiotics (the theory of signs), without which a creative presentation, i.e. the development of signs and messages, is hardly imaginable. We must therefore make greater use of semiotics as the communications science for our profession. The objects of research of that science are sign processes and the result should be an adequate understanding of the specific dynamics of signs. The pictorial presence of a visual statement in the public eye, in effect all optical appearances, have the character of signs. They say something definite; they communicate. This fact correlates with studies that conclude that almost 80 per cent of the information issued about a company is of a visual nature. This makes design to a marketing factor.

Im Zusammenhang mit der Entwicklung der Kommunikationsforschung stossen wir auf die moderne Semiotik, ohne die eine kreative Gestaltung, also die Entwicklung von Zeichen und Botschaften, kaum denkbar ist. Wir müssen deshalb verstärkt die Semiotik als Kommunikationswissenschaft für unseren Beruf fruchtbar machen. Ihr Untersuchungsgegenstand sind Zeichenprozesse. Man ist damit in der Lage, die spezifische Dynamik von Zeichen adäquat zu erfassen. Die bildliche Präsenz einer visuellen Aussage im öffentlichen Bereich, also sämtliche optisch in Erscheinung tretenden Elemente haben Zeichencharakter, sagen etwas Bestimmtes aus, kommunizieren. Studien besagen, dass fast 80 Prozent der Informationen über ein Unternehmen visueller Art sind. Dies macht den Corporate-Design-Gedanken zum Marktfaktor.

L'évolution de la recherche en communication nous conduit vers la sémiotique, sans laquelle on ne peut guère concevoir de réalisation créatrice, c'est-à-dire de développement de dessins et de messages. Notre profession doit ainsi s'efforcer de mieux tirer profit de la sémiotique en tant que science de la communication. Cette discipline a pour objet l'étude des processus des signes. Elle permet de saisir la dynamique spécifique des signes. La présence figurative d'un message visuel, tous les éléments qui se manifestent optiquement, ont le caractère de signe, expriment quelque chose de précis, communiquent. Cette réalité est exprimée par des études selon lesquelles presque 80% des informations concernant une entreprise sont de type visuel. Ainsi, l'idée du corporate design est un facteur de marché central.

6

The coming years will be marked by an important current development, namely that design is taking on a key role in marketing against a background of stronger competition, limited resources and narrowing markets. Design will develop into an important means of differentiation, contributing more and more to the competitive profiling of the company. Design supplies a clearly outlined image of a company as a whole, leading to both an outward and an inward corporate identity through its role in communication. One thing is certain: the association of design in all its aspects with company strategy will make it necessary for the designer and the manager to show their ability to communicate with each other.

Eine aktuelle Entwicklung wird die nächsten Jahre prägen: Vor dem Hintergrund stärkeren Wettbewerbs, begrenzter Ressourcen und enger werdender Märkte erhält Design als Marketingfaktor eine Schlüsselfunktion. Design wird sich zu einem wichtigen Differenzierungsinstrument entwickeln, das immer mehr zur Profilierung der Unternehmen im Wettbewerb beitragen kann. Design liefert ein fest umrissenes Bild des gesamten Unternehmens, das in seiner kommunikativen Umsetzung zur Corporate Identity nach aussen wie nach innen führt. Eines ist voraussehbar: Weil Design in seiner Gesamtbreite mit der Unternehmensstrategie verbunden ist, müssen in Zukunft Designer und Manager ihre Dialogfähigkeit unter Beweis stellen.

Une tendance déjà observée va marquer les années à venir: dans un contexte de concurrence accrue, de ressources limitées et de resserrement des marchés, le design devient un facteur-clé du marketing. Le design va devenir un instrument de différenciation important qui pourra de plus en plus contribuer à mettre en valeur l'entreprise par rapport à la concurrence. Le design apporte une image bien définie de toute l'entreprise. Appliquée à la communication, cette image conduit à l'affirmation de la corporate identity, aussi bien à l'extérieur qu'à l'intérieur. Le design dans son ensemble étant lié à la stratégie de l'entreprise, il est prévisible qu'à l'avenir les designers et les managers devront faire preuve de capacité à dialoguer.

7

The modern environment is strongly marked by concepts such as rationalism and functionalism in many of its outward aspects, taking little account of emotional needs. Industry being so much concerned to supply functionally efficient equipment, many areas of life suffer from a joyless environment. In response, there have been cautious attempts to modify the underlying ideological themes under the banner of ''postmodernism''. It would be more to the point to regard these problems as a challenge for the establishment of completely new principles. Despite the findings of environmental psychology, which concerns itself with the influence of the physical environment on human behaviour, we find that these basic human needs are hardly taken into consideration by manufacturers.

Die heutige Umweltgestaltung ist in weiten Bereichen von Begriffen wie Rationalismus und Funktionalismus geprägt. Sie nimmt wenig Rücksicht auf die emotionalen Bedürfnisse ihrer Benutzer. Eben weil die Industrie darauf fixiert ist, funktionsgerechte Einrichtungen zu liefern, hat dies in vielen Lebensbereichen zu einer freudlosen Umwelt geführt. So wird der Versuch unternommen, die erwähnten Leitbilder behutsam umzuformen und mit dem Etikett «Postmodernismus» zu versehen. Richtiger wäre, beides als Herausforderung für die Grundlegung eines gänzlich neuen Paradigmas zu betrachten. Trotz Erkenntnissen der Umweltpsychologie, die sich mit dem Einfluss der psychischen Umwelt auf das menschliche Verhalten beschäftigt, werden diese Bedürfnisse der Menschen von den Herstellern kaum wahrgenommen.

Dans bien des domaines, l'aménagement actuel de notre environnement est marqué par des considérations telles que le rationalisme ou le fonctionnalisme. Il n'est guère tenu compte des besoins émotionnels des usagers. C'est justement parce que l'industrie tient avant tout à créer des installations fonctionnelles que la joie est souvent absente de notre cadre de vie. On essaie de transformer soigneusement les idéaux mentionnés et de leur coller l'étiquette du «postmodernisme». Il serait plus judicieux de les considérer comme un défi pour établir un paradigme entièrement nouveau. Malgré les enseignements de la psychologie de l'environnement, qui étudie l'influence de l'environnement psychique sur le comportement humain, on constate que les industriels ne perçoivent guère les besoins fondamentaux de l'homme.

8

Many events are beyond the reach of immediate perception and are conveyed through the media. Examples are new images, happenings in space, artificial landscapes, robots, etc. This conveying of secondary experience is a characteristic of our times. When the horizon of human experience or culture broadens in such a dramatic way, the importance of the repertoire of signs increases likewise. The formation of a ''vicarious universe'', a world actuated by signs through global communication, is one of the key concepts for the characterization of our modern civilization. It means that the designer must be able to analyze, interpret and illustrate connections between developments.
We hope that the present work will make a small contribution to the understanding of this development.

Viele Ereignisse entziehen sich der unmittelbaren Wahrnehmung, sie werden von Medien vermittelt. So sind dies beispielsweise neue Bilder, Geschehnisse aus dem Weltall, künstliche Landschaften, Roboter usw. Diese Vermittlung von Sekundärerfahrung ist ein Charakteristikum unserer Zeit. Wenn sich der Erfahrungshorizont der Menschen oder der Kultur derart explosiv erweitert, so nimmt vor allem der Anteil des Zeichenrepertoires zu. Die Entstehung eines ''vicarious universe'', einer Welt aus Zeichen, ausgelöst durch weltweite Kommunikation, ist einer der Schlüsselbefunde zur Charakterisierung unserer modernen Zivilisation. Dies erfordert vom Designer die Fähigkeit, Zusammenhänge von Entwicklungen analysieren, interpretieren und veranschaulichen zu können.
Dazu leistet dieses Buch einen Beitrag.

Beaucoup d'événements ne sont pas perçus directement, mais par l'intermédiaire des médias: nouvelles images, aventure spatiale, paysages artificiels, robots, etc. Cet apport d'expériences «de seconde main» est caractéristique de notre époque. Quand l'horizon des expériences de l'homme ou de la civilisation s'élargit de manière aussi prodigieuse, c'est avant tout l'étendue du répertoire des signes qui augmente. L'apparition d'un «vicarious universe», d'un monde de signes engendré par la communication mondiale, constitue l'un des éléments-clé pour définir notre civilisation. Ainsi, le designer doit être capable d'analyser, d'interpréter et d'illustrer les événements et leur contexte.
Dans le cadre de cette évolution, le présent ouvrage se propose d'apporter une modeste contribution.

ISBN 3-85504-106-7
Printed in Switzerland

Contents

Inhalt

Sommaire

AD = Art Director / Directeur artistique
D = Designer / Gestalter / Maquettiste
Ph = Photographer / Fotograf / Photographe
Ar = Architect / Architekt / Architecte
A = Agency / Agentur / Agence

1. Introduction

1.1. Functions of visual communication

It is not often that one takes full account of the extreme importance of visual communication in our modern urban environment. Direction signs, traffic signs, company name plates and trademarks have come to be taken for granted and we scarcely realize the extent to which they govern our actions. This fact becomes most apparent when we have to find our bearings in a new environment such as a railway station or airport, where information systems of many kinds are used. Such systems came to the attention of a large public for the first time in the form of pictograms for the Olympic Games in Tokyo, Munich and Los Angeles. These were prime examples of the superiority of a pictorial language in overcoming familiar barriers of understanding.

Nevertheless, pictograms form only a small part, not even a typical part, of a pictorial language. In this context, the meaning of "picture" should not be too narrowly defined. For example, typography and alphabetic characters are also pictorial elements of communication. Pictograms are not, therefore, typical examples of a pictorial language, because they are conventional in their meaning, being based on explicit conventions, whereas pictorial language is essentially a natural language, governed by its own intrinsic rules. The development and acquisition of such a language follow the same basic principles as those of a spoken language. We encounter this natural language of pictures in children's drawings, in paintings, in holiday snapshots and press photos.

Advertisements, posters, brochures and catalogues are some further examples from a series which could be extended almost indefinitely.

1. Einleitung

1.1. Aufgaben der visuellen Kommunikation

Selten macht man sich die eminente Bedeutung der visuellen Kommunikation in unserer heutigen urbanen Umwelt wirklich bewusst. Hinweisschilder, Verkehrszeichen, Firmenschilder und Signets sind uns zur Selbstverständlichkeit geworden, und wir nehmen kaum noch das Ausmass wahr, in dem sie unser Verhalten steuern. Am ehesten wird man noch darauf aufmerksam, wenn man sich in einer neuen Umgebung orientieren muss, etwa auf einem Bahnhof oder einem Flughafen. Die verschiedensten visuellen Informationssysteme wurden in solchen Zusammenhängen geschaffen. Ins Bewusstsein einer breiteren Öffentlichkeit traten derartige Systeme erstmals im Zusammenhang mit den Piktogrammen für die Olympischen Spiele in Tokio, München oder Los Angeles. Gerade an diesen Beispielen zeigt sich die Überlegenheit einer bildlichen Sprache, die die herkömmlichen Sprachbarrieren leichter überwindet.

Dennoch bilden Piktogramme nur ein kleines – nicht einmal typisches – Segment einer bildlichen Sprache. Den Begriff des Bildes darf man dabei nicht zu eng auslegen. So sind beispielsweise auch Typografie und Schriftcharakter bildliche Elemente der Kommunikation. Piktogramme sind deswegen kein typisches Beispiel für eine bildliche Sprache, weil sie in ihrer Bedeutung konventionell sind, das heisst auf expliziten Übereinkünften beruhen. Die bildliche Sprache ist jedoch ihrem Wesen nach eine natürliche Sprache, die sich aus sich selbst heraus regelt. Sprachentwicklung wie Spracherwerb entsprechen in ihren Grundprinzipien denen der Umgangssprache. Dieser natürlichen Sprache der Bilder begegnen wir in Kinderzeichnungen wie in Gemälden, in Urlaubs- wie in Pressefotos.

Anzeigen, Plakate, Prospekte und Kataloge sind einige weitere Beispiele einer Reihe, die man beliebig fortsetzen könnte.

1. Introduction

1.1. Les fonctions de la communication visuelle

Il est rare que l'on prenne vraiment conscience de l'extrême importance de la communication visuelle dans notre environnement urbain actuel. La présence de panneaux indicateurs, de signalisation routière, d'enseignes et de logos nous paraît aller de soi et nous ne percevons pratiquement plus à quel point ils guident notre comportement. Il arrive encore qu'on les remarque si l'on doit s'orienter dans un lieu inconnu, comme par exemple un aéroport ou une gare. Les systèmes d'information visuels les plus divers ont été créés dans ce type de contexte. Un public plus large a pris conscience de leur existence pour la première fois avec les pictogrammes des Jeux Olympiques de Tokyo, Munich ou Los Angeles. Ces exemples montrent précisément la supériorité d'un langage figuratif qui surmonte les barrières linguistiques traditionnelles.

Néanmoins, les pictogrammes constituent un segment restreint – et pas même caractéristique – d'un langage figuratif. L'interprétation de la notion d'image ne doit pas être trop étroite. Ainsi, la typographie et les caractères d'écriture, par exemple, sont des éléments figuratifs de la communication. Les pictogrammes ne sont pas un exemple typique de langage figuratif car ils sont conventionnels dans leur signification, c'est-à-dire qu'ils sont fondés sur des conventions explicites. Toutefois, le langage figuratif est par essence un langage naturel qui se réglemente de lui-même. Le développement et l'acquisition du langage correspondent dans leurs principes fondamentaux à ceux du langage familier. Nous rencontrons ce langage naturel des images dans les dessins d'enfants comme dans les tableaux, dans les photos de vacances comme dans celles de la presse.

Les annonces, les affiches, les prospectus et les catalogues sont d'autres exemples d'une série que l'on pourrait prolonger à volonté.

Over and above this primary picture language there is an increasing use of systems of visual communication, of which the most widespread today is the system of traffic signs. The spread of such systems is closely connected with the increasing complexity of our environment, in which the sign takes on the function of orientation. The significance of trademarks and company logotypes should also be understood in this context. The consumer's need for orientation confronts the producer's need for presentation, not only to draw attention to his products but also to associate the prestige that his company may have acquired with the product itself. The overall image of a company has more than just an informative effect; it must also build up prestige. To a great extent, a company is judged by its outward appearance. This presentation is not least a matter of internal structure and the clear division of areas of operation.

Thus visual communication becomes an important instrument of marketing, because the orientation of business to the market requires the integrating force of an image based on clear principles. The objectives of such an image now go far beyond the traditional fields of marketing communications in publicity and sales promotion. Nowadays there are, for example, interesting fields of application in distribution, by no means limited to vehicle livery. Systems of visual communication can be of great usefulness in storage and in packaging and can also play a part in production, with beneficial effects on the working environment.

No doubt there are great differences here between different branches of industry, but on the whole something

Neben diese primäre Bildersprache treten in zunehmendem Masse visuelle Kommunikationssysteme, von denen das allgegenwärtigste heute das System der Verkehrszeichen ist. Die Ausbreitung derartiger Systeme steht in engem Zusammenhang mit der gesteigerten Komplexität der Umwelt, in der den Zeichen eine Orientierungsfunktion zukommt. In diesem Zusammenhang ist dann auch die Bedeutung von Markenzeichen und Signets zu sehen. Dem Orientierungsbedürfnis von seiten der Konsumenten steht das Darstellungsbedürfnis der Produzenten gegenüber, die nicht nur die Aufmerksamkeit auf ihr Produkt lenken möchten, sondern auch das Prestige, das etwa ein Unternehmen erworben hat, auf das einzelne Produkt übertragen wollen. Das integrierende Gesamterscheinungsbild eines Unternehmens wirkt jedoch nicht nur vermittelnd, sondern auch prestigebildend; ein Unternehmen wird zu einem grossen Teil danach eingeschätzt, wie es sich nach aussen hin präsentiert. Die Präsentation ist nicht zuletzt eine Frage der internen Struktur, der klaren Gliederung der Funktionsbereiche.

So wird die visuelle Kommunikation zu einem wichtigen Instrument des Marketings. Denn gerade die Ausrichtung der unternehmerischen Massnahmen am Markt benötigt die integrierende Kraft einer an klaren Prinzipien ausgerichteten Gestaltung. Die Aufgaben einer solchen Gestaltung gehen heute weit über die traditionellen Bereiche der Marketingkommunikation – also hauptsächlich Werbung und Verkaufsförderung – hinaus. So stellen sich heute beispielsweise auch interessante Aufgaben im Bereich der Distribution, die sich keineswegs nur auf die Beschriftung von Lieferfahrzeugen beschränken. Visuelle Kommunikationssysteme können bei der Lagerhaltung wie beim Warenumschlag von grossem Nutzen sein. Aber auch bei der Produktion können solche Systeme eine Rolle spielen und das Arbeitsklima positiv beeinflussen.

Zweifellos gibt es hier grosse Unterschiede zwischen den verschiedenen Branchen, aber insgesamt ergibt sich

Outre ce langage primaire des images, des systèmes de communication visuelle se développent toujours davantage: le plus omniprésent d'entre eux est celui de la signalisation routière. L'expansion de ce type de système est étroitement liée à la complexité accrue du cadre de vie, dans lequel le signe reçoit une fonction d'information. L'importance des marques de fabrique et des logos doit être considérée dans ce contexte. Face au besoin d'information du consommateur se trouve le besoin de présentation du producteur qui veut non seulement attirer l'attention sur son produit, mais aussi lui transférer le prestige d'une entreprise. Outre sa fonction médiatrice, l'image générale d'une entreprise contribue au développement du prestige; une entreprise est jugée dans une large mesure d'après l'image qu'elle présente à l'extérieur. La présentation dépend dans une certaine mesure de la structure interne, de l'articulation claire des domaines de fonction.

Ainsi, la communication visuelle devient un instrument important du marketing. En effet, l'orientation de la politique de l'entreprise selon le marché nécessite la puissance d'intégration d'une création guidée par des principes clairs. Aujourd'hui, les fonctions de ce type de création vont bien au-delà des domaines traditionnels de la communication en marketing – à savoir principalement la publicité et la promotion des ventes. Ainsi, par exemple, il existe des travaux intéressants dans le domaine de la distribution qui ne se limitent pas du tout à concevoir des inscriptions pour les véhicules de livraison. Les systèmes de communication visuelle peuvent se montrer fort utiles aussi bien pour le stockage que pour la rotation des marchandises. Néanmoins, ces systèmes peuvent aussi jouer un rôle au stade de la production et influencer favorablement l'atmosphère de travail.

Il existe sans aucun doute des différences considérables d'une branche à l'autre, mais dans l'ensemble l'impor-

Communication and advertising are changing today's residential areas, our urban environment, from systems of architectonics to systems of semiotics. We live not only in a world of housing but also in a world of signs, and we move not only through streets but through channels of communication.

Max Bense

Verkehr und Werbung verwandeln die heutigen Wohngebiete, unsere urbanistischen Systeme, aus architektonischen in semiotische Systeme. Wir bewohnen nicht mehr nur Hauswelten, wir bewohnen auch Zeichenwelten. Denn wir bewegen uns nicht nur durch Strassenzüge, sondern auch durch Kommunikationskanäle.

Max Bense

Les transports et la publicité transforment nos régions d'habitation actuelles, nos systèmes urbanistiques, de systèmes architecturaux en systèmes sémiotiques. Nous n'habitons plus seulement des mondes de maisons, nous habitons des mondes de signes. En effet, nous ne nous déplaçons pas seulement dans des rues, mais aussi dans des canaux de communication.

Max Bense

like the following illustration shows the importance of visual communication in the various areas of marketing.

The more complex the structure of an organization, the more important becomes the role of visual communication in its existence. This principle applies particularly to service organizations, where the customer, as an outsider, is offered aids to orientation. This sector provides numerous tasks for the designer, who in this case has to provide environmental design in the truest sense. Many promising starts have already been made in the service sector: airports and railway stations have already been mentioned as examples, but banks and postal services are also cases in point. In contrast to the commercial sector, e.g. supermarkets and department stores, where the possibilities of visual communication have been recognized and put into use at a very early stage, public institutions and authorities came very late to the same realization and it can hardly be said that everything is for the best in these sectors. As a positive example, the activities of public libraries and hospitals may be cited as approaches to specific problems of communication. In recent times, the authorities have paid more attention to these problems, thereby making a real contribution to the celebrated policy of "openness" towards the citizen. A genuine aspect of public work is the illumination of procedures through information capable of promoting the insight and understanding of the citizen. Such tasks make great demands on the designer and cannot be mastered with his traditional palette. The designer must learn to comprehend communication as an interaction, a process in which the recipient is also able to become active and participate in the flow of information. It is only in this way that the rapidly growing flood of information in many fields can be canalized; for the danger is great that

etwa folgendes Bild für die Bedeutung der visuellen Kommunikation in den verschiedenen Bereichen des heutigen Marketings.

Je komplexer die Struktur eines Unternehmens ist, um so bedeutungsvoller wird die Rolle der visuellen Kommunikation als Organisationshilfe. Dies gilt in besonderem Masse für den Dienstleistungsbereich, in dem die Kunden als Aussenstehende auf Orientierungshilfen angewiesen sind. Hier gibt es zahlreiche Aufgaben für den Designer, der hier im wahrsten Sinne Umweltgestaltung zu leisten hat. Vielfach wurden hier schon entscheidende Ansätze gemacht; als Beispiele wurden bereits Flughäfen und Bahnhöfe genannt, aber auch Banken und die Post sind in diesem Zusammenhang zu nennen. Während im kommerziellen Bereich, etwa bei Supermärkten und Warenhäusern, die Möglichkeiten der visuellen Kommunikation sehr früh erkannt und auch genutzt wurden, stellten sich Institutionen und Behörden sehr viel später darauf ein, und man kann heute kaum behaupten, dass hier alles zum besten stünde. Als positives Beispiel kann man die Aktivitäten im Bereich der öffentlichen Bibliotheken oder Krankenhäuser anführen, in denen die spezifischen kommunikativen Probleme dieses Bereichs angegangen werden. Es wäre an der Zeit, dass man sich auch in den Behörden mehr Gedanken um diese Probleme machte und damit wirklich einmal ein Stück der vielbeschworenen Bürgernähe praktizierte. Dies wäre eine echte Aufgabe von Öffentlichkeitsarbeit, der Durchschaubarmachung von Vorgängen, wobei man durch Information Einsicht und Verständnis des Bürgers fördern könnte. Derartige Aufgaben stellen hohe Anforderungen an den Designer, die sich nicht mehr mit dem traditionellen Instrumentarium bewältigen lassen. Der Gestalter muss lernen, die Kommunikation als Interaktion zu begreifen, als einen Prozess, in dem der Rezipient selbst aktiv werden kann und den Informationsfluss mitbestimmt. Die in vielen Bereichen enorm anwachsende Informationsflut kann nur auf diese Weise kanalisiert wer-

tance de la communication visuelle dans les différents secteurs du marketing peut être illustrée de la façon suivante.

Plus la structure d'une entreprise est complexe, plus le rôle de la communication visuelle dans le soutien à l'organisation devient essentiel. Tel est le cas en particulier dans le secteur des services, où le client non spécialiste a besoin qu'on l'aide à s'orienter. Le designer a ici de nombreuses tâches à accomplir: il doit véritablement aménager l'environnement. De nombreuses approches décisives ont déjà été faites dans ce domaine; nous avons déjà mentionné les aéroports et les gares à titre d'exemple, mais il convient de citer également les banques et la poste. Si dans le secteur commercial (supermarchés, grands magasins...) on a très tôt reconnu et utilisé les possibilités de la communication visuelle, les institutions et les administrations ont été beaucoup plus lentes, et l'on ne peut pas dire aujourd'hui que la situation soit brillante. Citons néanmoins les efforts remarquables faits dans le domaine des bibliothèques et des hôpitaux publics, où l'on a abordé les problèmes de communication spécifiques à ces institutions. Le moment est venu qu'une réflexion sur ce sujet s'engage aussi dans les administrations: il ne suffit pas de proclamer la nécessité de se rapprocher du citoyen, encore doit-on agir. Tel pourrait être l'objet d'une campagne d'explication des processus qui susciterait la compréhension du citoyen. Le designer se trouve là devant une tâche difficile pour laquelle les instruments traditionnels dont il dispose sont insuffisants. Le créateur doit apprendre à concevoir la communication comme une interaction, un processus dans lequel le récepteur peut devenir lui-même actif et influencer le flux d'information. Il n'existe pas d'autre moyen de canaliser le véritable torrent qui grossit

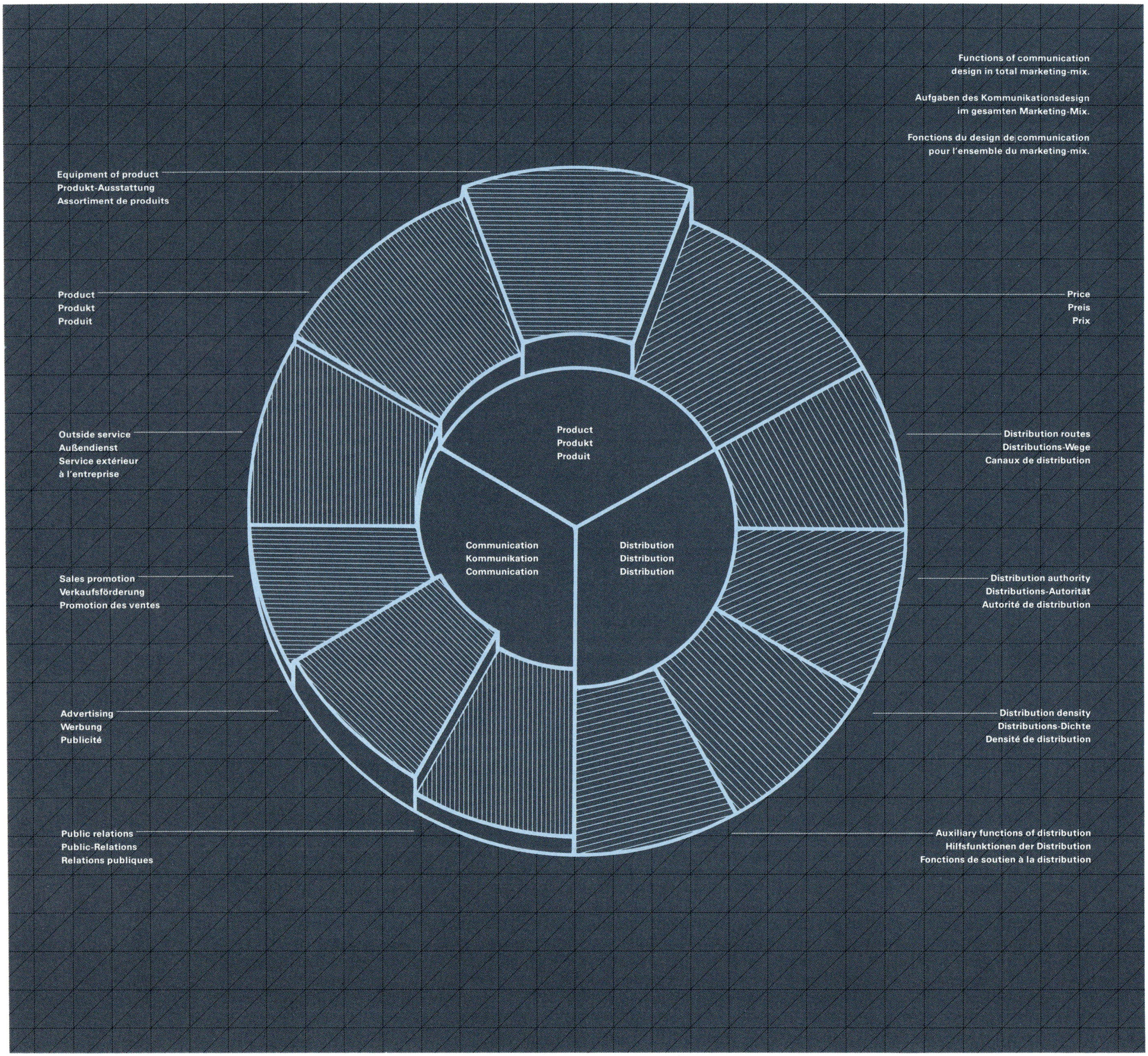
Functions of communication design in total marketing-mix.
Aufgaben des Kommunikationsdesign im gesamten Marketing-Mix.
Fonctions du design de communication pour l'ensemble du marketing-mix.
Equipment of product
Produkt-Ausstattung
Assortiment de produits
Product
Produkt
Produit
Price
Preis
Prix
Outside service
Außendienst
Service extérieur à l'entreprise
Distribution routes
Distributions-Wege
Canaux de distribution
Product
Produkt
Produit
Communication
Kommunikation
Communication
Distribution
Distribution
Distribution
Sales promotion
Verkaufsförderung
Promotion des ventes
Distribution authority
Distributions-Autorität
Autorité de distribution
Advertising
Werbung
Publicité
Distribution density
Distributions-Dichte
Densité de distribution
Public relations
Public-Relations
Relations publiques
Auxiliary functions of distribution
Hilfsfunktionen der Distribution
Fonctions de soutien à la distribution

information, simply through its quantity, can turn into its opposite and lead to total confusion.

The consequences for the designer's self-image and for design education are covered at the end of this book. At this point it must, however, be made quite clear that the following comments apply not only to the commercial artist or graphic designer but are made with the professional communicator in mind. This is the person who, on the basis of fundamental knowledge of the process of communication, can provide the decisive stimulus in a wide variety of fields. In addition to the entire spectrum of marketing work, mention may be made here of publicity for associations, institutions and political parties, and also architecture, town planning and urban development. In all these fields of activity and many more, the importance of visual communication is increasing. At the same time, one cannot assume that the visual elements of communication are of overriding importance but must endeavour to integrate them into the general communicative concept.

This approach requires a general theoretical basis for communication in all its practical applications — an extremely difficult task, which is the responsibility of the science of modern communications.

1.2. Communications based on theories

The solution of this problem is a challenge that must now be faced by communicators and designers, who cannot claim to have achieved any satisfactory results so far. The theory of communications is not to be completed by a few simple models and the systematization of the processes and influences concerned. On the other hand, it would be a mistake to regard these models as too unproductive to deserve consideration. They provide

den, denn die Gefahr ist gross, dass Information allein durch ihre Quantität ins Gegenteil umschlägt und zu völliger Desorientierung führt.

Ich werde erst am Schluss dieser Publikation auf die Konsequenzen für das Selbstbild des Gestalters und für seine Ausbildung eingehen. Es soll aber hier schon deutlich gesagt werden, dass sich die folgenden Ausführungen nicht nur auf Werbegrafiker oder Grafik-Designer beziehen, sondern das Bild eines Kommunikationsfachmannes vor Augen haben, der aufgrund seiner fundamentalen Kenntnisse des Kommunikationsprozesses in den verschiedensten Bereichen entscheidende Impulse geben kann. Neben dem gesamten Spektrum der Marketingaufgaben seien hier als weitere Tätigkeitsbereiche die Öffentlichkeitsarbeit für Verbände, Institutionen und Parteien genannt, daneben aber auch Architektur, Stadtplanung und Stadtentwicklung. In allen diesen und noch vielen anderen Bereichen nimmt die Bedeutung der visuellen Kommunikation zu. Man kann jedoch nicht von einem Primat der visuellen Elemente der Kommunikation ausgehen, sondern muss ihre Integration in das kommunikative Gesamtkonzept anstreben.

Dies setzt eine gemeinsame theoretische Basis für die Kommunikation in all ihren konkreten Erscheinungsformen voraus, eine äusserst diffizile Aufgabe, die der Kommunikationswissenschaft zufällt.

1.2. Kommunikation basiert auf Theorien

Die Lösung dieser Aufgabe ist eine Herausforderung, der sich Kommunikation und Design heute stellen müssen,und es kann keine Rede davon sein, dass dies bereits befriedigend gelungen ist. Die Kommunikationstheorie erschöpft sich nicht in einigen simplen Kommunikationsmodellen und der Systematisierung der dabei ablaufenden Prozesse und wirksam werdenden Einflüsse. Doch es muss zugleich davor gewarnt werden, diese Modelle für zu unergiebig zu halten, um sich mit ihnen zu beschäftigen. Sie

dans certains secteurs: par sa quantité même, l'information risque de se transformer en son contraire et de conduire à une désorientation complète.

C'est à la fin du présent ouvrage que je traiterai des conséquences de cette situation pour l'image que le créateur a de lui-même et pour sa formation. Néanmoins, il convient de préciser dès maintenant que les réflexions qui suivent ne concernent pas seulement le graphiste de publicité ou le graphic designer, mais aussi tout spécialiste de la communication capable d'exercer une influence décisive dans les domaines les plus variés en raison de ses connaissances fondamentales du processus de communication. Outre l'ensemble des activités de marketing, nous citerons les relations publiques pour les associations, les institutions et les partis, sans oublier l'architecture et l'urbanisme. Dans tous ces secteurs, et dans bien d'autres encore, la communication visuelle prend une importance croissante. Toutefois, il n'est pas possible de poser comme principe de base la primauté des éléments visuels: il faut s'efforcer de les intégrer dans le contexte global de la communication.

Pour mener à bien une telle entreprise, il est nécessaire d'établir au préalable une base théorique commune à toutes les formes concrètes de communication, tâche extrêmement ardue qui incombe à la science de la communication.

1.2. La communication est fondée sur des théories

L'accomplissement de cette mission est un défi que la communication et le design devraient relever aujourd'hui, car ils ne l'ont pas encore fait. La théorie de la communication ne se limite pas à quelques modèles simples de communication et à la systématisation des processus et des influences qu'ils représentent. Néanmoins, il faut se garder de considérer ces modèles comme trop improductifs pour être étudiés. A bien des égards, ils constituent des hypothèses fondamentales qui, si elles ne sont jamais suffisantes,

many basic propositions, which may well be inadequate but are not therefore to be disregarded. It has become fashionable to be dismissive of such "universal formulae", but fashion should not influence anyone who wishes to work with precision. Scientific principles never become old-fashioned; at most they are replaced by better ones or further developed through progress in knowledge. Our future professional image will be served best by carrying out basic research, not by standing aside. Unfortunately the science of semiotics, one of the most promising bases of communications science, has come under suspicion of being merely a fashionable trend. The fact that this accusation is all too often justified is not the fault of semiotics itself but of some of its practitioners. On the one hand there is the purely scientific approach, by which the subject is isolated as a sterile academic discipline, turned in on itself and incapable of any practical value.

On the other hand, there are practitioners who are unable to make use of the theory but simply wear the giant's robe of pseudoscience and do nothing more than play with scientific concepts. Both cases are typical examples of fashionable trends which do more harm than good to the meaningful development of sign theory. But fashion is ephemeral and time will tell what is really lasting in the science of semiotics.

Semiotics still has a somewhat marginal position in communications science, not least because of the dubious character it has acquired for the reasons given above, but clear evidence of an increasingly serious approach to the theory of signs can be observed. At the same time, there is much confusion about the real value

bilden vielfach grundlegende Voraussetzungen, die zwar niemals ausreichend sein können, nichtsdestoweniger aber unabdingbar sind. Es ist Mode geworden, über solche «Allerweltsformeln» nachsichtig und besserwissend hinwegzugehen, doch wer präzise arbeiten muss, sollte sich von solchen Moden nicht beeinflussen lassen. Wissenschaftliche Grundlagen werden niemals altmodisch, sie werden höchstens durch bessere ersetzt oder durch Erkenntnisfortschritte weiterentwickelt. Unserem zukünftigen Berufsbild ist also nur gedient, wenn wir nicht abseits stehen, sondern endlich eigene Grundlagenforschung betreiben. Leider ist gerade die Semiotik, eine der vielversprechendsten Basistheorien in der Kommunikationswissenschaft, in den Verdacht geraten, eine Modeerscheinung zu sein. Dass dies bedauerlicherweise oft zutreffend ist, liegt nicht an der Semiotik selbst, sondern am Umgang mit ihr. Auf der einen Seite steht die rein wissenschaftliche Behandlung, in der sich die Thematik verselbständigt und sich eine sterile Wissenschaftsdisziplin immer wieder nur selbst reproduziert, ohne für die Praxis fruchtbar werden zu können.

Auf der anderen Seite steht eine Praxis, die unfähig ist, diese Theorie zu verarbeiten, doch aber dessenungeachtet das pseudowissenschaftliche Mäntelchen umhängt und nichts weiter als den Ausverkauf wissenschaftlicher Begriffe betreibt. In beiden Fällen handelt es sich um typische Modeerscheinungen, die einer sinnvollen Entwicklung der Zeichentheorie mehr schaden als nützen. Aber Modeerscheinungen gehen vorbei, und die Zeit wird weisen, was an der Semiotik tatsächlich Bestand hat.

Noch nimmt die Semiotik in den Kommunikationswissenschaften eine gewisse Aussenseiterposition ein, was nicht zuletzt am oben skizzierten Charakter dieser Wissenschaftsdisziplin liegt. Doch es sind deutliche Anzeichen einer zunehmenden ernsthaften Auseinandersetzung mit der Zeichentheorie zu beobachten. Vielfach herrscht jedoch noch Unklarheit über

n'en sont pas moins indispensables. La mode voudrait que l'on fasse mine d'ignorer avec indulgence et condescendance ces «formules insignifiantes». Pourtant, quiconque veut travailler de manière précise ne doit pas céder à cette tentation. Les bases scientifiques ne se démodent jamais: tout au plus sont-elles remplacées par d'autres, meilleures, ou perfectionnées par les progrès de la connaissance. L'image future de notre profession a tout à gagner si nous ne restons pas en marge, mais lançons plutôt, enfin, notre propre recherche fondamentale. Malheureusement, l'une des théories les plus prometteuses de la science de la communication, la sémiotique, est parfois soupçonnée de n'être qu'une mode. Il est regrettable que ce reproche soit souvent fondé, car en fait la sémiotique elle-même ne devrait pas être contestée, mais plutôt la façon dont on la traite. D'une part se trouve l'approche purement scientifique: le sujet devient autonome, et une discipline scientifique stérile ne fait que se perpétuer sans pouvoir devenir féconde pour la pratique.

D'autre part, on trouve une pratique incapable d'assimiler la théorie, mais qui malgré tout se voile d'une aura pseudo-scientifique et ne fait rien d'autre que brader des notions scientifiques. Dans les deux cas nous assistons à des phénomènes de mode typiques qui font plus de tort que de bien à un développement raisonnable de la théorie des signes. Toutefois, les modes passent, et les aspects valables de la sémiotique résisteront au temps.

Parmi les sciences de la communication, la sémiotique garde encore une position marginale, due partiellement à la situation esquissée plus haut. Néanmoins, certains indices montrent clairement qu'une réflexion de plus en plus sérieuse est en cours au sujet de la théorie des signes. Une grande incertitude demeure quant à la valeur de

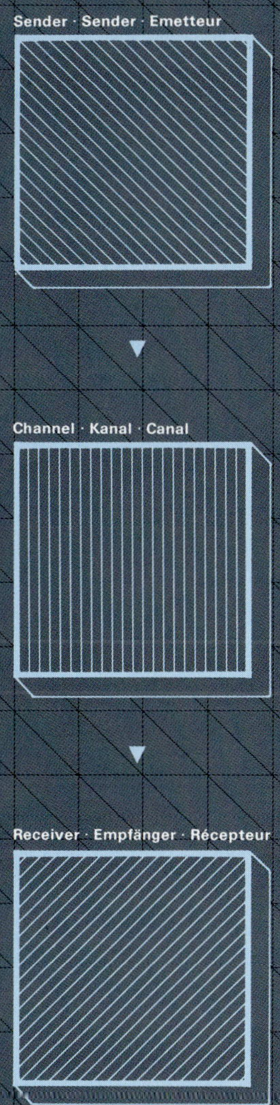

Model of information theory
Modell der Informationstheorie
Modèle de la théorie de l'information

of semiotics for communications, or more precisely, about the relationship between the processes of communications and of signs. A brief explanation of this point follows.

A very simple yet precise idea of the communications process is provided by the basic model of mathematical information theory.

Information theory owes its existence to the concerns of electrical transmission of news. In the simple model of news transmission there is a transmitter sending signals through a channel to a receiver. The nature of the signals is determined by the characteristics of the channel, for example sound waves in the air, electrical impulses via a cable or printing ink on paper. News must always be transformed in such a way that it can be transmitted, for example from alphabetical characters into Morse code for telegrams. This process is called coding. It is always based on a repertoire consisting of the signals possible in a given channel. The signals available in the repertoire are given meanings by means of a code, whereby they become signs. It is always the case that they are signs only for the human sender or receiver, while for the technical equipment they always remain signals. Bearing in mind the possibility that transmission through the channel may be disturbed by outside influences, we obtain the following differentiated model of the whole process of communication (next page).

The problem for information theory lies in the assurance of agreement between the transmitted and the received signal, even when the channel is disturbed. This central problem is approached from two sides: those of encoding and decoding. The work of

den Stellenwert einer Semiotik für die Kommunikation oder, genauer, über das Verhältnis von Kommunikationsprozess und Zeichenprozess. Dieser Punkt soll im folgenden kurz geklärt werden.

Eine recht einfache und dennoch zugleich präzise Vorstellung vom Kommunikationsprozess vermittelt das Modell, vom dem die mathematische Informationstheorie ausgeht.

Ihre Entstehung verdankt die Informationstheorie der Beschäftigung mit Problemen der elektrischen Nachrichtenübertragung. Im einfachen Modell der Nachrichtenübertragung gibt es ein Sendegerät, das Signale über einen Kanal an ein Empfangsgerät vermittelt. Welcher Art diese Signale sind, bestimmen die Eigenschaften des Kanals, beispielsweise Schallwellen in der Luft, Stromimpulse über ein Kabel oder Druckfarbe auf Papier. Eine Nachricht muss daher immer so umgewandelt werden, dass sie durch den Kanal übertragen werden kann, bei Telegrammen beispielsweise von Schriftzeichen ins Morsealphabet. Dieser Vorgang wird Codierung genannt. Die Codierung beruht immer auf einem Repertoire, das durch die in einem Kanal möglichen Signale gebildet wird. Den im Repertoire verfügbaren Signalen werden durch einen Code Bedeutungen zugeordnet; dadurch werden die Signale zu Zeichen. Zeichen können sie allerdings nur für einen menschlichen Sender oder Empfänger werden, für die technischen Geräte bleiben sie immer Signale. Berücksichtigt man nun auch noch die Möglichkeit, dass die Übertragung im Kanal durch äussere Einflüsse gestört sein kann, so ergibt sich das folgende, differenzierte Modell des gesamten Kommunikationsprozesses (siehe nächste Seite).

Für die Informationstheorie liegt das Problem bei der Sicherung der Übereinstimmung zwischen gesendetem und empfangenem Signal, auch wenn der Kanal gestört ist. Dieses zentrale Problem wurde von zwei Seiten angegangen: von der Encodierung und von der Decodierung her. Die Arbeiten

la sémiotique pour la communication, ou plus précisément quant au rapport existant entre le processus de la communication et le processus du signe. Nous allons éclaircir ce point ci-après.

Le modèle dont découle la théorie de l'information mathématique donne une représentation très simple mais très précise du processus de la communication.

La théorie de l'information doit son origine à l'étude des problèmes de la transmission électrique des informations. Dans le modèle simple de cette transmission, il existe un appareil émetteur qui transmet des signaux à un appareil récepteur par l'intermédiaire d'un canal. La nature des signaux est déterminée par le canal: ondes sonores dans l'air, impulsions électriques dans un câble ou encre d'imprimerie sur du papier, etc. Ainsi, une information doit toujours être transformée de sorte qu'elle puisse être transmise par le canal donné. Pour un télégramme, par exemple, on convertit les caractères en alphabet morse. Ce processus s'appelle le codage. Le codage a toujours pour base un répertoire constitué par les signaux transmissibles par un canal. Un code permet d'attribuer des significations aux signaux disponibles dans le répertoire: les signaux deviennent ainsi des signes. Néanmoins, ils ne sont signes que pour un émetteur ou un récepteur humain; pour les appareils, ils restent des signaux. Si l'on prend en considération le fait que la transmission dans le canal risque d'être perturbée par des influences extérieures, on obtient le modèle suivant, plus élaboré, de l'ensemble du processus de communication (page suivante).

La théorie de l'information doit assurer la conformité entre le signal envoyé et le signal reçu, même si le canal subit des perturbations. Ce problème central a été abordé de deux côtés: celui de l'encodage et celui du décodage. Les travaux de Norbert Wiener pour le filtrage, le lissage et le

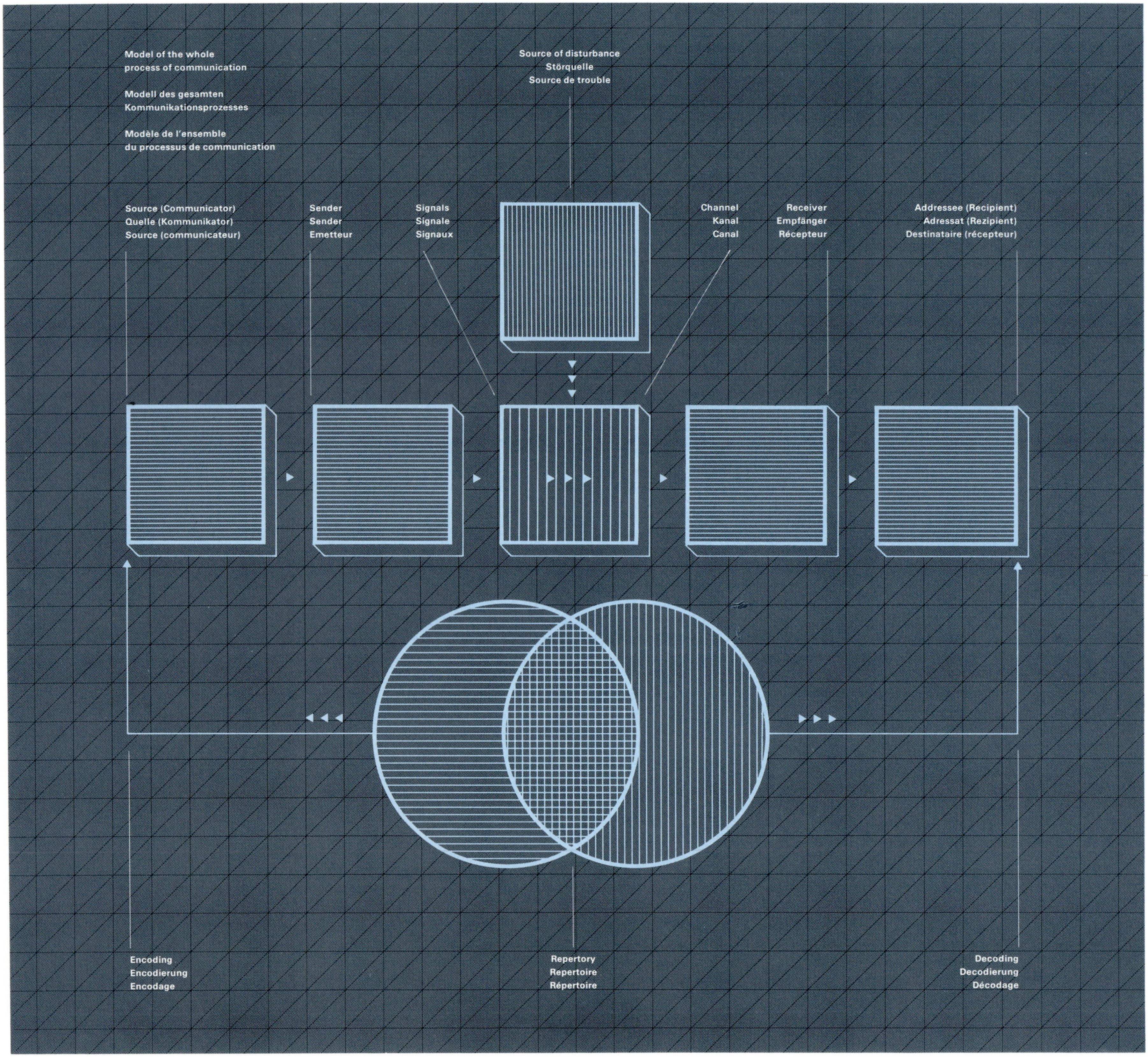
Model of the whole
process of communication
Modell des gesamten
Kommunikationsprozesses
Modèle de l'ensemble
du processus de communication
Source of disturbance
Störquelle
Source de trouble
Source (Communicator)
Quelle (Kommunikator)
Source (communicateur)
Sender
Sender
Emetteur
Signals
Signale
Signaux
Channel
Kanal
Canal
Receiver
Empfänger
Récepteur
Addressee (Recipient)
Adressat (Rezipient)
Destinataire (récepteur)
Encoding
Encodierung
Encodage
Repertory
Repertoire
Répertoire
Decoding
Decodierung
Décodage

Norbert Wiener on the filtering, smoothening and regulation of feedback in the reception of signals led to the development of cybernetics. Claude E. Shannon, on the other hand, was concerned with optimal encoding so as to make news less sensitive to disturbances, thereby creating the bases of mathematical information theory.

There is no doubt that important contributions to communications science have been made in the field of information theory; but their important effects on the practice of communications have been largely limited to technical matters, while applications to communications itself appear to be hardly relevant to practice, owing to their high level of formalization. The reason for this contrast lies in the basic difference between technical and communicative coding.

The technical process of transmission often requires multiple coding, for example sounds into letters, letters into Morse code, Morse code into electrical impulses, and back again. This technical form of coding produces a complete conversion of all the information from one sign system into another. For this purpose, the repertoire and rules of conversion are clearly established, so that a loss of information can occur only as a result of "interference", that is to say a disturbance of the channel.

In the communication process, on the other hand, coding does not mean conversion from one sign system to another, but the conversion of a complex reality into a less complex system of signs. Thus communications always involves a reduction of complexity, which occurs in a series of steps (next page).

Perception directed towards a section of reality is always partial, but the part perceived is still infinitely great, since perception in itself has no distinct

Norbert Wieners zur Filterung, Glättung und Regelung durch Rückkopplung beim Empfang von Signalen führten zur Entwicklung der Kybernetik. Claude E. Shannon dagegen beschäftigte sich mit der optimalen Encodierung, um die Nachricht gegen Störungen unempfindlicher zu machen, und schuf dabei die Grundlagen der mathematischen Informationstheorie.

Zweifellos wurden im Bereich der Informationstheorie wichtige Beiträge für die Kommunikationswissenschaft geleistet. Doch ihre immensen Auswirkungen auf die Praxis der Kommunikation beschränken sich weitgehend auf technische Aspekte, Übertragungen auf die Kommunikation an sich erscheinen angesichts des hohen Formalisierungsniveaus der Informationstheorie kaum praxisrelevant. Der Grund dafür liegt im prinzipiellen Unterschied zwischen technischer und kommunikativer Codierung.

Der technische Prozess der Übertragung erfordert oft eine mehrfache Codierung, beispielsweise Laute in Buchstaben, Buchstaben in Morsezeichen, Morsezeichen in Stromimpulse und zurück. Eine solche technische Form der Codierung stellt eine vollständige Umsetzung der gesamten Information einer Nachricht von einem Zeichensystem in ein anderes dar. Dabei sind Repertoire und Umsetzungsregeln eindeutig festgelegt, so dass ein Informationsverlust nur durch «Rauschen», also die Störung des Kanals, entsteht.

Im Kommunikationsprozess dagegen handelt es sich bei der Codierung jedoch nicht um eine Umsetzung von einem Zeichensystem in ein anderes, sondern um die Umsetzung einer komplexen Realität in ein weniger komplexes Zeichensystem. Daher bedeutet Kommunikation immer zugleich Reduktion von Komplexität. Diese Reduktion erfolgt in verschiedenen Stufen (siehe nächste Seite).

Die auf einen Ausschnitt der Realität gerichtete Wahrnehmung erfasst stets nur einen Teil der Realität. Dieser Teil ist jedoch immer noch unend-

réglage par rétroaction à la réception des signaux ont donné naissance à la cybernétique. Claude E. Shannon s'est en revanche consacré à l'encodage optimal permettant de rendre l'information moins sensible aux interférences, jetant ainsi les bases de la théorie de l'information mathématique.

La science de la communication a sans aucun doute beaucoup bénéficié des enseignements de la théorie de l'information. Néanmoins, ses répercussions considérables sur la pratique de la communication se limitent généralement aux aspects techniques. La théorie de l'information ayant un niveau élevé de formalisation, des transferts à la communication en tant que telle ne semblent guère utiles pour la pratique. Ce décalage provient de la différence de principe existant entre le codage technique et le codage en communication.

Le processus technique de la transmission nécessite souvent un codage multiple, comme par exemple les sons en lettres, les lettres en signaux morse, les signaux morse en impulsions électriques, et l'inverse. Cette forme technique du codage représente une transposition complète de l'ensemble de l'information contenue dans un message d'un système de signes dans un autre. Le répertoire et les règles de transposition sont fixés clairement: ainsi, toute perte d'information ne provient que du «bruit», c'est-à-dire d'une perturbation du canal.

En revanche, dans le processus de la communication, le codage ne sert pas à transposer un système de signes dans un autre, mais une réalité complexe dans un système de signes moins complexe. En conséquence, la communication implique toujours en même temps une réduction de la complexité. Cette réduction se déroule en plusieurs étapes (page suivante).

La perception, dirigée vers un fragment de la réalité, n'en saisit jamais qu'une partie. Néanmoins, cette partie reste immensément grande, car la

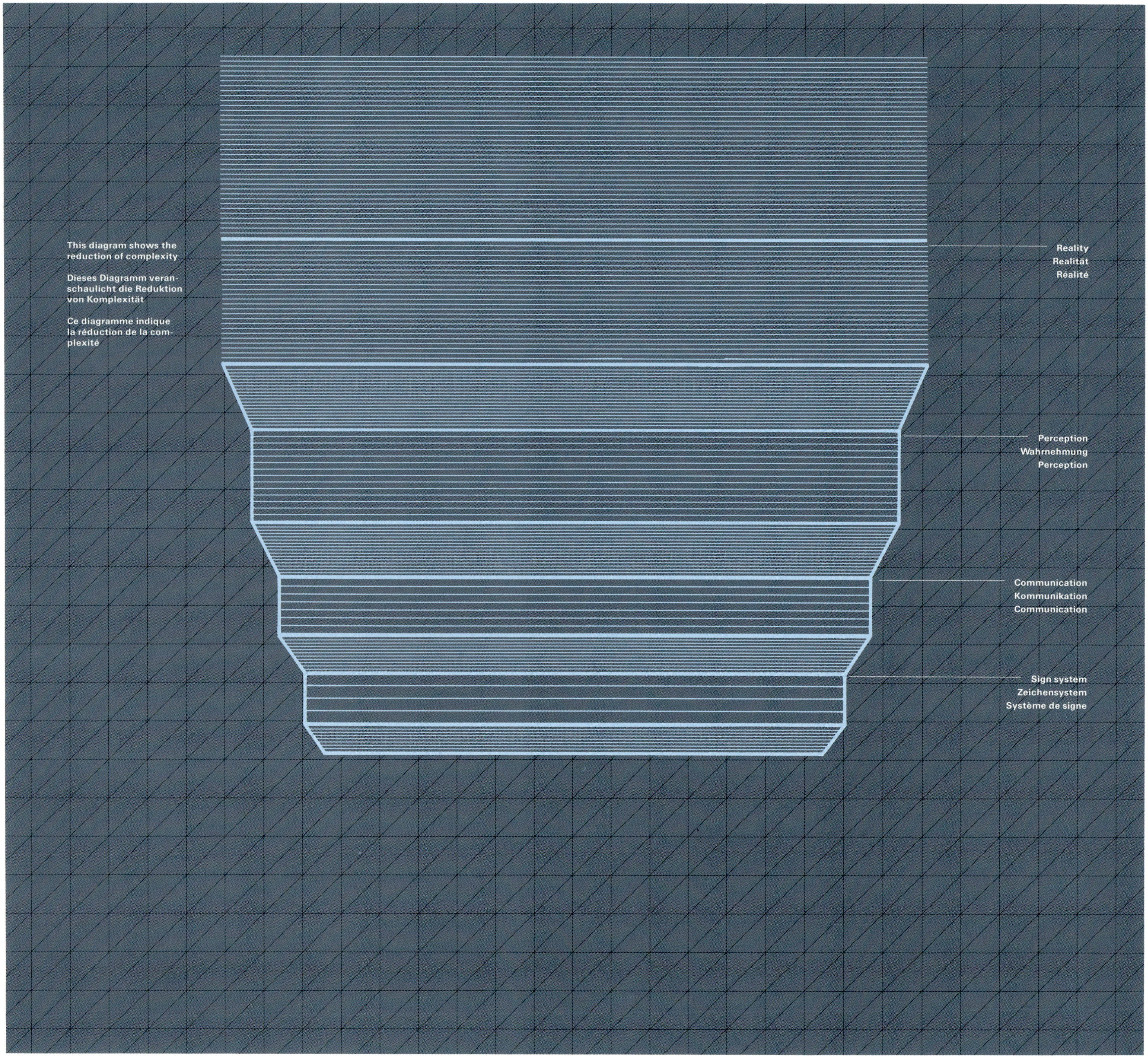

This diagram shows the reduction of complexity

Dieses Diagramm veranschaulicht die Reduktion von Komplexität

Ce diagramme indique la réduction de la complexité

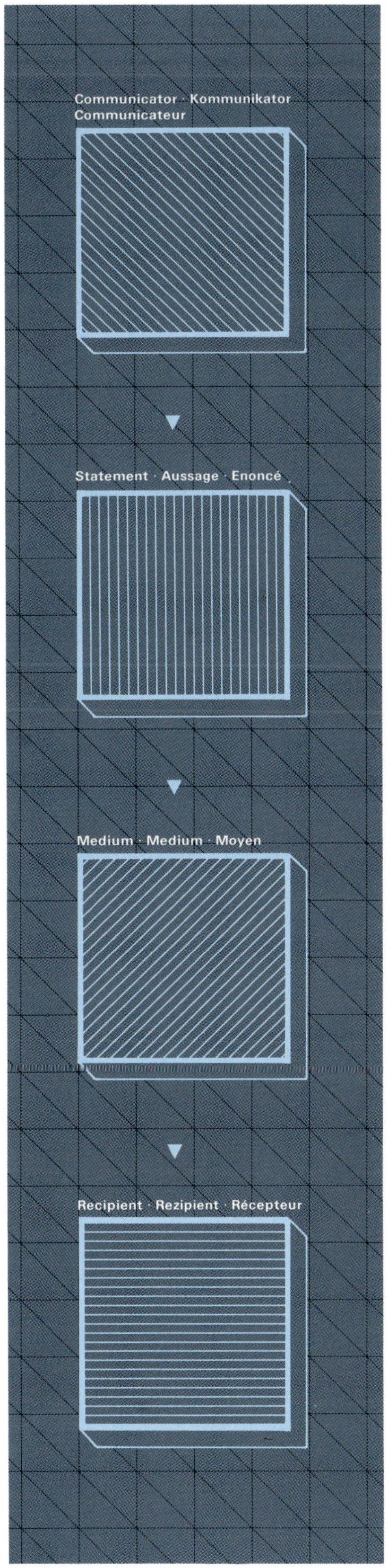

items. In communication, however, it is always necessary to pick out single, differentiable elements, in order to be able to make them objects of communication. The choice of the way of communication, i.e. the sign system, means further reduction, since each sign system can apprehend only certain aspects of an object, namely those to which its signs refer. Taking as an example a personal portrait and the person's name: these two signs from different systems both refer to the same object but supply very different kinds of information.

With regard to the relationship between encoding and decoding, a further problem arises in the communication process. The repertoire and the rules of conversion are not categorically established and cannot be so except in special cases, for example in science, by means of definitions.

Yet even if the purely material repertoire were identical for communicator and recipient, and the rules of conversion categorically formulated, the elements would still refer to differently perceived reality. Since in fact the two specified conditions are not fulfilled, there are several levels at which communication may be disturbed, and of these, "interference" in the strictly technical sense causes the least of the practical and theoretical problems.

The most important resulting consequence for communications science is that encoding and decoding cannot in principle be regarded as one and the same. This identity is, however, tacitly assumed in the most widely used model of mass communications, where the subject under consideration is simply the "statement".

To be precise, one must distinguish between the statement "as intended

lich gross, da die Wahrnehmung an sich noch keine diskreten Elemente enthält. Bei der Kommunikation müssen jedoch notwendigerweise einzelne unterscheidbare Elemente herausgegriffen werden, um sie zum Gegenstand der Kommunikation machen zu können. Die Wahl der Vermittlungsart, also des Zeichensystems, bedeutet dabei wiederum eine Reduktion, weil jedes Zeichensystem immer nur bestimmte Aspekte der Objekte, auf die sich seine Zeichen beziehen, erfassen kann. Nehmen wir als Beispiel das Bild einer Person und ihren Namen; diese beiden Zeichen aus verschiedenen Systemen beziehen sich auf das gleiche Objekt, liefern jedoch sehr unterschiedliche Informationen.

Im Hinblick auf das Vehältnis von Encodierung und Decodierung tritt im Kommunikationsprozess ein weiteres Problem auf. Repertoire und Umsetzungsregeln sind nicht eindeutig festgelegt und lassen sich auch nur in besonderen Fällen – etwa im Bereich der Wissenschaften durch entsprechende Definitionen – festlegen.

Doch selbst wenn das rein materiale Repertoire bei Sender und Empfänger identisch und die Umsetzungsregeln eindeutig formuliert wären, so beziehen sich die Elemente immer noch auf eine unterschiedlich wahrgenommene Wirklichkeit. Da aber schon die beiden genannten Bedingungen nicht zutreffen, gibt es mehrere Ebenen, auf denen die Kommunikation gestört sein kann, wobei das «Rauschen» im strengen Sinne der Nachrichtentechnik die geringsten praktischen und theoretischen Schwierigkeiten bereitet.

Als wichtigste Konsequenz für die Kommunikationswissenschaft ergibt sich daraus, dass Encodierung und Decodierung nicht prinzipiell als identisch angesehen werden können. Eine solche Identität wird von dem meistverwendeten Modell der Massenkommunikation stillschweigend vorausgesetzt, wenn hier einfach von der «Aussage» die Rede ist.

Wenn man präzise sein will, muss man zwischen der «Aussage, wie sie

perception en tant que telle ne contient pas encore d'éléments discrets. Dans la communication, il est nécessaire de choisir des éléments différentiables isolés pour en faire l'objet de la communication. Le choix du type de transmission, c'est-à-dire du système de signes, implique encore une fois une réduction, car tout système de signes ne peut saisir que certains aspects déterminés des objets auxquels ces signes se rapportent. Prenons par exemple la photographie d'une personne et son nom: ces deux signes qui appartiennent à des systèmes différents se rapportent au même objet mais apportent des informations très différentes.

Le processus de la communication présente un autre problème lié au rapport existant entre l'encodage et le décodage. Le répertoire et les règles de transposition ne sont pas établis clairement et ne peuvent être fixés que dans des cas particuliers, comme par exemple dans le domaine des sciences, où des définitions adéquates existent.

Toutefois, même si le répertoire purement matériel était identique pour l'émetteur et le récepteur, et même si les règles de transposition étaient formulées sans équivoque, les éléments se rapporteraient toujours à une réalité perçue de différentes manières. Etant donné que les deux premières conditions elles-mêmes ne sont pas remplies, il existe plusieurs niveaux où la communication risque d'être perturbée, le «bruit» au sens le plus strict de la technique des communications ne représentant que la moindre difficulté pratique et théorique.

Pour la science de la communication, il s'ensuit principalement que l'encodage et le décodage ne peuvent être considérés comme identiques dans leur principe. On admet tacitement cette identité dans le schéma de communication de masse le plus utilisé lorsqu'on parle simplement de l'«énoncé».

Pour être précis, il faut distinguer l'«énoncé comme le communicateur

by the communicator" and the statement "as understood by the recipient", and the model should be accordingly modified to agree with the one used in the theory of information (see illustration).

What has all this to do with semiotics?

Semiotics is the theory of signs. A statement can be regarded as a complex of signs and thus semiotically analyzed. Semiotics treats a sign not as a static object but as a dynamic process. In this science, a sign is not to be considered in isolation from its practical application, the situation in which it is used. For the communicator and the recipient, this situation is fundamentally different, which is why encoding and decoding must be treated as two different processes, in which there must consequently be two different signs. That which connects these two sign processes in the process of communication is the identity of the sign carrier, its purely material aspect, such as the typographic characters on paper or the grid of light and dark on the video screen.

The difference between the physical character of a sign and mental conceptions of it goes back to Saussure and has found general recognition in semiotics. The terms significat and significant have been accepted to denote this difference. The significant is the purely material sign carrier, while the significat is the conception of an object associated with the sign carrier. How the significat appears in a concrete case varies with the recipient and depends on the social and individual circumstances of literacy and socialization. The most important prerequisite for communication consists in the ability to give a common meaning, within a given bandwidth of variations, to individual significats. Thus, if I say "dog", I can assume that

der Kommunikator meint», und der «Aussage, wie sie der Rezipient versteht», unterscheiden. Entsprechend wäre dieses Modell in Übereinstimmung mit dem von der Informationstheorie benutzten zu modifizieren (siehe Abbildung).

Was hat dies nun alles mit der Semiotik zu tun?

Die Semiotik ist die Lehre von den Zeichen. Die Aussage kann als ein Komplex von Zeichen angesehen und somit semiotisch analysiert werden. Die Semiotik behandelt ein Zeichen nicht als statischen Gegenstand, sondern als dynamischen Prozess. Ein Zeichen ist für sie nicht unabhängig von seiner konkreten Verwendung, der Situation, in der es gebraucht wird, zu sehen. Diese Situation ist für Kommunikator und Rezipient grundsätzlich unterschiedlich, weshalb man Encodierung und Decodierung als zwei verschiedene Zeichenprozesse gebrauchen muss, in denen es folglich auch zwei verschiedene Zeichen geben muss. Was diese beiden Zeichenprozesse im Kommunikationsprozess verbindet, ist die Identität der Zeichenträger, der rein materiellen Seite des Zeichens, also etwa die Buchstaben auf dem Papier oder die Verteilung von Hell und Dunkel auf einem Bildschirm.

Die Unterscheidung zwischen der physischen Beschaffenheit eines Zeichens und psychischen Vorstellung davon geht auf Saussure zurück und hat in der Semiotik allgemeine Anerkennung gefunden, und es haben sich dafür die Bezeichnungen Signifikant und Signifikat durchgesetzt. Der Signifikant ist also der rein materielle Zeichenträger, während das Signifikat die Vorstellung von einem Objekt, die man damit verbindet, ist. Wie dieses Signifikat konkret aussieht, ist individuell verschieden und hängt von den gesellschaftlichen und individuellen Umständen des Spracherwerbs und der Sozialisation ab. Die wichtigste Voraussetzung für die Kommunikation besteht darin, dass man innerhalb einer gewissen Bandbreite der Variation individueller Signifikate diese als intersubjektiv übereinstimmend auffassen kann. Wenn ich also «Hund»

l'entend» de l'«énoncé comme le récepteur le comprend». En conséquence, il faudrait modifier ce schéma d'après celui utilisé dans la théorie de l'information (voir illustration).

Quel rapport tout cela a-t-il avec la sémiotique?

La sémiotique est la théorie des signes. L'énoncé peut être considéré comme un ensemble de signes et, partant, peut être analysé sémiotiquement. La sémiotique ne considère pas un signe comme un objet statique, mais plutôt comme un processus dynamique. Le signe ne doit pas être pris indépendamment de son application concrète, de la situation dans laquelle il est utilisé. Cette situation est fondamentalement différente pour le communicateur et le récepteur: l'on traitera donc l'encodage et le décodage comme deux processus distincts dans lesquels doivent se trouver, par conséquent, deux signes distincts. Dans la communication, ces deux processus de signes sont liés par l'identité du support de signes, par l'aspect purement matériel du signe, c'est-à-dire, entre autres, par les lettres sur le papier ou par la répartition du clair et du sombre sur un écran.

La distinction entre la constitution physique d'un signe et sa représentation psychique remonte à Saussure: elle est largement reconnue en sémiotique, où les termes signifiant et signifié se sont imposés. Ainsi, le signifiant est le support purement matériel du signe, tandis que le signifié est la représentation d'un objet qu'on lui associe. L'apparence concrète de ce signifié varie selon les individus et dépend des circonstances sociales et individuelles de l'acquisition du langage et de la socialisation. La première condition de la communication, c'est que les signifiés puissent être compris intersubjectivement de manière concordante à l'intérieur d'une certaine fourchette de variations individuelles. Ainsi, quand je dis «chien», je

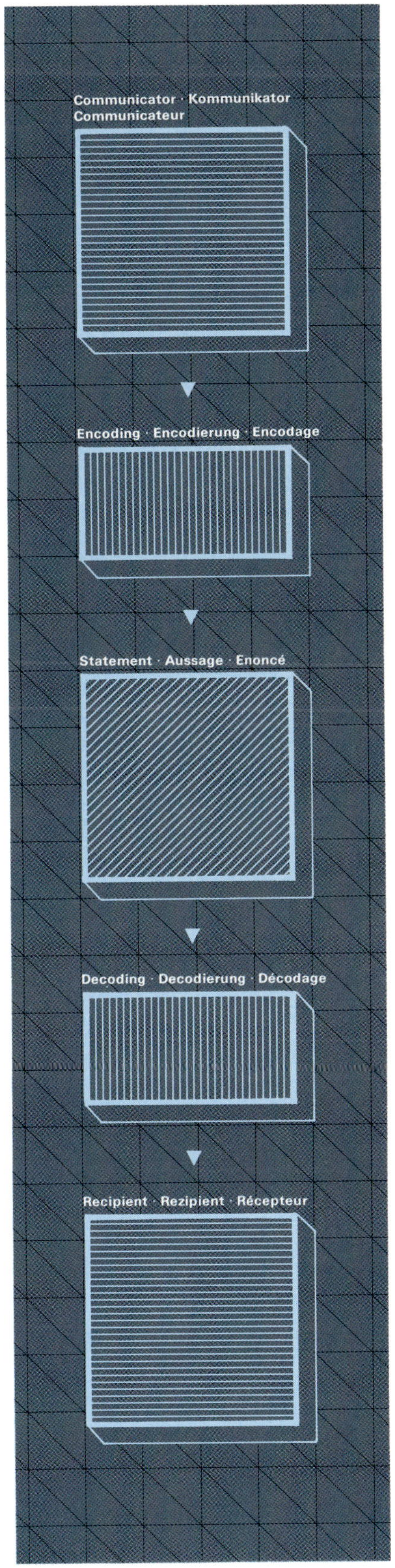

all English-speaking people associate the same idea with this word, even if they imagine quite different examples of the class of dogs and the word arouses quite different associations for each person. In this context one speaks of the significat as a "cultural unit".

By accepting a cultural unit one can construct a common significat for the communication process and thereby establish *one* sign. This kind of construction ist helpful for many questions of communications science and often absolutely necessary. It almost always provides the solution for the optimization of communications.

The following graphic model is intended to illustrate once more the manner in which the sign functions in the communicative process (next page).

The significant is here taken to be a kind of prism. Through the choice of sign carrier and its placing within the process of communication, the communicator specifies the object as a portion of reality and, at the same time, the point of view from which it is seen. For the sender and recipient of communication, only the significant is identical, while the significats, being images of the object, differ owing to differences in the point of view.

To return from these considerations, which affect the process of communication in general and are generally still underestimated in practice, to the subject of visual communication, brief reference must be made to the role of the process of selection which accompanies the process of communication and has already been briefly mentioned. In this first approach we looked at the selection by the communicator. In the field of mass communications, which are of primary interest in this connection, the selection made

sage, so kann ich davon ausgehen, dass alle deutschsprechenden Personen damit die gleiche Vorstellung verbinden, auch wenn sie ganz unterschiedliche Exemplare der Gattung Hund vor Augen haben und ganz unterschiedliche Assoziationen geweckt werden. Man spricht in diesem Zusammenhang vom Signifikat als einer kulturellen Einheit.

Durch die Annahme einer kulturellen Einheit kann man für den Kommunikationsprozess ein gemeinsames Signifikat konstruieren und so an *einem* Zeichen festhalten. Für viele Fragen der Kommunikationswissenschaft ist eine solche Konstruktion auch hilfreich, oft sogar notwendig. Für Probleme der Optimierung der Kommunikation verbaut sie jedoch fast immer die Lösung.

Das folgende grafische Modell soll die Funktionsweise des Zeichens im kommunikativen Prozess noch einmal veranschaulichen (siehe nächste Seite).

Der Signifikant wird hier als eine Art Prisma aufgefasst. Durch die Wahl des Zeichenträgers und dessen Plazierung im Kommunikationsprozess bestimmt der Kommunikator das Objekt als Ausschnitt aus der Wirklichkeit und zugleich den Blickwinkel, unter dem das Objekt betrachtet wird. Identisch ist für die Kommunikationspartner nur der Signifikant, die Signifikate, hier als Bilder vom Objekt, sind aufgrund des unterschiedlichen Blickwinkels verschieden.

Um hier von diesen Überlegungen, die den Kommunikationsprozess ganz allgemein betreffen und deren Bedeutung für die Praxis der Kommunikation heute noch meistens unterschätzt wird, zurückzukommen auf die visuelle Kommunikation, sei kurz auf die Rolle der Selektionsprozesse eingegangen, die den Kommunikationsprozess begleiten und die im vorangegangenen kurz angesprochen wurden. Der Ausgangspunkt war die Selektion durch den Kommunikator. Im Rahmen der Massenkommunikation – und die ist im gegebenen Zusammenhang von vorrangigem Interesse – spielt jedoch

peux partir du principe que tous les francophones y associent la même représentation, même s'ils voient des exemplaires très différents du genre chien et si les associations que ce mot éveille varient considérablement d'une personne à l'autre. Dans ce contexte, on parle du signifié comme unité culturelle.

En adoptant une unité culturelle, on peut construire un signifié commun pour le processus de communication et ainsi retenir *un seul* signe. Pour de nombreuses questions de la science de la communication, une telle construction est d'un grand secours, quand elle n'est pas nécessaire. Toutefois, elle compromet presque toujours la solution des problèmes d'optimisation de la communication.

Le schéma suivant illustre une fois encore le mode de fonctionnement du signe dans le processus de la communication (page suivante).

Le signifiant est conçu ici comme une sorte de prisme. En choisissant le support du signe et sa position dans le processus de communication, le communicateur détermine l'objet comme fragment de la réalité et choisit l'angle selon lequel il est observé. Pour le destinataire, seul le signifiant est identique. Les signifiés, qui sont ici des images de l'objet, sont différents car l'angle d'observation est différent.

Après ces considérations sur le processus de communication en général, dont l'importance pour la pratique est le plus souvent sous-estimée aujourd'hui, revenons à la communication visuelle en évoquant brièvement le rôle des processus de sélection qui accompagnent le processus de communication et dont nous avons rapidement fait mention ci-dessus. Le point de départ était la sélection par le communicateur. Dans le contexte de la communication de masse – qui nous intéresse particulièrement ici –, c'est cependant le choix effectué par le

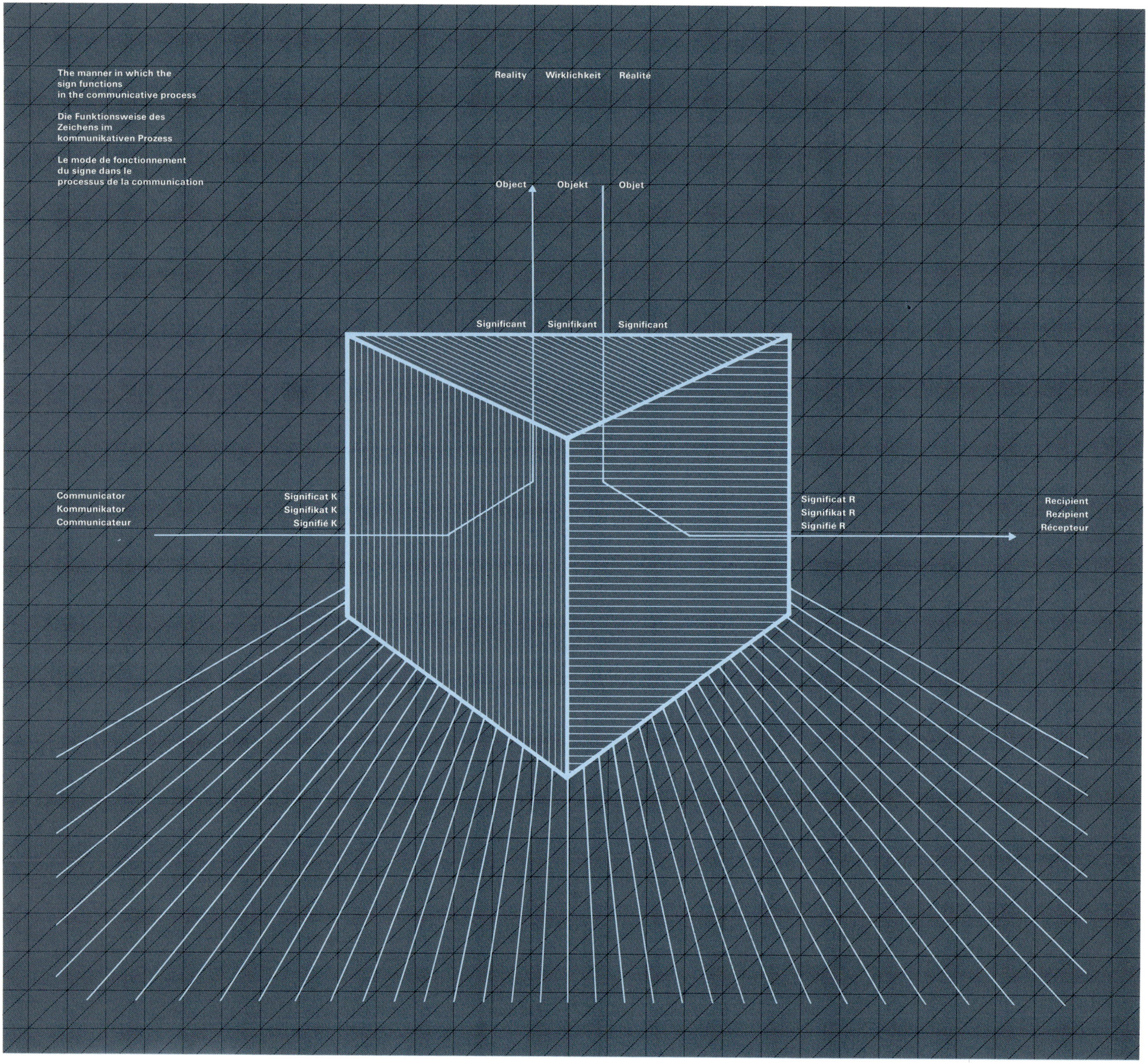

The manner in which the sign functions in the communicative process

Die Funktionsweise des Zeichens im kommunikativen Prozess

Le mode de fonctionnement du signe dans le processus de la communication

by the recipient plays the greater part. The communication process does not begin to exist until the recipient turns his mind to a statement. This attention depends on a number of factors, which thereby become determinants of communication. In addition to sheer attentiveness, which depends on external factors such as volume in speech or design features in visual communication, numerous purely personal factors come into effect here. The recipient's needs, interests and attitudes largely determine his behaviour in the field of communications. The science of communications has concerned itself very thoroughly with the extent of such influences and their investigation has made up a large part of the work of that discipline.

It would lead too far to go more deeply into this area of communications science, but the theories and models developed in this connection are frequently notable for their practical relevance.

1.3. Suggestions for design practice

Problems of transfer in the exchange of ideas are responsible for the well-known fact that this genuine practical relevance has not so far had very much practical effect. It may well seem paradoxical that the very science of communications is unable to communicate its findings, but experience shows that this is the case. The reasons are manifold, but an attempt should be made to explain at least some of the main ones and perhaps make a small contribution to overcoming the difficulties concerned.

There is absolutely no doubt that one of the reasons is a misunderstanding of science, awakening false expectations, which are then inevitably disappointed, leading to a rejection of

die Auswahl durch den Rezipienten die grössere Rolle, erst durch seine Zuwendung zu einer Aussage kommt der Kommunikationsprozess zustande. Diese Zuwendung hängt von zahlreichen Faktoren ab, die damit zu Determinanten der Kommunikation werden. Neben dem Aufmerksamkeitswert, der auf äussere Faktoren – wie Lautstärke bei der Sprache oder Gestaltungsmerkmale bei visueller Kommunikation – zurückgeht, spielen hier zahlreiche persönlichkeitsspezifische Faktoren hinein. Bedürfnisse, Interessen und Einstellungen des Rezipienten bestimmen weitgehend sein Kommunikationsverhalten. Die Kommunikationswissenschaft hat sich sehr eingehend mit solchen Einflussgrössen befasst, und ihre Erforschung macht einen grossen Teil der Arbeit in dieser Disziplin aus.

Es würde zu weit führen, näher auf diesen Bereich der Kommunikationswissenschaft einzugehen, doch die in diesem Zusammenhang entwickelten Theorien und Modelle zeichnen sich häufig durch sehr konkrete Praxisrelevanz aus.

1.3. Denkanstösse für die Designpraxis

Dass sich diese real gegebene Praxisrelevanz bisher nicht stärker auf die tatsächliche Praxis ausgewirkt hat, macht die vorhandenen Transferprobleme offenkundig. Zwar erscheint es paradox, dass gerade die Kommunikationswissenschaft nicht in der Lage sein sollte, ihre Erkenntnisse über die Kommunikation auch zu kommunizieren, doch die Erfahrung lehrt, dass dem so ist. Die Gründe dafür sind vielschichtig, doch es soll versucht werden, wenigstens einige der Hauptursachen zu erklären und vielleicht einen kleinen Beitrag zur Überwindung der Schwierigkeiten zu leisten.

Eine der Ursachen liegt ganz sicher in einem falschen Wissenschaftsverständnis, das falsche Erwartungen weckt, die dann notwendigerweise enttäuscht werden, was in der Konsequenz zu einer Ablehnung der Wissenschaft führt. So haben blinde Wissenschaftsgläubigkeit und totale Ab-

destinataire qui joue le rôle le plus important: le processus de communication ne s'engage que lorsque le récepteur tourne son attention vers un énoncé. De nombreux facteurs déterminants pour la communication interviennent. Outre la valeur de certaines données extérieures qui contribuent à attirer l'attention – intensité sonore de la parole, caractéristiques de forme dans la communication visuelle – bien des facteurs purement personnels entrent ici en ligne de compte. Les besoins, les intérêts et les opinions du récepteur déterminent dans une large mesure sa manière de communiquer. La science de la communication a étudié en détail ces facteurs d'influence et continue d'y consacrer une part considérable de sa recherche.

Nous n'irons pas plus avant dans ce domaine au risque de dépasser le cadre du présent ouvrage. Relevons néanmoins que les théories et les schémas élaborés à ce propos sont souvent d'une grande importance pour la pratique.

1.3. Suggestions pour la pratique

Si cette importance véritable n'a pas eu jusqu'à présent un impact plus profond sur la pratique, c'est précisément qu'il existe des problèmes de transfert. Il semble sans doute paradoxal que la science de la communication elle-même ne soit pas capable de communiquer ses connaissances en matière de communication, et pourtant l'expérience nous montre que tel est le cas. Les raisons de cet état de choses sont complexes; nous allons néanmoins nous efforcer d'éclaircir les causes principales et – peut-être – d'apporter une modeste contribution à la solution des problèmes.

L'une de ces causes est sans aucun doute une compréhension erronée de la science qui suscite des attentes mal fondées, nécessairement déçues, ce qui conduit à son rejet. Ainsi, la foi

science. Blind faith and total rejection of science thus have the same cause, namely a lack of understanding. It is the duty of science to demonstrate its principles, and thereby its possibilities and limits. A few general and easily understood explanations of the nature of science therefore seem appropriate.
Science by its nature is a working method based on three fundamental principles:

Systematization, formation of theories, empirical checking

One of the most important consequences of this approach is that science can never make any claim to absolute validity in its results. Scientists must therefore always attempt to clarify the conditions under which given statements are valid. One can speak of a scientific advance only when all of the three fundamental principles have been observed. Systematization is certainly useful but in itself it cannot create a scientific method. Similarly, it is not enough to develop a conclusive theory, for all theories must be verified by empirical means. At the same time, the value of empirical tests is extremely doubtful without a theoretical basis and methodical system. In modern market research in particular—the very field in which one is mainly concerned with visual communication—all kinds of semi or pseudoscientific models and methods are to be found, and it is these which have led to much of the discredit of scientists among creative people. Instead of a clear presentation of the preconditions and limits of validity of the results, one is often presented with exaggerated assertions. In the face of justified criticism, the theorist then often withdraws behind the curtain of a form of conceptualization which is incomprehensible to the layman, thus putting an end to the possibility of discussion.

lehnung der Wissenschaft die gleiche Ursache, nämlich mangelndes Verständnis. Es ist Aufgabe der Wissenschaft, ihre Prinzipien und damit ihre Möglichkeiten und Grenzen aufzuzeigen. Einige allgemeine und allgemein verständliche Erläuterungen zum Wesen der Wissenschaft erscheinen daher angebracht.
Wissenschaft ist ihrem Wesen nach eine Arbeitsmethode, die auf drei Grundprinzipien basiert:

Systematisierung, Theorienbildung, Empirische Überprüfung

Eine der wichtigsten Konsequenzen dieser Betrachtungsweise besteht darin, dass Wissenschaft niemals einen Anspruch auf absolute Gültigkeit ihrer Ergebnisse erheben kann. Sie muss daher immer versuchen, die Voraussetzungen, unter denen bestimmte Aussagen gültig sind, zu klären. Wissenschaftlich kann ein Vorgehen nur dann genannt werden, wenn es den drei genannten Grundprinzipien entspricht, und zwar allen. Systematisierung ist sicher nützlich, aber allein für sich kann sie nicht den Anspruch der Wissenschaftlichkeit erheben. Ebenso genügt es nicht, eine in sich schlüssige Theorie zu entwikkeln, sie muss auch empirisch überprüfbar sein. Aber auch der Stellenwert empirischer Tests ist ohne theoretische Begründung und methodische Systematisierung äusserst zweifelhaft. Insbesondere in der heutigen Markt- und Werbeforschung – also dem Bereich, in dem man sich hauptsächlich mit der visuellen Kommunikation auseinandersetzt – kann man die verschiedensten Typen halb- oder gar pseudowissenschaftlicher Modelle und Methoden antreffen, und gerade sie haben zu einer Diskreditierung der Wissenschaft bei den Kreativen erheblich beigetragen. Statt Voraussetzungen und Grenzen der Gültigkeit von Ergebnissen deutlich zu machen, werden nicht selten überzogene Behauptungen aufgestellt. Gegenüber berechtigter Kritik zieht man sich dann oft hinter das Imponiergehabe einer für Laien unverständlichen Begriffsbildung zurück, so dass die Argumentation undurchschaubar ist.

absolue dans la science et son rejet total ont la même origine, à savoir un manque de compréhension. Il incombe à la science de faire connaître ses principes et, ce faisant, ses possibilités et ses limites. Il paraît donc judicieux d'apporter ici quelques explications générales et compréhensibles par tous sur la nature de la science.
La science est par nature une méthode de travail fondée sur trois principes de base:

Systématisation, formation de théories, vérification empirique

L'une des conséquences principales de cette manière de voir est que la science ne peut jamais prétendre à l'absolue validité de ses résultats. Dès lors, elle doit toujours s'efforcer de préciser les conditions dans lesquelles certains énoncés sont valables. Un procédé peut seulement être considéré comme scientifique s'il répond à chacun des trois principes de base. La systématisation est sans aucun doute utile, mais elle ne peut prétendre en soi au caractère scientifique. De même, il ne suffit pas d'élaborer une théorie convaincante: elle doit pouvoir être prouvée empiriquement. Toutefois, la valeur des essais empiriques est plus qu'incertaine sans justification théorique ni systématisation méthodique. Dans le domaine de l'analyse des marchés et de la publicité, où la communication visuelle joue un rôle primordial, on rencontre souvent aujourd'hui des schémas ou des méthodes peu ou même pseudoscientifiques qui contribuent largement à discréditer la science aux yeux des créateurs. Au lieu de préciser les conditions et les limites de la validité des conclusions, il n'est pas rare que l'on présente des affirmations absolues. Devant des critiques justifiées, on se réfugie souvent derrière une terminologie incompréhensible et impressionnante qui obscurcit l'argumentation.

For me, the field to which the concept of function applies has not ceased to expand . . . To consider another aspect: the communicative dimension. That is to say: what meaning design can convey. For every design is at the same time a communication. It directly conveys information of different kinds.

Dieter Rams

Für mich hat sich der Bereich, auf den der Begriff Funktion zutrifft, immer mehr erweitert . . .
Um einen weiteren Aspekt anzusprechen: die kommunikative Dimension. Das heisst: Was kann Design zu verstehen geben? Denn jedes Design ist immer zugleich Kommunikation. Es übermittelt direkt Informationen verschiedener Art.

Dieter Rams

Pour moi, le domaine auquel s'applique la notion de fonction n'a cessé de s'élargir...
Abordons un autre aspect: la dimension de la communication. C'est-à-dire: le design, que peut-il faire comprendre? En effet, chaque design est toujours aussi communication.
Il transmet directement des informations de différentes natures.

Dieter Rams

It would, however, be a mistake to accept this accusation without reserve. The use of an exact terminology is in all cases essential to science.

Theories must be based on well-defined concepts, which must be used for verbal precision. The conversion of scientific terms into everyday language, which is indispensable for their transfer into practice, brings the loss not only of a part of a theory's precision, but often also of the whole basis of discussion. The scientist therefore finds himself in a real dilemma: if he argues with scientific exactitude he is not understood, while if he uses everyday language he loses precision and lays himself open to learned criticism. It is not hard to understand that a scientist who finds himself in a vulnerable position will retreat to the sure ground of exact terminology. Consequently, there will always be some elements not easily explained, where science must hope to be taken on trust by the practitioner. This is not to expect a blind trust, because theory must meet the requirements of empirical evidence and it must be possible to formulate empirically valid hypotheses in everyday language. Basically, therefore, mistrust of a theory is justified when none of its assertions can be checked.

Conversely, tests without theoretical backing are to be treated with extreme caution, since the underlying theory always provides the conditions under which the given results obtain their validity. Basically there are no scientific findings which can be free of conditions and lay claim to universal validity. Especially in the field of commercial research and experiments in classic design, the limits of validity of the results are very narrowly drawn, sometimes so narrowly that they exclude the normal communications sit-

Es wäre jedoch falsch, diesen Vorwurf zu pauschalieren. Immerhin gehört die Verwendung einer exakten Terminologie zu den Voraussetzungen der Wissenschaft.

Theorien bauen auf wohldefinierten Begriffen auf, und nur mit der Verwendung dieser Begriffe ist eine sprachliche Präzisierung möglich. Mit einer Umsetzung in die Umgangssprache, die für den Transfer in die Praxis unerlässlich ist, geht nicht nur ein Teil der Präzision einer Theorie verloren, oft geht damit auch die Grundlage der Argumentation verloren. Der Wissenschaftler befindet sich also in einem echten Dilemma: Argumentiert er wissenschaftssprachlich exakt, so bleibt er unverständlich, argumentiert er allgemeinverständlich, so gibt er die Präzision auf und wird wissenschaftlich angreifbar. Von daher ist es nur zu leicht zu verstehen, dass sich ein Wissenschaftler, wenn er angegriffen wird, auf den sicheren Boden der exakten Terminologie zurückzieht. Es wird also immer einen nicht leicht erklärbaren Rest geben, wo die Wissenschaft auf das Vertrauen des Praktikers angewiesen ist. Das verlangt jedoch kein blindes Vertrauen, denn die Theorie muss die Forderung der empirischen Überprüfbarkeit erfüllen, und prüfbare Hypothesen müssen umgangssprachlich formulierbar sein. Grundsätzlich ist also Misstrauen gegenüber einer Theorie dann angebracht, wenn sie keine prüffähigen Aussagen macht.

Umgekehrt sind aber auch Tests ohne theoretische Fundierung mit äusserster Vorsicht zu behandeln, denn die zugrunde liegende Theorie gibt stets die Voraussetzungen an, unter denen bestimmte Ergebnisse Gültigkeit haben. Es gibt grundsätzlich keine wissenschaftlichen Erkenntnisse, die voraussetzungsfrei wären, also allgemeine Gültigkeit in Anspruch nehmen könnten. Gerade im Bereich der kommerziellen Forschung und insbesondere bei Experimenten nach klassischem Design sind die Grenzen der Gültigkeit von Ergebnissen recht eng gezogen, nicht selten sogar so eng, dass die normale Kommunikations-

Néanmoins, il serait abusif de généraliser ce reproche. L'emploi d'une terminologie exacte est une nécessité dans le domaine scientifique.

Les théories se fondent sur des notions bien définies dont l'emploi est nécessaire à l'obtention de toute précision linguistique. La transposition en langage courant, indispensable pour les applications pratiques, entraîne non seulement une perte partielle de la précision de la théorie, mais aussi, fréquemment, la perte de la base de l'argumentation. Ainsi le chercheur est-il confronté à un dilemne: s'il argumente en termes scientifiquement exacts, on ne le comprend pas; s'il argumente de manière à être entendu par tous, il renonce à la précision et risque d'être mis en cause sur le plan scientifique. Dès lors, on comprendra aisément qu'un chercheur se retire sur le terrain relativement sûr de la terminologie exacte quant il est attaqué. Il restera donc toujours un domaine difficile à expliquer où la science a besoin de la confiance du praticien. Toutefois, cette confiance ne doit pas nécessairement être aveugle: la théorie doit résister à l'épreuve empirique, et les hypothèses vérifiables doivent pouvoir être formulées en langage courant. En somme, la méfiance vis-à-vis d'une théorie est justifiée si ses énoncés ne peuvent être vérifiés dans la pratique.

Inversement, les essais sans fondement théorique sont à considérer avec la plus grande circonspection car la théorie donne toujours les conditions dans lesquelles certaines conclusions sont valables. Par principe, il n'existe pas de notions scientifiques indépendantes de toutes conditions qui pourraient en quelque sorte revendiquer une validité générale. Dans le domaine de la recherche commerciale, et en particulier dans les expériences de design classique, les limites de la validité des conclusions sont très étroites, souvent à tel point que la situation normale de communication n'y trouve

uation. The exposition and clarification of preconditions for research and testing with visual communications material is important to creative people because they are thereby saved from being subordinated to an arbitrary judgement. When they know the conditions under which a design has been rejected, they can work purposefully on an improvement, which may possibly consist of changing the said preconditions. It is only on this basis that the relationship between science and creativity can be made fruitful.

A major obstacle to understanding between science and creativity is also erected by a widely prevalent concept of creativity which places it in sharp contrast to logic, under the motto of "divergent thinking". Creativity in this sense is generally equated with intuition and associated with an almost neurotic urge to innovate. In this sense, it is only the unusual, the surprising and the unprecedented that are recognized as being truly innovative. To earn the title of "creative", the solution to a problem must be both original and unconventional. To forestall any misunderstanding at this point I must emphasize that I neither question the role of intuition, nor undervalue the criterion of originality. The question is rather to demonstrate the negative effects of the dominance of these principles and to formulate an alternative concept of creativity.

It is precisely the application of scientific pretensions to "innovative techniques" that has contributed much to perpetuating the "myth of creativity", and to diminishing the readiness of creative people to have any dealings with science. Thus a well-known author asserts that "conscious thought, and verbalized thought in particular, play only a subordinate role in the decisive phase of the creative act". He even cites scientific results as evi-

situation nicht hineinpasst. Die Bekanntgabe und Klärung der Voraussetzungen von Untersuchungen und Tests mit visuellem Kommunikationsmaterial ist für den Kreativen schon deshalb von Bedeutung, weil er dann den Ergebnissen nicht wie einem Urteilsspruch unterworfen ist. Wenn er die Bedingungen kennt, unter denen etwa ein Entwurf abgelehnt wurde, so kann er gezielt an einer Verbesserung arbeiten, die dann möglicherweise auch darin besteht, dass er die Voraussetzungen ändert. Nur auf dieser Basis kann das Verhältnis zwischen Wissenschaft und Kreativität fruchtbar werden.

Ein entscheidendes Hindernis für die Verständigung zwischen Wissenschaft und Kreativen bildet aber auch ein in der Praxis verbreiteter Kreativitätsbegriff, der unter dem Stichwort «divergentes Denken» die Kreativität in einen scharfen Gegensatz zur Logik stellt. Kreativität in diesem Sinne wird weitgehend mit Intuition gleichgesetzt und mit einem fast neurotischen Zwang zur Innovation verbunden, wobei als innovativ meist nur das Ungewöhnliche, Überraschende und nie Dagewesene anerkannt wird. Originell und unkonventionell muss eine Lösung sein, der man das Prädikat «kreativ» zuspricht. Damit keine Missverständnisse aufkommen – ich möchte hier weder die Rolle der Intuition in Frage stellen noch das Kriterium der Originalität abwerten. Es geht vielmehr darum, die negativen Auswirkungen der Dominanz dieser Prinzipien aufzuzeigen und ein alternatives Konzept von Kreativität zu formulieren.

Gerade die mit wissenschaftlichem Anspruch auftretenden «innovativen Techniken» haben viel dazu beigetragen, den «Mythos von der Kreativität» zu festigen und die Bereitschaft der Kreativen, sich mit Wissenschaft auseinanderzusetzen, zu mindern. So meint ein bekannter Autor, dass «das bewusste Denken und das verbale Denken im besonderen in der entscheidenden Phase des schöpferischen Aktes nur eine untergeordnete Rolle» spielen. Er zitiert gar wissen-

pas sa place. Une information claire sur les conditions régissant les recherches et les expériences menées en communication visuelle est importante pour le créateur, car il n'est alors pas soumis aux conclusions comme si elles constituaient un verdict. S'il connaît les circonstances dans lesquelles un projet a été rejeté, il peut travailler à une amélioration spécifique qui pourra même éventuellement consister en une modification des conditions initiales. C'est uniquement sur cette base que le rapport entre la science et la créativité peut être fructueux.

L'entente entre la science et les créateurs est entravée par un autre obstacle important: une conception de la créativité répandue dans la pratique selon laquelle logique et créativité sont diamétralement opposées (idée de la «pensée divergente»). Dans cette acception, la créativité est considérée comme synonyme d'intuition et liée à une contrainte presque névrotique d'innover. Seuls l'inhabituel, le surprenant et l'inédit peuvent être reconnus comme novateurs. Pour qu'une solution puisse recevoir le label «créatif», il faut qu'elle soit originale et non conventionnelle. Pour éviter tout malentendu, je précise que je ne cherche nullement ici à remettre en cause le rôle de l'intuition ou à dénigrer le critère de l'originalité. Bien plus, mon intention est de montrer les répercussions négatives de la prédominance de ces principes et de formuler une autre conception de la créativité.

L'apparition des «techniques novatrices» à prétention scientifique a précisément contribué à perpétuer le «mythe de la créativité» et à rendre les créateurs plus réticents vis-à-vis des questions scientifiques. Ainsi, selon un auteur connu, «la pensée consciente et la pensée verbale ne jouent qu'un rôle secondaire, en particulier dans la phase décisive de l'acte créateur». Il cite même des résultats

Functionality is an important requirement of design. This cannot be denied, but we do not wish to stay with yesterday's problems but pursue today's and tomorrow's questions. In an advanced industrial society, correct functional design is no longer a great achievement, for most products have reached the stage of maturity. The various versions or brands of a given product have almost identical techniques and main qualities. It is therefore to be assumed that their functional design will also be more or less indistinguishable.

Werner Kroeber-Riel

Funktionalität ist ein wichtiger Anspruch an das Design. Dagegen ist nichts zu sagen. Aber wir wollen uns nicht mit Problemen von gestern aufhalten, sondern Fragestellungen von heute und morgen verfolgen:
In einer fortgeschrittenen Industriegesellschaft ist die funktionsgerechte Gestaltung keine grosse Errungenschaft mehr. Denn die meisten Produkte sind heute ausgereift. Die verschiedenen Ausführungen beziehungsweise Marken eines Produkts besitzen fast die gleiche Technik, die gleichen substantiellen Eigenschaften. Es ist deswegen damit zu rechnen, dass bei funktionaler Gestaltung auch ein zum Verwechseln ähnliches Design herauskommt.

Werner Kroeber-Riel

Le design doit répondre à certaines exigences de fonction. A cela nous n'avons pas d'objections. Néanmoins, nous ne voulons pas nous attarder sur les problèmes d'hier; au contraire, nous voulons aborder les questions d'aujourd'hui et de demain: dans une société industrialisé avancée, le fait de parvenir à une conception fonctionnelle n'est plus un exploit. En effet, la plupart des produits sont aujourd'hui parfaitement au point. Les différents modèles ou marques d'un produit possèdent presque les mêmes caractéristiques fondamentales. En conséquence, il est à prévoir qu'une conception fonctionnelle aboutisse à un design quasi-similaire.

Werner Kroeber-Riel

dence that "too much knowledge of a subject can block the thought processes". From the scientific point of view, these so-called "creative techniques" are nothing but a systematization of the "traditional spinning of the web", as formulated in the same book. There is nothing against the organization of intuition, but the danger of this point of view is that the creative person's reservations about science appear to be justified scientifically. The crucial misunderstanding in this way of thinking lies in the associated assumption that creativity is entirely, or at least mainly, intuitive. According to this doctrine, intuition can be described as "the ability to come to conclusions, or make important decisions, without consciously formulating all the preconditions or being clear in detail about the reasons leading to these decisions". One may thoroughly endorse this description of intuition, but would have to be very much opposed to logic not to draw the conclusion that intuition is therefore nothing more than an emergency solution, to be applied when sure grounds for decision are lacking. Intuition accordingly plays a part in science and technology only in the early stages of a project and is replaced by more precise methods during the course of development.

In view of the tasks that visual communication today poses for design, it would seem to be a pure anachronism to cling doggedly to the principle of intuition. Modern creativity already makes much use of the findings of science in order to gather information about its subject and make the preconditions of design decisions clear, both to the designer himself and to the client. There are scientific methods which not only serve to analyze the subject but also penetrate very

schaftliche Ergebnisse, die belegen sollen, «dass zuviel Wissen über ein Objekt den Denkprozess blockieren kann». Unter wissenschaftlichem Aspekt sind diese sogenannten «kreativen Techniken» nichts weiter als eine Systematisierung, eine Systematisierung des «traditionellen Spinnens», wie er im gleichen Buch formuliert. Nichts gegen die Organisation der Intuition, aber das Gefährliche an dieser Betrachtungsweise liegt darin, dass die Reserve der Kreativen gegenüber der Wissenschaft auch noch scheinbar wissenschaftlich legitimiert wird. Das entscheidende Missverständnis dieser Denkweise liegt in der damit verbundenen Annahme, Kreativität sei nur oder zumindest hauptsächlich intuitiv. Nach dieser Lehre kann man «Intuition als die Fähigkeit beschreiben, zu Schlussfolgerungen zu kommen oder wichtige Entscheidungen zu treffen, ohne alle Voraussetzungen bewusst zu formulieren oder sich im einzelnen klar über die Gründe zu sein, die zu dieser Entscheidung geführt haben». Man kann dieser Beschreibung der Intuition durchaus zustimmen, aber man muss der Logik schon sehr feindlich gegenüberstehen, wenn man aus dieser Formulierung dann nicht den Schluss zieht, dass Intuition nichts weiter ist als eine Notlösung, wenn gesicherte Entscheidungsgrundlagen fehlen. Entsprechend spielt die Intuition in Wissenschaft und Technologie nur in typischen Frühstadien eine Rolle und wird im Laufe der Entwicklung durch präzise Methoden ersetzt.

Angesichts der Aufgaben, die sich heute für die Gestaltung der visuellen Kommunikation stellen, erscheint es als reiner Anachronismus, an der Intuition als Prinzip krampfhaft festzuhalten. Die moderne Kreativität bedient sich heute schon sehr wohl der Erkenntnisse der Wissenschaft, um Informationen über ihr Objekt zu sammeln und die Voraussetzungen gestalterischer Entscheidungen sich selbst – ebenso wie dem Auftraggeber – transparent zu machen. Es gibt wissenschaftliche Methoden, die nicht nur der Analyse des Gegenstandes dienen, sondern sehr weit in den

scientifiques d'après lesquels «une connaissance trop parfaite d'un objet peut bloquer le processus de pensée». Du point de vue scientifique, les prétendues «techniques créatives» ne sont qu'une systématisation, une systématisation du «délire traditionnel», comme il l'exprime dans le même livre. Bien qu'il ne condamne pas l'organisation de l'intuition, ce point de vue est dangereux dans la mesure où il semble légitimer scientifiquement la réserve montrée par les créateurs vis-à-vis de la science. Cette façon de penser est liée au malentendu qui consiste à dire que la création est seulement, ou principalement, intuitive. Selon cette théorie, on peut «décrire l'intuition comme étant la capacité à tirer des conclusions ou à prendre des décisions importantes sans formuler consciemment toutes les conditions préalables ou sans connaître précisément les motifs qui ont entraîné cette décision». On peut admettre pleinement une telle description de l'intuition. Néanmoins, il faudrait être farouchement opposé à toute logique pour ne pas en déduire que l'intuition n'est qu'un pis-aller auquel on a recours en l'absence d'éléments de décision plus sûrs. D'ailleurs, dans les domaines scientifique et technique, l'intuition joue un rôle uniquement dans les stades préliminaires, pour être remplacée par des méthodes plus précises au cours du développement.

Devant les tâches à accomplir aujourd'hui dans le domaine de la communication visuelle, il semble tout à fait anachronique de se cramponner au principe de l'intuition. La créativité utilise déjà avec bonheur les enseignements de la science pour rassembler des informations sur son objet et pour déterminer les conditions préalables à des décisions – dans son propre intérêt et dans celui du client. Il existe des méthodes scientifiques qui permettent d'analyser l'objet, mais qui permettent aussi d'aller au fond du

deeply into the design process itself, without encroaching in the very least into the domain of creativity. I refer principally to semiotics, which will be covered in detail in the following pages. But first, a few basic observations.

What has so far hindered the long overdue process of transfer of knowledge from science to design? I was once admonished by the "high priests of semiotics" for the inadmissible activity of associating their scientific discipline too literally and directly with everyday practice. In return, I would like to ask what justification the science of semiotics has for its existence if it cannot be applied in a realistic manner to practical concerns? On the other hand, design practitioners have objected that many of the demonstrated connections had to be initiated by a process of study. It may also be that many of the observations are only too self-evident, so that "do-it-yourself" answers are accepted as sufficient. The following considerations should strengthen the designer's competence, therefore, in that they are based on a comprehensive theory which gives them a new value. This connection of ideas should be borne in mind throughout.

For this purpose it is essential to start by going somewhat more deeply into semiotic theory. At the same time, it would seem impossible to discuss the matter in formal scientific terms. My presentation of the subject therefore follows a middle way between scientific exactitude, which cannot exist without a certain basis of defined concepts, and easy everyday language, but without enirely turning aside from scientific concepts.

eigentlichen Prozess der Gestaltung eindringen, ohne den Spielraum der Kreativität im geringsten einzuengen. Ich meine hier vor allem die Semiotik, die ich im folgenden ausführlich behandeln werde. Doch zuvor möchte ich noch einige grundsätzliche Bemerkungen machen.

Was hat bisher den längst überfälligen Transformationsprozess erschwert? Von den «Gralshütern der wahren Semiotik» als Wissenschaftsdisziplin wurde mir einmal der Vorwurf gemacht, es sei unzulässig, die semiotische Theorie so konkret und direkt mit der Praxis zu verknüpfen, wie ich das tue. Doch ich möchte fragen, was eine Semiotik überhaupt für eine Existenzberechtigung hat, wenn sie nicht konkret auf eine Praxis bezogen werden kann. Umgekehrt wurde mir von Praktikern gesagt, dass viele der aufgezeigten Zusammenhänge erst einen Lernprozess auslösen müssten. Darüber hinaus kann es sein, dass manche der Beobachtungen nur zu selbstverständlich sind, man glaubt weiterhin mit sogenannten «Hausrezepten» weiterkommen zu können. Die nachfolgenden Überlegungen stärken deshalb die Kompetenz des Gestalters, weil sie auf einer umfassenden Theorie basieren und von daher einen neuen Stellenwert erhalten. Man muss diesen Zusammenhang grundsätzlich mitberücksichtigen.

Es ist daher unerlässlich, zunächst etwas intensiver auf die semiotische Theorie als solche einzugehen.
Es erscheint jedoch im gegebenen Zusammenhang unmöglich, dabei wissenschaftlich vollständig zu argumentieren. Die folgende Darstellung der Semiotik ist also in gewisser Weise eine Gratwanderung zwischen wissenschaftlicher Genauigkeit – für die auf ein gewisses Fundament definierter Begriffe nicht verzichtet werden kann – und umgangssprachlicher Verständlichkeit – für die auf eine vollständige Ableitung der Begriffe verzichtet werden muss.

processus de la conception sans entraver le moins du monde le libre jeu de la créativité. Je pense ici en particulier à la sémiotique dont je traiterai en détail ci-après. Permettez-mois cependant de faire au préalable quelques remarques fondamentales.

Pourquoi a-t-il été si difficile jusqu'à présent d'engager un processus de transformation qui se fait attendre depuis longtemps? Les «défenseurs de la vraie sémiotique», discipline scientifique, m'ont un jour reproché de rattacher la théorie de la sémiotique à la pratique de manière trop concrète et directe. La question que je pose est alors la suivante: comment la sémiotique peut-elle justifier son existence si elle ne peut être appliquée concrètement à la pratique? Inversement, des praticiens m'ont dit que beaucoup des corrélations exposées devraient d'abord déclencher un processus d'apprentissage. En outre, il est possible que certaines observations semblent tellement évidentes que l'on croit pouvoir continuer à progresser à l'aide de ce que l'on appelle les «recettes maison». Les considérations qui suivent renforcent les compétences du créateur car elles se fondent sur une théorie complète et acquièrent dès lors une nouvelle valeur. Cet élément doit être pris en considération.

En conséquence, il est indispensable de s'attarder sur la théorie sémiotique. Le contexte du présent ouvrage ne permet pas d'apporter une argumentation scientifique complète.
Dans la présentation de la sémiotique qui va suivre, nous allons donc emprunter en quelque sorte une voie moyenne entre la précision scientifique – pour laquelle il n'est pas possible de renoncer à une base de notions bien définies – et un langage compréhensible par tous – pour lequel on renoncera à certaines disgressions.

To its advantage, semiotics is a mosaic of terminology and methods that can help us clarify and understand the role of meaning as embodied in the semiosis of consumer behaviour as well as research behaviour.

David Glen Mick

Die Semiotik hat den Vorteil, dass sie uns ein Mosaik von Begriffen und Methoden liefert, um die Rolle der Bedeutung zu erklären, wie sie in den Zeichenprozessen des Konsumentenverhaltens wie des Verhaltens der Forscher zum Ausdruck kommt.

David Glen Mick

La sémiotique présente l'avantage d'offrir une mosaïque de notions et de méthodes permettant d'expliquer le rôle du sens tel qu'il s'exprime dans les processus de signes aussi bien du comportement des consommateurs que du comportement des chercheurs.

David Glen Mick

2. The basics of a theory of signs

2.1. Is there a language of images?

Let us make the purpose of these considerations clear once again. We are seeking a theory of visual communications, which will allow a general systematization for the treatment of all problems arising in this connection and, at the same time, can be applied in an entirely practical way to the business of design in its widest variety of uses. It is clear that this can be achieved only within the framework of a general theory of communications, applicable to the specific problems of visual communication. Semiotics is here regarded as an appropriate theory.

Semiotics is concerned with sign systems in an all-inclusive way. In the application of theory to the problems of specific sign systems, the semiotics of pictorial signs can be directed towards the formulation of specific theories in the area of language. Owing to the outstanding importance of the sign system of language, the formation of theories has advanced particularly far in this respect. The science of linguistics comprises a wide variety of models for the description of language, mostly known as grammars. The most commonly known is school grammar, which may not be quite up to date as a linguistic model; but to be able to describe pictorial sign systems at least on this theoretical level would be a major advance for visual communications. Transformational generative grammar may be mentioned as a topical model in linguistics. The value of scientific models cannot, however, be determined by topicality but depends once and for all on whether they can be meaningfully applied to a given practical situation. In this respect, school grammar has lost nothing of its value.

2. Die Grundlagen der Zeichentheorie

2.1. Gibt es eine Sprache der Bilder?

Besinnen wir uns noch einmal auf das Ziel unserer Überlegungen. Gesucht ist eine Theorie der visuellen Kommunikation, die eine umfassende Systematisierung bei der Behandlung aller in diesem Zusammenhang auftauchenden Probleme erlaubt und gleichzeitig ganz konkret auf die Praxis der Gestaltung bei den unterschiedlichsten Aufgabenstellungen bezogen werden kann. Wir sind uns darüber klar, dass dies nur im Rahmen einer allgemeinen Kommunikationstheorie geleistet werden kann, die auf die spezifischen Probleme der visuellen Kommunikation übertragbar ist. Als eine solche Theorie wird hier die Semiotik angesehen.

Die Semiotik beschäftigt sich ganz allgemein mit Zeichensystemen. Bei der Übertragung auf die Problematik spezifischer Zeichensysteme kann sich eine Semiotik der bildlichen Zeichen an der spezifischen Theorienbildung im Bereich der Sprache orientieren. Aufgrund der herausragenden Bedeutung des Zeichensystems Sprache ist hier die Theorienbildung besonders weit fortgeschritten. Die Linguistik kennt die verschiedensten Modelle zur Beschreibung der Sprache, die meist als Grammatiken bezeichnet werden. Am geläufigsten ist hier die Schulgrammatik, die zwar als linguistisches Modell nicht gerade aktuell ist, aber es wäre für die visuelle Kommunikation schon ein gewaltiger Fortschritt, das bildliche Zeichensystem wenigstens auf dieser theoretischen Ebene beschreiben zu können. Als ein aktuelles Modell in der Linguistik wäre hier die generative Transformationsgrammatik zu nennen. Der Wert wissenschaftlicher Modelle kann jedoch nicht anhand der Aktualität bestimmt werden, sondern hängt einzig und allein davon ab, dass sie in einer bestimmten Situation sinnvoll auf die Praxis angewendet werden können. Und in dieser Hinsicht hat auch die Schulgrammatik nichts von ihrem Wert verloren.

2. Les fondements de la théorie des signes

2.1. Existe-t-il un langage des images?

Rappelons l'objectif de notre réflexion: nous cherchons une théorie de la communication visuelle permettant une systématisation complète du traitement de tous les problèmes pouvant surgir dans ce contexte. En outre, cette théorie doit pouvoir s'appliquer concrètement à la pratique de la conception, même si les missions qui lui sont confiées sont des plus diverses. Il est entendu que cet objectif ne peut être atteint qu'avec une théorie générale de la communication pouvant être transposée aux problèmes spécifiques de la communication visuelle. La sémiotique semble répondre à ces exigences.

D'une manière générale, la sémiotique se consacre aux systèmes de signes. Lors du transfert à la problématique de systèmes de signes spécifiques, une sémiotique des signes figuratifs peut se laisser guider par la théorie spécifique élaborée dans le domaine de la langue. En raison de l'importance considérable de la langue comme système de signes, la théorie dans ce domaine est particulièrement avancée. La linguistique connaît les modèles les plus divers pour décrire la langue: on les appelle généralement des grammaires. La plus courante d'entre elles est la grammaire scolaire, qui n'est certes pas à jour en tant que modèle linguistique. Néanmoins, si le système de signes figuratifs pouvait être décrit à ce niveau théorique, ce serait un progrès considérable pour la communication visuelle. La grammaire transformationnelle générative est un modèle très actuel en linguistique. Toutefois, la valeur des modèles scientifiques n'est pas déterminée par leur actualité. Elle se mesure uniquement à la possibilité de les appliquer utilement dans une situation pratique donnée. A cet égard, la grammaire scolaire n'a rien perdu de sa valeur.

In order to be able to develop a grammar of pictorial language, it is first necessary to name the conditions which must underlie such a description. There follows a brief summary of the conditions formulated by the linguist Manfred Bierwisch. It is only necessary to substitute "semiotic" for "linguistic" and "sign system" for "language" to obtain the semiotic programme:

1. The linguistic description of a language must declare all properties which determine how any expression of that language is built up and thus how it is understood. The description must show what elements comprise an expression and what relationship one expression has to other expressions.

2. The description must cover *all* possible expressions. This means, empirically, that the actual subject of the description of the language is not any given expressions but the rules under which these expressions are formed. Theoretically speaking, it means that the description of the language is by its nature a system of rules, which produce the infinite quantity of expressions of a language and thus confer their structural description.

3. Every natural language is a particular coinage from the mint of general human capacity for speech, and in all its particularities it shows the lines of this general conditionality. Following this assumption, the description must, in each case, satisfy certain general conditions.

The language of images, like everyday language, is a natural one. As we know, the use of a natural language is completely independent of a mastery of its grammar. Every child learns its language without any knowledge of grammar. Nevertheless, there is no doubt that linguistic competence and

Wenn im folgenden versucht wird, eine Grammatik der bildlichen Sprache zu entwickeln, so sind zunächst die Bedingungen zu nennen, die an eine solche Beschreibung gestellt werden müssen. Ich will hier kurz die Bedingungen zitieren, die der Linguist Manfred Bierwisch formuliert hat. Man braucht hier nur statt «linguistisch» «semiotisch» und statt «Sprache» «Zeichensystem» zu setzen, um das Programm der Semiotik zu haben:

1. Die linguistische Beschreibung einer Sprache muss für beliebige Äusserungen dieser Sprache alle Eigenschaften angeben, die festlegen, wie diese Äusserungen aufgebaut sind und also verstanden werden. Sie muss zeigen, aus welchen Elementen eine Äusserung besteht, welche Relation eine Äusserung zu anderen Äusserungen hat.

2. Die Beschreibung muss *alle* möglichen Äusserungen erfassen. Das bedeutet empirisch, dass der eigentliche Gegenstand der Sprachbeschreibung nicht beliebig gegebene Äusserungen sind, sondern die Regeln, nach denen diese Äusserungen gebildet werden. Theoretisch bedeutet es, dass die Sprachbeschreibung die Form eines Regelsystems hat, das die – unendliche – Menge von Äusserungen einer Sprache erzeugt und ihnen dabei ihre Strukturbeschreibung zuordnet.

3. Jede einzelne natürliche Sprache ist eine besondere Ausprägung im Rahmen der allgemeinen menschlichen Sprachfähigkeit und zeigt in all ihren Besonderheiten eben die Züge dieser allgemeinen Bedingtheit. Dieser Annahme entsprechend muss die Beschreibung jeder Einzelsprache bestimmten allgemeinen Bedingungen genügen.

Die Sprache der Bilder ist wie die Umgangssprache eine natürliche Sprache. Nun ist die Benutzung einer natürlichen Sprache unabhängig von der Beherrschung ihrer Grammatik. Jedes Kind lernt die Sprache ohne Kenntnisse der Grammatik. Doch ohne Zweifel steigt mit der Beherr-

Avant de prétendre élaborer une grammaire du langage figuratif, nous devons préciser les conditions que doit remplir une telle description. Je vais citer ici brièvement les conditions énumérées par le linguiste Manfred Bierwisch. Il suffit de remplacer «linguistique» par «sémiotique» et «langue» par «système de signes» pour obtenir le programme de la sémiotique:

1. La description linguistique d'une langue doit indiquer pour chaque énoncé de cette langue toutes les caractéristiques qui déterminent la façon dont il est structuré et, partant, la façon dont il est compris. Cette description doit montrer de quels éléments un énoncé est constitué et quelle relation existe entre un énoncé et d'autres énoncés.

2. La description doit comprendre *tous* les énoncés possibles. Empiriquement, cela signifie que l'objet véritable de la description de la langue n'est pas constitué par certains énoncés donnés, mais par les règles selon lesquelles ces énoncés sont construits. Théoriquement, cela signifie que la description de la langue a la forme d'un système de règles qui engendre la quantité – infinie – des énoncés d'une langue et leur attribue en même temps leur description structurelle.

3. Toute langue naturelle est une expression particulière dans le cadre général de la faculté humaine du langage et montre justement, dans toutes ses particularités, les traits caractéristiques de cette relativité générale. A partir de cette hypothèse, la description de toute langue doit satisfaire à certaines conditions générales.

La langue des images, comme la langue familière, est une langue naturelle. Or, l'utilisation d'une langue naturelle est indépendante de la maîtrise de sa grammaire. Tout enfant apprend sa langue sans connaître la grammaire. Cependant, il ne fait aucun doute que la maîtrise des règles

the ability fo find the best forms for given communications grow with an understanding of the rules.

The situation of visual communications is characterized by the fact that everyday pictorial language has developed with unimaginable dynamics in recent times, while its theoretical treatment is still in its early stages. In the following pages, some basic principles will be worked out for the formation of a theory in parallel with linguistics.

An important precondition for a linguistically exact working method is a distinction between the levels at which the description of a language is made. The following principal levels, here placed in relation to systems of analysis and levels of imagery, can be distinguished:

Levels of language
Sounds
Sound formations
Concepts
Statements

Systems of analysis
Phonology
Morphology
Lexicology
Syntax

Levels of imagery
Elements of perception
Figures, patterns
Represented objects
Images

Just as the development of modern linguistics had its origin in phonology, the attempt to make a semiotic analysis of images must first begin at the level of elements of perception.
But even at this basic level, there are various possible approaches, which

schung der Regeln die Sprachkompetenz, die Fähigkeit, für bestimmte Mitteilungen die optimale Form zu finden.

Die Situation der visuellen Kommunikation ist dadurch gekennzeichnet, dass sich die bildliche Umgangssprache innerhalb kurzer Zeit mit unvorstellbarer Dynamik entwickelt hat, während ihre theoretische Aufarbeitung noch in den ersten Anfängen steckt. Im folgenden sollen einige Grundprinzipien der Theorienbildung parallel zur Linguistik herausgearbeitet werden.

Eine wesentliche Voraussetzung für eine linguistisch exakte Arbeitsweise ist die Unterscheidung der Ebenen, auf denen die Beschreibung einer Sprache erfolgt. Folgende Hauptebenen, die hier gleich in Beziehung zu Analysesystemen und Bildebenen gesetzt werden, kann man somit unterscheiden:

Sprachebenen
Laute
Lautgestalten
Begriffe
Aussagen

Analysesysteme
Phonologie
Morphology
Lexikologie
Syntax

Bildebenen
Wahrnehmungselemente
Figuren, Muster
Abgebildete Gegenstände
Bilder

Wie die Entwicklung der modernen Linguistik von der Phonologie ihren Ausgang nahm, so sollte sich der Versuch einer semiotischen Analyse von Bildern zunächst mit der Ebene Wahrnehmungselemente auseinandersetzen.
Aber schon auf dieser grundlegenden Ebene sind verschiedene Betrach-

améliore la compétence linguistique, la capacité de trouver la forme la plus appropriée à l'expression de certains messages.

La situation de la communication visuelle est caractérisée en ce que la langue familière figurative s'est développée rapidement, avec un grand dynamisme, alors que son élaboration technique n'en est qu'à ses balbutiements. Nous allons dégager ci-après quelques principes de base de la formation de la théorie, parallèlement à la linguistique.

Pour procéder selon une méthode de travail linguistiquement exacte, il est nécessaire de différencier les niveaux auxquels nous allons décrire la langue. Il est possible de distinguer les principaux niveaux suivants, présentés ici en corrélation avec les systèmes d'analyse et les niveaux d'image:

Niveaux linguistiques
sons
formes des sons
concepts
énoncés

Systèmes d'analyse
phonologie
morphologie
lexicologie
syntaxe

Niveaux d'image
éléments de perception
figures, motifs
objets représentés
images

Le développement de la linguistique moderne ayant son origine dans la phonologie, la tentative d'une analyse sémiotique des images doit commencer par le niveau des éléments de perception.

Néanmoins, il existe déjà à ce niveau fondamental plusieurs variantes d'ob-

can be explained by means of the simple communications model.

Depending on the perspective from which we view this process, the basic elements, whether sounds or images, look very different.

Language	*Image*
articulated (Speaker)	designed (Designer)
acoustic (Air vibrations)	optical (Light waves)
auditive (Listener)	visual (Viewer)

Theoretically speaking, the analysis can begin at any of these points. There are two reasons for starting from the auditive, or the visual. First, the act of communication is always angled towards the recipient, and secondly, the number of elements to be analyzed in the auditive-visual field is less than in either of the other two pairs of elements. Thus, the same visual effect can be achieved through widely different imaging techniques, for example a given colour impression through the application of mixed colouring matter, the spinning of a top, the projection of various coloured lights or the printing of a set of colour separations. In the same way, we obtain similar visual effects by means of photographic printing, watercolour painting or chemical etching.

With the restriction of the analysis to the visual area, the consideration of graphic techniques *per se* becomes irrelevant in this context—even though nothing more than graphic techniques is taught at many art colleges under the ambitious title of "visual communications". All the same, the fallacious use of a term should not prevent us from ever using it in the correct context. The use of the terms "pictorial

tungsweisen möglich, die man anhand des einfachen Kommunikationsmodells verdeutlichen kann.

Je nachdem, aus welcher Perspektive ich diesen Prozess betrachte, stellen sich die grundlegenden Elemente, seien es nun Laute oder Bildelemente, sehr unterschiedlich dar.

Sprache	*Bild*
artikulatorisch (Sprecher)	gestalterisch (Gestalter)
akustisch (Luftvibrationen)	optisch (Lichtwellen)
auditiv (Hörer)	visuell (Betrachter)

Theoretisch kann die Analyse an jedem dieser Punkte ansetzen. Zwei Gründe sprechen dafür, vom Auditiven bzw. Visuellen auszugehen. Zum einen ist der Kommunikationsakt immer im Hinblick auf den Empfänger angelegt, zum andern ist die Zahl der zu analysierenden Elemente im auditiv-visuellen Bereich geringer als etwa im akustisch-optischen oder im artikulatorisch-gestalterischen Bereich. So kann man den gleichen visuellen Eindruck durch die verschiedensten gestalterischen Techniken erzielen, etwa einen bestimmten Farbeindruck durch den Auftrag gemischter Körperfarben, durch Kreiselmischung, durch Projektion verschiedener Lichtfarben oder durch Zusammendruck eines Farbsatzes. Ebenso erreiche ich den gleichen visuellen Effekt beispielsweise durch Hartkopieren einer Fotografie, durch eine Tuschzeichnung oder mit Hilfe einer Ätzung.

Mit einer Einschränkung der Analyse auf den visuellen Bereich wird zugleich die Behandlung grafischer Techniken als solcher für den gegebenen Zusammenhang als irrelevant erklärt, auch wenn unter dem anspruchsvollen Begriff der «visuellen Kommunikation» an vielen Kunsthochschulen nichts weiter als grafische Techniken gelehrt werden. Doch die fälschliche Verwendung eines Begriffes sollte uns nicht davon abhalten,

servation, illustrées par ce simple schéma de la communication:

Selon la perspective que je choisis pour observer ce processus, les éléments fondamentaux, qu'ils soient des sons ou des éléments d'image, se présentent sous des aspects fort différents.

Langue	*Image*
articulatoire (orateur)	morphologique (dessinateur)
acoustique (vibrations de l'air)	optique (ondes lumineuses)
auditif (auditeur)	visuel (observateur)

Théoriquement, l'analyse peut se fonder sur n'importe lequel de ces points. Deux raisons nous entraînent à prendre pour base l'auditif ou le visuel. D'une part, l'acte de communication est toujours orienté vers le récepteur et, d'autre part, le nombre d'éléments à analyser est plus faible dans le domaine audio-visuel que dans les domaines acoustico-optique ou articulo-morphologique. Ainsi, il est possible d'obtenir la même impression visuelle par des techniques morphologiques très différentes: par exemple, une impression de couleur peut être obtenue par l'application de différentes couleurs opaques mélangées, par un mélange centrifuge, par la projection de différentes couleurs lumineuses ou par l'impression simultanée d'une gamme de clichés. Pareillement, la copie dure d'une photographie, un dessin à l'encre de Chine et une gravure peuvent donner le même effet visuel.

En limitant l'analyse au domaine visuel, on déclare que l'étude des techniques graphiques n'est pas pertinente dans le contexte donné, même si la notion prétentieuse de «communication visuelle» ne recouvre souvent que l'enseignement de techniques graphiques dans de nombreuses écoles des beaux-arts. Toutefois, l'uti-

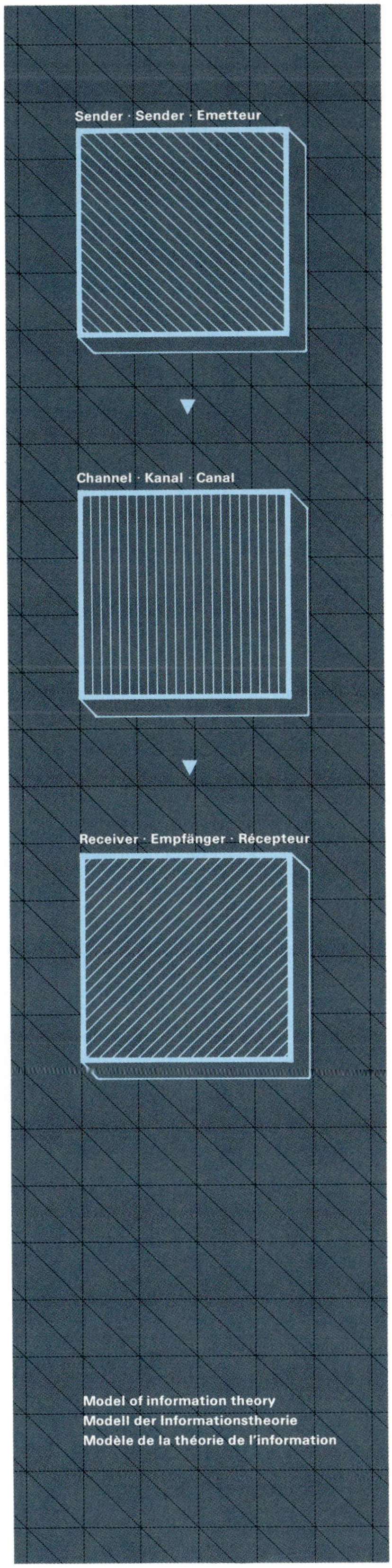

Model of information theory
Modell der Informationstheorie
Modèle de la théorie de l'information

communication" and "visual communication" in the present work can easily be justified against the given background. "Figurative" or "pictorial communication" refers to the entire process of communication (sender, channel, recipient), in so far as its figurative or pictorial elements convey independent information. In "visual communication", the centre of gravity lies in the analysis of the process with regard to the recipient.

In the linguistic analysis of language, a phenomenon occurs that should be borne in mind during the search for the elements of visual communication: namely, that the number of elements becomes smaller as the level chosen for description becomes lower. Thus phonology, as the lowest level of categorization, numbers only about 30 phonemes, or significant sounds, for most languages. Phonemes are classes of sounds. In principle, the number of possible sounds is infinite, but their arrangement into classified phonemes is made on the basis of different characteristics. A distinction is made between free, facultative and positional variants on the one hand, and relevant variants on the other. Sounds can, in fact, be quite different one from another without necessarily forming different phonemes. Examples of free, facultative variants are the different pronunciations of "a" in different regions of a country. Positional variants occur in the combination of phonemes: for example, "a" before "r" sounds different from "a" after "r". Variations of sound that distinguish one phoneme from another must therefore be sought: in linguistics, these variations are known as distinctive characteristics. In German, for example, the change from "a" to "o" is easily recognized, but in Danish there is an intermediate phoneme which is written "å". Different distinctive characteristics apply in the two languages.

ihn auch einmal im richtigen Zusammenhang zu nennen. Die Verwendung der Begriffe «bildliche Kommunikation» und «visuelle Kommunikation» in der vorliegenden Arbeit lässt sich vor dem skizzierten Hintergrund leicht begründen. «Bildliche Kommunikation» betrifft den gesamten Kommunikationsprozess – also Sender, Kanal und Empfänger –, sofern in ihm bildliche Elemente eigenständige Information übertragen. Bei «visueller Kommunikation» liegt der Schwerpunkt bei der Analyse dieses Prozesses im Hinblick auf den Empfänger.

Bei der linguistischen Analyse der Sprache auf den verschiedenen Ebenen taucht ein Phänomen auf, das man bei der Suche nach den Elementen visueller Kommunikation berücksichtigen sollte: Die Zahl der Elemente ist um so kleiner, je niedriger die Beschreibungsebene gewählt wird. So weist die Phonologie als unterste Ebene für die meisten Sprachen nur um 30 Phoneme, also Bedeutung tragende Laute, auf. Phoneme sind Klassen von Lauten. Denn prinzipiell ist die Zahl möglicher Laute unendlich, ihre Zuordnung zu bestimmten Phonemen erfolgt aufgrund unterscheidender Merkmale, wobei man zwischen freien fakultativen und positionellen Varianten einerseits und relevanten Varianten anderseits unterscheiden muss. Laute können also durchaus unterschiedlich klingen, ohne dass sie verschiedene Phoneme bilden. Freie fakultative Varianten sind beispielsweise die unterschiedlichen Aussprachen des «a» in verschiedenen Regionen. Positionelle Varianten entstehen bei der Kombination mit andern Phonemen, so klingt das «a» vor einem «r» anders als nach einem «r». Es müssen daher Lautvariationen gesucht werden, die ein Phonem von anderen unterscheiden; solche Variationen werden in der Linguistik distinktive Merkmale genannt. Im Deutschen lässt sich beispielsweise der Übergang von «a» zu «o» leicht markieren, im Dänischen dagegen liegt zwischen diesen beiden Phonemen noch ein weiteres, nämlich das «å». Es gelten also andere distinktive Merkmale.

lisation erronée d'une notion ne doit pas nous empêcher de la reprendre, pour une fois, dans le contexte qui doit être le sien. Le tableau que nous avons brossé justifie aisément l'utilisation des expressions «communication figurative» et «communication visuelle». La «communication figurative» se rapporte à tout le processus de communication – émetteur, canal et récepteur –, dans la mesure où des éléments figuratifs y transmettent une information qui leur est propre. Dans la «communication visuelle», l'analyse du processus est axée principalement sur le récepteur.

Dans l'analyse de la langue à ses différents niveaux, l'on distingue un phénomène qui doit être pris en considération lors de la recherche des éléments de communication visuelle: le nombre d'éléments est d'autant plus petit que le niveau de description choisi est bas. Ainsi, la phonologie, niveau le plus bas, ne présente dans la plupart des langues qu'environ 30 phonèmes, c'est-à-dire des éléments porteurs de sens.
Les phonèmes sont des classes de son. Par principe, le nombre de sons possibles est infini; leur classification en phonèmes se fait selon certains traits distinctifs: l'on distinguera ici, d'une part, les variantes facultatives libres et les variantes positionnelles et, d'autre part, les variantes pertinentes. Ainsi, des sons peuvent être différents sans constituer pour autant des phonèmes distincts. Les variantes facultatives libres sont par exemple les prononciations différentes du «a» d'une région à l'autre. Les variantes positionnelles naissent de la combinaison avec d'autres phonèmes: ainsi, le «a» n'a pas le même son quand il est placé avant un «r» que quand il se trouve après celui-ci. Dès lors, il faut chercher des variations de sons qui différencient un phonème des autres; en linguistique, on nomme ces variations des traits distinctifs. Dans la langue française, par exemple, il est facile de remarquer le passage du «a» au «o», alors qu'en danois il existe un autre phonème intermédiaire, le «å»: ainsi, d'autres traits distinctifs s'appliquent.

Applying this principle to the semiotic analysis of images, it can be seen that one should begin by looking for the distinctive characteristics of the elements, rather than their specific forms of appearance. A study of the current findings of perception psychology shows that there are such characteristics for visual elements as well as for phonemes. However, before going into this matter, we must explain the connection with semiotics, which here plays the part of the interpreting theory. Unfortunately we cannot do without this basis of theory—though it may seem rather dry to the practical man—because otherwise it would be impossible to explain the comprehensive character of its subsequent application to practice.

2.2. The threefold reference of the sign

2.2.1. How can signs be defined?

When we speak of semiotics we must bear in mind that there is no uniform theory. Semiotics is a scientific discipline in which there are very many different theories. Despite similar terminology, and to some extent similar concepts, there are substantial differences between the different approaches to the subject.

This means that the meaning of a term or concept can be defined only within the framework of the theory in question. As already explained in the introduction, the value of a theory depends entirely on how far it makes an advance of knowledge possible in a given connection. Consequently there is no theory for which "sole rights" can be claimed.

If, therefore, the following explanations are based on the theory of signs of the American philosopher Charles S. Peirce, this implies no evaluation of other semiotic theories. It means no

Übertragen auf die semiotische Analyse von Bildern bedeutet dies, dass man zunächst weniger nach konkreten Erscheinungsformen der Elemente als nach deren distinktiven Merkmalen suchen muss. Dass es solche Merkmale auch für visuelle Elemente gibt, zeigt das Studium der aktuellen Erkenntnisse der Wahrnehmungspsychologie. Doch ehe darauf eingegangen werden kann, muss zunächst einmal die Semiotik, die hier als vermittelnde Theorie fungiert, im Zusammenhang dargestellt werden. Leider kann auf diese – für den interessierten Praktiker zweifellos recht nüchterne – theoretische Fundierung hier nicht verzichet werden, da sonst der umfassende Charakter der nachfolgenden Übertragung auf die Praxis der visuellen Kommunikation nicht erklärt werden könnte.

2.2. Die dreifache Beziehung des Zeichens

2.2.1. Wie lassen sich Zeichen definieren?

Wenn man von der Semiotik spricht, muss man wissen, dass es sich dabei nicht um eine einheitliche Theorie handelt, sondern um eine wissenschaftliche Disziplin, in der die verschiedensten Theorien zu finden sind. Trotz ähnlicher Terminologie, ja teilweise gleichen Begriffen, gibt es erhebliche Unterschiede zwischen den verschiedenen Ansätzen.

Die Bedeutung eines Begriffes kann also immer nur im Rahmen der jeweiligen Theorie erklärt werden. Es wurde bereits darauf hingewiesen, dass der Wert einer Theorie nur davon abhängt, inwieweit sie in einem gegebenen Zusammenhang Erkenntnisfortschritte ermöglicht, folglich gibt es keine Theorie, die einen «Alleinvertretungsanspruch» stellen könnte.

Wenn sich also die folgenden Ausführungen auf die Zeichentheorie des amerikanischen Philosophen Charles S. Peirce stützen, so beinhaltet dies keine Bewertung anderer Theorien. Es bedeutet nicht mehr und nicht weniger, als dass ich persönlich im Peirceschen Modell des Zeichenprozesses

Transposées à l'analyse sémiotique des images, ces considérations signifient qu'il faut d'abord rechercher les traits distinctifs des éléments plutôt que leurs manifestations concrètes. Les connaissances actuelles en psychologie de la perception prouvent que ces traits existent aussi pour les éléments visuels. Cependant, avant d'entrer dans ce domaine, il est nécessaire de présenter la sémiotique, qui nous sert ici de théorie médiatrice. Cette base théorique – sans doute rébarbative pour le praticien – est malheureusement indispensable: sans elle, il ne serait pas possible d'expliquer le caractère global de la transposition à la pratique de la communication visuelle qui va suivre.

2.2. La triple relation du signe

2.2.1. Comment définir les signes?

Quand on parle de la sémiotique, il faut savoir qu'il ne s'agit pas d'une théorie uniforme, mais plutôt d'une discipline scientifique dans laquelle on trouve les théories les plus diverses. Malgré une terminologie similaire et des concepts partiellement semblables, il existe des écarts considérables entre les différentes approches.

La signification d'un concept ne peut ainsi être expliquée que dans le cadre d'une théorie donnée. Dans l'introduction, nous avons souligné que la valeur d'une théorie ne dépend que de sa capacité à permettre des progrès de la connaissance dans un contexte donné. Il n'existe dès lors aucune théorie qui pourrait prétendre à une «représentation exclusive».

Ainsi, le fait que les considérations ci-après se fondent sur la théorie des signes de Charles S. Peirce, philosophe américain, ne suppose pas une évaluation des autres théories. Ce

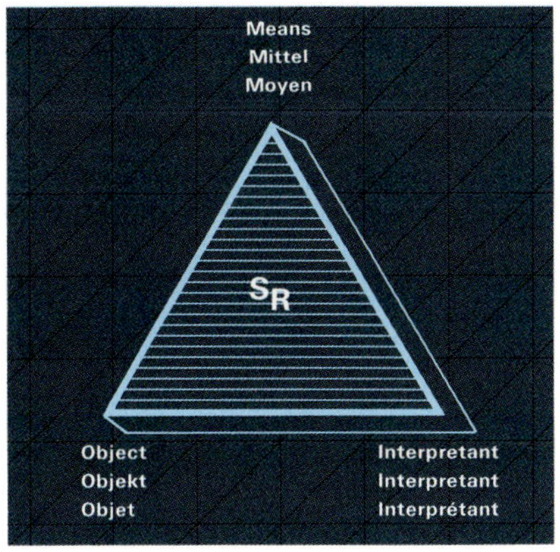

A sign exists only through the interaction of these three components, which constitute the sign-process.

Ein Zeichen konstituiert sich nur im Zusammenwirken dieser drei Komponenten, die den Zeichenprozess ausmachen.

Un signe ne se constitue qu'en cas de symbiose entre les trois éléments qui composent le processus du signe.

more and no less than that I personally find the best possibility of practical application in Peirce's model of the sign process.

Peirce regards a sign not as a static phenomenon but as a dynamic process, in which a trichotomy or threefold reference comes into effect (see illustration).

This model is known as the "triadic sign relation". The medium for the sign can be any material object, its qualities or a material event, so long as it is interpreted only as a sign, that is to say, is so regarded that it stands for something else, namely its object.

For example, when Robinson Crusoe discovers the remains of a fire on the beach, he sees it not as such but as a sign of the presence of people on the island, where he had thought he was alone. In contrast to the communication process, the sign process does not *assume the existence of a communicator* and *a recipient. The ashes of the fire are a sign, even if the cannibals who made the fire did not have any communicative intention. Conversely, the bottle-post which Crusoe throws in the sea is a sign, even if nobody ever receives it.*

The concept of interpretants, the third element of the sign relation, is often misunderstood. In no case should the interpretant be confused with the interpreter, who is the sign user, whether as producer (communicator) or recipient of the sign. The interpretant is the system within which meaning is allotted to a sign. The following example should make this point clear:

The Greek term "helios" can be translated as "sun" and the object, the sun, can be applied to it without further explanation. Nevertheless, the meaning of "helios" is not even approximately comprehended by the translation into English.

am ehesten die Möglichkeit einer Übertragung auf die Praxis der visuellen Kommunikation sehe.

Peirce betrachtet ein Zeichen nicht als ein statisches Phänomen, sondern als einen dynamischen Prozess, in dem eine dreifache Beziehung wirksam wird (siehe Abbildung).

Dieses Modell wird als «triadische Zeichenrelation» bezeichnet. Mittel zum Zeichen kann jeder materielle Gegenstand, seine Eigenschaften oder ein materielles Ereignis sein, sobald es nur als Zeichen interpretiert wird, das heisst, sobald man es so sieht, dass es für etwas anderes, nämlich sein Objekt, steht.

Wenn beispielsweise Robinson die Feuerstelle am Strand entdeckt, so sieht er sie nicht nur als solche, sondern als ein Zeichen für die Anwesenheit von Menschen auf der Insel, auf der er sich allein glaubte. Im Gegensatz zum Kommunikationsprozess setzt der Zeichenprozess nicht Kommunikator und *Rezipient voraus. Die Feuerstelle ist ein Zeichen, auch wenn die Kannibalen, von denen sie stammte, keine kommunikativen Absichten damit verbanden. Umgekehrt ist auch die Flaschenpost, die Robinson dem Meer anvertraute, ein Zeichen, auch wenn niemand es jemals empfängt.*

Das Konzept vom Interpretanten, dem dritten Element der Zeichenrelation, ist oft missverstanden worden. Auf keinen Fall darf der Interpretant mit dem Interpreten – also dem Zeichenbenutzer, sei es nun der Kommunikator als Zeichenproduzent oder der Rezipient als Zeichenempfänger – verwechselt werden. Der Interpretant ist vielmehr das System, in dem einem Zeichen Bedeutung zugeordnet wird. Folgendes Beispiel soll dies veranschaulichen:

Der griechische Begriff «helios» kann mit «Sonne» übersetzt werden, und man kann ihm auch ohne weiteres das Objekt Sonne zuordnen. Doch damit ist die Bedeutung von «helios» auch nicht annähernd erfasst.

choix signifie ni plus ni moins que je vois dans le modèle de Peirce du processus des signes la plus grande probabilité de pouvoir opérer une transposition à la pratique de la communication visuelle.

Peirce considère un signe non pas comme un phénomène statique, mais comme un processus dynamique dans lequel opère une triple relation (voir illustration).

Ce schéma est appelé «relation triadique du signe». Le moyen du signe peut être tout objet matériel, ses propriétés, ou un événement matériel, dès lors qu'il n'est interprété que comme signe, c'est-à-dire dès lors qu'on le voit comme représentant autre chose, à savoir son objet.

Par exemple, quand Robinson découvre le foyer sur la plage, il ne le considère pas seulement comme tel, mais comme un signe de la présence d'hommes sur l'île où il se croyait seul. A la différence du processus de la communication, le processus des signes ne présuppose pas l'existence d'un communicateur et *d'un récepteur. Le foyer est un signe, même si les cannibales qui l'ont créé n'avaient pas l'intention de l'utiliser pour communiquer. Inversement, le message dans une bouteille que Robinson confie à la mer est aussi un signe, même si personne ne le reçoit jamais.*

Le concept de l'interprétant, le troisième élément de la relation du signe, est souvent mal compris. L'interprétant ne doit en aucun cas être confondu avec l'interprète – c'est-à-dire l'utilisateur du signe, que ce soit le communicateur, producteur de signes, ou le récepteur, récepteur de signes. L'interprétant est le système dans lequel on attribue un sens à un signe. Prenons l'exemple suivant:

Le concept grec «helios» peut être traduit par «soleil», et l'on peut d'emblée lui attribuer l'objet soleil. Toutefois, on est ainsi bien loin d'avoir saisi le sens de «helios».

The true meaning is revealed only by the addition of the interpretant, which in this case is formed by the culture and outlook of the ancient world. Even so, there is only a certain approximation, because although we may appreciate the idea of a sun-god intellectually, we can never experience it immediately.

The interpretant comprises the possibility of replacing one sign by another, a process which always comes into use when there is some question about the meaning of a sign. Thus a lexicon, for example, represents a collection of realized interpretants: "realized" because interpretants are only possibilities of replacement. In the sign process, interpretants are usually only actualized, that is to say, the meaning is taken without being named. The interpretant comprises still more, explaining at the same time why one and the same material sign can denote different objects, by providing the sign system from which each meaning is obtained. In this connection one often speaks of the context, which can also be determined by the situation.

In order to understand the further differentiation of the triadic sign relation and appreciate the resulting consequences, one must know the philosophical bases of the theory, at least in broad outline.

2.2.2. A brief excursion into philosophy

Charles Sanders Peirce, an American philosopher and natural scientist, is held to be the founder of pragmatism and must also be regarded as the true founder of modern semiotics, even though the title is often given to Charles W. Morris. In fact, Morris expressly refers to the work of Peirce.

Philosophical pragmatism has nothing to do with "getting down to brass tacks", as "pragmatism" is generally understood in everyday language. In

Erst die Hinzunahme des Interpretanten, der hier durch die Kultur und das Weltbild der Antike gebildet wird, erschliesst die Bedeutung. Allerdings auch dann nur mit einer gewissen Annäherung, weil wir die Vorstellung eines Sonnengottes zwar intellektuell nachvollziehen, aber niemals unmittelbar erleben können.

Der Interpretant beinhaltet die Möglichkeit, ein Zeichen durch ein anderes Zeichen zu ersetzen, ein Vorgang, der immer dann einsetzt, wenn nach der Bedeutung eines Zeichens gefragt wird. So stellt zum Beispiel ein Lexikon eine Sammlung realisierter Interpretanten dar. «Realisiert» deshalb, weil Interpretanten nur die Möglichkeit der Ersetzung sind. Üblicherweise werden im Zeichenprozess Interpretanten nur aktualisiert, das heisst, die Bedeutung wird erfasst, ohne dass man sie noch einmal benennt. Der Interpretant umfasst aber noch mehr. Er erklärt zugleich, warum ein und dasselbe (materielle) Zeichen verschiedene Objekte bezeichnen kann, indem er das Bezugssystem angibt, aus dem sich die jeweilige Bedeutung ergibt. In diesem Zusammenhang spricht man oft vom Kontext, der auch durch die Situation bestimmt sein kann.

Um die weitere Differenzierung der triadischen Zeichenrelation verstehen und die sich daraus ergebenden Konsequenzen nachvollziehen zu können, muss man die philosophischen Grundlagen dieser Theorie zumindest in groben Zügen kennen.

2.2.2. Ein kleiner Ausflug in die Philosophie

Charles Sanders Peirce, ein amerikanischer Philosoph und Naturwissenschaftler, gilt als der Begründer des Pragmatismus und ist als eigentlicher Begründer der modernen Semiotik zu sehen, auch wenn als solcher oft Charles W. Morris bezeichnet wird. Morris bezieht sich jedoch ausdrücklich auf Peirce.

Der philosophische Pragmatismus hat nichts mit der Hemdsärmeligkeit zu tun, die den «Pragmatiker», so wie dieser Begriff in der Umgangssprache

Ce n'est que par l'apport de l'interprétant, ici constitué de la civilisation et de la philosophie de l'antiquité, que le sens peut être déduit. Toutefois, nous restons encore dans une certaine approximation, car si nous pouvons comprendre intellectuellement la représentation d'un dieu soleil, nous ne pourrons jamais en faire l'expérience directe.

L'interprétant donne la possibilité de remplacer un signe par un autre, un procédé auquel on a toujours recours quand on cherche le sens d'un signe. Ainsi un dictionnaire, par exemple, représente une collection d'interprétants réalisés. «Réalisés», parce que les interprétants ne sont que la possibilité de la substitution. En général, dans le processus du signe, les interprétants sont seulement actualisés, c'est-à-dire que le sens est saisi sans qu'on le nomme encore une fois. Néanmoins, l'interprétant apporte davantage. Il explique aussi pourquoi un même signe (matériel) peut désigner différents objets, en ce qu'il indique le système de référence duquel découle le sens correspondant. On parle souvent ici de contexte, qui peut également être déterminé par la situation.

Pour comprendre les subtilités de la relation triadique du signe et pour pouvoir suivre les conclusions qui en sont tirées, il est nécessaire de connaître au moins sommairement les fondements philosophiques de cette théorie.

2.2.2 Une petite digression philosophique

Charles Sanders Peirce, philosophe et naturaliste américain, est tenu pour le fondateur du pragmatisme, et peut aussi être considéré comme le véritable fondateur de la sémiotique moderne, même si ce titre est souvent attribué à Charles W. Morris. Pourtant, Morris se réfère expressément à Peirce.

Le pragmatisme philosophique n'a rien à voir avec l'idée que l'on se fait familièrement de la personne «pragmatique» qui n'hésite pas à retrousser ses manches. Pour mettre en lumière

I am, as far as I know, a pioneer, or rather a backwoodsman, in the work of clearing and opening up what I call semiotic, that is the doctrine of the essential nature and fundamental varieties of possible semiosis.

Charles Sanders Peirce

Ich bin, soviel ich weiss, ein Pionier, fast ein Hinterwäldler, bei der Arbeit, das zu klären und offenzulegen, was ich Semiotik nenne. Nämlich die Lehre vom Wesen und der grundlegenden Vielfalt möglicher Zeichenprozesse.

Charles Sanders Peirce

Je suis, pour autant que je sache, un pionnier, presque un homme des bois, dans le travail qui consiste à exposer ce que j'appelle la sémiotique. A savoir la théorie de la nature et de la multiplicité sous-jacente des processus de signes possibles.

Charles Sanders Peirce

order to point out this difference, Peirce coined the expression "pragmaticism" in his later work. This philosophical orientation directs thought toward action; every finding is aligned with concrete action and action is an important precondition for perception. If, for example, a Stone Age man is interested in the nature of a stone, his concern is what he can do with that stone. Thus he cannot know the nature of the stone until he takes action and registers the effect. I can be said to know an object when I know its effect.

Semiotics takes up special position within the framework of pragmatism, because perceptions cannot be made or conveyed except by means of signs. Peirce treats semiotics as logic, i.e. an instrument of perception or realization. The most important precondition of scientific work is verbal precision, with which Peirce concerned himself in a consistent manner. As a result, none of his terms is unsharp or could be regarded as superfluous. True to the principles of pragmatism, they always refer to concrete action. In complete contrast, one must regretfully conclude that semiotics as widely practised today is declining into pure jargon. If one wishes to be precise one can hardly avoid the terms coined by Peirce, but these are without value if they are not related to the underlying principles, which can, in fact, be generally understood if properly presented.

The constantly recurring theme of triads, or threefold relations, to be found in Peirce's work is based on his belief that everything can be traced back to three basic categories of existence. That which he calls a *First* is the pure existence of a thing, unconnected with any relationship to anything else. In relation to action, pure existence presents nothing but possibilities,

verwendet wird, auszeichnet. Um diesen Unterschied herauszustellen, hat Peirce in seinen späteren Arbeiten den Begriff Pragmatizismus geprägt. Diese philosophische Richtung orientiert das Denken am Handeln, jede Erkenntnis ist auf konkretes Handeln ausgerichtet, und Handeln ist eine wichtige Voraussetzung für die Erkenntnis. Wenn beispielsweise der Steinzeitmensch an der Beschaffenheit eines Steines interessiert ist, so geht es ihm darum, was er mit diesem Stein anfangen kann. Erkennen kann er diese Beschaffenheit aber nur dann, wenn er handelt und die Wirkung registriert. Ich kenne einen Gegenstand dann, wenn ich seine Wirkung kenne.

Im Rahmen der Pragmatik nimmt die Semiotik eine besondere Stellung ein, da alle Erkenntnis nur durch Zeichen gewonnen und über Zeichen vermittelt werden kann. Peirce behandelt die Semiotik als eine Logik, das heisst ein Instrument der Erkenntnis. Die wichtigste Voraussetzung wissenschaftlichen Arbeitens ist die sprachliche Präzision, um die sich Peirce konsequent bemüht. Keiner seiner Begriffe ist daher unscharf oder könnte als überflüssig angesehen werden. Sie sind getreu dem Grundsatz der Pragmatik immer auf konkretes Handeln bezogen. Ganz im Gegensatz dazu muss man heute leider feststellen, dass die Semiotik, so wie sie vielfach betrieben wird, zu einer reinen Terminologie verkommt. Zwar kann man, wenn man genau sein will, kaum auf die von Peirce geprägten Begriffe verzichten, doch sind diese wertlos, wenn man sie nicht auf die zugrunde liegenden Prinzipien bezieht. Und diese Prinzipien sind durchaus auch allgemeinverständlich darstellbar.

Die bei Peirce immer wieder anzutreffenden Triaden, dreistelligen Beziehungen, beruhen darauf, dass für ihn alles Existierende auf drei Grundkategorien des Seins zurückgeführt werden kann. Die *Erstheit* ist die reine Existenz einer Sache, unabhängig von jeglicher Beziehung zu irgend etwas anderem. In bezug auf das Handeln stellt die reine Existenz immer nur

cette différence, Peirce a forgé la notion de pragmaticisme dans ses travaux tardifs. Cette doctrine oriente la pensée vers l'action; tout enseignement est axé sur l'action concrète, et l'action est une condition importante de la connaissance. Par exemple, si l'homme de l'âge de pierre s'intéresse à la nature d'une pierre, il veut savoir ce qu'il peut en faire. Il ne peut cependant connaître cette nature que s'il agit et enregistre l'effet produit. Je ne connais un objet que quand je connais son effet.

Dans le cadre de la pragmatique, la sémiotique occupe une place particulière, car toute connaissance ne peut être acquise qu'à travers les signes et ne peut être transmise que par les signes. Peirce utilise la sémiotique comme une logique, c'est-à-dire un instrument de la connaissance. La principale condition préalable au travail scientifique est la précision linguistique, que Peirce s'efforce d'atteindre par une recherche conséquente. Dès lors, aucun de ses concepts n'est imprécis ou pourrait être considéré comme superflu.
Fidèles au principe fondamental de la pragmatique, ils se rapportent toujours à l'action concrète. Au contraire, force est malheureusement de constater que la sémiotique a souvent tendance aujourd'hui à se dégrader en une terminologie pure. Pour être précis, il est sans aucun doute indispensable d'utiliser les concepts formés par Peirce, mais ces notions n'ont aucune valeur si elles ne se rapportent pas aux principes fondamentaux. Or, il est possible d'exposer ces principes de façon qu'ils soient compréhensibles par tous.

Les triades, ces relations triples qui reviennent fréquemment chez Peirce, sont fondées sur le fait que pour lui, tout ce qui existe peut être rapporté à trois catégories fondamentales de l'être. La *priméité* est l'existence pure d'une chose, indépendante de toute relation à quoi que ce soit d'autre. Par rapport à l'agir, l'existence pure ne re-

since action makes existence into a fact, and thereby what he calls a *Second.* In the Second, a thing is always placed in relation to another. Let us take as an example the stone which was found by our Stone Age man. As pure existence, it harbours many possibilities: it can be used as an axe to fell trees; as a weapon to kill wild beasts; as a millstone, a ploughshare or a hammer. All these functions are, in themselves, Seconds, because by their nature they set the stone into relationship with other things, be it the timber, the grain or the soil. Nevertheless, the Second is only the act *per se,* the deed. *Action,* on the other hand, is the *Third,* for in his actions man produces the third element, which is the relationship between the First and the Second. Behind the character of the Third there always stands reason, the recognition of possibilities and their utilization. The perception of an object is a Second, where the relationship exists only between the perceiver and the object, while the perception of the possible functions of an object is a Third: it is a realization.

All the triads proposed by Peirce relate to these three basic forms of existence. The relationships can most easily be derived from concepts of possibility, fact and reason; but the terms feeling, experience and law are also among the basic categories. It is easier to understand the differentiation of the triadic sign relationship against this background of terminology.

2.2.3. The dynamics of the sign process

In the triadic sign relationship, the sign — every sign — is understood as a process, in which three references come into effect: those to the medium, the object and the interpretant. Thus the sign is basically a trichot-

Möglichkeiten dar, denn im Handeln wird die Existenz zur Wirklichkeit und damit zur *Zweitheit.* In der Zweitheit wird eine Sache immer in Beziehung zu einer anderen gesetzt. Nehmen wir als Beispiel wieder den Stein, den unser Steinzeitmensch gefunden hat. Als reine Existenz birgt er viele Möglichkeiten: Er kann als Axt benutzt werden, um Bäume zu fällen; er kann als Waffe dienen, um Tiere zu erlegen; er kann als Mahlstein eingesetzt werden, als Pflugschar oder als Hammer. Alle diese Funktionen sind für sich genommen Zweitheiten, weil sie ihrem Wesen nach den Stein in Beziehung zu anderen Dingen setzen, sei es zum Holz des Baumes, zum Getreidekorn oder zum Erdreich. Zweitheit ist allerdings nur die Handlung an sich, die Aktion. Das Handeln dagegen ist eine *Drittheit,* denn im Handeln stellt der Mensch als drittes Element die Beziehung zwischen den beiden Elementen her. Hinter der Seinsweise der Drittheit steht immer die Vernunft, das Erkennen der Möglichkeiten und deren Nutzung. Die Wahrnehmung eines Gegenstandes ist eine Zweitheit, die Beziehung besteht nur zwischen der wahrnehmenden Person und dem Gegenstand, das Wahrnehmen der möglichen Funktionen eines Gegenstandes ist dagegen eine Drittheit, es ist die Erkenntnis.

Alle Triaden, die Peirce aufstellt, sind auf diese drei Grundformen des Seins bezogen, wobei sich die jeweiligen Beziehungen am ehesten aus den Begriffen Möglichkeit, Wirklichkeit und Vernunft ableiten lassen; aber auch die Bezeichnungen Gefühl, Erfahrung und Gesetz treffen auf die Grundkategorien zu. Vor diesem Hintergrund lässt sich nun die Differenzierung der triadischen Zeichenrelation leichter verstehen.

2.2.3. Von der Dynamik des Zeichenprozesses

In der triadischen Zeichenrelation wird das Zeichen – jedes Zeichen – als Prozess verstanden, in dem drei Beziehungen zur Wirkung kommen: die Beziehung zu den Mitteln, zum Objekt und zum Interpretanten. Das Zeichen ist also grundsätzlich eine Dritt-

présente jamais que des possibilités, car dans l'agir, l'existence devient réalité, et ainsi *secondéité.* Dans la secondéité, chaque chose est toujours placée en relation avec une autre. Reprenons l'exemple de la pierre trouvée par notre homme de l'âge de pierre. En tant qu'existence pure, elle recèle maintes possibilités: elle peut être utilisée comme hache, pour abattre des arbres; elle peut être utilisée comme arme, pour tuer des animaux; elle peut être utilisée comme meule, comme soc ou comme marteau. Toutes ces fonctions, prises en tant que telles, sont des secondéités, car par leur nature, elles mettent la pierre en relation avec d'autres choses, que ce soit le bois de l'arbre, le grain de céréale ou la terre. Toutefois, la secondéité n'est que l'action en tant que telle. L'agir, en revanche, est une *tiercéité,* car en agissant, l'homme, troisième élément, crée la relation entre les deux autres. Derrière la manière d'être de la tiercéité se trouve toujours la raison, la reconnaissance des possibilités et leur utilisation. La perception d'un objet est une secondéité, la relation n'existe qu'entre la personne qui perçoit et l'objet; en revanche, la perception des fonctions possibles d'un objet est une tiercéité, c'est la cognition.

Toutes les triades établies par Peirce se réfèrent à ces trois formes fondamentales de l'être, les relations respectives pouvant être déduites au mieux des concepts de possibilité, réalité et raison; cependant, les désignations émotion, expérience et loi correspondent aussi aux catégories fondamentales. Ces éléments étant posés, il est plus facile de comprendre la relation triadique du signe.

2.2.3. De la dynamique du processus du signe

Dans la relation triadique du signe, le signe – chaque signe – est compris comme un processus dans lequel opèrent trois relations: la relation aux moyens, à l'objet et à l'interprétant. Le signe est donc fondamentalement une tiercéité, il est fondé sur la raison

What has changed is our attitude both to mass products and to works of "fine art". The differences between the two have become smaller or disappeared altogether. At the same time, the time scale, the lines of descent, the before and after, have also become unrecognizable. We have now obtained what the enlightened and enlightening culture of the Sixties demanded, namely the end of the traditional division between primitive products for the ignorant masses and difficult products for the educated public with good taste.

Umberto Eco

Was sich verändert hat, ist unser Verhältnis zu den Massenprodukten wie unser Verhältnis zu den Werken der «hohen Kunst». Die Unterschiede sind kleiner geworden oder verschwunden. Doch mit den Unterschieden sind auch die Zeitbezüge, die Abstammungslinien, das Vorher und Nachher unkenntlich geworden. Wir haben bekommen, was die aufgeklärte und aufklärerische Kultur der sechziger Jahre verlangt hatte, nämlich das Ende der traditionellen Zweiteilung in einerseits primitive Produkte für blöde Massen und anderseits diffizile Produkte für das gebildete Publikum mit dem feinen Geschmack.

Umberto Eco

Ce qui a changé, c'est notre rapport aux produits fabriqués en série, ainsi que notre rapport aux œuvres du «grand art». Les différences se sont estompées, voire effacées. Mais avec les différences, les références temporelles, les sources d'inspiration, l'avant et l'après sont devenus méconnaissables. Nous avons obtenu ce que la culture éclairée et rationaliste des années soixante avait exigé: la fin de la distinction traditionnelle entre, d'une part, des produits primitifs pour des masses ignorantes, et d'autre part des produits recherchés pour un public cultivé au goût raffiné.

Umberto Eco

omy, based on the perceiving reason. The sign process is called semiosis and its analysis is the aim of semiotics in the narrower sense. The relations to the means, the object and the interpretant form the three dimensions of the semiosis, whose three areas of investigation equate with semiotics: syntactics, semantics and pragmatics. These three terms go back to Charles W. Morris and are generally accepted in semiotics. At the same time, they are among the most misused of all terms. Everyone wishing to assume the mantle of semiotics fills these terms with his own ideas, which in most cases are derived from everyday language.

Morris himself drew back from this terminology in his later writings because its terms had become meaningless slogans through undisciplined use. The terms are used here in the hope that, one day, semiotics will acquire a uniform terminology. Here the words syntactics, semantics and pragmatics are used — in accordance with Morris — for the analysis of the individual references of the sign.

Signs and their syntactic background

In syntactics, the sign is studied in relation to the medium of which it consists, the purely material aspect of the sign. Syntactics draws up the catalogue of elements, the repertoire, and specifies the rules under which larger sign complexes can be formed from these elements. Since practically every sign complex can be reinvestigated as a single sign, and conversely practically every sign element can be divided into partial signs, the factor of analysis plays a decisive role in syntactics. Its levels are built up in a hierarchical way, that is to say that the syntagms or combinations of one

heit, es beruht auf der erkennenden Vernunft. Der Zeichenprozess wird Semiose genannt, seine Analyse ist das Ziel der Semiotik im engeren Sinne. Die Beziehungen zu Mittel, Objekt und Interpretant bilden die drei Dimensionen der Semiose, denen drei Untersuchungsbereiche der Semiotik entsprechen: Syntaktik, Semantik und Pragmatik. Die Begriffe der Syntaktik, Semantik und Pragmatik gehen auf Charles W. Morris zurück und haben sich in der Semiotik allgemein durchgesetzt. Sie gehören jedoch gleichzeitig zu den am meisten missbrauchten Begriffen. Jeder, der sich mit dem Mantel der Semiotik schmücken möchte, füllt diese Begriffe mit seinen eigenen Vorstellungen, die meist nur umgangssprachlich motiviert sind.

Morris selbst rückte in seinen späteren Arbeiten von dieser Terminologie ab, weil sie durch den undisziplinierten Umgang zu nichtssagenden Schlagworten geworden waren. Wenn diese Begriffe hier dennoch verwendet werden, so geschieht dies in der stillen Hoffung, dass die Semiotik eines Tages vielleicht doch zu einer einheitlichen Terminologie finden wird. Hier werden die Bezeichnungen Syntaktik, Semantik und Pragmatik – in Übereinstimmung mit Morris – für die Analyse der einzelnen Beziehungen des Zeichens verwendet.

Zeichen und ihr syntaktischer Hintergrund

In der Syntaktik wird das Zeichen im Hinblick auf die Mittel untersucht, aus denen es besteht. Sie beschäftigt sich also mit der rein materiellen Seite des Zeichens. Sie stellt den Katalog der Elemente auf, das Repertoire, und nennt die Regeln, nach denen aus den Elementen grössere Zeichenkomplexe gebildet werden, liefert also auch den Code. Da fast jeder Zeichenkomplex wieder als einheitliches Zeichen untersucht und umgekehrt fast jedes Zeichenelement in weitere Teilzeichen zerlegt werden kann, spielt in der Syntaktik die Ebene der Analyse eine entscheidende Rolle. Diese Ebenen sind hierarchisch aufgebaut, das heisst, die Syntagmen, die Kombinationsformen einer Ebene, bilden die Paradigmen,

cognitive. On appelle le processus du signe sémiose, et son analyse est le but de la sémiotique au sens strict. Les relations aux moyens, à l'objet et à l'interprétant constituent les trois dimensions de la sémiose, auxquelles correspondent trois domaines de recherche de la sémiotique: la syntactique, la sémantique et la pragmatique. Les concepts syntactique, sémantique et pragmatique datent de Charles W. Morris et se sont largement imposés en sémiotique. Ils comptent néanmoins parmi ceux qui sont le plus souvent utilisés de manière erronée. Toutes les personnes qui se targuent de faire de la sémiotique accomodent ces concepts selon leurs propres idées, qui bien souvent ne sont motivées que par le parler d'usage.

Dans ses derniers travaux, Morris lui-même a abandonné cette terminologie, car le manque de discipline dans son utilisation en avait fait un ensemble de mots vide de sens. Si nous utilisons néanmoins ces concepts ici, c'est dans l'espoir secret qu'un jour la sémiotique trouvera une terminologie uniforme. Nous utiliserons ici les termes syntactique, sémantique et pragmatique – au sens de Morris – pour l'analyse des différentes relations du signe.

Les signes et leur arrière-plan syntactique

En syntactique, on examine les moyens dont le signe est constitué. La syntactique s'intéresse donc à l'aspect purement matériel du signe. Elle établit le catalogue des éléments, le répertoire, et indique les règles selon lesquelles on construit, à partir des éléments, de plus grands complexes de signes: ainsi, elle fournit également le code. Comme presque chaque complexe de signes peut être étudié comme un seul signe et, inversement, presque chaque élément de signe peut être décomposé en signes partiels, le niveau de l'analyse joue un rôle décisif en syntactique. Ces niveaux sont ordonnés de façon hiérarchique, c'est-à-dire que les syntagmes, les formes de combinaison, constituent un niveau, et les

level form the paradigms or elements of the next higher level.

According to their function, the sign elements are divided into three types:

Qualisign	Sinsign	Legisign

Signs and their semantic background
Semantics is concerned with the relation between the sign and the object signified. The method of questioning is: what does the sign signify? And how does it do that? The point of gravity here lies with the "how" of signification. This method of questioning is not yet concerned with meaning, which cannot become manifest except in relation to the user, or to an underlying system. It must be emphasized that this way of looking at signs is not a common property of semiotics but a specific of the triadic relationship. From most other approaches, semantics is defined as the area in which one is concerned with meaning. In linguistics in particular, semantics is understood as a theory of meaning. In accordance with the relation to the object, the triadic sign relation distinguishes three types of signification:

Icon	Index	Symbol

This triad is one of the most widely known of semiotic divisions and here, too, we come across undisciplined usage, bordering on sheer arbitrariness — particularly in the use of the term "icon", under which it is often thought that all figurative signs can be subsumed. It must be admitted that Morris, with his explanations of the iconic sign, is not entirely blameless in this respect. We must here make it clear that pictorial signs also exist under all three descriptive headings, just as there are verbal icons. More details of this point will be given with the aid of concrete examples.

die Elemente der nächsthöheren Ebene.

Nach ihrer Funktion werden die Zeichenelemente in drei Zeichenarten eingeteilt:

Qualizeichen	Sinzeichen	Legizeichen

Zeichen und ihr semantischer Hintergrund
Die Semantik befasst sich mit der Beziehung zwischen Zeichen und bezeichnetem Objekt. Die Fragestellung lautet: Was bezeichnet das Zeichen? Und wie tut es das? Der Schwerpunkt liegt dabei auf dem Wie der Bezeichnung. Die Fragestellung hat noch nichts mit der Bedeutung zu tun, da sich Bedeutung immer erst in bezug auf den Benutzer oder ein zugrundeliegendes System manifestieren kann. Es muss darauf hingewiesen werden, dass diese Betrachtungsweise keineswegs ein Allgemeingut der Semiotik ist, sondern ein Spezifikum der triadischen Zeichenrelation. Von den meisten anderen Ansätzen wird Semantik als der Bereich definiert, der sich mit der Bedeutung befasst, insbesondere im Bereich der Linguistik wird Semantik als Bedeutungstheorie aufgefasst. Nach der Beziehung zum Objekt unterscheidet die triadische Zeichenrelation drei Bezeichnungsarten:

Ikon	Index	Symbol

Diese Triade gehört zu den bekanntesten semiotischen Unterscheidungen, und auch hier treffen wir wieder auf die undisziplinierte Begriffsverwendung, die an reine Willkür grenzt. Dies gilt insbesondere für den Begriff des Ikons, unter dem man nicht selten alle bildlichen Zeichen subsumieren will. An diesem Zustand ist allerdings Morris mit seinen Ausführungen zum ikonischen Zeichen nicht ganz unschuldig. Es muss hier festgehalten werden, dass auch bildliche Zeichen in allen drei Bezeichnungsarten vorkommen können, ebenso wie es sprachliche Ikons gibt. Doch darauf wird noch ausführlicher an konkreten Beispielen eingegangen.

paradigmes, les éléments, le niveau supérieur.

Selon leur fonction, les éléments de signe sont répartis en trois catégories de signes:

Qualisigne	Sinsigne	Légisigne

Les signes et leur arrière-plan sémantique
La sémantique étudie la relation entre le signe et l'objet désigné. Les termes du problème sont les suivants: qu'est-ce que désigne le signe? Et comment cette désignation se fait-elle? L'important est ici le comment de la désignation. La question ne porte pas encore sur le sens, car il ne peut se manifester qu'en rapport avec l'utilisateur ou un système sous-jacent. Signalons que cette approche n'est pas commune en sémiotique: elle constitue un trait caractéristique de la relation triadique du signe. En général, la sémantique est plutôt considérée comme le domaine de l'étude du sens. En linguistique, notamment, la sémantique est comprise comme la théorie du sens. La relation triadique du signe opère une distinction entre trois types de désignation, selon la relation à l'objet:

Icône	Indice	Symbole

Cette triade est une des distinctions sémiotiques les plus connues. Ici encore, on rencontre un manque de discipline dans l'utilisation des concepts qui confine au pur arbitraire. C'est souvent le cas de la notion d'icône, à laquelle on veut souvent subordonner tous les signes figuratifs. Néanmoins, Morris lui même, par ses considérations sur le signe iconique, a une part de responsabilité dans cet état des choses. Soulignons ici que des signes figuratifs peuvent aussi se trouver dans les trois types de désignation, tout comme il existe des icônes linguistiques. Nous reviendrons plus en détail à cette question à l'aide d'exemples concrets.

Signs and their pragmatic background

Pragmatics is only indirectly concerned with the user of signs. In the foreground of this area is the analysis of the systems within which signs receive their meaning. For example, a STOP signboard receives its meaning from the exactly defined system of traffic signs. If I change systems and put the STOP sign in front of a special offer in a supermarket, for example, the meaning of the sign also changes. Sign systems can be described in accordance with the degree of their openness, that is to say in accordance with the distinctness of meaning of the signs occurring in them. Thus art, for example, is a very open system, in which meaning is generally conveyed only in terms of feelings and is highly subjective. On the other hand, the aim of everyday language is intersubjective agreement, although it generally suffices when the exactness of meaning is good enough for understanding. Not so for science, which is directed towards verbal precision and therefore defines its terms, constructing closed systems.

With regard to the type of conveyance of meaning which rules in them, three kinds of system can be distinguished:

Connotation Denotation Precision

All in all, the triadic sign relationship represents a very complicated system of classification, which nevertheless can be traced back to a relatively simple basic structure. This structure is founded on the fact that the relation of the sign to the medium, the object and the interpretant is repeated in each stage of refinement, while the three basic categories of existence remain the common points of reference.

This can be illustrated graphically (see next page).

Zeichen und ihr pragmatischer Hintergrund

Die Pragmatik setzt sich nur indirekt mit dem Zeichenbenutzer auseinander. Im Mittelpunkt der Analyse stehen in diesem Bereich die Systeme, in denen die Zeichen ihre Bedeutung erhalten. So bezieht beispielsweise das STOP-Schild seine Bedeutung aus dem exakt definierten System der Verkehrszeichen. Wechsle ich nun dieses System, indem ich etwa ein STOP-Schild in einem Supermarkt vor einem Sonderangebot anbringe, so ändert sich auch die Bedeutung dieses Zeichens. Zeichensysteme können nach dem Grad ihrer Offenheit beschrieben werden, also nach der Bestimmtheit der Bedeutung der in ihnen auftretenden Zeichen. So ist etwa die Kunst ein sehr offenes System, in dem Bedeutung meist nur gefühlsmässig vermittelt wird und in hohem Mass subjektiv ist. Dagegen zielt die Umgangssprache auf intersubjektive Übereinstimmung, gibt sich jedoch damit zufrieden, wenn die Genauigkeit der Bedeutung zur Verständigung ausreicht. Nicht so die Wissenschaft, die auf sprachliche Präzision angewiesen ist und daher ihre Begriffe definiert, also somit geschlossene Systeme konstruiert.

In Hinblick auf die Art der Bedeutungsvermittlung, die in ihnen dominiert, lassen sich drei Systemtypen unterscheiden:

Konnotation Denotation Präzision

Insgesamt stellt sich die triadische Zeichenrelation als ein recht kompliziertes System der Klassifikation von Zeichen dar, das allerdings auf eine relativ einfache Grundstruktur zurückgeführt werden kann. Diese Grundstruktur ergibt sich daraus, dass sich die Beziehungen des Zeichens zu Mittel, Objekt und Interpretant in den einzelnen Feinbezügen wiederholen, wobei der gemeinsame Bezugspunkt die drei Grundkategorien des Seins sind.

Die Grafik soll dies veranschaulichen (siehe nächste Seite).

Les signes et leur arrière-plan pragmatique

La pragmatique n'a qu'un rapport indirect avec l'utilisateur du signe. Au centre de l'analyse pragmatique se trouvent les systèmes dans lesquels les signes reçoivent leur sens. Par exemple, le panneau STOP tire son sens du système exactement défini de la signalisation routière. Si je change ce système, en plaçant par exemple un panneau STOP devant une offre spéciale dans un supermarché, le sens du signe est modifié. On peut décrire les systèmes de signes selon leur degré d'ouverture, c'est-à-dire selon la précision du sens des signes qui s'y manifestent. L'art, par exemple, est un système très ouvert, dans lequel le sens est généralement transmis par l'émotion et avec une grande subjectivité. En revanche, le parler d'usage vise à la concordance intersubjective, mais se contente d'une précision du sens qui suffit à la compréhension. Tel n'est pas le cas de la science, qui a besoin de la précision linguistique et définit par conséquent ses concepts, construisant des systèmes fermés.

On distingue trois types de systèmes selon le type de transmission du sens qui domine:

Connotation Dénotation Précision

La relation triadique du signe se présente comme un système de classification des signes très complexe qui repose néanmoins sur une structure de base relativement simple. Cette structure apparaît du fait que les relations du signe au moyen, à l'objet et à l'interprétant se répètent dans les différentes sous-références, tandis que le point de référence commun est constitué par les trois catégories fondamentales de l'être.

Illustration schématique (voir page suivante).

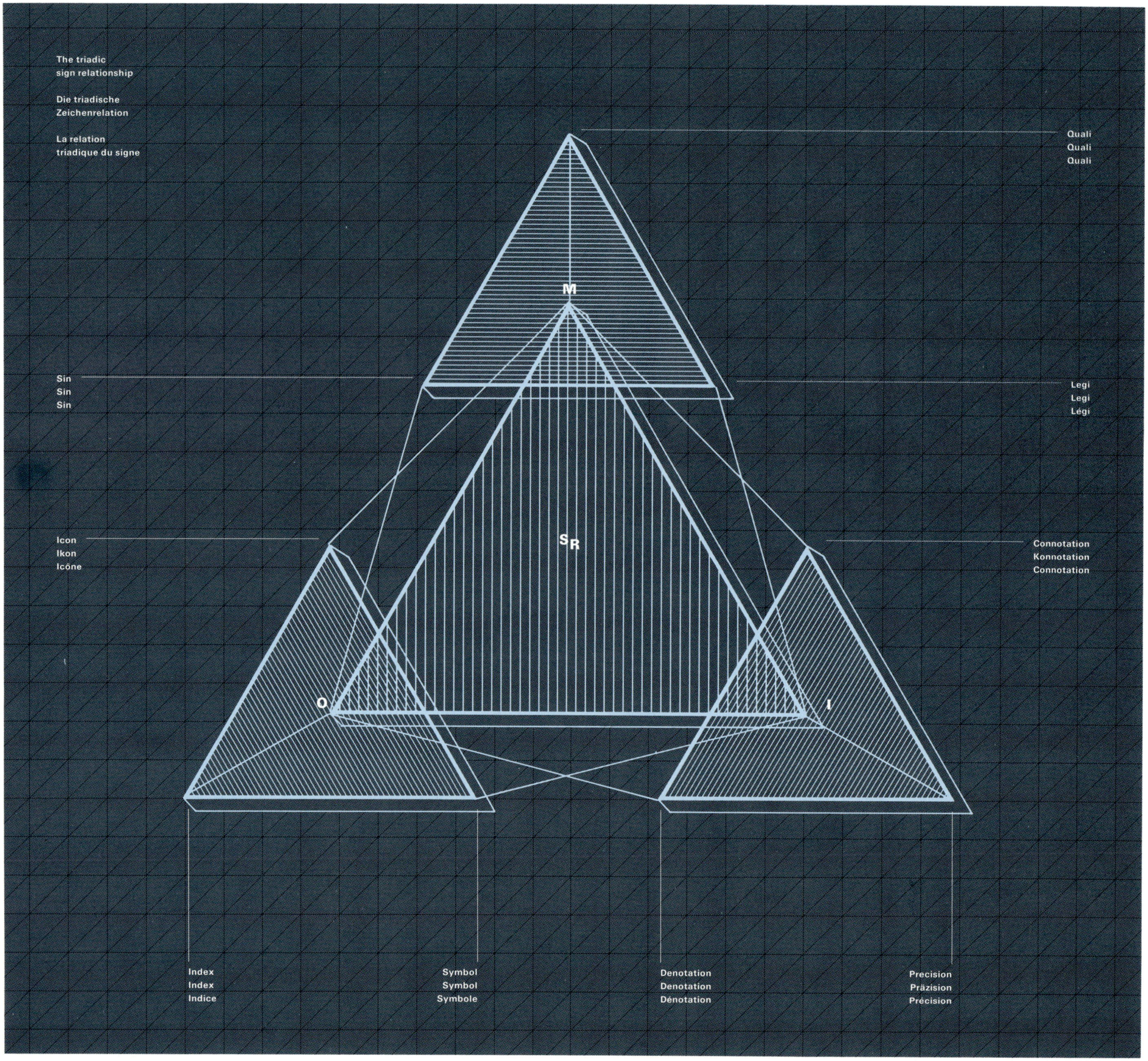
The triadic
sign relationship
Die triadische
Zeichenrelation
La relation
triadique du signe
Quali
Quali
Quali
M
Sin
Sin
Sin
Legi
Legi
Légi
Icon
Ikon
Icône
S_R
Connotation
Konnotation
Connotation
O
I
Index
Index
Indice
Symbol
Symbol
Symbole
Denotation
Denotation
Dénotation
Precision
Präzision
Précision

To conclude these theoretical explanations, reference must once again be made to an important point for the correct understanding of semiotics: a concrete sign always stands in a three-way relationship and can be fully comprehended only by means of all three references. The division into three relationships is therefore an analytical construct. There is no sign which is merely a qualisign or an icon: each sign can only be so described with regard to individual aspects. Moreover, the arrangement of signs into areas of reference is not always unambiguous. In the practice of communication, we are almost always concerned with mixed forms of signs, where one can discern only certain points of gravity. It is Peirce's view that, with regard to the representation of an object, the most complete signs are those in which iconic, indexical and symbolic elements are evenly balanced. This is valid for representation in practice, i.e. for logotypes and trademarks. For purposes of communication, the prominence of individual elements appears to be more suitable, because in this way the intentions of the communicator can be emphasized.

This view presupposes the communicator's purposeful use of signs. In the field of visual communications, the use of signs is usually still quite naive. Such an evaluation is by no means negative but refers to the immediacy of the communication, that is to say an absence of theoretical reflection. Theory, as we know, is not an essential condition for successful communication, but there is no doubt that it improves the communicator's position. In the following pages we intend to show how semiotics, as a grammar of visual communication, can contribute to such an improvement.

The following levels of description serve as a precondition:
Texture level: *Perception elements*
Structure level: *Figures and patterns*
Object level: *Objects*
Statement level: *Relations between objects*

Zum Schluss dieser theoretischen Ausführungen sei noch auf einen wichtigen Punkt zum richtigen Verständnis der Semiotik hingewiesen: Ein konkretes Zeichen steht immer in allen drei Beziehungen und kann nur durch alle vollständig erfasst werden. Die Trennung der einzelnen Bezüge ist also ein analytisches Konstrukt. Es gibt kein Zeichen, das ein Qualizeichen oder ein Ikon wäre, ein Zeichen kann nur im Hinblick auf einzelne Aspekte als Qualizeichen oder Ikon bezeichnet werden. Darüber hinaus ist auch die Einordnung innerhalb eines Zeichenbezuges nicht immer eindeutig, wir haben es vielmehr in der Praxis der Kommunikation fast immer mit Mischformen zu tun, bei denen man nur Schwerpunkte erkennen kann. Im übrigen ist Peirce der Ansicht, dass in bezug auf die Repräsentation eines Objektes die vollkommensten Zeichen diejenigen sind, in denen sich ikonische, indexikalische und symbolische Elemente die Waage halten. Dies gilt für die Repräsentation, in der Praxis also besonders für Signets und Marken. Für die Kommunikation erscheint die Herausstellung einzelner Elemente angemessener, weil dies die Intentionen des Kommunikators zum Ausdruck kommen lässt.

Dies setzt den gezielten Zeichengebrauch durch den Kommunikator voraus. Im Bereich der visuellen Kommunikation ist der Zeichengebrauch normalerweise noch recht naiv, was keine negative Wertung sein soll, sondern sich auf die Unmittelbarkeit, das heisst Fehlen theoretischer Reflexion, bezieht. Nun ist die Theorie zwar keine Voraussetzung für eine gelungene Kommunikation, aber sie verbessert zweifellos die Position des Kommunikators. Wie die Semiotik in Form einer Grammatik der visuellen Kommunikation dazu beitragen kann, soll im folgenden dargestellt werden.

Als Beschreibung dienen folgende Beschreibungsebenen:
Texturebene: *Wahrnehmungselemente*
Strukturebene: *Figuren und Muster*
Gegenstandsebene: *Gegenstände*
Aussageebene: *Beziehungen zwischen Gegenständen*

Pour conclure ces considérations théoriques, ajoutons un point important pour une bonne compréhension de la sémiotique: un signe concret se trouve toujours dans les trois relations et ne peut être saisi complètement qu'avec leur totalité. La division des différentes références est une construction analytique. Il n'existe aucun signe qui soit un qualisigne ou une icône: un signe ne peut être défini comme qualisigne ou icône qu'en considération d'aspects particuliers. En outre, la classification dans une référence de signe n'est pas toujours sans équivoque: dans la pratique de la communication, on rencontre presque toujours des formes mélangées où l'on ne peut reconnaître que les éléments les plus marqués. De surcroît, Peirce est d'avis que dans la représentation d'un objet, les signes les plus complets sont ceux dans lesquels les éléments iconiques, indiciaires et symboliques sont en équilibre. Ceci vaut pour la représentation, c'est-à-dire, dans la pratique, particulièrement pour les logos et les marques. La mise en évidence d'éléments distincts semble mieux adaptée à la communication, car elle permet de faire ressortir les intentions du communicateur.

A cette fin, le communicateur doit faire du signe une utilisation choisie. Dans le domaine de la communication visuelle, l'utilisation du signe demeure très naïve, ce qui n'est pas une appréciation défavorable, mais se réfère plutôt au caractère immédiat, c'est-à-dire a l'absence de réflexion théorique. Certes, la théorie n'est pas la condition d'une communication réussie, mais améliore la position du communicateur. Nous allons montrer ci-dessous comment la sémiotique, forme de grammaire de la communication visuelle, peut y contribuer.

Les niveaux de description suivants serviront de préalable:
niveau de la texture: *éléments de la perception*
niveau de la structure: *figures et modèles*
niveau de l'objet: *objets*
niveau de l'enoncé: *relations entre les objets*

1

2

3

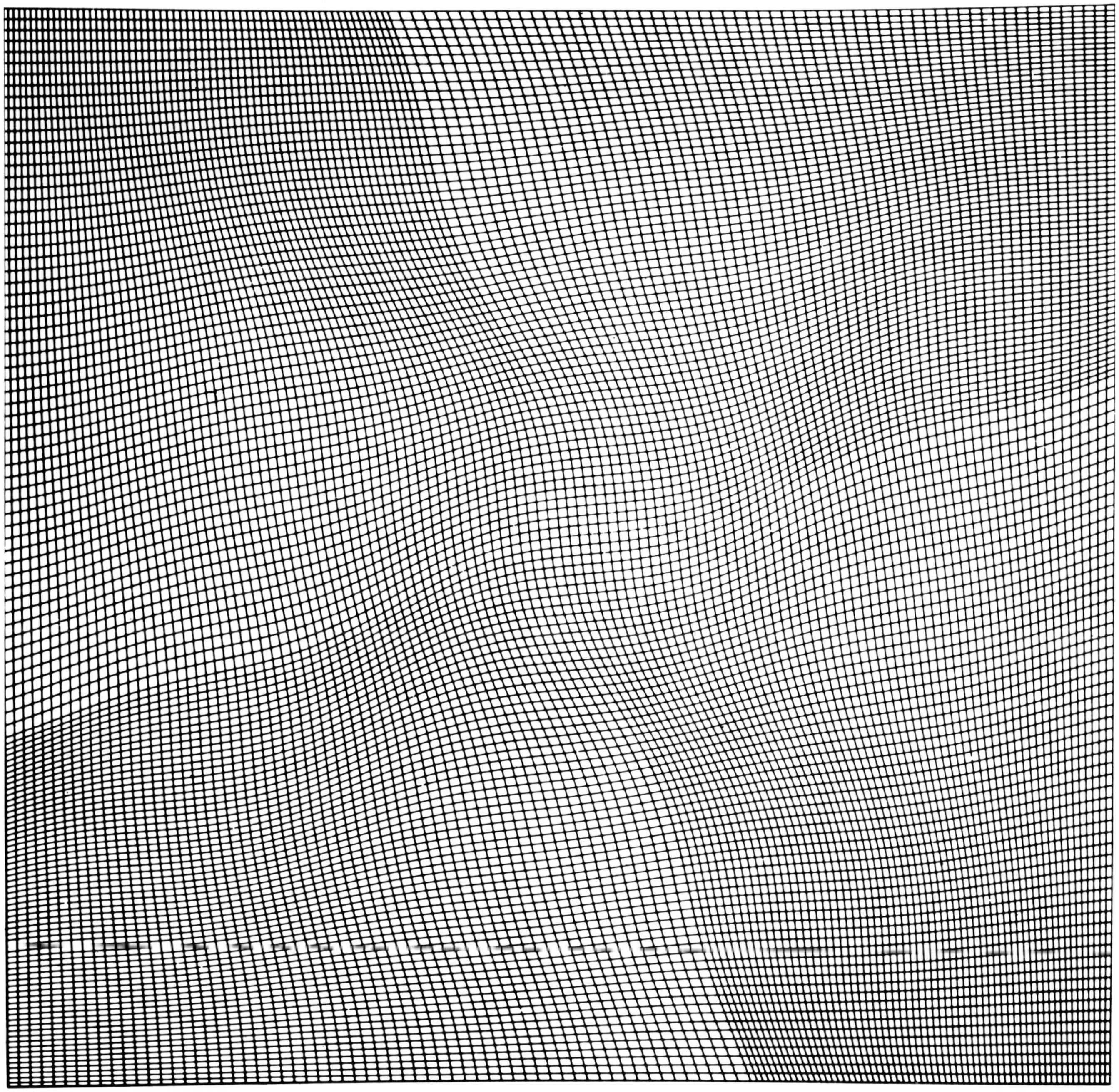

4

François Morellet 1
Kroehl Design 2, 3
Mitsuo Katsui 4

The discovery of texture has become a characteristic factor of contemporary design. New processes of serialization and networking form important bases for sign theory and practice. One of the most fascinating contributions is to be found in the work of Morellet.
At left: example of a uniformly altered structure (surface).
At right, one above another: change-over from one gradient of texture to another (edge), sudden alteration (break) and a continuous alteration (curvature).

Die Entdeckung der Textur ist für das Design unserer Zeit zum kennzeichnenden Faktor geworden. Neue Verfahren der Seriation und der Netzkonstruktion bilden wichtige Grundlagen für Zeichentheorie und -praxis. Einen der faszinierendsten Beiträge finden wir im Werk von Morellet.
Linke Seite: Beispiel einer gleichmässig veränderten Struktur (Oberfläche).
Die rechte Seite zeigt untereinanderstehend: Sprung von einem in einen anderen Texturgradienten (Kante), eine plötzliche Änderung (Knick) und zuletzt eine kontinuierliche Veränderung (Wölbung).

La découverte de la texture est devenue un facteur déterminant pour le design moderne. Les nouveaux procédés de sériation et de construction de réseaux constituent une base importante de la théorie et de la pratique du signe. L'œuvre de Morellet représente une des contributions les plus fascinantes en la matière.
Gauche: exemple d'une structure transformée uniformément (surface).
Droite, verticalement: passage d'un gradient de texture à l'autre (arête), changement subit (coude) et enfin, changement continu (courbure).

Osamu Kataoka AD 5
Koji Kanai / Satoshi Inoue D
Chieko Iwagami AD 6
Otl Aicher D 7–10

On the products shown here, we see the simplest elements of perception, representing, in their graphic transcriptions, the basic elements of pictorial signs. These elements are completed through the addition of colour.
At right, the Maack company's range of gift wrapping paper provides an example of the systematic use of textures, which have been produced with the aid of a CAD system. This has made possible 1225 different combinations of colours. In addition, a file is created for more than 4 billion proposals, showing the direction for future development.

Wir sehen auf den hier vorgestellten Produkten einfachste Wahrnehmungselemente, die in ihren grafischen Transkriptionen die Grundelemente bildlicher Zeichen darstellen. Bei Ergänzung durch Farbe sind diese Grundelemente vollständig.
Die auf der rechten Seite gezeigte Geschenkpapierkollektion der Firma Maack ist ein Beispiel für die systematische Nutzung von Texturen, die mit Hilfe eines CAD-Rechners festgelegt wurden. Damit sind 1225 verschiedene Farbkombinationen möglich geworden. Darüber hinaus sind die Grundlagen für über 4 Milliarden Vorschläge dokumentiert, die die Richtung für die zukünftige Entwicklung festlegen.

Ces produits représentent les plus simples des éléments de la perception qui, grâce à leur transcription graphique, illustrent les éléments fondamentaux des signes figuratifs, complétés dans leur représentation par un ajoût de couleur.
A droite, la collection de papier-cadeau de l'entreprise Maack illustre l'utilisation systématique de textures, déterminées à l'aide d'un calculateur CAD. Cette démarche a permis de créer 1225 assortiments de couleurs. La documentation de base permet en outre d'envisager plus de quatre milliards de propositions, annonciatrices de l'orientation future.

5

6

7

8

9

10

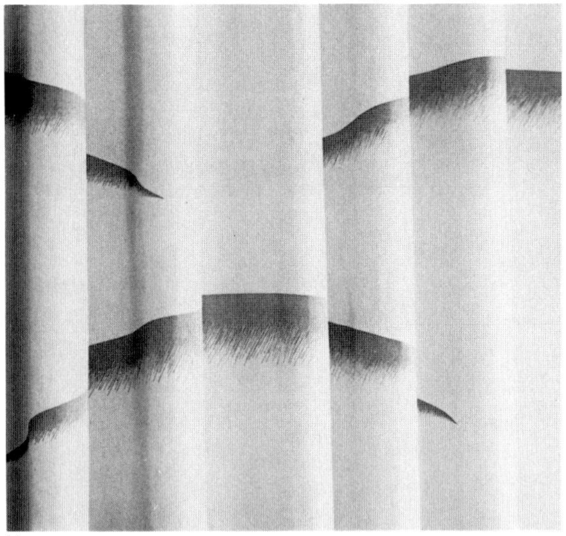
11

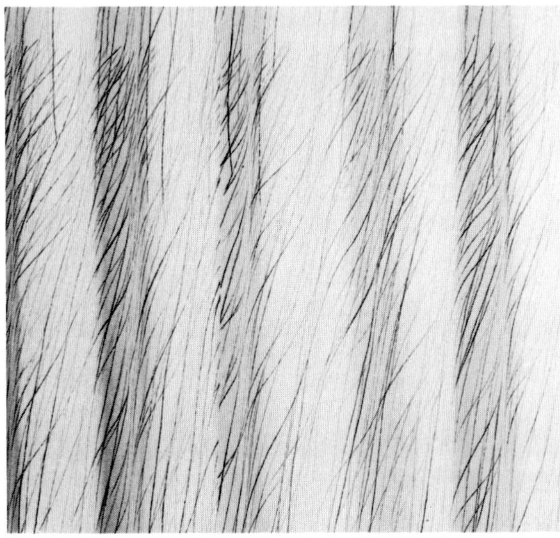
12

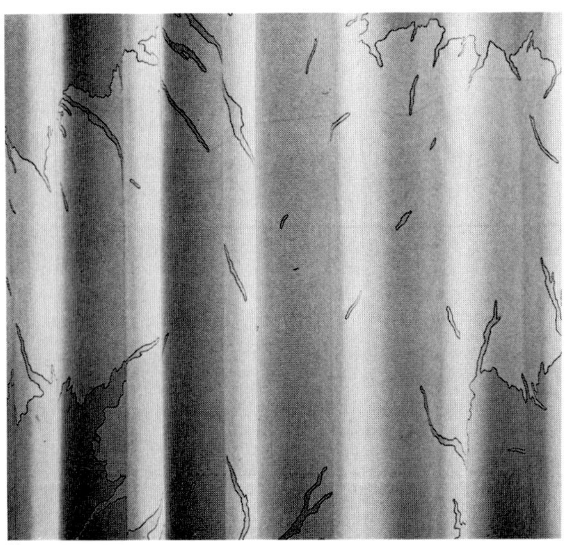
13

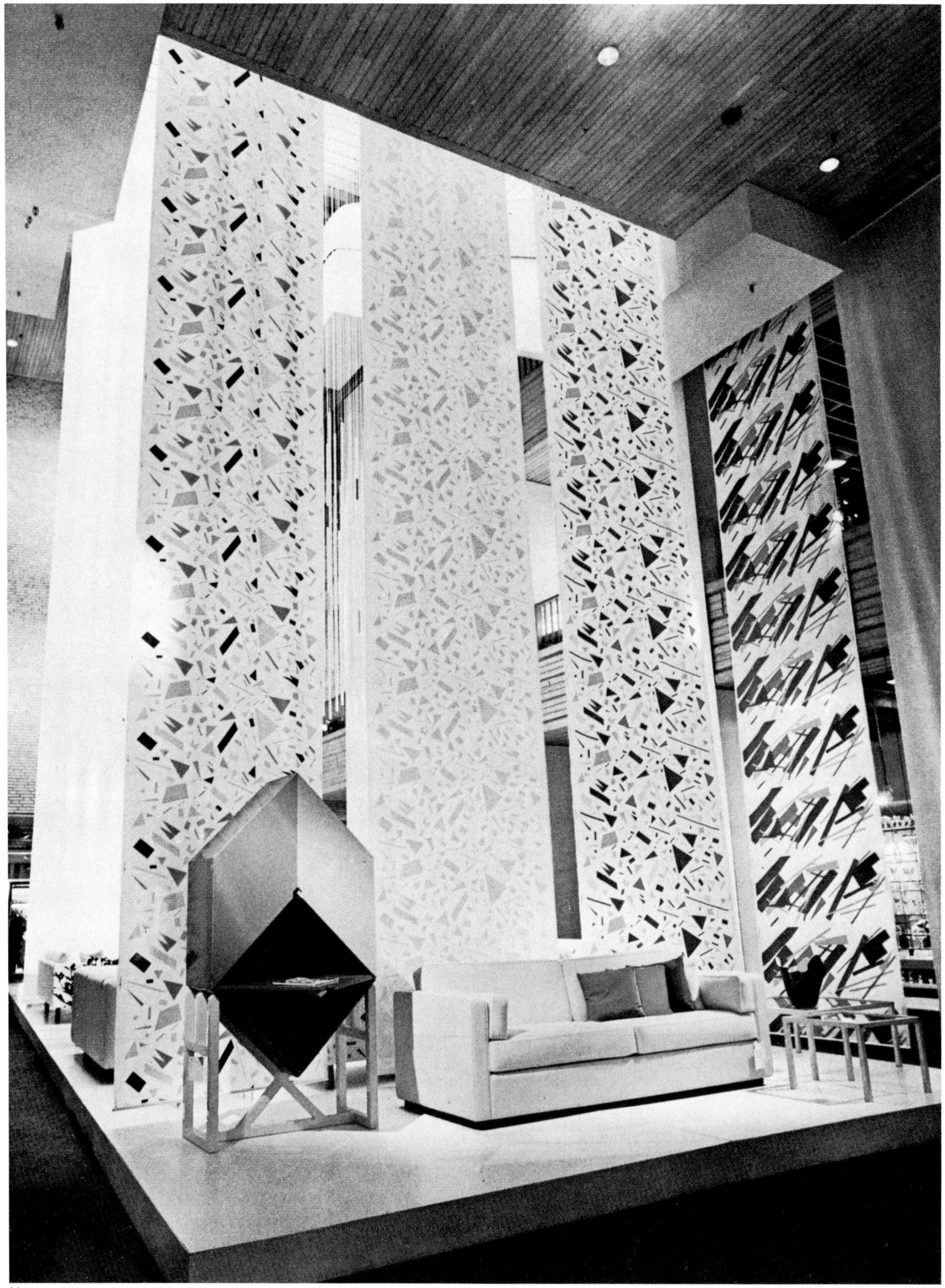
14

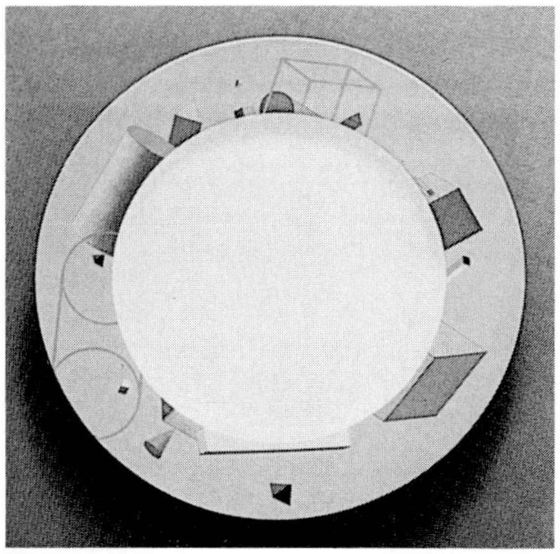
15

16

18

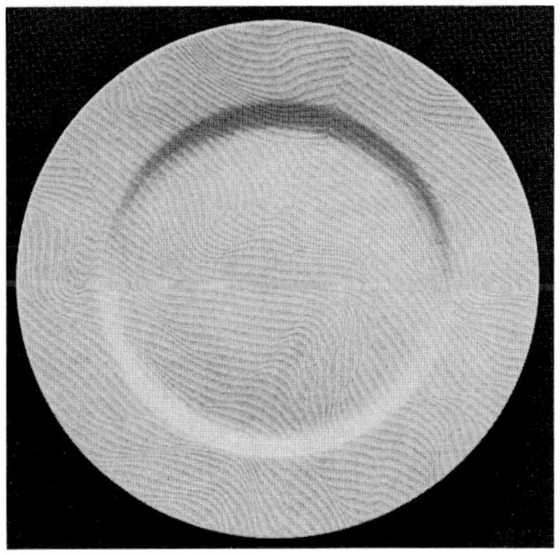
17

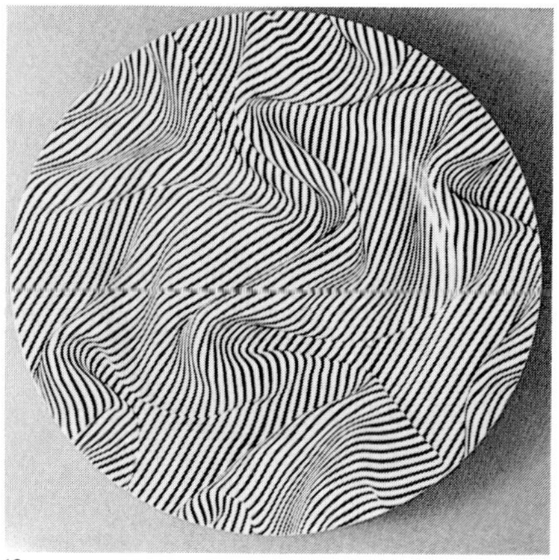
19

20

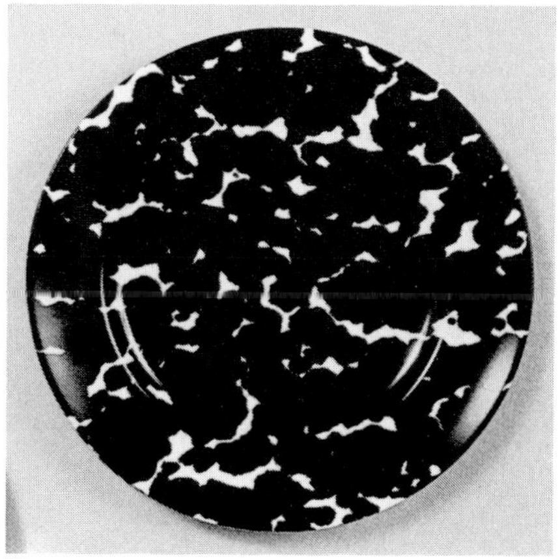
21

Hiroshi Awatsuji	D 11–13
Ole Hertz	D 14
Steven Holl	D 15, 16
Robert Haussmann	D 17, 19
Hans Hollein	D 18
Robert Venturi	D 20, 21

Textures are elements of perception
Texture corresponds to a structuring of the surfaces of real objects. The fields of application are universal, as demonstrated by the examples from the manufacturing and textile sectors. Progressive design can make our product environment more varied and agreeable.

Texturen sind Wahrnehmungselemente
Der Textur entspricht eine Strukturierung der Flächen realer Objekte. Die Anwendungsbereiche sind universell, wie die Beispiele aus dem Manufaktur- und Textilsektor belegen. Fortschrittliches Design kann unsere Produktumwelt vielfältiger und freudiger machen.

Les textures sont des éléments de la perception
A chaque structure correspond une structuration des superficies des objets réels. Les domaines d'application sont universels, comme le montrent les exemples puisés dans le secteur de la manufacture et du textile. Un design orienté vers le progrès permet de diversifier et d'égayer le monde dans lequel évoluent les produits.

Nikken Sekkei D 22
Georg Stärk Ph 23
Toshihiro Katayama D 24

22

23

24

Figures and patterns
All the principles mentioned are encountered today in architecture and interior design. As can be clearly seen, the planned organization of elements of perception leads, at the next level, to the formation of figures and structures. Outlines are produced of a refined internal structure, formed of edges, creases, gradients and curvatures. This is perceived by the viewer as a multiplicity of forms.

Figuren und Muster
Alle die vorgenannten Prinzipien begegnen uns heute in Architektur und Interior-Design. Die planmässige Organisation von Wahrnehmungselementen führt – wie man deutlich sehen kann – auf der nächsten Ebene zur Ausbildung von Figuren und Strukturen. Es entstehen Umrisse von einer raffinierten internen Struktur, die durch Kanten, Knicke, Neigungen und Wölbungen gebildet wird. Sie wird vom Betrachter als Formenvielfalt wahrgenommen.

Figures et modèles
Les principes susmentionnés apparaissent tous dans le domaine de l'architecture et du design d'intérieur modernes. L'organisation méthodique des éléments de la perception entraîne – comme on le voit très clairement – la formation, dès le niveau suivant, de figures et de structures. D'où la naissance de contours d'une structure interne fine et subtile, composée d'arêtes, de coudes, de pentes et de courbures. L'observateur la perçoit en tant que multiplicité de formes.

25

Woddy Pirtle D 25
François Robert Ph 26

According to J. J. Gibson, all the elementary impressions of the visual world can be reduced to textures and gradients of textures. As can be seen from this example, figures and patterns are formed from lines, outlines and forms. These create the conditions for the formation of objects. The dynamic impression of an architectural design (at right) is perceived as a result of gradients of density (distancing).

Nach J. J. Gibson können alle elementaren Eindrücke der visuellen Welt auf Textur und Texturgradienten zurückgeführt werden. Wie bei diesem Beispiel ersichtlich, sind es Linien, Umrisse und Formen, die sich zu Figuren und Mustern formieren. Sie bilden die Voraussetzung für die Abbildung von Gegenständen oder Objekten. Für die Wahrnehmung entsteht der dynamische Eindruck einer Architektur (rechte Seite) als Ergebnis von Dichtegradienten (Entfernung).

Selon J. J. Gibson, toute impression élémentaire, déclenchée par le monde visuel, trouve son origine dans la texture et les gradients de texture. Cet exemple illustre en effet que les lignes, les contours et les formes deviennent figures et modèles. L'œil perçoit l'impression dynamique d'une architecture (à droite) qui est l'aboutissement des gradients de densité (distance).

26

François Morellet 27
Etsushi Kiyohara D 28
Osamu Furumura D 29
Hideki Fujii Ph 30

The principle of texture, whereby the syntagms of the lower stage provide the construction of the next, is illustrated once again on the following pages. The organization of screen dots (textures) has its own aesthetic attraction. At the next higher level, however, these patterns (dot densities) provide the conditions for the representation of concrete objects. Finally it is shown how border lines between various textures make up outlines (next page).

Das Prinzip der Textur, wobei die Syntagmen der unteren Stufe den Aufbau der nächsten Stufe bilden, wird auf den nachfolgenden Seiten noch einmal veranschaulicht. Die Organisation von Rasterpunkten (Texturen) hat einen eigenen ästhetischen Reiz. Auf der nächsthöheren Ebene jedoch bilden diese Muster (Punktdichte) die Voraussetzung für die Abbildung von konkreten Objekten. Zum Schluss wird verdeutlicht, wie Begrenzungslinien zwischen verschiedenen Texturen Umrisse bilden (nächste Seite).

Les pages suivantes illustrent le principe de la texture, selon lequel les syntagmes du degré le plus bas constituent la structure du degré suivant. L'organisation de points de trame (textures) possède son propre attrait esthétique. Au niveau suivant, toutefois, ces motifs (densité des points) constituent la condition de la représentation d'objets concrets. Pour terminer, l'on montre comment des lignes de démarcation entre différentes textures constituent des contours (page suivante).

27

28

29

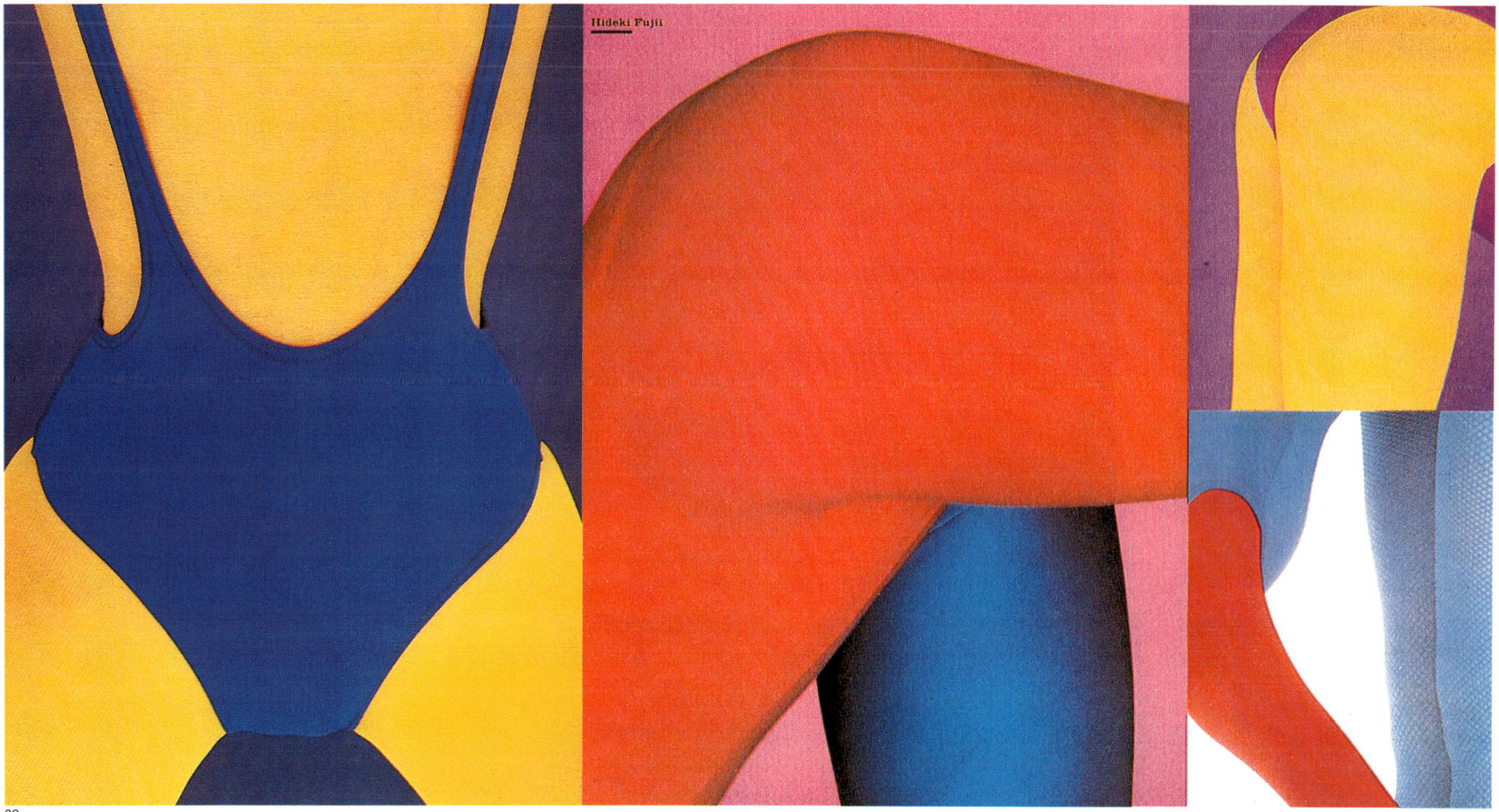

30

IAGP D 31
Evans & Southerland D 32

Exactly in accordance with the principles described, the computer equipped with measuring data produces precise relief pictures (topography of the Antarctic icecap) or coloured models of flying objects.
Thus the classes mentioned form the elements of the visual field, allowing a description of *every* possible illustration.

Genau nach den bereits geschilderten Prinzipien erzeugt der Computer anhand von Messdaten exakte Reliefbilder (Topographie des antarktischen Eisschildes) oder farbige Flugkörpermodelle.
Die vorgenannten Klassen bilden also die Elemente des visuellen Bereichs, sie erlauben die Beschreibung *jeder* möglichen Abbildung.

C'est précisément en fonction des principes énoncés plus tôt que, sur la base de mesures précises, l'ordinateur produit des images en relief (topographie des glaces qui recouvrent l'Antarctique) ou des modèles en couleur d'objets volants.
Les classes prénommées constituent donc les éléments du domaine visuel, et permettent la description de *toute* représentation possible.

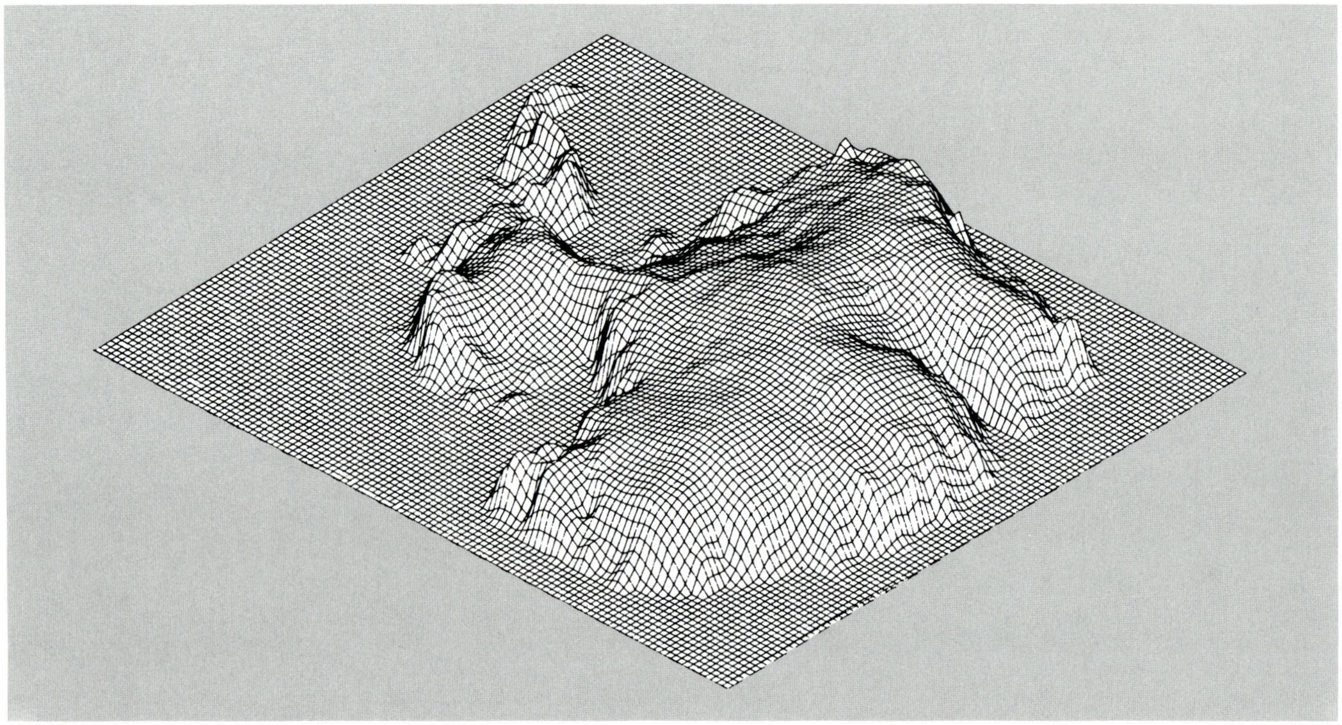

31

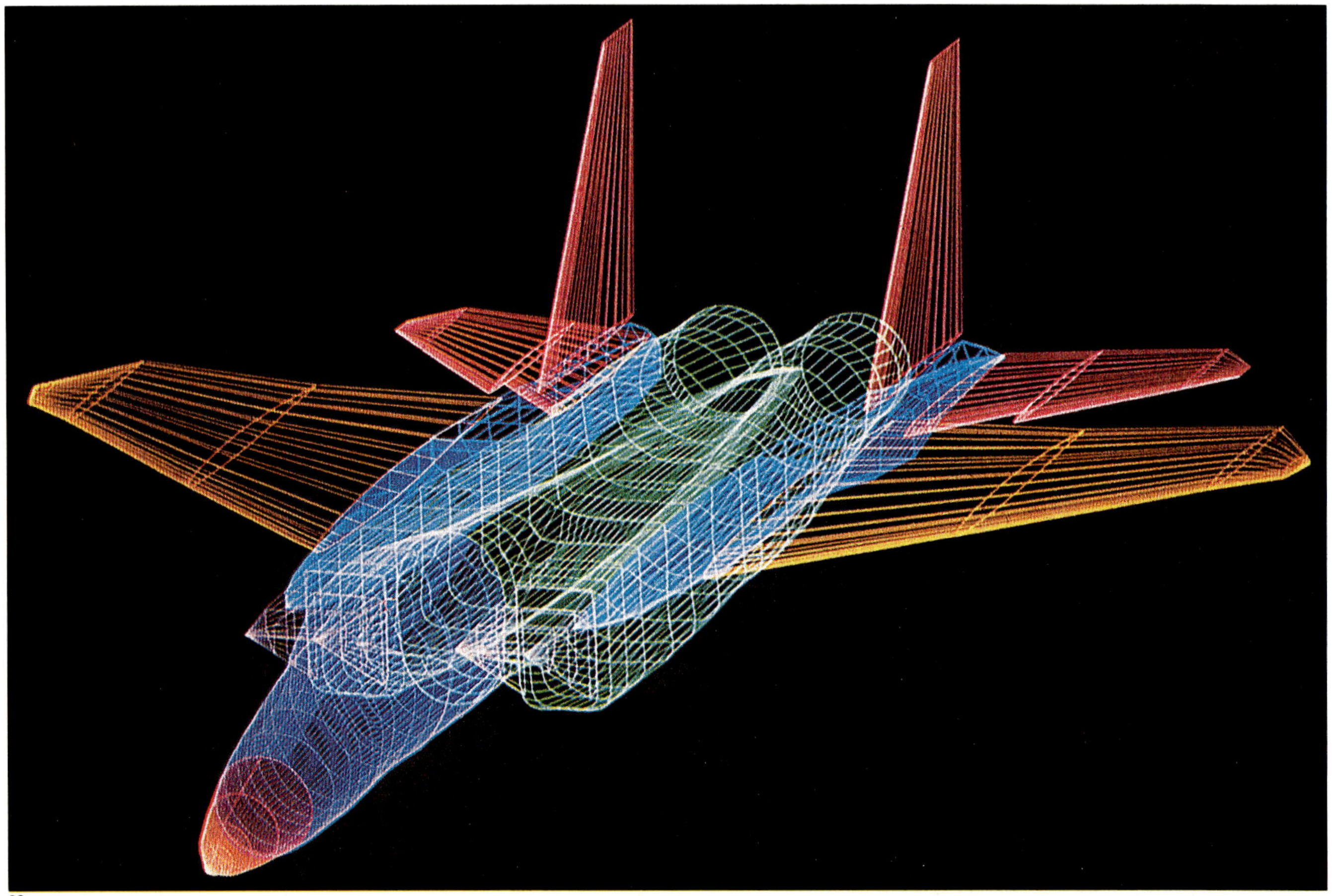

32

Jay Maisel Ph 33
Tatsushiro Inuyama AD 34
Minsei Tominaga Ph

At a further level — the fourth — pictorial statements are made possible through the representation of relationships between objects. Basic rules for the formation of such statements are supplied by means of perspective and gradients of texture. In a most striking manner, the two subjects shown here grasp such connections. A company signalizes the close connection between itself and NASA. The symbol of a cosmetics firm also produces a relationship between the product and certain of its characteristics. Basic rules for the formation of such statements are supplied by means of perspective and gradients of textutre.

Auf einer weiteren – der vierten – Ebene werden durch die Abbildung von Beziehungen zwischen Gegenständen bildliche Aussagen möglich. Grundlegende Regeln für die Bildung solcher Aussagen werden durch die Perspektive und die Texturgradienten geliefert. Mit geradezu lapidaren Mitteln greifen die beiden hier abgebildeten Sujets solche Zusammenhänge auf: Ein Unternehmen signalisiert die zwischen dem Konzern und der NASA bestehende enge Verbindung. Auch beim Motiv einer Kosmetikfirma entsteht eine Relation zwischen Produkt und bestimmten Produkteigenschaften. Grundlegende Regeln für die Bildung solcher Aussagen werden durch die Perspektive und die Texturgradienten geliefert.

Au quatrième niveau, la représentation des relations entre objets permet de réaliser des énoncés figuratifs. La perspective et les gradients de texture fournissent les règles de base de tels énoncés. C'est avec des moyens extrêmement réduits que les deux sujets ici représentés illustrent ce phénomène: une entreprise signale l'existence de liens étroits qui la lient à la NASA. Le thème choisi par une entreprise de produits cosmétiques établit aussi un lien entre le produit, et certaines de ses qualités. La perspective et le gradient de texture fournissent les règles qui sont à la base de la formation des énoncés de ce type.

33

34

In my opinion, the goods produced today for our people in the USSR are not yet good enough. The job of design is to ensure that the goods sold, like the production tools used by the workers, meet the needs of the user . . . We now need designers for industry, fashion and graphics, and we need product designers. The most important thing is to bring in new ideas.

Yuri Soloviev

Ich bin der Meinung, dass die Waren, die heute für unser Volk in der UdSSR produziert werden, noch nicht gut genug sind. Aufgabe des Designs ist es, dafür zu sorgen, dass die Waren, die gekauft werden, wie auch die Produktionseinrichtungen, mit denen die Arbeiter in den Werken zu tun haben, den Bedürfnissen der Verbraucher entsprechen . . . Wir brauchen jetzt Designer für die Industrie, für Mode, für Grafik, und wir brauchen Produkt-Designer. Das wichtigste ist jetzt, dass neue Ideen eingebracht werden.

Yuri Soloviev

A mon avis, les produits fabriqués aujourd'hui en URSS pour notre peuple ne sont pas encore assez bons. Le design a pour mission de faire en sorte que les produits destinés à la vente, tout comme les équipements de production utilisés par les travailleurs dans les usines, répondent aux besoins des consommateurs... Nous avons actuellement besoin de designers pour l'industrie, la mode, les arts graphiques, et nous avons besoin de product-designers. Aujourd'hui, le plus important, c'est l'apport de nouvelles idées.

Yuri Soloviev

3. Better communication through purposeful use of signs

3.1. The meaning of syntactics

3.1.1. Basic elements of pictorial signs

Scientific theories are usually formed on the basis of analyses and, at this point, I will use an analysis in order to develop the grammar of pictorial language from semiotics. The object of analysis here is a wide variety of motifs with an increasing degree of complexity.

The first step in the analysis of an image consists of ascertaining the elements of which that image is composed. For a long time, any attempts to identify dots, lines and geometrical shapes as image elements have proved utterly fruitless. One must therefore find another starting point in the search for elementary signs. This starting point must be perception, allowing use to be made of the findings of the psychology of perception. Many theorists of visual communication have already recognized these findings, but when one considers their attempts to apply them to practice, one gets the impression that research into perception has not yet passed the stage of gestalt psychology. The basic approach of J. J. Gibson to this matter may not represent the most up-to-date state of science but it allows some very concrete applications to the practical problems of visual communication. In association with semiotic theory, a comprehensive grammar of pictorial language can be built upon this basis, allowing elements of perception to be investigated with regard to their elementary sign character.

As is shown by linguistics, there is a need to distinguish between different levels of analysis. Every combination

3. Bessere Kommunikation durch gezielte Zeichenverwendung

3.1. Was verstehen wir unter Syntaktik?

3.1.1. Grundelemente bildlicher Zeichen

Wissenschaftliche Theorien entstehen meist auf der Grundlage von Analysen, und ich möchte daher eine Analyse benutzen, um die Grammatik der bildlichen Sprache von der Semiotik her zu entwickeln. Analysegegenstand sind dabei die verschiedensten Motive mit zunehmendem Komplexitätsgrad.

Der erste Schritt für die Analyse eines Bildes besteht in der Feststellung der Elemente, die das Bild ausmachen. Als absolut erfolglos haben sich in vielen Jahren die Versuche erwiesen, Punkte, Linien und geometrische Flächen als Bildelemente zu identifizieren. Man muss also bei der Suche nach elementaren Zeichen anders beginnen. Ausgangspunkt muss dabei die Wahrnehmung sein, wo man die Ergebnisse der Wahrnehmungspsychologie heranziehen kann. Dies haben bereits viele Theoretiker der visuellen Kommunikation erkannt. Doch sieht man sich die Versuche einer Übertragung auf die Praxis an, so hat man den Eindruck, die Erforschung der Wahrnehmung sei bisher nicht über den Stand der Gestaltpsychologie hinausgekommen. Zwar ist auch der hier zugrundegelegte Ansatz von J. J. Gibson nicht der allerneueste Stand der Wissenschaft, aber er erlaubt sehr konkrete Übertragungen auf praktische Probleme der visuellen Kommunikation. In Verbindung mit der semiotischen Theorie lässt sich auf dieser Grundlage eine umfassende Grammatik der bildlichen Sprache aufbauen. Dabei werden Wahrnehmungselemente auf ihren elementaren Zeichencharakter hin untersucht.

Im Zusammenhang mit der Linguistik wurde auf die Notwendigkeit der Unterscheidung der Analyseebenen hingewiesen. Jede Kombination von

3. Une meilleure communication par une utilisation choisie du signe

3.1. Que comprenons-nous par la syntactique?

3.1.1. Eléments fondamentaux des signes figuratifs

Les théories scientifiques se forment le plus souvent sur la base d'analyses, et j'aimerais en conséquence utiliser une analyse pour développer la grammaire de la langue figurative à partir de la sémiotique. Cette analyse porte sur les motifs les plus variés avec un degré de complexité croissant.

La première étape de l'analyse d'une image consiste à reconnaître ses éléments constitutifs. Pendant plusieurs années, l'on a tenté en vain d'identifier des points, des lignes et des surfaces géométriques comme éléments de l'image. Il convient donc de commencer ailleurs la recherche de signes élémentaires. Le point de départ doit être la perception, et l'on peut ici reprendre les résultats de la psychologie de la perception, comme l'ont déjà discerné beaucoup de théoriciens de la communication visuelle. Toutefois, si l'on considère les tentatives de transfert à la pratique, on a l'impression que l'étude de la perception n'est pas encore allée au-delà du niveau de la «Gestaltpsychologie». Sans doute l'approche de J. J. Gibson qui nous sert ici de base ne constitue-t-elle pas l'état de la science le plus récent, mais elle permet néanmoins d'opérer des transferts très concrets à des problèmes pratiques de la communication visuelle. Avec la théorie sémiotique, cette base permet de bâtir une grammaire complète de la langue figurative. Dans ce contexte, l'on examinera le caractère de signe élémentaire des éléments de perception.

Dans le contexte de la linguistique, l'on a mentionné la nécessité de la distinction des niveaux d'analyse. Chaque combinaison d'éléments de

Wolf Lommel / Annette Meisen AD 35, 36
Detlef Trefz Ph
TBWA A

The fourth level, now reached, characterized by relationships between objects, is of central interest for communications research. Umberto Eco describes this level as sufficient for a semiotics of visual communication, but an exact analysis is quite impossible without recourse to the lower levels. These are therefore treated in equal detail on the preceding pages. The advertisements shown here are examples of a regular pictorial statement. The following basic syntactical rule can be established for the levels of statement which are decisive for a theory of visual communication. A regular pictorial statement always consists of Qualisigns, Sinsigns and Legisigns.

Die jetzt erreichte vierte Ebene, die durch Beziehungen zwischen Gegenständen gekennzeichnet ist, ist von zentralem Interesse für die Kommunikationsforschung. Umberto Eco bezeichnet diese Ebene als ausreichend für eine Semiotik der visuellen Kommunikation. Eine exakte Analyse ist jedoch ohne Rückgriff auf die niedrigeren Ebenen gar nicht möglich. Deshalb wurden diese auch so ausführlich auf den vorangegangenen Seiten behandelt.
Die hier abgebildeten Anzeigen sind Beispiele einer regulären bildlichen Aussage. Für die Aussageebene, die entscheidend ist für eine Theorie der visuellen Kommunikation, kann man die folgende syntaktische Grundregel aufstellen. Eine reguläre bildliche Aussage besteht immer aus Quali-, Sin- und Legizeichen.

Caractérisé par les relations entre objets, ce quatrième niveau revêt un aspect essentiel pour la recherche sur la communication. Selon Umberto Eco, ce niveau permet déjà une sémiotique de la communication visuelle. Une analyse exacte n'est toutefois pas possible sans les niveaux inférieurs, qui ont donc fait l'objet d'une attention toute particulière aux pages précédentes.
Les annonces représentées ici illustrent un énoncé classique. Voici la règle syntaxique de base, applicable au niveau d'énoncé se révélant déterminant pour la théorie de la communication visuelle. Un énoncé classique est toujours composé de qualisignes, de sinsignes et de légisignes.

35

36

A

B

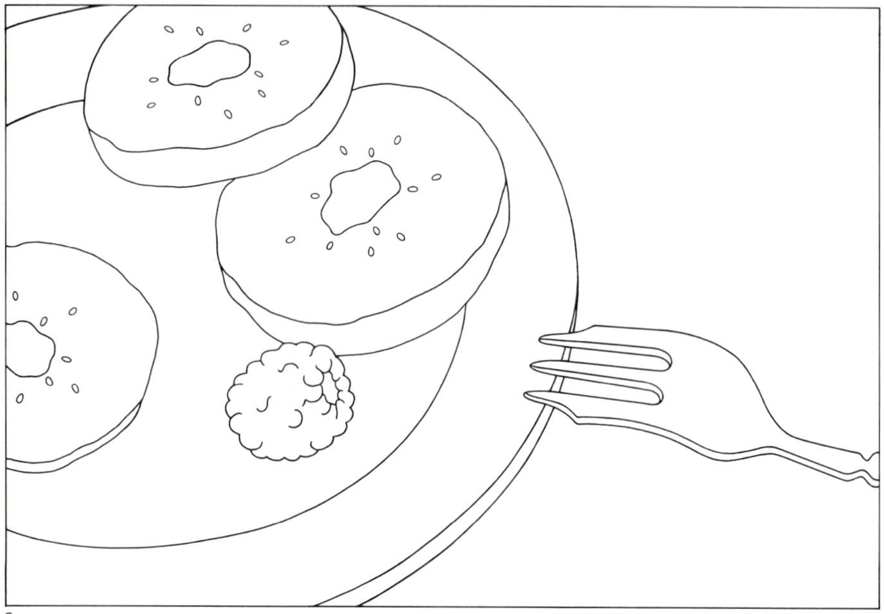
C

D

A Example of a regular pictorial statement
Beispiel einer regulären bildlichen Aussage
Exemple d'un énoncé figuratif classique
B Example of various Qualisigns
Beispiel verschiedener Qualizeichen
Exemple de qualisignes différents
C Example of available Sinsigns
Beispiel vorhandener Sinzeichen
Exemple de sinsignes existants
D Example for Legisign (perspective)
Beispiel für Legizeichen (Perspektive)
Exemple de légisignes (perspective)

The analysis of pictorial statements has so far always fallen down on the translation of pictorial content into categories of speech. Such a translation is based on a subjective process of interpretation. In the examples shown here, the question is to identify and classify the concrete forms of appearance of the pictures on the basis of the signs.

Die Analyse bildlicher Aussagen scheiterte bisher immer an der Umsetzung von Bildinhalten in sprachliche Kategorien. Diese Umsetzung basiert auf einem subjektiven Interpretationsprozess. Bei den hier gezeigten Beispielen geht es darum, die konkreten Erscheinungsformen der Bilder aufgrund der Zeichen zu identifizieren und zu klassifizieren.

Jusqu'à présent, l'analyse des énoncés figuratifs a toujours échoué à cause de la transposition de contenus d'image en catégories linguistiques. Cette transposition se base sur un processus subjectif d'interprétation. Ces exemples visent, en partant des signes, à identifier l'apparence extérieure concrète des images, et à les classer.

A

B

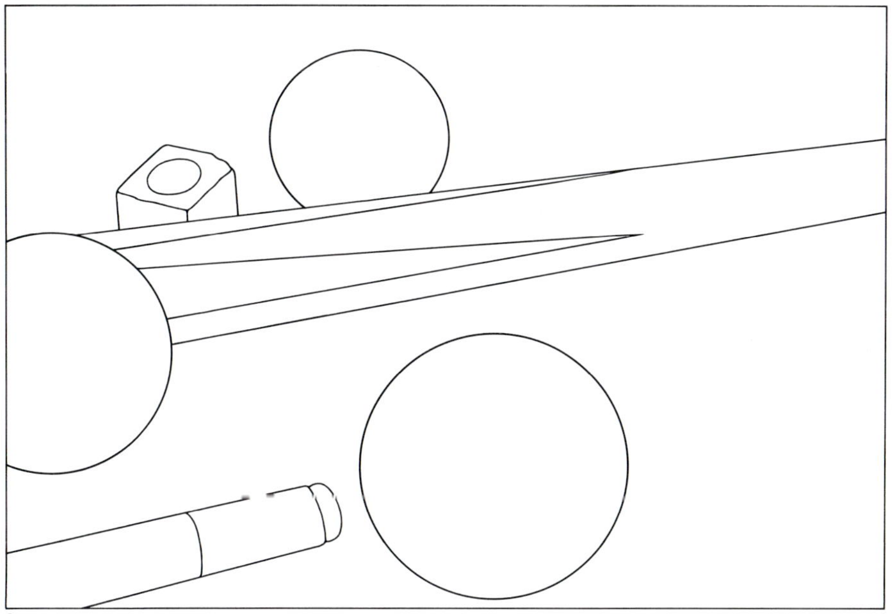
C

D

A Example of a regular pictorial statement
Beispiel einer regulären bildlichen Aussage
Exemple d'un énoncé figuratif classique
B Example of various Qualisigns
Beispiel verschiedener Qualizeichen
Exemple de qualisignes différents
C Example of available Sinsigns
Beispiel vorhandener Sinzeichen
Exemple de sinsignes existants
D Example for Legisign (perspective)
Beispiel für Legizeichen (Perspektive)
Exemple de légisignes (perspective)

As pictures are gaining ever greater importance in advertising, future research must start at this point. The instrumentarium of analysis is in a position to evaluate the design's firmness, its inner meaning and its conveyance of connotations, in short the communicative performance of pictorial statements.

Da Bilder in der Werbung immer mehr an Bedeutung gewinnen, muss die Forschung in Zukunft an dieser Stelle ansetzen. Das Analyseinstrumentarium ist in der Lage, Gestaltfestigkeit, Prägnanz, Vermittlung von Konnotationen, kurz, die kommunikative Leistung von Bildaussagen zu bewerten.

Etant donné le rôle croissant des images dans la publicité, il faut qu'à l'avenir, la recherche se fonde sur celles-ci. Ses instruments d'analyse sont en mesure d'évaluer la solidité de la morphologie, la pénétration, la transmission de connotations, bref, l'efficacité de communication déployée par certains énoncés figuratifs.

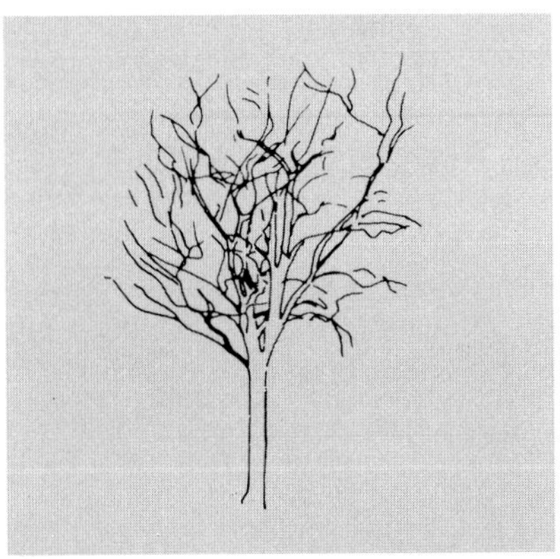

of sign elements can be regarded as a unified sign at the next higher level, and therefore treated as an element in itself. It is true that elements at different levels are all based on the same principles, but their concrete expression is different from one level to the next. For communications, the most important level is the one where statements are formed. In the concluding analysis, therefore, that is the only level to be considered.

The first kind of sign required for the formulation of pictorial expressions is that of elements of perception, known as textures. In practice, they allow recognition of the material from which something is made. In semiotics, such signs are known as Qualisigns. According to Peirce, a Qualisign is "a quality which is a Sign". It cannot actually act as a sign until it is embodied in a concrete form; but the embodiment has nothing to do with its character as a sign. Colours, textures and patterns are examples of Qualisigns. An essential feature of the Qualisign is its generality. Thus it does not stand for a given object but for a class of objects, which it signifies independently of its concrete form.

In contrast to this, the second kind of sign, known as a Sinsign, signifies only the form. The visual Sinsign presupposes the existence of Qualisigns, which take on concrete form through structuring. The sign itself consists of this concrete form, not of the underlying qualities. Sinsigns do not signify qualities or conditions but individual objects, the term Sinsign having the same derivation as "singular". At the level of statements, representations of objects can also be Qualisigns, namely when the representation refers to a class of objects, not to the single object. In this case the form

Zeichenelementen kann auf der nächsthöheren Ebene als einheitliches Zeichen und damit selbst wieder als Element behandelt werden. Zwar beruhen die Elemente auf den verschiedenen Ebenen auf denselben Prinzipien, doch ist ihre konkrete Ausprägung von Ebene zu Ebene unterschiedlich. Für die Kommunikation ist die wichtigste Ebene diejenige, auf der Aussagen gebildet werden. Bei der abschliessenden Analyse wird daher nur sie berücksichtigt.

Die erste Zeichenart, die zur Formulierung bildlicher Aussagen notwendig ist, sind Wahrnehmungselemente, die Texturen genannt werden. Sie lassen praktisch den Stoff erkennen, aus dem etwas besteht. Diese Zeichen werden in der Semiotik «Qualizeichen» genannt. Nach Peirce ist ein Qualizeichen «eine Qualität, die ein Zeichen ist». Es kann nicht tatsächlich als Zeichen wirken, solange es nicht in eine konkrete Gestalt gefasst ist; aber die Konkretisierung hat nichts mit seinem Charakter als Zeichen zu tun. Farben, Texturen und Muster sind Beispiele für Qualizeichen. Ein wesentliches Merkmal des Qualizeichens ist seine Allgemeinheit. Es steht also nicht für einen bestimmten Gegenstand, sondern für eine Klasse von Gegenständen, die es unabhängig von seiner konkreten Form bezeichnet.

Im Gegensatz dazu bezeichnet die zweite Zeichenart nur die Form, diese Zeichenart wird «Sinzeichen» genannt. Das visuelle Sinzeichen setzt das Vorhandensein von Qualizeichen voraus, die durch Strukturierung eine konkrete Form annehmen. Das Zeichensein besteht in ebendieser konkreten Form, nicht aber in den zugrunde liegenden Qualitäten. Sinzeichen bezeichnen nicht Qualitäten oder Zustände, sondern einzelne Objekte. Der Begriff «Sinzeichen» leitet sich von singulär ab. Auf der Aussagenebene können Darstellungen von Gegenständen durchaus auch Qualizeichen sein. Nämlich dann, wenn diese Darstellung nicht auf den einzelnen Gegenstand, sondern auf eine Klasse von Gegenständen verweist. Dabei kann dann die Form variieren, ohne

signe peut être traitée au niveau immédiatement supérieur comme signe uniforme, et ainsi comme élément. Si les éléments reposent sur les mêmes principes aux différents niveaux, leur expression concrète varie toutefois d'un niveau à l'autre. Pour la communication, le niveau le plus important est celui auquel les énoncés sont formés. C'est donc le seul que nous retiendrons en dernière analyse.

Le premier type de signe indispensable à la formulation d'énoncés figuratifs est constitué d'éléments de perception nommés textures. Pour ainsi dire, ces textures permettent de reconnaître de quelle matière une chose est composée. En sémiotique, ces signes sont appelés «qualisignes». Selon Peirce, un qualisigne est «une qualité qui est un signe». Il ne peut pas réellement agir comme signe avant de se matérialiser; mais cette matérialisation n'a rien à voir avec son caractère de signe. Les couleurs, les textures et les motifs sont des exemples de qualisignes. L'un des traits essentiels du qualisigne est sa généralité. Ainsi, il ne représente pas un objet déterminé, mais une classe d'objets qu'il désigne indépendamment de sa forme concrète.

En revanche, le deuxième type de signe désigne uniquement la forme; il est appelé «sinsigne». Le sinsigne visuel présuppose l'existence de qualisignes qui prennent une forme concrète par la structuration. L'être signe est justement constitué par cette forme concrète, et non pas par les qualités sous-jacentes. Les sinsignes ne désignent pas des qualités ou des états, mais des objets individuels. La notion de «sinsigne» est dérivée de singulier. Au niveau de l'énoncé, des représentations d'objets peuvent être aussi des qualisignes, lorsqu'elles ne renvoient pas à l'objet individuel, mais à une classe d'objets. D'ailleurs, la

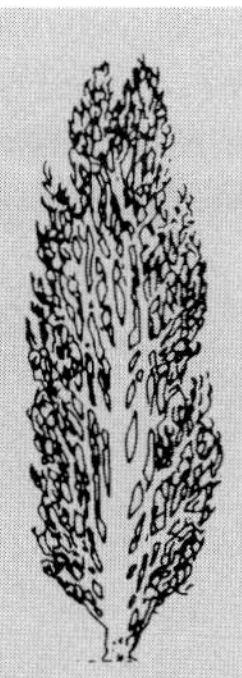

Poplar · Pappel · Peuplier

Oak · Eiche · Chêne

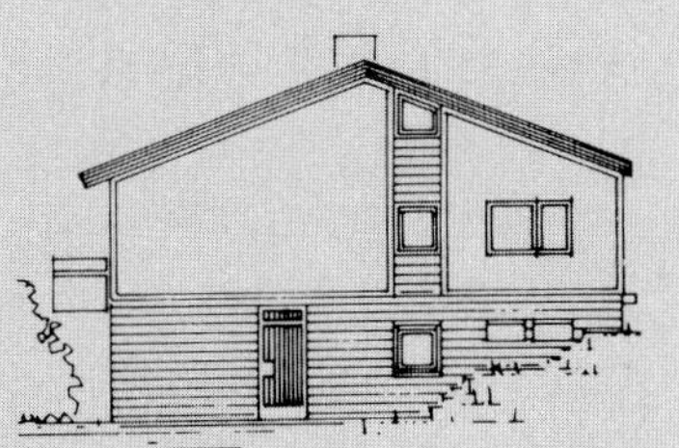

House · Haus · Maison

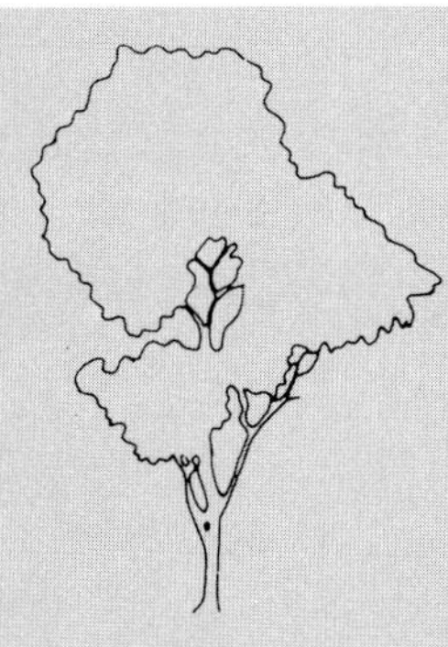

Tree · Baum · Arbre

may vary without alteration to the object, as shown in the two examples.

On the other hand, in the following examples the variations of form signify different objects, as is recognizable from the specific method of representation.

Now, whether a sign is to be regarded as general or specific, that is to say as Qualisign or Sinsign, can be decided only on the basis of the given connection. The third elementary kind of sign, known as the Legisign, does not signify any objects but creates the relationships between objects. In the pictorial sign system, this is done by the perspective or the gradient of texture, meaning the increasing density of texture with increasing distance.

The term "Legisign" is derived from the Latin *lex, legis* (law), because Legisigns are always based on laws. In the cases of perspective and gradient of texture we are concerned with the laws of perception. There is, however, another variant of the Legisign, based on accepted conventions, not natural laws. The most widely used of these Legisigns is script, but they also include logotypes, coats of arms and flags. What all these signs have in common is that they each belong to a system of conventions which assigns to them their function. The triad of Qualisign, Sinsign and Legisign can easily be referred back to the three basic forms of existence and, against this background, is once again explained on the basis of first principles. The Qualisign is, by its nature, only a possibility, while the Sinsign refers to the concrete reality of an object. The Legisign results from the recognition of the laws of perception and is therefore an achievement of reason. The correctness of this theory is confirmed by experience with pictorial communication in the field of

dass sich das Objekt verändert, wie dies bei den beiden Beispielen auf der linken Seite der Fall ist.

Dagegen bezeichnen bei den hier gezeigten Beispielen die Formvariationen unterschiedliche Objekte, was aufgrund der spezifischen Darstellungsweise erkennbar ist.

Ob nun ein Zeichen als allgemein oder als spezifisch, also als Quali- oder als Sinzeichen anzusehen ist, kann nur aus dem jeweils gegebenen Zusammenhang entschieden werden. Die dritte elementare Zeichenart, das «Legizeichen», bezeichnet keine Gegenstände, sondern stellt Beziehungen zwischen Gegenständen her. Im bildlichen Zeichensystem leistet dies die Perspektive oder der Texturgradient, die Zunahme der Dichte einer Textur bei zunehmender Entfernung.

Der Begriff «Legizeichen» ist von *lex, legis* (Gesetz) abgeleitet, weil Legizeichen immer auf Gesetzen beruhen. Im Falle der Perspektive und des Texturgradienten handelt es sich dabei um Gesetzmässigkeiten der Wahrnehmung. Es gibt jedoch noch eine andere Variante des Legizeichens. Es beruht nicht auf Naturgesetzen, sondern auf Konventionen. Das verbreitetste dieser Legizeichen ist die Schrift, aber auch Signets, Wappen oder Flaggen gehören zu dieser Gruppe. Allen diesen Zeichen ist gemeinsam, dass sie jeweils einem System von Konventionen angehören, das ihnen ihre Funktion zuweist. Die Triade, die Quali-, Sin- und Legizeichen zusammen bilden, lässt sich leicht auf die drei Grundformen des Seins zurückführen und wird vor diesem Hintergrund noch einmal vom Prinzip her erläutert. Das Qualizeichen ist seinem Wesen nach lediglich eine Möglichkeit, erst das Sinzeichen bezieht sich auf die konkrete Wirklichkeit eines Objekts. Das Legizeichen resultiert aus der Erkenntnis der Gesetzmässigkeiten der Wahrnehmung und ist von daher eine Leistung der Vernunft. Die Richtigkeit dieser theoretischen Ableitung wird durch Erfahrungen bestätigt, die mit bildlicher Kommunikation im Rahmen der

forme peut varier sans que l'objet ne change, ce qui est le cas dans ces deux exemples.

En revanche, dans les exemples montrés ici, les variations de forme désignent des objets différents, ce qui est visible en raison du mode de représentation spécifique.

Seul un contexte donné permet de déterminer si un signe est général ou spécifique, c'est-à-dire s'il est un qualisigne ou un sinsigne. Le troisième type de signe élémentaire, le «légisigne», ne désigne pas d'objets, mais établit des liens entre eux. Dans le système de signes figuratifs, c'est le rôle de la perspective ou du gradient de texture, c'est-à-dire l'augmentation de la densité d'une texture avec l'éloignement.

La notion de «légisigne» est dérivée de *lex, legis* (loi), car les légisignes reposent toujours sur des lois. Dans le cas de la perspective et des gradients de texture, il s'agit des lois de la perception. Toutefois, il existe une autre variante du légisigne qui n'est pas fondée sur des lois naturelles, mais sur des conventions. Le plus répandu de ces légisignes est l'écriture, mais les logos, les armoiries ou les drapeaux appartiennent aussi à ce groupe. Tous ces signes ont en commun le fait qu'ils appartiennent chacun à un système de conventions qui leur assigne leur fonction. La triade constituée par les qualisignes, les sinsignes et les légisignes se ramène facilement aux trois formes de l'être: dans ce contexte, reprenons l'explication de son principe. Le qualisigne, par essence, n'est qu'une possibilité. Le sinsigne, lui, est lié à la réalité concrète d'un objet. Le légisigne résulte de la cognition des lois de la perception, et constitue donc un effort de la raison. La justesse de cette déduction théorique est confirmée par des expériences de communication visuelle menées dans le cadre de

37

38

天に。地に。旅は、胸いっぱいの感動を吸い込む。
The Beverly Hill
NORTHWEST ORIENT

39

PHOTOGRAPHY Jimmy Williams Raleigh, North Carolina

40

Arthur Meyerson	Ph	37
Kazumasa Nagai	D	38
Yuichi Yukawa	AD	39
Hiroyuki Negishi	Ph	
Charlotte White	D	40
Jimmy Williams	Ph	

These examples also show regular pictorial statements, producing a dynamic picture formation through the conscious use of Legisigns. For the pictorial sign system, the perspective, together with the gradients of texture, is certainly the most important convention (it could also probably be understood as a natural law), but there are also conventions which are based on the size or the arrangement of the elements.

Auch bei diesen Beispielen handelt es sich um reguläre bildliche Aussagen, bei denen durch den bewussten Einsatz von Legizeichen ein dynamischer Bildaufbau entsteht. Für das bildliche Zeichensystem ist die Perspektive zusammen mit dem Texturgradienten wohl die wichtigste Konvention (man könnte sie wahrscheinlich auch als Naturgesetz auffassen); es gibt aber auch Konventionen, die auf der Grösse oder der Anordnung der Elemente beruhen.

Ces exemples illustrent aussi des énoncés figuratifs classiques, dans le cadre desquels une structure dynamique de l'image est rendue possible grâce au recours conscient à des légisignes. La plus importante des conventions (ou à la limite, des lois naturelles) pour le système figuratif de signes, est l'alliance de la perspective et du gradient de texture. Il existe toutefois aussi des conventions qui se basent sur la grandeur, ou la classification des éléments.

UNESCO and aid to developing countries, where it has been found that natives having no experience in the use of figurative signs are often unable to understand perspective and the relative sizes of objects in pictures.

This makes it plain that the associated schemata of interpretation are not innate qualities but must be seen as results of a learning process in which conventions are internalized. The three kinds of sign — Qualisign, Sinsign and Legisign — cover all conceivable sign elements, thus forming the basis of every pictorial statement. In addition, syntactics must be able to provide the rules by which such statements are formed.

3.1.2. Should syntactical rules be followed or discarded?

Just as grammar gives the rules by which sentences are formed from various kinds of words, so there is a syntax of pictorial sign systems underlying the syntagms of the individual levels of description. No system has yet been worked out for these rules and there is certainly a need for more comprehensive preparatory work, both theoretical and empirical, before such a system can be devised. There are, however, some interesting starting points from which one can see the form which such rules would take. For the level of statement, the following ground rule can be formulated:

"Every regular pictorial statement contains all three kinds of sign. The number of Qualisigns is unlimited, while the number of Sinsigns is limited to the number of objects shown. Legisigns can occur only in one expression."

One becomes really conscious of these rules only through consideration of deviations from them. Such deviations can be classified into three categories: "incomplete representation", "replacement of an expected sign by

UNESCO und organisierter Entwicklungshilfe gemacht wurden: Eingeborene, die keine Erfahrung im Umgang mit bildlichen Zeichen hatten, waren vielfach nicht in der Lage, Perspektive und im Bild enthaltene Grössenverhältnisse richtig zu interpretieren.

Hier wird deutlich, dass die entsprechenden Interpretationsschemata nicht angeboren sind, sondern nur als Ergebnis eines Lernprozesses gesehen werden können, in dem Konventionen verinnerlicht werden. Die drei Zeichenarten – Qualizeichen, Sinzeichen und Legizeichen – erfassen alle nur denkbaren Elemente von Zeichen und bilden somit die Grundlage jeder bildlichen Aussage. Die Syntaktik muss aber auch die Regeln angeben können, nach denen solche Aussagen gebildet werden.

3.1.2. Soll man syntaktische Regeln einhalten oder verwerfen?

Wie die Grammatik die Regeln angibt, nach denen aus den verschiedenen Wortarten Sätze gebildet werden, so gibt es auch eine Syntax bildlicher Zeichensysteme, die den Syntagmen der einzelnen Beschreibungsebenen zugrunde liegen. Ein System dieser Regeln ist bis heute noch nirgends ausgearbeitet worden, und es bedarf sicher noch umfangreicher theoretischer und empirischer Vorarbeiten, ehe man dazu in der Lage sein wird. Es gibt aber interessante Ansatzpunkte, die die Form solcher Regeln erkennen lassen. Für die Aussagenebene kann man folgende Grundregel formulieren:

«Jede reguläre bildliche Aussage enthält alle drei Zeichenarten. Dabei ist die Zahl der Qualizeichen unbegrenzt, während die Zahl der Sinzeichen auf die Anzahl der dargestellten Objekte begrenzt ist. Legizeichen können immer nur in einer Ausprägung auftreten.»

Man wird sich dieser einfachen Regeln eigentlich erst richtig bewusst, wenn man die Abweichungen davon betrachtet. Solchen Abweichungen lassen sich drei Kategorien zuordnen: «unvollständige Abbildung»,

l'UNESCO et d'organisations d'aide au développement: des indigènes sans expérience des signes figuratifs n'étaient généralement pas capables d'interpréter correctement la perspective et les rapports de grandeur contenus dans une image.

Il apparaît clairement ici que les schémas d'interprétation nécessaires ne sont pas innés, mais qu'ils peuvent seulement être considérés comme le résultat d'un processus d'apprentissage au cours duquel des conventions sont intériorisées. Les trois types de signes – qualisignes, sinsignes et légisignes – comprennent tous les éléments imaginables de signes et constituent ainsi la base de tout énoncé figuratif. Cependant, la syntactique, qui s'occupe du discours lui-même, doit aussi pouvoir indiquer les règles selon lesquelles ces énoncés sont construits.

3.1.2. Faut-il observer des règles syntactiques ou les rejeter?

Tout comme la grammaire donne des règles selon lesquelles on construit des phrases à partir des différents types de mots, il existe aussi une syntaxe des systèmes de signes figuratifs sous-jacente aux syntagmes des différents niveaux de description. L'on n'a pas encore élaboré de système de règles dans ce domaine, et bien des travaux préliminaires théoriques et empiriques seront encore nécessaires à cet effet. Il existe néanmoins des approches intéressantes qui permettent de déceler la forme de ces règles. Pour le niveau de l'énoncé, on peut formuler la règle fondamentale suivante:

«Tout énoncé figuratif régulier comprend trois types de signes. Le nombre de qualisignes est illimité, alors que le nombre de sinsignes est limité par le nombre des objets représentés. Les légisignes ne peuvent jamais apparaître que sous une seule expression.»

On ne comprendra bien ces règles qu'en observant ses dérogations, qui peuvent appartenir à trois catégories différentes: «reproduction incom-

As already demonstrated in the experimental part of these explanations, Qualisigns remain strictly limited to their function as "medium". As signs, they are absolutely independent of their concrete form. Thus they always signify only a general category — the material or the condition — but never a concrete object.
The strong emotional effect can be put to good use in advertising, as is shown by the example from a paper manufacturer (The Art of Strathmore). Qualisigns are most likely to be characteristics of abstract painting.

Wie bereits bei dem experimentellen Teil dieser Ausführungen dargestellt, bleiben Qualizeichen allein auf ihre Funktion als «Mittel» beschränkt. Als Zeichen sind sie absolut unabhängig von ihrer jeweiligen konkreten Form. Sie bezeichnen daher immer nur eine allgemeine Kategorie – das Material oder den Zustand –, aber niemals ein konkretes Objekt.
Die starke emotionale Wirkung kann in der Werbung gut genutzt werden, wie das Beispiel eines Papierherstellers (The Art of Strathmore) belegt. Am ehesten sind Qualizeichen Kennzeichen abstrakter Malerei.

Comme nous l'avons déjà démontré dans la partie expérimentale de ces propos, les qualisignes restent limités exclusivement à leur fonction de «support». En tant que signe, ils sont absolument indépendants de leur forme concrète. Ainsi ne désignent-ils jamais qu'une catégorie d'ordre général – le matériau, l'état – sans jamais s'attacher à un objet concret.
La publicité peut faire très bon usage de l'impact émotionnel, comme l'illustre l'exemple d'un fabricant de papier (The Art of Strathmore). Ce sont les qualisignes qui caractérisent le mieux la peinture abstraite.

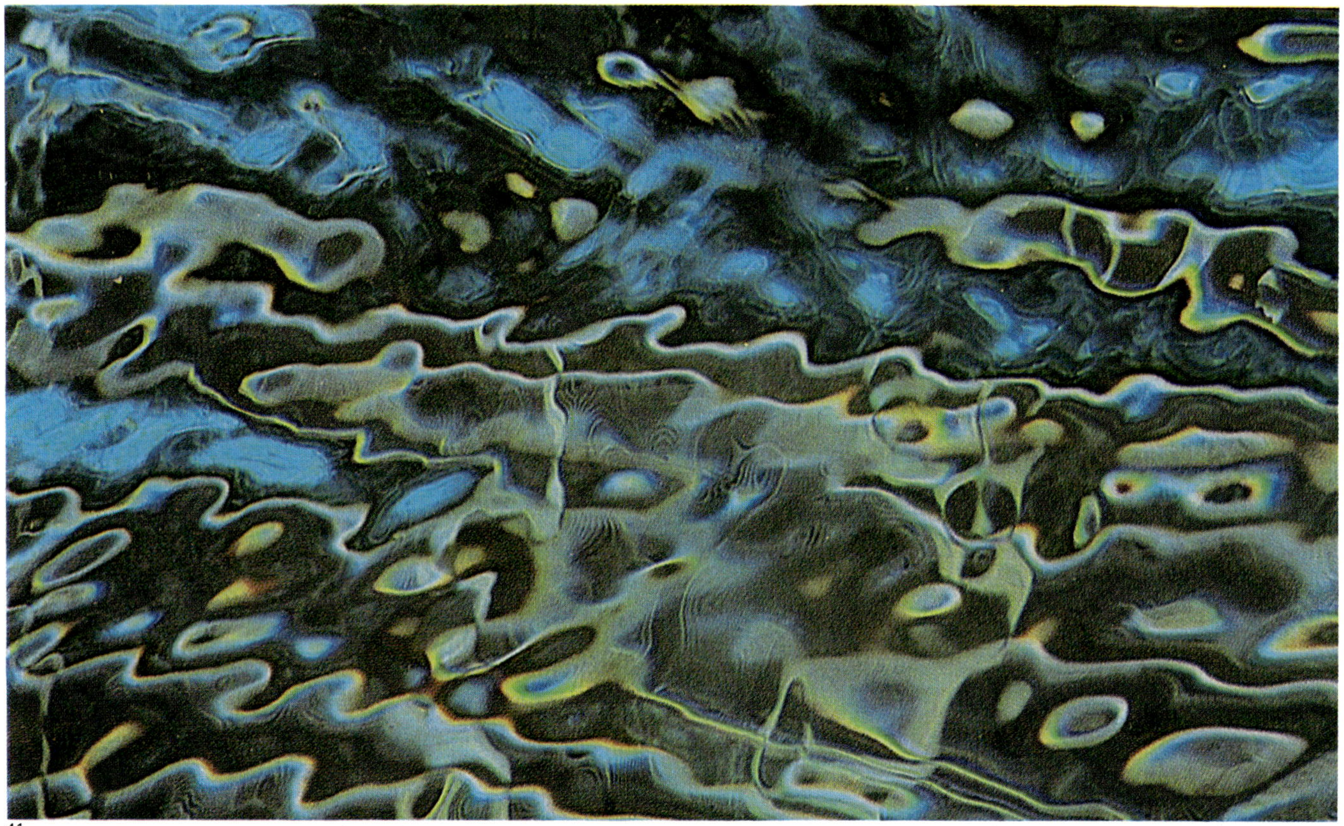

41

42

43

Kathleen Bick	Ph	41
Yoji Yamamoto	Ph	42
Shu Kataoka	D	43
Mike Scricco	AD	44
Michael Furman	Ph	

44

It must be repeated that a complete statement consists of Quali-, Sin- and Legisigns. In the foregoing example two of these elements were missing, which means that, in the semiotic sense, the statement is incomplete. These advertising subjects also show the reduction of the pictures to outlines. Thus the Qualisign is eliminated and only Sinsigns are formed.

Es muss wiederholt werden, dass eine vollständige Aussage aus Quali-, Sin- und Legizeichen besteht. Beim vorhergehenden Beispiel fehlten zwei dieser Elemente, also war im semiotischen Sinne diese Aussage unvollständig. Auch bei diesen Anzeigenmotiven handelt es sich um die Reduktion der Bilder auf Umrisslinien. Damit werden die Qualizeichen eliminiert, und es werden nur Sinzeichen gebildet.

Réitérons qu'un énoncé complet est composé de qualisignes, de sinsignes et de légisignes. Deux de ces éléments manquaient dans l'exemple précédent. Du point de vue sémiotique, cet énoncé est donc incomplet. Ces motifs publicitaires reviennent également à une réduction des images à leur simple contour. Ceci permet d'éliminer les qualisignes, pour ne produire que des sinsignes.

45

46

47

Masaaki Izumiya D 45–47
Barbara Nessim D 48

Whether we are concerned with showing people or products, the subjects have lost none of their completeness for the viewer. As the following pages also show, the reduction of the means produces an unfortunately neglected instrumentarium of differentiation of graphic means of communication.

Ob es sich um die Wiedergabe von Personen oder Produkten handelt, für den Rezipienten haben die Sujets nichts von ihrer Vollständigkeit eingebüsst. Durch die Reduktion der Mittel entsteht – wie auch die nachfolgenden Seiten zeigen – ein leider vernachlässigtes Differenzierungsinstrumentarium grafischer Mittel für die Kommunikation.

Pour le destinataire, l'intégrité des sujets reste intacte, qu'il s'agisse de la représentation de personnes ou de produits. Comme le montrent les pages suivantes, la réduction des moyens entraîne, au détriment de la communication, une diminution des possibilités de différentiation de la part des supports graphiques.

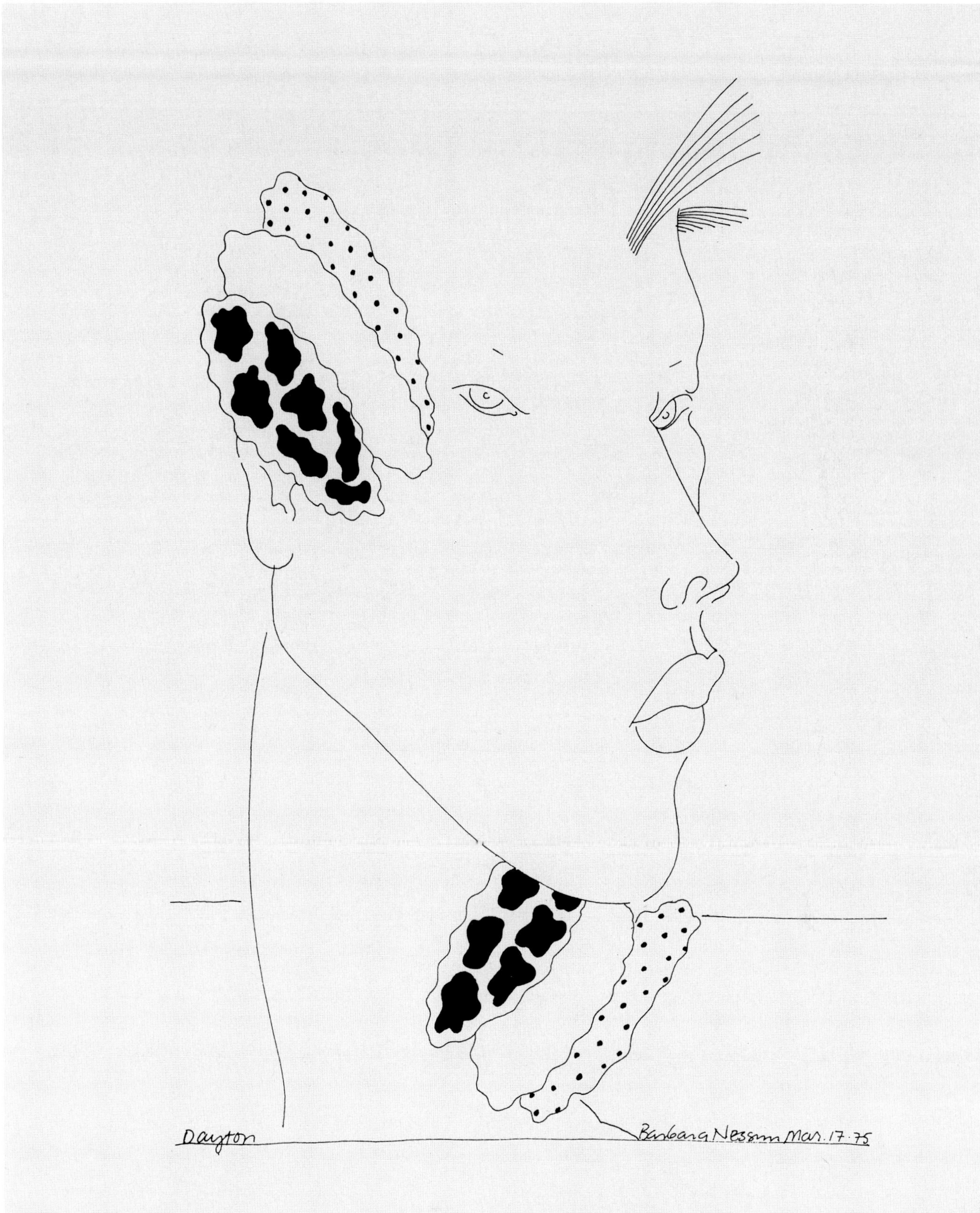

48

Pat Burnham D 49
Zenji Funabashi D 50
Ikko Tanaka D 51–53

Great complexity of pictorial representations in advertising can be a particularly negative factor. It destroys the effect which is achieved by a big picture as such. The incompleteness of these statements results from a lack of Legisigns such as perspective and texture gradient; but for this very reason, they lose nothing of their communicative effectiveness. It follows from the results of information research that the objects shown on the left, which have a freer and more picturesque form, are more effective with regard to information of an emotional nature; while the graphics on the right are better suited to conveying practical information.

Insbesondere die grosse Komplexität bildlicher Darstellungen in der Werbung kann ein negativer Faktor sein. Er macht die Wirkung, die ein grosses Bild für sich genommen erzielt, wieder zunichte. Die Unvollständigkeit dieser Aussagen beruht auf dem Fehlen von Legizeichen, wie Perspektive oder Texturgradient. Aber gerade deswegen büssen sie nichts von ihrer kommunikativen Leistungsfähigkeit ein. Ergebnisse zur Informationsvermittlung belegen, dass die links abgebildeten Objekte, in mehr malerischer, freier Form wiedergegeben, im Hinblick auf emotionale Information leistungsfähiger sind, während die rechts stehenden Grafiken hinsichtlich sachlicher Information besser abschneiden.

En publicité, la grande complexité de représentations figuratives peut constituer un facteur négatif. En effet, il redétruit l'impact qu'une grande image aurait obtenu en tant que telle. Ces énoncés sont incomplets parce qu'ils ne contiennent pas de légisignes, comme la perspective ou le gradient de texture. C'est en revanche précisément pour cette raison qu'il ne perdent rien de leur efficacité au niveau de la communication. Des études sur la transmission de l'information prouvent que la capacité d'information émotionnelle des objets représentés à gauche, sous une forme plus pittoresque et plus libre, est supérieure à celle des graphiques reproduits du côté droit qui, pour leur part, transmettent davantage d'informations objectives.

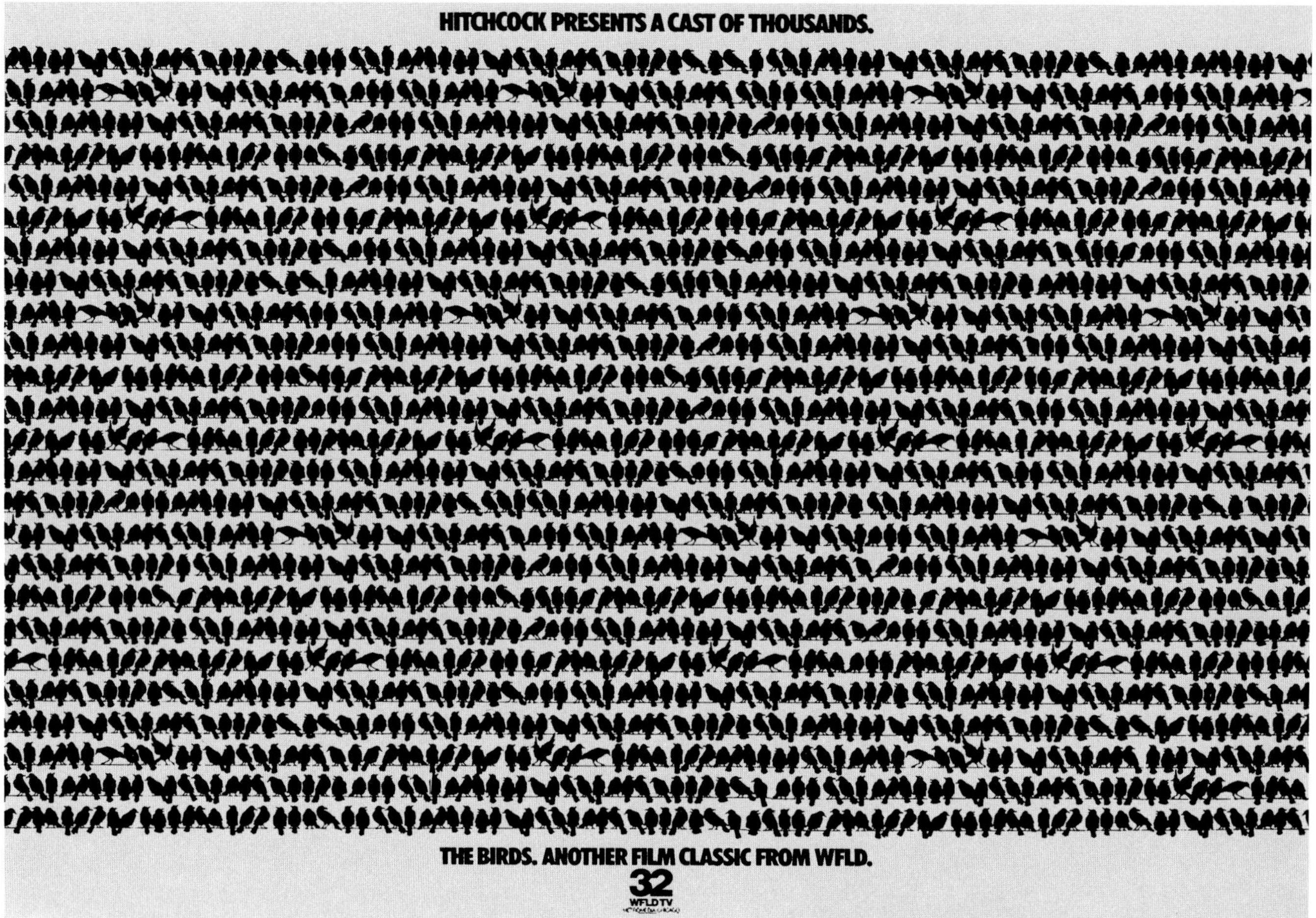

49

50

Nihon Buyo
UCLA
Asian Performing Arts
Institute 1981
Los Angeles
Washington, D.C.
New York

51

Tradition et Nouvelles Techniques
12 Graphistes Japonais
22 Octobre–15 Novembre '84
Les Ateliers

52

53

54

55

Nikon
SAVING THE WORLD'S BIRDS
Saving the World's Birds
Salvando los pájaros del mundo
Voor de vogels van onze aarde
Pour les oiseaux du monde
Für den weltweiten Schutz der Vögel
INTERNATIONAL COUNCIL FOR BIRD PRESERVATION

56

57

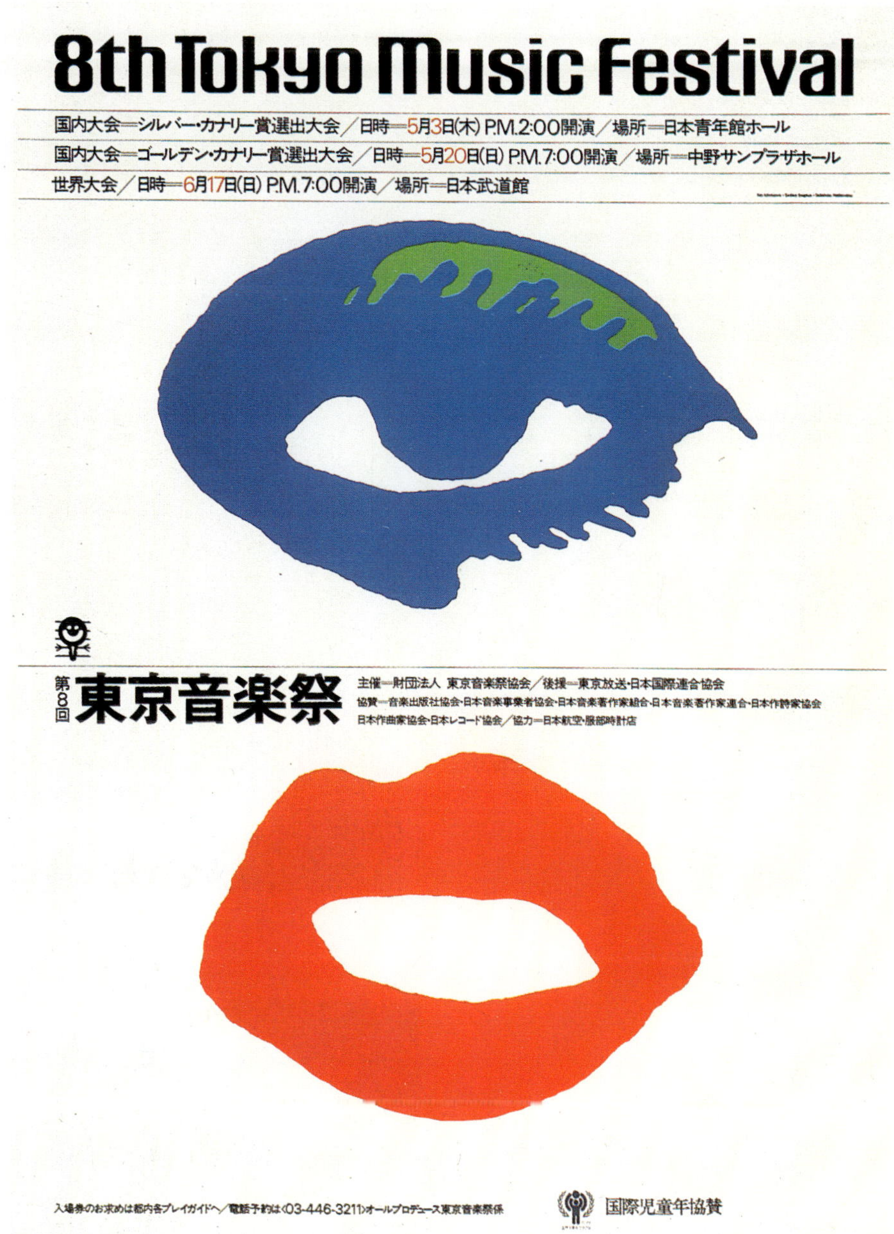

58

Otl Aicher D 54, 55
Ryohei Kojima D 56
Per Arnoldi D 57
Sadao Sugaya D 58

These pictures again document the superiority of painting and drawing techniques for the best representation of certain statements — whether it be a series of exhibition panels about medieval life or the illustration of details of bird species. The uniformity of photographic images must lead to a "poverty of sameness" ("Elend der Einheit") as a leading scientist predicts. With an increasing overload of information, there is a danger of losing creativity. We need a greater variability of pictorial signs.

Auch diese Bilder dokumentieren die Überlegenheit von Maltechnik und Zeichnung, um bestimmte Aussagen zu optimieren, ob es um den dramaturgischen Aufbau von Ausstellungstafeln über mittelalterliches Leben geht oder um die Vermittlung von Objektdetails bestimmter Vogelarten. Die Gleichförmigkeit fotografischer Bildgestaltung muss in den nächsten Jahren zu einem «Elend der Einheit» führen, wie ein bekannter Wissenschaftler voraussagt. Bei einer zunehmenden Informationsüberlastung ist ein Mangel an Kreativität gefährlich. Wir brauchen eine grössere Variabilität bildlicher Zeichen.

Qu'il s'agisse de la construction dramaturgique de panneaux d'exposition sur la vie au Moyen Age, ou de la transmission de détails précis concernant certaines espèces d'oiseaux, ces images permettent de constater, une fois de plus, la supériorité de la technique picturale et du dessin. Selon un éminent scientifique, l'uniformité de l'architecture de l'image photographique conduira rapidement à la «misère de l'unité». Un manque de créativité peut s'avérer dangereux en temps de surinformation croissante. Un pluralisme accru des signes figuratifs s'impose.

The following advertisements and posters clearly show that photography can also be used creatively. Here, too, it is a question of an incompleteness in pictorial signs. Their communicative performance is particularly high because they catch the eye and are very well remembered. The series for Jourdan shoes is based on this principle: namely, the lack of a person or object, which must have been present from the pictorial association.

Die nachfolgenden Anzeigen und Plakate belegen deutlich, dass Fotografie auch kreativ eingesetzt werden kann.
Auch hier geht es um eine Unvollständigkeit bildlicher Zeichen. Ihre kommunikative Leistung ist besonders hoch, weil sie den Blick fesseln und sehr gut erinnert werden. Die Serie für Jourdan-Schuhe ist auf diesem Prinzip aufgebaut: nämlich dem Fehlen einer Person oder eines Gegenstandes, der aus dem bildlichen Zusammenhang heraus eigentlich vorhanden sein müsste.

Les affiches et annonces suivantes prouvent que la photographie peut également être utilisée de manière créative.
L'on retrouve ici l'état incomplet des signes figuratifs. Leur pouvoir de communication est particulièrement élevé, car ils retiennent l'attention et s'inscrivent dans la mémoire. La série des chaussures Jourdan se fonde sur ce principe: il manque une personne ou un objet qui, d'après le contexte, devrait figurer sur l'image.

59

60

61

62

Tsuyoshi Fukuda D 59, 60
Katsumi Asaba D 61
Peter Hendrie Ph 62

This form of incompleteness also shows the syntactical possibilities of modern picture design.

Auch diese Form der Unvollständigkeit belegt die syntaktischen Möglichkeiten moderner Bildgestaltung.

Cette forme d'état incomplet prouve également les possibilités syntactiques du design actuel.

63

Wilson McLean D 63
Mathias Bapst AD 64
Jürgen Tapprich Ph
Lester Feldman AD 65
Bruno Ph
Shigeru Shikooma AD 66
Seiji Yamada Ph

The full use of syntactical rules can also be demonstrated here, where the Qualisigns, which denote a lake or a continent, are replaced by another object. From this connection of two signs for the same object there ensues an especially effective centering of publicity on the object-statement in view.

Die Ausschöpfung syntaktischer Regeln kann auch hier demonstriert werden. Dabei werden die Quali-Zeichen, die einen See oder einen Kontinent bezeichnen, durch ein anderes Objekt ersetzt. Aus dieser Verknüpfung zweier Zeichen für das gleiche Objekt ergibt sich eine besonders werbewirksame Zentrierung auf die beabsichtigte Objektaussage.

L'utilisation de toutes les règles syntactiques est également démontrée ici. L'on remplace les qualisignes qui désignent un lac ou un continent par un autre objet. Cette combinaison de deux signes pour le même objet permet un centrage d'une grande efficacité publicitaire sur l'énoncé de l'objet recherché.

Johnnie Walker. The Nr. 1 Scotch Whisky.
Das beste Glas Whisky, das je umgestossen wurde.

64

CHIVAS REGAL
BLENDED SCOTCH
WHISKY
Not all men dream of castles.

65

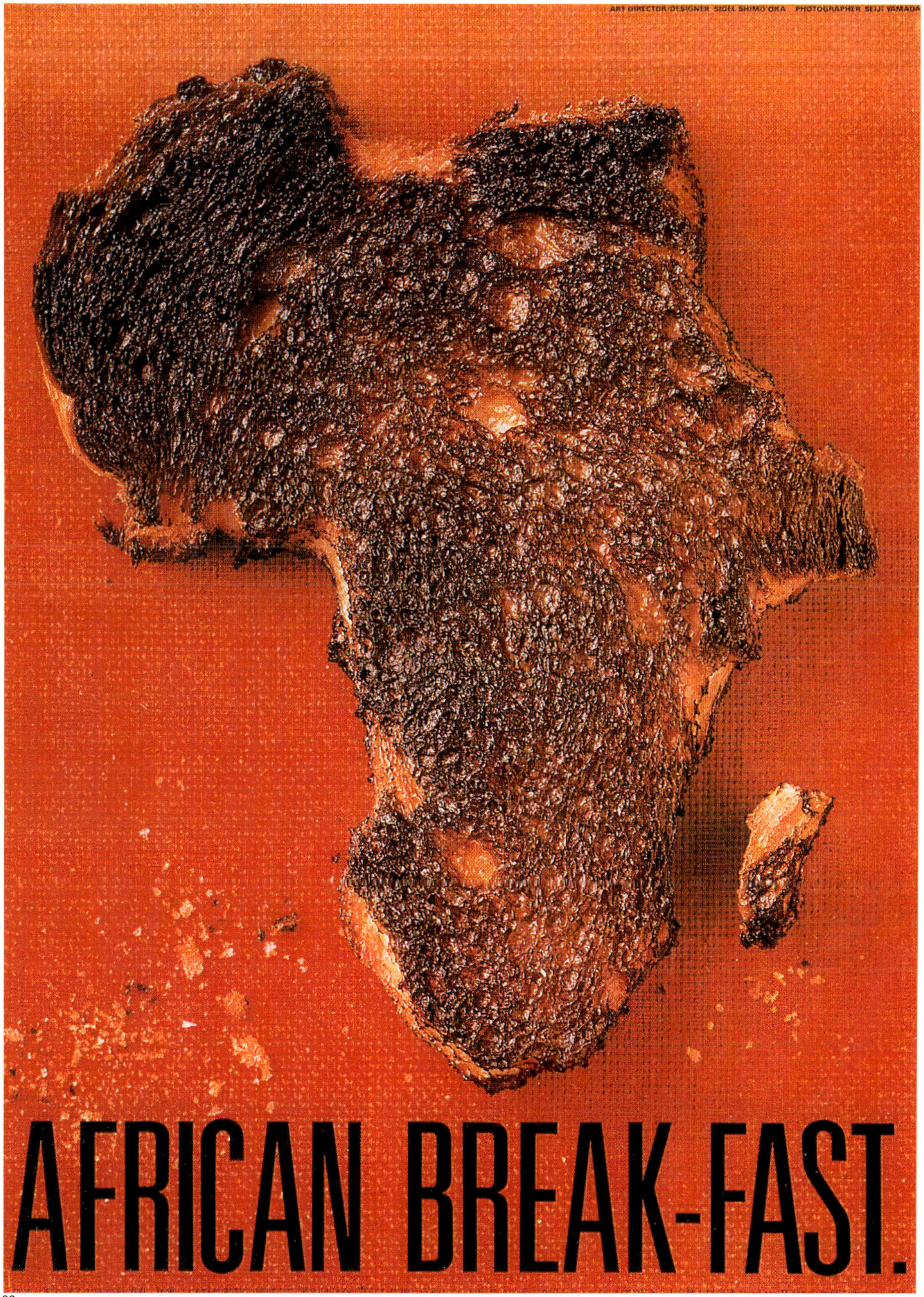
ART DIRECTOR/DESIGNER SIGEL SHIMO'OKA PHOTOGRAPHER SEIJI YAMADA
AFRICAN BREAK-FAST.

66

Vance Jonson D 67
Koji Fujimori D 68
Rob Boezewinkel AD 69

These pictorial statements can also be said to involve the creative use of signs. New analyses of effect show that the use of signs is regular to a percentage of more than 90. Theoretical considerations, however, indicate a greater communicative performance ability in syntactically irregular use of signs. Such advertising statements at first represent a certain obstacle to perception, but if such a picture comes once into view it is fixed for a particularly long time and leads to considerable values with regard to information processing.

Auch bei diesen bildlichen Aussagen kann man von kreativer Zeichenverwendung sprechen. So belegen neue Wirkungsanalysen, dass die Zeichenverwendung zu über 90 Prozent regulär ist. Theoretische Überlegungen deuten aber auf eine grössere kommunikative Leistungsfähigkeit syntaktisch irregulärer Zeichenverwendung hin. Solche Werbeaussagen stellen zunächst ein gewisses Wahrnehmungshindernis dar, kommt ein solches Bild aber erst einmal in den Blick, so wird es besonders lange fixiert und führt zu beachtlichen Werten bezüglich der Informationsverarbeitung.

Ces énoncés figuratifs témoignent aussi d'une utilisation créative du signe. Des analyses d'efficacité récentes prouvent que l'utilisation des signes est régulière dans plus de 90% des cas. Toutefois, des considérations théoriques indiquent que l'utilisation syntactique irrégulière des signes est plus efficace pour la communication. S'il est difficile de percevoir ce type d'énoncé publicitaire au premier abord, une fois l'image enregistrée, elle se fixe durablement et produit des valeurs d'assimilation de l'information excellentes.

67

TAIWA

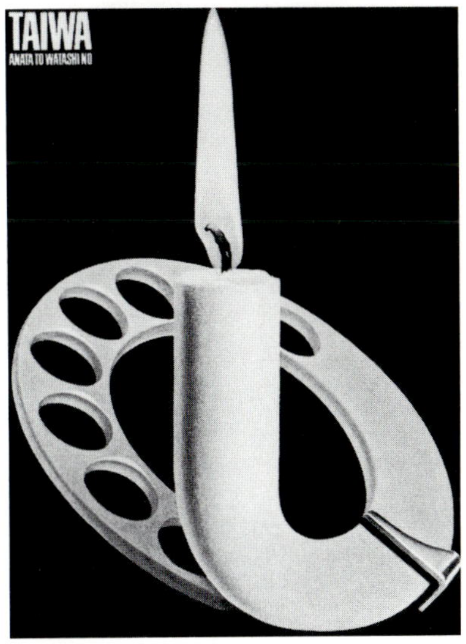
TAIWA
ANATA TO WATASHI NO

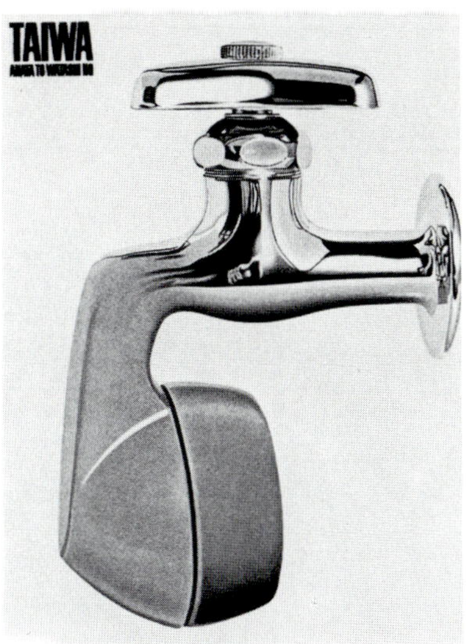
TAIWA

68

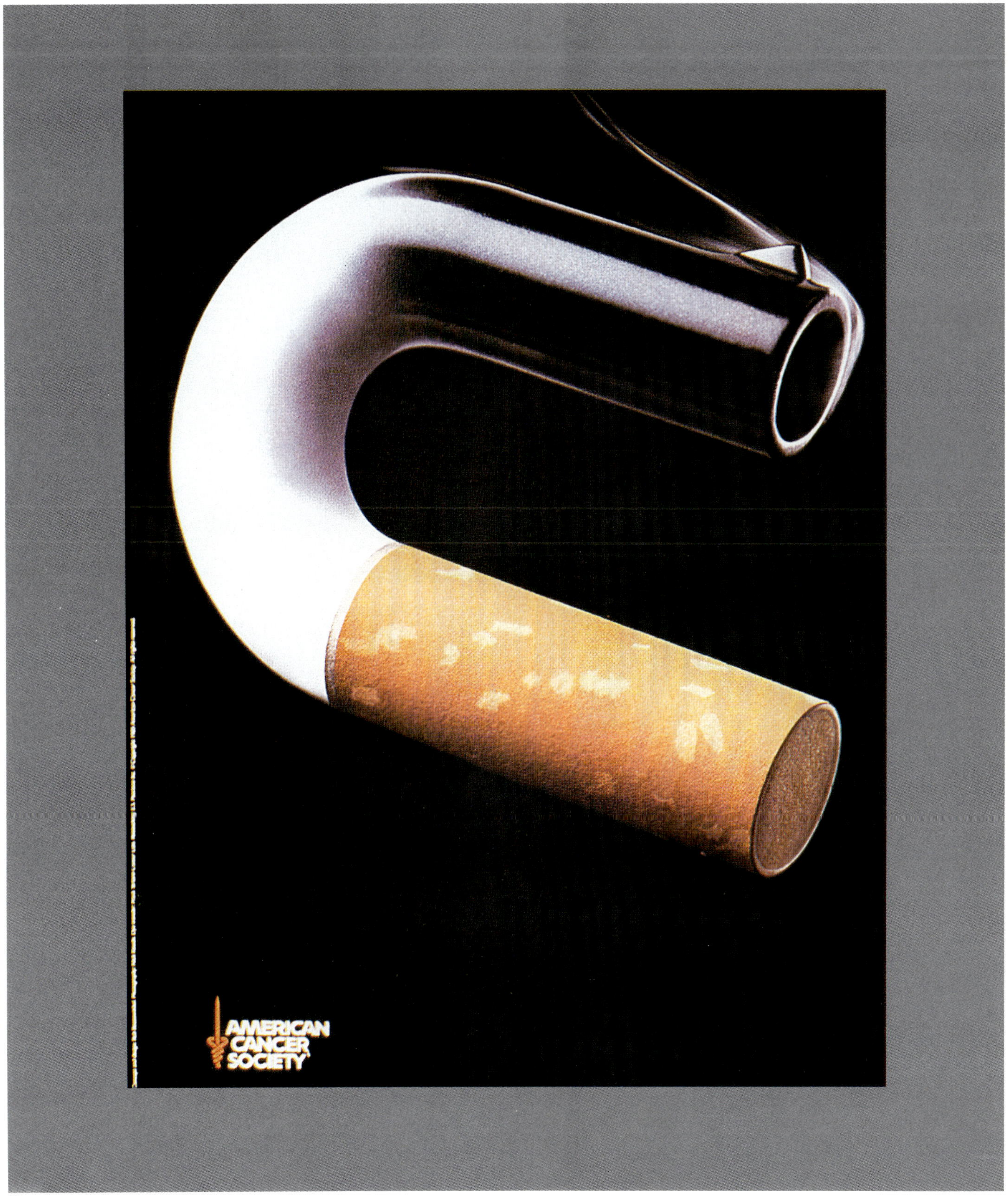
AMERICAN
CANCER
SOCIETY

69

Phil Weiner / Bruce Arendash	D	70, 71
Hiro	Ph	
Ian Potter	AD	72
FCO	A	
Manfred Rieker	Ph	73
TEAM/BBDO	A	
George Simmons	D	74, 75
Clint Clemens	Ph	

The overloading of information has taken on considerable proportions. Pictures conceived in a novel way greatly improve advertising effectiveness. This principle also applies to outdoor advertising. Thus these examples can be called semiotic paradoxes. Normally the poster site is the material sign-carrier and the printed paper has the function of illustration. Here, on the other hand, the site itself becomes the sign for the holding power of an adhesive or serves for the attachment of a real piece of coachwork.

Die Informationsüberlastung hat beträchtliche Ausmasse angenommen. Neuartig konzipierte Bilder verbessern die Werbewirksamkeit erheblich. Dies gilt auch für die Aussenwerbung. So kann man diese Beispiele als semiotische Paradoxie bezeichnen. Normalerweise ist die Plakatwand der materielle Zeichenträger, das bedruckte Papier hat eine Abbildungsfunktion. Hier hingegen wird die Plakatwand zum Zeichen für die Haftkraft eines Klebstoffes oder dient zur Aufhängung einer realen Karosserie.

L'excès d'information a pris des proportions considérables. Les images de conception novatrice améliorent sensiblement l'efficacité de la publicité. Il en va de même pour la publicité extérieure. L'on peut dire de ces exemples qu'ils constituent des paradoxes sémiotiques. Normalement, le mur d'affichage est le support de signes matériel et le papier imprimé a une fonction d'illustration. Ici, en revanche, le mur d'affichage est utilisé comme signe du pouvoir adhésif d'une colle ou sert à accrocher une véritable carrosserie.

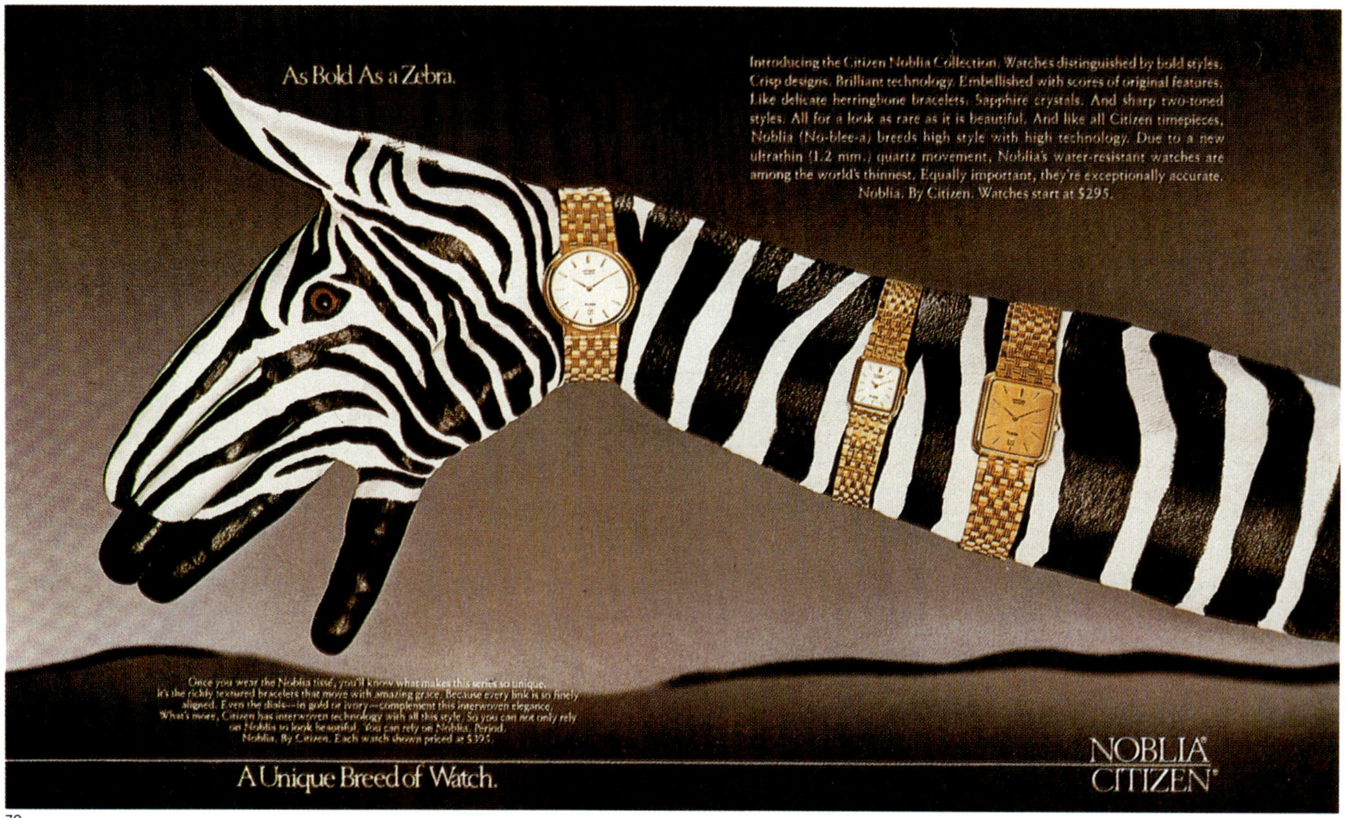

70

71

72

73

74

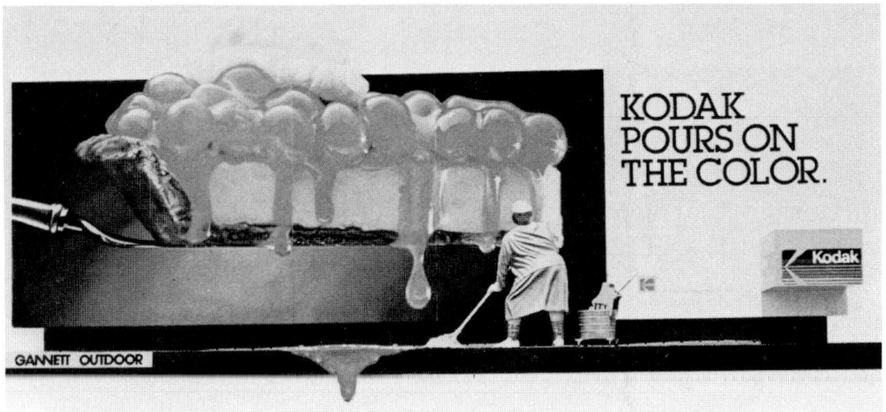

75

Poul Henningsen	D	76
Kit Hinrichs / Lenore Bartz	D	77
Laurie Rubins	D	78, 80
James Sebastian / Pen-Ek Ratanaruang	D	79
Bruce Wolf	Ph	

The following brochures and folders clearly show the underlying pictorial grammar. The opposition of two kinds of signs (the photo of a lamp and the technical drawing of light flow) is presented. The works photo and the strong graphics of a detail, below, also reflect this principle. Research has shown that the credibility of advertising statements can thereby be increased. Finally, the fusion of two sign relations in a single subject is documented, as in the painted background to photographed ceramic ware or its transfer to a textile manufacturer's brochure (Martex) (next page).

Die nachfolgenden Broschüren und Prospekte belegen deutlich die hier zugrunde gelegte bildliche Grammatik. Die Gegenüberstellung zweier Zeichenarten (das Foto einer Lampe und die technische Zeichnung des Lichtverlaufs). Auch das darunter stehende Werksfoto und die strenge Grafik eines Details reflektieren dieses Prinzip. Dadurch kann die Glaubwürdigkeit von Werbeaussagen erhöht werden, wie aus Untersuchungen hervorgeht.
Zum Schluss wird die Verschmelzung zweier Zeichenbezüge in einem einzigen Sujet dokumentiert, so ist es der gemalte Hintergrund zur fotografierten Keramikware oder deren Wechsel auf der Broschüre eines Textilherstellers (Martex) (nächste Seite).

Les brochures et les prospectus suivants illustrent clairement la grammaire figurative présentée ici. L'opposition de deux types de signe (la photo d'une lampe et le dessin technique du parcours de la lumière).
La photo suivante et la graphique rigoureuse d'un détail reflètent ce principe. On peut ainsi accroître la crédibilité d'énoncés publicitaires, comme le montrent certaines études.
Le dernier exemple illustre la fusion de deux références de signe dans un seul sujet, ainsi l'arrière plan peint de la céramique photographiée ou ce qui la remplace dans la brochure d'un producteur de textiles (Martex) (page suivante).

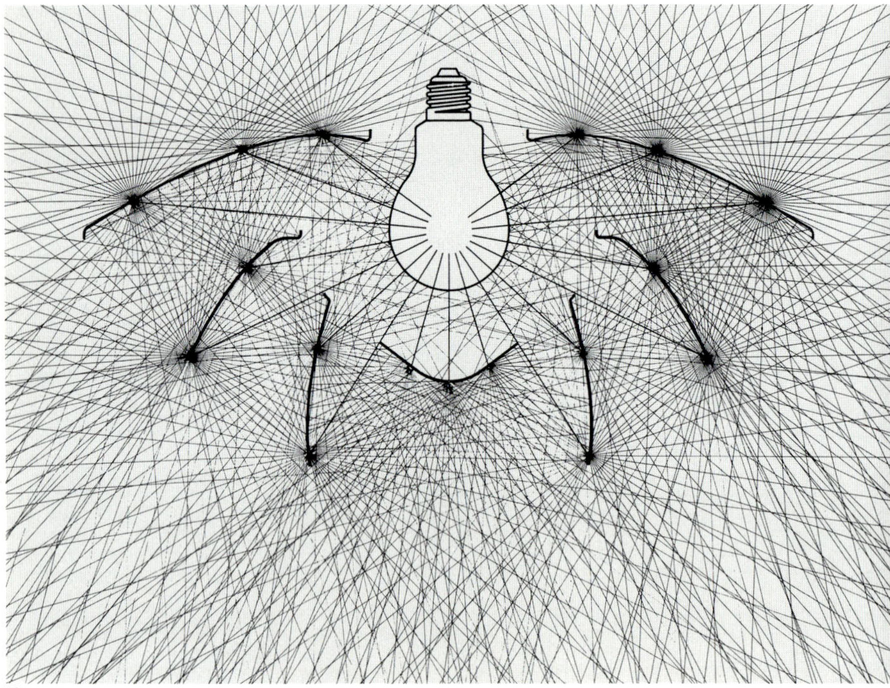

76

THEMES
< Existing fine art should not be precluded from annual reports. In a position essay on future changes in its industry, Crocker Bank used this work, which was part of a series created for New York's Museum of Modern Art.
> Stepping away from the expected renews excitement. Highland Energy depicted its heavy drilling rigs in pastel shades and bold geometric shapes.

77

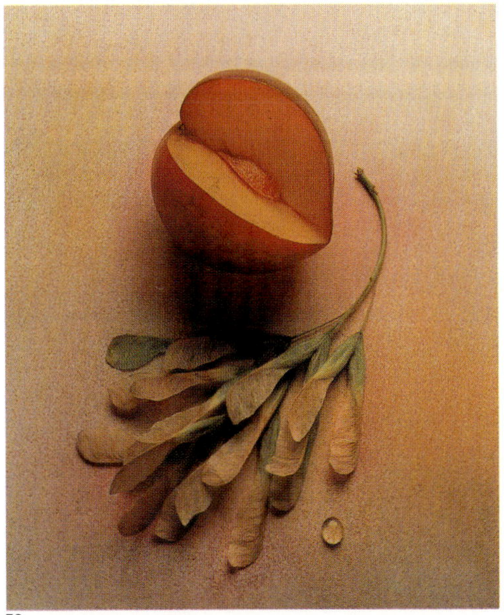

78

79

80

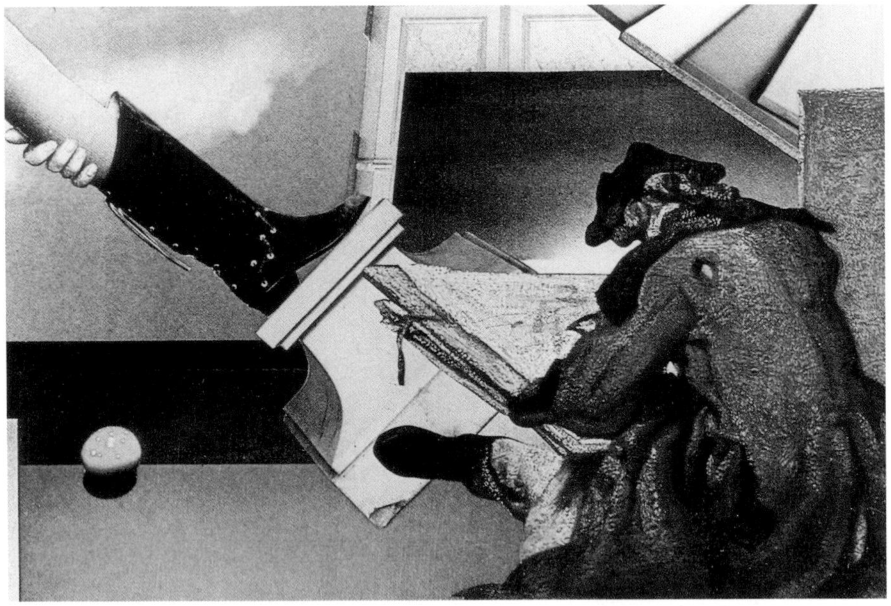

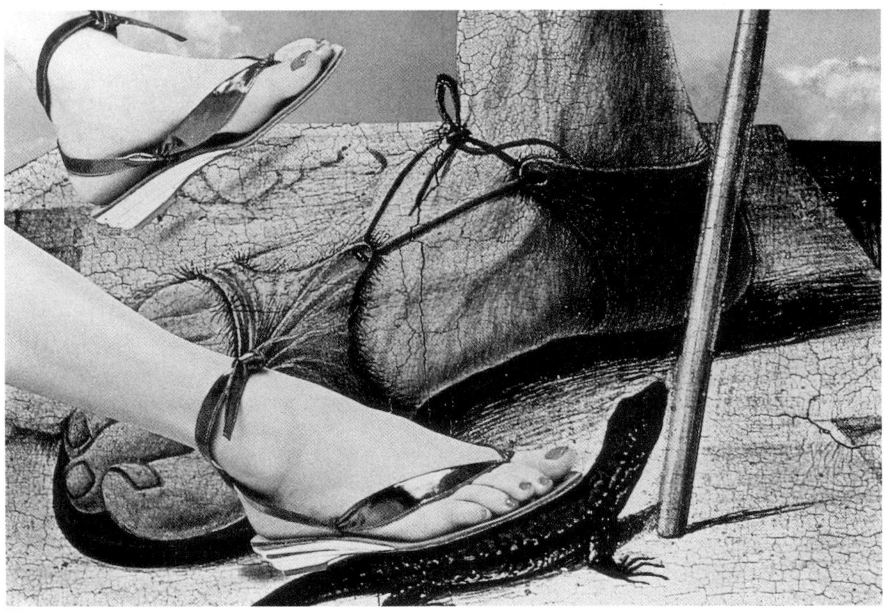

81

Roman Cieslewicz D 81
René Magritte 82
Henry Wolf Ph 83

Today we have reached a turning-point in advertising, where this question becomes ever more important: How can advertising effectiveness be raised still further through unusual picture composition?
The irregular linking of classical picture elements with topical photo cuts for Jourdan shoes combines to make a novel but thoroughly realistic complete picture.

Wir sind heute an einem Wendepunkt der Werbung angelangt, wo die Frage immer wichtiger wird: Wie kann man durch ungewöhnliche Bildkompositionen die Werbewirkung steigern?
Die irregulären Verknüpfungen klassischer Bildelemente mit aktuellen Fotoausschnitten für Jourdan-Schuhe fügen sich zu einem neuartigen, aber durchaus noch realistischen Gesamtbild zusammen.

Nous sommes arrivés aujourd'hui à un tournant de la publicité, où la question suivante prend une importance croissante: comment accroître l'efficacité publicitaire par l'utilisation de compositions graphiques inhabituelles?
Les liaisons irrégulières d'éléments d'image classiques avec des fragments de photo actuels pour les chaussures Jourdan composent une image d'ensemble novatrice mais qui reste tout à fait réaliste.

82

These advertisements give evidence of a direct relationship with art, whether we see parallels with the work of René Magritte or Max Ernst. Surrealism uses similar principles.

Wer diese Anzeigen betrachtet, wird eine direkte Beziehung zur Kunst feststellen, ob es sich nun um Parallelen im Werk von René Magritte oder Max Ernst handelt. Der Surrealismus arbeitete mit ähnlichen Prinzipien.

En observant cette annonce, l'on remarque immédiatement un lien avec l'art, qu'il s'agisse de parallèles avec l'œuvre de René Magritte ou de Max Ernst. Le surréalisme a travaillé avec des principes similaires.

83

Takushi Mizuno AD 84
Bishin Jyumonji Ph
Ishii Tsukasa AD 85
Koguro Toru Ph
Masaaki Izumiya AD 86, 87

If the desired effect is to proceed from advertising which is perceived for only a few seconds, the designer must understand the rules of human perception and also the breaking of those rules. The following pages show some tricks with our world of perception.

Wenn nur wenige Sekunden lang wahrgenommene Werbung die angestrebte Wirkung entfalten soll, dann muss der Gestalter die Gesetze menschlicher Wahrnehmung, aber auch das Durchbrechen ihrer Regeln kennen. Die nächsten Seiten belegen einige Tücken unserer Wahrnehmungswelt.

Pour qu'une publicité aperçue seulement quelques secondes puisse exercer l'effet recherché, le designer doit connaître les lois de la perception humaine, mais il doit aussi savoir comment les transgresser. Les pages suivantes illustrent quelques pièges de la perception.

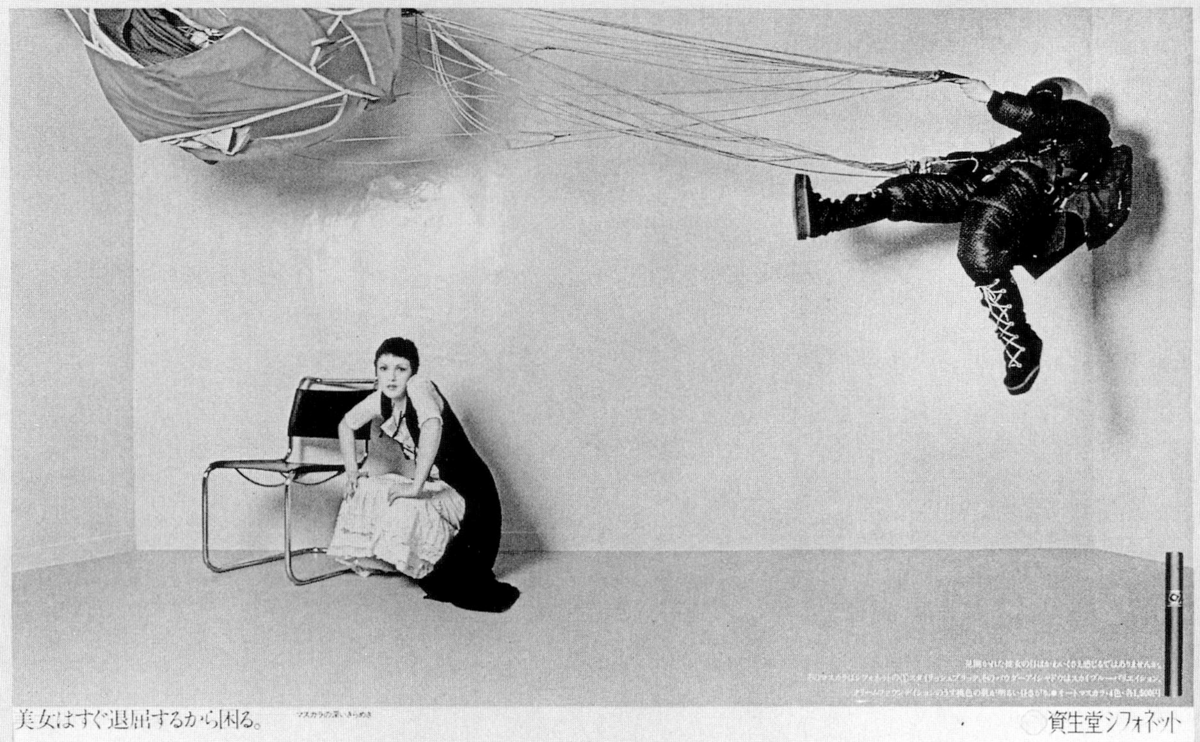

84/85

The creation of an independent, emotionally anchored market position will become ever more important in the future. This is possible with more than simply verbal information. The establishment of inner images of brands is primarily a question of pictures.
The degree of complexity of such pictures should not, however, be too great, since the recipient in search of novelty begins to break away at the point where he suspects that he has found the key answer.

Der Aufbau einer eigenständigen emotionalverankerten Marktposition wird in Zukunft immer wichtiger. Dies ist aber nicht nur mit verbalen Informationen möglich. Die Verankerung innerer Markenbilder ist in erster Linie auf Bilder angewiesen.
Der Komplexitätsgrad solcher Bilder darf aber nicht zu hoch sein, da der Rezipient auf der Suche nach Neuigkeiten bereits dort abzubrechen beginnt, wo er vermutet, die schlüssige Antwort gefunden zu haben.

Le développement d'une position de marché indépendante et présentant une charge affective va prendre à l'avenir une importance croissante. Toutefois, les informations verbales n'y suffisent pas. La fixation d'images de marque internes dépend avant tout des images.
Le degré de complexité de ces images ne doit pas être trop élevé, car le récepteur avide de nouveauté commence déjà à abandonner quand il pense avoir trouvé la réponse appropriée.

86/87

another" and "irregular connection of partial signs". In a figurative or pictorial representation, Qualisigns may be reduced but not eliminated. Their reduction leads to forms of abstraction but without loss of the completeness and regularity of the representation. On the other hand, a lack of Sinsigns makes it impossible to identify concrete objects. Incomplete statements of this kind are made, for example, by abstract painting. A special kind of incompleteness is shown by motifs where an object can be clearly identified from the pictorial context even though both Qualisign and Sinsign for it are lacking. A statement is also incomplete if it lacks a Legisign, such as perspective or other form of arrangement of the pictorial elements.

A replacement is made when a sign which would be expected in the given context is replaced by another. In most cases these exchanged signs are Qualisigns, such as textures and patterns, but Sinsigns can also be replaced.

The commonest form of deviation from the syntactical rules of pictorial communication is irregular connection. This occurs, for example, when various Sinsigns are connected together in order to represent an object.

The irregular connection of various partial signs makes clear the unity of the object meant by the total sign. The association of two perspectives makes the identification of a real form impossible. This principle can quite often be observed in cubist and surrealist pictures, which sometimes unite a whole series of perspectives into one system.

Deviations from the rule that a Sinsign can only ever signify one object are found in the well-known optical illusions from the field of traditional

«Ersetzung eines gegebenen Zeichens durch ein anderes» sowie «irreguläre Verknüpfung von Teilzeichen». Qualizeichen sind in einer bildlichen Darstellung nur reduzierbar, nicht aber eliminierbar. Ihre Reduktion führt zu Abstraktionsformen, bei denen jedoch die Vollständigkeit und Regularität der Abbildung nicht verlorengeht. Dagegen macht das Fehlen von Sinzeichen die Identifizierung konkreter Objekte unmöglich. Unvollständige Aussagen dieser Art liefert beispielsweise die abstrakte Malerei. Eine besondere Art der Unvollständigkeit zeigen Motive, wo sowohl Quali- als auch Sinzeichen für einen Gegenstand fehlen, der aus dem bildlichen Kontext heraus eindeutig zu identifizieren ist. Unvollständig ist eine Aussage auch beim Fehlen eines Legizeichens, wie der Perspektive oder einer anderen Form der Zuordnung der Abbildungselemente.

Ersetzungen bestehen darin, dass ein aufgrund des gegebenen Kontextes zu erwartendes Zeichen durch ein anderes ersetzt wird. Meist handelt es sich bei den ausgetauschten Zeichen um Qualizeichen, also Texturen oder Muster, aber auch Sinzeichen können ersetzt werden.

Die häufigste Form der Abweichung von den syntaktischen Regeln der bildlichen Kommunikation ist die irreguläre Verknüpfung. Sie liegt beispielsweise dann vor, wenn verschiedene Sinzeichen zur Darstellung eines Objekts verknüpft werden.

Die irreguläre Verknüpfung verschiedener Teilzeichen verdeutlicht die Einheit des vom Gesamtzeichen gemeinten Gegenstandes. Die Verknüpfung zweier Perspektiven macht die Identifizierung einer realen Form unmöglich. Dieses Prinzip kann man relativ oft bei Bildern des Kubismus und des Surrealismus beobachten, die manchmal eine ganze Reihe von Perspektiven in einem System vereinen.

Abweichungen von der Regel, dass ein Sinzeichen immer nur ein Objekt bezeichnen könne, bilden die aus der traditionellen Wahrnehmungspsychologie wohlbekannten Kippfiguren.

plète», «remplacement d'un signe attendu par un autre», et «jonction irrégulière de signes partiels». Il est possible de réduire le nombre de qualisignes dans une représentation figurative, mais non de les éliminer. Cette réduction conduit à des formes d'abstraction dans lesquelles l'intégralité et la régularité de la reproduction ne sont pas perdues. En revanche, l'absence de sinsignes rend impossible l'identification d'objets concrets. La «peinture abstraite», par exemple, présente des énoncés incomplets de ce type. Un type particulier de non-intégralité est illustré par des motifs dans lesquels manquent des qualisignes et des sinsignes d'un objet qui peut être identifié sans équivoque à partir du contexte. Un énoncé est également incomplet s'il manque un légisigne, comme la perspective ou une autre forme d'organisation des éléments de reproduction.

Il y a remplacement quand un signe auquel on s'attend en raison du contexte est remplacé par un autre. Les signes remplacés sont le plus souvent des qualisignes, donc des textures ou des motifs; toutefois, les sinsignes peuvent aussi être remplacés.

La forme la plus courante de dérogation aux règles syntactiques de la communication figurative est la jonction irrégulière. Elle apparaît, par exemple, quand différents sinsignes sont liés à la reproduction d'un objet.

La jonction irrégulière des signes différents partiels illustre l'unité de l'objet signifié par le signe complet. La jonction de deux perspectives rend impossible l'identification d'une forme réelle. On observe assez souvent ce principe dans des toiles cubistes et surréalistes qui réunissent parfois toute une série de perspectives dans un seul système.

Les figures réversibles, bien connues dans la psychologie de la perception traditionnelle, constituent des dérogations à la règle qui veut qu'un sinsigne

88

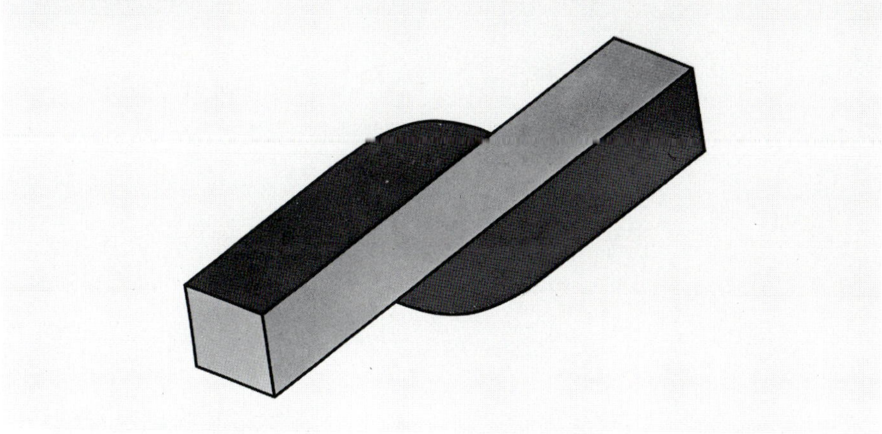

89

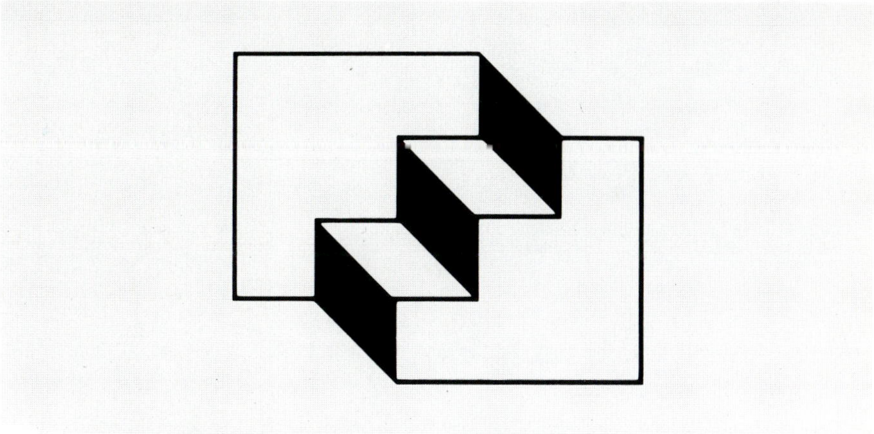

90

Dennis Merritt	D	88
Dan Vermillion	Ph	
Tetsuhiro Seki	D	89
Felipe Taborda	D	90
Richard (Dick) Hess	D	91
Jurriaan Schrofer	D	92
Shigeo Fukuda	D	93, 94

The section concerning the irregular use of signs closes with the above advertisement, which visualizes a company's change of premises. What is irregular in this theme is the linking of two Legisigns (perspectives), together with the linking of two Sinsigns (forms) below. It can be seen that an outline can never represent two objects at the same time. This explains the phenomenon of optical illusions.

Mit obenstehender Anzeige, die den Umzug einer Firma visualisiert, soll der Teil irregulärer Zeichenverwendung abschliessen. Irregulär an diesem Motiv ist die Verknüpfung von zwei Legizeichen (Perspektiven). Irregulär ist aber auch die darunter stehende Verknüpfung zweier Sinzeichen (Formen). Nachfolgend ersieht man, dass eine Umrisslinie niemals zwei Objekte gleichzeitig kennzeichnen kann, das erklärt das Phänomen der Kippfiguren.

L'annonce ci-dessus, qui illustre le déménagement d'une entreprise, achève la partie consacrée à l'utilisation irrégulière du signe. Dans ce motif, la liaison de deux légisignes (perspectives) est irrégulière. Une irrégularité se trouve également au-dessous dans la jonction de deux sinsignes (formes). Ensuite, l'on voit qu'une ligne de contour ne peut jamais indiquer simultanément deux objets, ce qui explique le phénomène des figures réversibles.

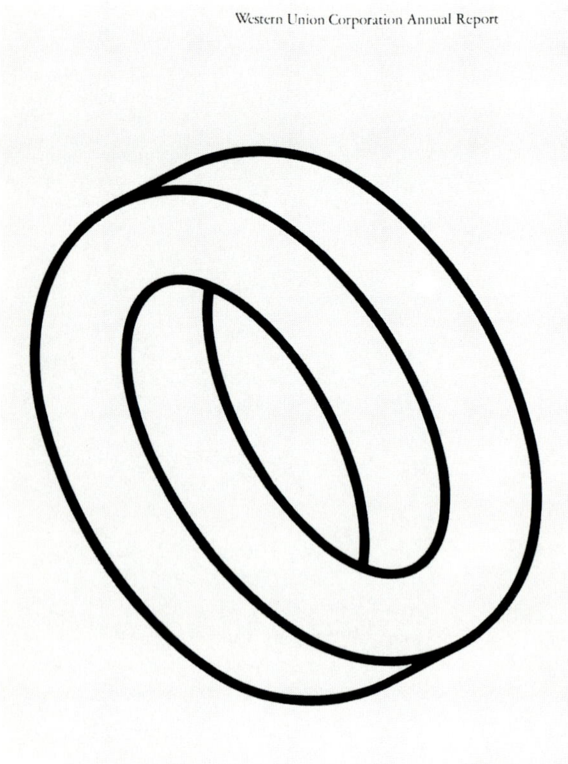

91

92

93

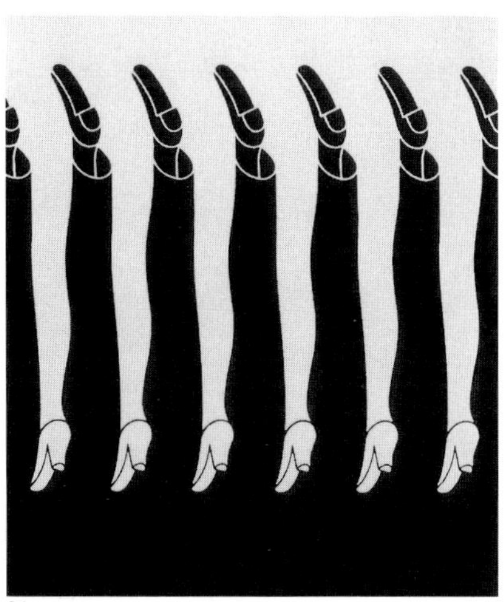

94

perception psychology. In visual apprehension, the human eye can easily identify both the objects of such a sign but can never see them both at once.

The rules and deviations shown here are, as mentioned, all at the level of statements. Both the signs and the rules at other levels certainly rest on the same principles, but they have a different form. In the following section, at least the basic structure of the levels of analysis for visual communication is described.

3.1.3. The levels of description

The first, that is the lowest, level of description is formed by the fundamental elements of perception. These elements are textures and patterns which allow the nature of objects to be recognized. The verbal equivalents of these signs are mostly adjectives, e.g. stony, earthy, rough, smooth, etc. At the level of statement such signs could only be Qualisigns but here they have the character of Sinsigns because they supply different characteristics and separate different conditions. In fact, this first level of description cannot offer anything more, because here only textures *per se* can be comprehended.

At the second level, structures can be recognized from variations in the gradient of textures. These can be traced back to a relatively narrow repertoire. The texture gradient consists of the increasing density and decreasing size of the individual texture elements. The nature of this change characterizes the various possibilities of formation of structure. Thus the rate of the gradient expresses the angle of slope of surfaces. If this rate is constant, the surface is straight, but if the rate is changing, we obtain a curvature. Curvature presupposes a constant rate of

In der visuellen Auffassung ist der Mensch sehr wohl in der Lage, beide Objekte eines solchen Zeichens zu identifizieren, er kann sie jedoch niemals gleichzeitig sehen.

Die hier gezeigten Regeln und Abweichungen liegen, wie gesagt, alle auf der Ebene der Aussagen. Zwar beruhen sowohl die Zeichen als auch die Regeln anderer Ebenen auf den gleichen Prinzipien, doch sie haben eine andere Form. Im folgenden soll wenigstens der Grundaufbau der Analyseebenen für die visuelle Kommunikation beschrieben werden.

3.1.3. Die Ebenen der Beschreibung

Die erste, also unterste Ebene der Beschreibung wird durch die grundlegenden Elemente der Wahrnehmung gebildet. Diese grundlegenden Elemente sind die Texturen, Muster, die die Beschaffenheit von Gegenständen erkennen lassen. Die sprachliche Entsprechung dieser Zeichen sind am ehesten Adjektive, beispielsweise das Steinige, das Erdige, das Rauhe, das Glatte usw. Auf der Aussagenebene könnten solche Zeichen nur Qualizeichen sein, hier jedoch haben sie Sinzeichencharakter, weil sie unterscheidende Merkmale liefern, unterschiedliche Zustände trennen. Mehr kann diese Ebene auch nicht leisten, da auf ihr nur Texturen an sich erfasst werden können.

Auf der zweiten Ebene lassen sich aufgrund von Variationen des Texturgradienten Strukturen erkennen, die sich auf ein relativ eng begrenztes Repertoire zurückführen lassen. Der Texturgradient besteht in der Zunahme der Dichte und einer Abnahme der Grösse der einzelnen Texturelemente. Die Art dieser Änderung kennzeichnet die verschiedenen Möglichkeiten der Strukturbildung. So bringt die Geschwindigkeit des Gradientenverlaufs die Neigung von Oberflächen zum Ausdruck. Ist diese Geschwindigkeit konstant, so erscheint die Oberfläche plan; verändert sich jedoch die Geschwindigkeit, so erkennen wir eine Wölbung. Die Wölbung setzt eine kontinuierliche

ne puisse jamais désigner qu'un seul objet. Visuellement, l'homme est tout à fait capable d'identifier les deux objets de ce type de dessin, mais il ne peut jamais les voir simultanément.

Toutes les règles et leurs dérogations présentées ici se trouvent, répétons-le, au niveau des énoncés. Si les signes et les règles à d'autres niveaux reposent sur les mêmes principes, elles ont toutefois une autre forme. Nous allons décrire ci-après la structure de base des niveaux d'analyse pour la communication visuelle.

3.1.3. Les niveaux de description

Le premier niveau de description, c'est-à-dire le plus bas, est constitué par les éléments fondamentaux de la perception. Ces éléments sont les textures, les motifs qui permettent de reconnaître la nature des objets. Les équivalents linguistiques les plus proches de ces signes sont des adjectifs, comme par exemple pierreux, terreux, rugueux, lisse, etc. Au niveau de l'énoncé, ces signes ne peuvent être que des qualisignes; ici, toutefois, ils ont le caractère de sinsignes, car ils fournissent des traits distinctifs, ils séparent des états différents. Ce niveau ne peut apporter davantage, car seules les textures en tant que telles peuvent y être enregistrées.

Au deuxième niveau, en raison de variations du gradient de texture, l'on reconnaît des structures qui peuvent être ramenées à un répertoire assez limité. Le gradient de texture est constitué par une augmentation de la densité et une diminution de la taille des éléments de texture. Le type de cette modification caractérise les différentes possibilités de la formation de structure. Ainsi, la vitesse de déroulement du gradient exprime l'inclinaison de la surface. Si cette vitesse est constante, la surface paraît plane; si elle varie, nous observons une courbure. La courbure suppose une variation continue de la vitesse; une

John Snyder Ph 95
Ingo Heintzen AD 96, 97
SMS A
Hans Hansen Ph

These examples are given to show the hierarchical nature of picture formation. At the lowest level Quali-signs are formed. On this basis, there is the representation of qualities, the mediation of the material or substance of which an object consists. In these advertisements, various qualities of bakery products are conveyed in the best way.

Mit diesen Beispielen soll der hierarchische Aufbau der Bilder dokumentiert werden. Auf der niedrigsten Ebene bilden sich Quali-Zeichen. Auf ihnen beruht die Darstellung von Beschaffenheiten, die Vermittlung des Materials oder der Substanz, aus der ein Gegenstand besteht. Bei unseren Anzeigen werden verschiedene Qualitäten von Backwaren optimal vermittelt.

Ces exemples illustrent la structure hiérarchique des images. Au niveau le plus bas se forment des qualisignes. C'est sur eux que se fonde la représentation de caractéristiques, l'information sur le matériau ou la substance dont est fait un objet. Nos annonces renseignent de manière optimale sur les différentes qualités de pain et pâtisserie.

95

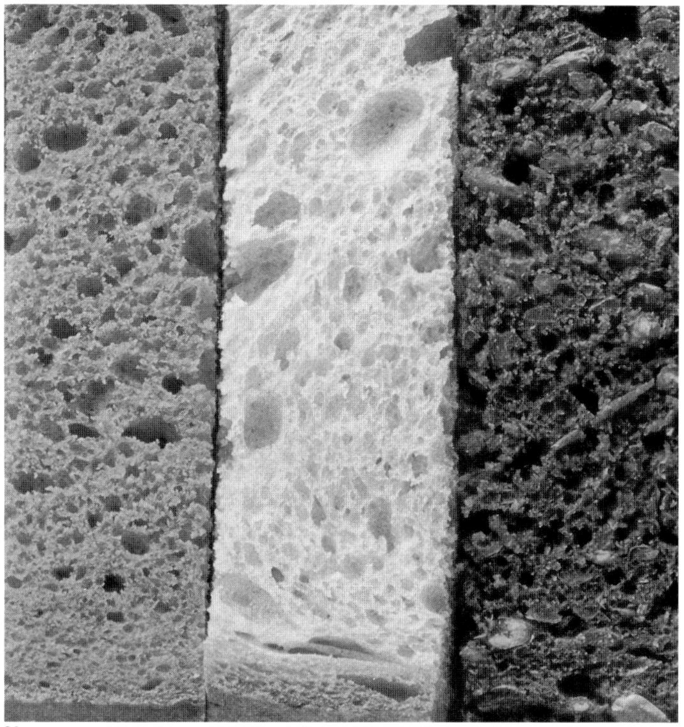

96

97

Arnold Saks AD 98
Dick Frank Ph

The Sinsigns of this lowest level provide the concrete form of textures, i.e. the elements of recognition. This kind of sign can also be expressed in adjectives, as denoting the metallic, the fabric, the wooden, etc. Our brochure title-page shows that statements capable of saying something about the quality of the product concerned can be made only through the conjunction of textures.

Die Sinzeichen dieser untersten Ebene bilden die konkrete Form der Texturen. Die Elemente also, die etwas erkennen lassen. Man kann diese Zeichenart auch in Adjektiven ausdrücken. Sie bezeichnet das metallische, stoffliche, hölzerne usw. Unser Prospekttitel zeigt, dass nur durch das Aneinanderstossen von Texturen Aussagen entstehen, die etwas über die Qualität des betreffenden Produkts aussagen können.

Les sinsignes de ce niveau inférieur constituent la forme concrète des textures. Il s'agit donc des éléments qui permettent d'identifier quelque chose. On peut aussi exprimer ce type de signe en adjectifs. Il désigne ce qui est métallique, en tissu, en bois, etc. Le titre de notre prospectus montre que seule l'opposition de textures génère des énoncés qui peuvent renseigner sur la qualité du produit en question.

98

Gina Morehead	D	99
Jimmy Williams	Ph	
Michael Schirner	D	100
KKG	A	
Daimler Benz	Ph	101

On this page we move again to the level of texture, in order to document once again the capacity of textures and colours to convey qualities. The recipient experiences the fabric character directly, feeling the density and colour quality of the material. On the facing page we find the next level of representation. The various gradients of texture provide structure, thereby forming qualities such as surface inclination, curvature, creases and edges. These are called the levels of structure, here showing details and the exactness of the workmanship.

Auf dieser Seite bewegen wir uns noch auf der Texturebene, um noch einmal zu dokumentieren, inwieweit Texturen und Farben in der Lage sind, Qualitäten zu vermitteln. Der Rezipient erlebt den stofflichen Charakter unmittelbar, er spürt förmlich Dichte und Farbigkeit des Materials. Auf der gegenüberliegenden Seite begegnen wir der nächsten Darstellungsebene. Die verschiedenen Texturgradienten strukturieren Texturen und bilden damit Eigenschaften wie Oberflächenneigung, Wölbung, Knicke und Kanten ab. Man nennt dies die Strukturebene, die hier Details zeigt, und Exaktheit der Verarbeitung.

Sur cette page, nous restons au niveau de la texture pour illustrer encore dans quelle mesure les textures et les couleurs peuvent transmettre des qualités. Le récepteur perçoit directement la nature de la matière, il sent presque la densité et la couleur du matériau. Sur la page opposée, nous rencontrons le niveau suivant du niveau de représentation. Les différents gradients de texture structurent des textures et constituent ainsi des caractéristiques comme l'inclinaison de la surface, la courbure, les coudes et les angles. Il s'agit du niveau de structure, qui montre ici des détails et l'exactitude de la finition.

99

100

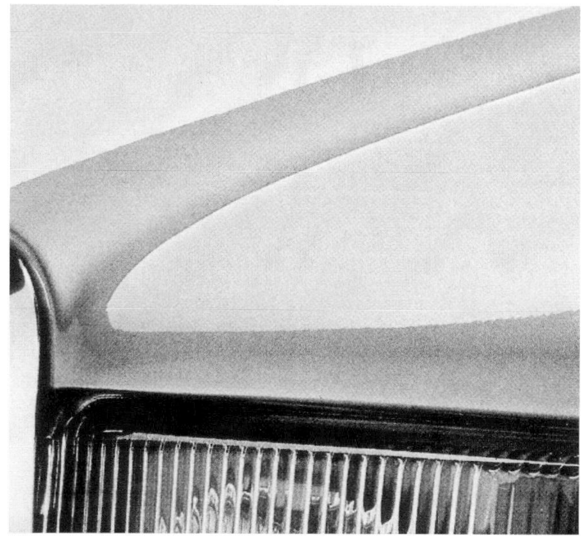

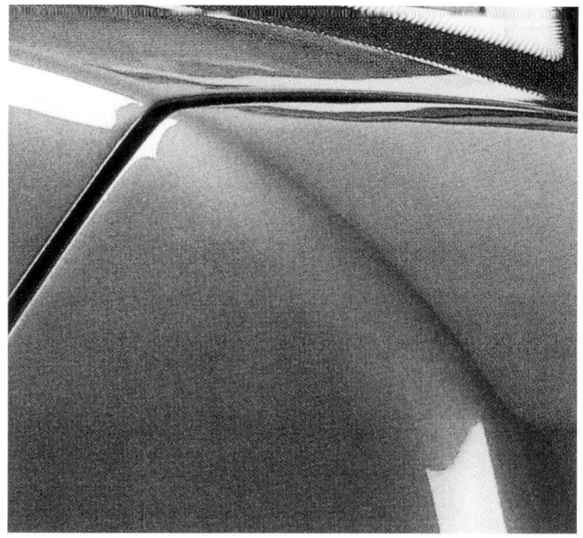

101

102

Manfred Rieker Ph 102
Barry Shepard AD 103, 104
Bob Bender Ph

Here again, details are at first shown, but we leave this description level of changing perspectives and reach the illustration of an object at the third level. Here the syntagms exactly designate the object, this being the realization.

Auch hier werden zunächst Details gezeigt, aber wir verlassen diese Beschreibungsebene wechselnder Perspektiven und befinden uns mit der Abbildung eines Objekts auf der dritten Ebene. Hier bezeichnen die Syntagmen exakt den Gegenstand, man bezeichnet dies als Realisierung.

Ici également, l'on montre d'abord des détails, mais nous quittons ce niveau de description de perspectives changeantes et nous nous trouvons au troisième niveau, avec la reproduction d'un objet. Les syntagmes désignent ici exactement l'objet; c'est ce que l'on nomme la réalisation.

103

104

To page 97 / zu Seite 97 / à la page 97

The pictorial sign stands for the same object in all three cases. The fact that the pictorial information conveyed is nevertheless different is due to the choice of different Qualisigns.

Das bildliche Zeichen steht in allen drei Fällen für das gleiche Objekt. Dass die vermittelte bildliche Information trotzdem unterschiedlich ist, liegt an der Wahl unterschiedlicher Qualizeichen.

Dans les trois cas, le signe figuratif représente le même objet. Le choix de qualisignes différents explique que l'information figurative transmise soit différente.

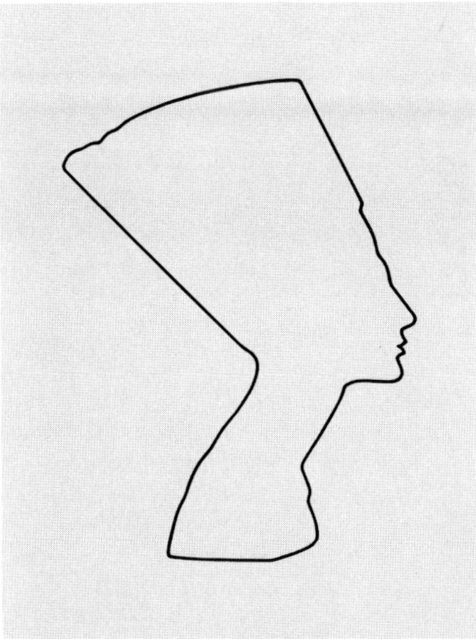

change, while a sudden change is perceived as a bump or an edge.

In this way, all the elements of the second level of description are given and they contain the preconditions for any conceivable form.

With the realization of form, the third level is already reached. On the basis of the outline, which in fact is a graphic convention to show the junction of two textures, concrete objects can be recognized at this level. The choice of graphic technique for visualization is irrelevant to the identification of the objects. At this level, it makes no difference whether the Sinsign is based on graphic reduction to an outline, an artistic imitation of light and shade, or a photographic reproduction of light values (as the illustration shows on this page).

As soon as we have points of reference for the relationship between the objects of a figurative representation, we find ourselves at the level of statements, which must be regarded as the most important for an analysis of visual communication. The sign elements and rules of combination for this level have already been explained in some detail.

Since we have now reached the level which we need to analyze, we can break off the series of levels at this point, but it could easily be continued. The next level is that of the self-contained image or picture, which can certainly contain many figurative statements and consists of their totality. Forms of connection of statements are also of interest here. The level of the image is followed by that of the series of images, which also has its own laws. There then follows the continuous transfer to the analysis of moving pictures, in which the hierarchy of levels is continued.

Veränderung der Geschwindigkeit voraus, eine plötzliche Änderung wird als Knick oder Kante wahrgenommen.

Damit sind alle Elemente der zweiten Beschreibungsebene gegeben, sie enthalten die Voraussetzungen für jede nur denkbare Form.

Mit der Realisierung der Form ist jedoch bereits die dritte Ebene erreicht. Aufgrund der Umrisslinie, die als Linie natürlich nur in der grafischen Konvention existiert und in der Realität durch das Aufeinandertreffen zweier Texturen entsteht, lassen sich auf dieser Ebene konkrete Gegenstände erkennen. Für eine Identifizierung der Gegenstände ist es unerheblich, auf welche grafische Technik die Visualisierung zurückgeht. Es macht für das Sinzeichen dieser Ebene keinen Unterschied, ob es jetzt auf der grafischen Reduktion auf eine Umrisslinie, einer zeichnerischen Imitation von Hell und Dunkel oder einer fotografischen Reproduktion der Lichtwerte beruht (wie aus der Abbildung auf dieser Seite hervorgeht).

Sobald es Anhaltspunkte für die Beziehung zwischen den Gegenständen einer bildlichen Darstellung gibt, befinden wir uns auf der Ebene der Aussagen, die als die wichtigste für eine Analyse der visuellen Kommunikation angesehen werden muss. Zeichenelemente und Kombinationsregeln dieser Ebene wurden bereits etwas ausführlicher behandelt.

Die Reihe der Ebenen soll hier, da wir die uns interessierende Analyseebene erreicht haben, abgebrochen werden. Sie lässt sich jedoch ohne weiteres fortsetzen. Die nächste Ebene ist die des abgeschlossenen Bildes, das ja viele bildliche Aussagen enthalten kann und aus deren Gesamtheit besteht. Hier interessieren dann auch Formen der Verknüpfung von Aussagen. Auf die Bildebene folgt die Ebene der Bilderserien, die ebenfalls wieder eigenen Gesetzmässigkeiten folgt. Damit wäre dann der kontinuierliche Übergang zur Filmanalyse gegeben, in der die Hierarchie der Ebenen fortgesetzt wird.

modification soudaine sera perçue comme un coude ou une arête.

Nous avons maintenant tous les éléments du deuxième niveau de description; ils comprennent les conditions préalables à toute forme possible.

Avec la réalisation de la forme, nous atteignons déjà le troisième niveau. Sur la base de la ligne de contour, qui n'existe naturellement que par convention graphique et apparaît dans la réalité par le contact de deux textures différentes, il est possible de distinguer des objets concrets à ce niveau. Pour l'identification des objets, la technique graphique qui est à la base de la visualisation ne joue aucun rôle. Pour le sinsigne de ce niveau, il est indifférent qu'il soit fondé sur la réduction graphique à une ligne de contour, sur une imitation graphique de clair et de sombre ou sur une reproduction photographique des valeurs lumineuses (comme illustré sur cette page).

Dès qu'il existe des points de repère pour la relation entre les objets d'une représentation figurative, nous nous trouvons au niveau des énoncés, qui doit être considéré comme le plus important pour une analyse de la communication visuelle. Nous avons déjà traité plus en détail des éléments de signe et des règles de combinaison de ce niveau.

Nous pouvons interrompre ici notre étude des différents niveaux, car nous avons atteint celui qui nous intéresse pour l'analyse. Poursuivons néanmoins: le niveau suivant est celui de l'image achevée, qui peut contenir beaucoup d'énoncés figuratifs et qui est constituée par leur totalité. Les formes de jonction des énoncés sont ici également intéressantes. Au niveau de l'image succède celui des séries d'images, qui de même suit ses propres lois. L'on arrive ainsi à la transition progressive vers l'analyse de film, dans laquelle se poursuit la hiérarchie des niveaux.

105

Kroehl Design A, B, C, D, E, 105

The automobile shown here can be analysed at four levels.
- A The first level is described as texturing
- B The second level as structuring
- C The third level as realization
- D The fourth level as "relativization"
- E At the final level there is a change in the object of representation, which is here a brochure.

Das hier abgebildete Auto kann man auf vier Ebenen analysieren.
- A Die erste Ebene bezeichnet man als Texturierung
- B Die zweite Ebene bezeichnet man als Strukturierung
- C Die dritte Ebene bezeichnet man als Realisierung
- D Die vierte Ebene bezeichnet man als Relativierung
- E Bei der abschliessenden Abbildung wechselt das Objekt der Darstellung, das hier ein Prospekt ist.

On peut analyser la voiture représentée ici à quatre niveaux.
- A Le premier niveau est nommé texturation
- B Le second niveau est nommé structuration
- C Le troisième niveau est nommé réalisation
- D Le quatrième niveau est nommé relativisation
- E Dans la dernière image, l'objet de la représentation (ici un prospectus) change.

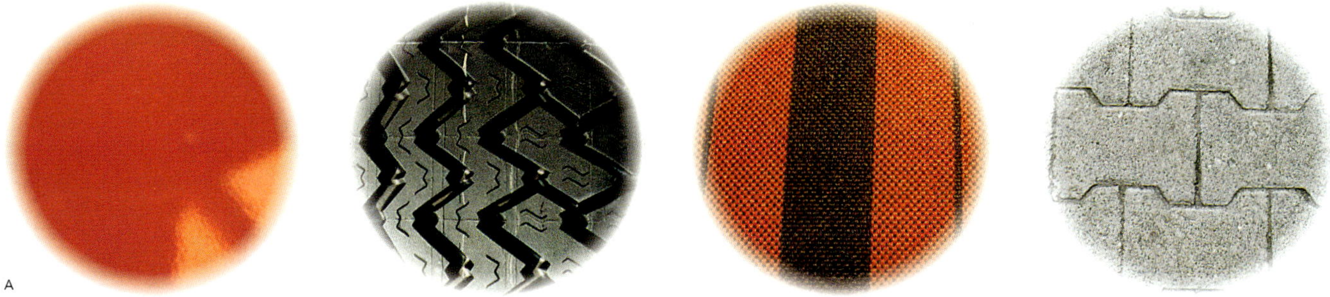

A

B

C

D

E

On this page the illustration shows the build-up of levels of analysis once more, by means of a concrete example.

In this connection, reference must once more be made to the fact that Qualisigns, Sinsigns and Legisigns can be distinguished at each level. These kinds of signs are, however, expressed differently and associated by different rules at each level. In the classification of signs it is therefore an essential condition that the level under consideration be named. A sign that is a Sinsign at one level may well function as a Qualisign at another.

This point makes it clear that, despite the foundations established for a syntactics of visual communication, there is still a great deal to be done before the instrumentarium of analysis can be regarded as complete. To summarize, it can be said that syntactics is concerned only with the formal aspects of figurative communication. The substantial aspects are to be discussed in the next chapter.

3.2. What do we understand by semantics?

3.2.1. The semantic dimension

Semantics is usually described as the study of meaning, a term which is encountered in particular in the context of "Product Semantics", an American development. For semiotics based on the triadic relationship of signs, this definition is inapplicable, since here the meaning is obtained only after the analysis of a sign in all three dimensions. In the second dimension, semiotics is concerned solely with the possibilities of the description of an object.

Semantics characterizes signs on the basis of their reference to the object signified. This may relate to the medium, the object or the interpretant. Depending on the kind of relationship concerned, one can make a distinction between Icon, Index and Symbol. This distinction has certainly found the widest recognition and attention

Auf dieser Seite wird der Aufbau der Analyseebenen noch einmal an einem konkreten Beispiel veranschaulicht.

In diesem Zusammenhang ist noch einmal darauf hinzuweisen, dass man auf jeder der Ebenen Quali-, Sin- und Legizeichen unterscheiden kann. Diese Zeichen sind jedoch auf jeder Ebene anders ausgeprägt und werden nach anderen Regeln verknüpft. Bei der Klassifizierung von Zeichen ist es daher unabdingbare Voraussetzung, jeweils auch die Ebene zu benennen. Denn was auf der einen Ebene ein Sinzeichen ist, kann auf einer anderen Ebene als Qualizeichen fungieren.

Damit wird klar, dass trotz den erarbeiteten Grundlagen für eine Syntaktik der visuellen Kommunikation noch viel zu leisten ist, ehe man von einer Vollständigkeit des Analyseinstrumentariums ausgehen kann. Zusammenfassend kann man also sagen, dass die Syntaktik nur die formalen Aspekte bildlicher Kommunikation behandelt. Inhaltliche Aspekte werden im nächsten Kapitel erörtert.

3.2. Was verstehen wir unter Semantik?

3.2.1. Die semantische Dimension

Die Semantik wird meist als die Lehre von der Bedeutung bezeichnet, insbesondere im Rahmen der in den USA entwickelten «Product Semantics» kann man diese Begriffsverwendung antreffen. Für eine Semiotik auf der Basis der triadischen Zeichenrelation ist diese Bestimmung unzutreffend, denn für sie ergibt sich die Bedeutung erst aus der Analyse eines Zeichens in allen drei Dimensionen. In der zweiten Dimension behandelt sie lediglich die Möglichkeiten der Bezeichnung von Objekten.

Die Semantik charakterisiert Zeichen aufgrund ihrer Beziehung zum bezeichneten Objekt, das wiederum auf Mittel, Objekt oder Interpretant bezogen sein kann. Je nach Art dieser Beziehung kann man zwischen Ikon, Index und Symbol unterscheiden. Diese Unterscheidung hat wohl die weiteste Anerkennung und Beach-

Sur cette page, illustrons encore la structure des niveaux d'analyse à l'aide d'un exemple concret.

Il convient de répéter ici qu'il est possible de différencier à chaque niveau des qualisignes, des sinsignes et des légisignes. Toutefois, à chacun de ces niveaux, les signes s'expriment différemment et sont liés selon des règles différentes. Pour toute classification des signes, il est dès lors indispensable de désigner au préalable le niveau considéré. En effet, ce qui est un sinsigne à un niveau donné peut avoir fonction de qualisigne à un autre niveau.

Ainsi, même si l'on a jeté les bases d'une syntactique de la communication visuelle, il reste manifestement beaucoup à faire avant que l'on puisse prétendre disposer d'un ensemble d'instruments d'analyse complet. En résumé, disons que la syntactique ne traite que des aspects relatifs à la forme de la communication figurative. Nous étudierons les aspects ayant trait au fond dans le chapitre suivant.

3.2. Que comprenons-nous par la sémantique?

3.2.1. La dimension sémantique

Le plus souvent, la sémantique est considérée comme la théorie du sens; on rencontre notamment cette définition dans le contexte de la «product semantics» élaborée aux Etats-Unis. Il ne convient pas de définir ainsi une sémiotique fondée sur la relation triadique du signe, car pour elle le sens n'apparaît qu'à partir de l'analyse d'un signe dans l'ensemble des trois dimensions. Dans la deuxième dimension, elle ne considère que les possibilités de la désignation d'objets.

La sémantique caractérise les signes sur la base de leur relation avec l'objet désigné, qui pour sa part peut être en relation avec le moyen, l'objet ou l'interprétant. Selon la nature de ce rapport, on peut différencier entre l'icône, l'indice et le symbole. Cette distinction est sans doute la plus largement reconnue et respectée dans la

in the literature of semiology, to such an extent that the whole science is sometimes reduced to this formula. Nevertheless there is no other part of sign theory that has been so often and so fundamentally misunderstood. An example of this misunderstanding is the commonly encountered differentiation between the iconic as a figurative or pictorial sign and the symbolic as a verbal sign.

3.2.2. How objects are represented by signs

In the Icon, an object is used as a means of signifying another object, as for example when an object is made to stand for a whole series of concrete objects as a general type. The relation of the Icon to the object signified is one of similarity. Three kinds of Icons are to be distinguished: *Images* reproduce the simple perception qualities of an object, whether such an object actually exists in reality or not. The objects of images can therefore be understood only as possibilities, which contain the offer of identification, of reference to the given situation. In advertising, this applies particularly to the use of protagonists whose function is to address the target group. *Diagrams* reduce the image to the relationship between parts of the object, these being reproduced in abstract form. This form of sign is a means of characterizing the relationships as the most important object of the representation. This applies, for example, to transport connection maps, storage plans and the like. *Metaphors* show the primarily intended qualities of an object through a parallel with something else. In this case, the iconic principle of the use of an object as pure medium in the sign process becomes particularly apparent.

In the Index, by contrast, the object refers to itself. The Index is thus a sign of the real existence of its object. One could also say that it is caused by

tung in der semiotischen Literatur gefunden. Wobei die Semiotik allerdings oft nur auf diesen Aspekt reduziert worden ist. Kein anderer Teil der Zeichentheorie ist aber auch so oft und so gründlich missverstanden worden. So beispielsweise auch die häufig anzutreffende Differenzierung zwischen ikonischen als bildlichen Zeichen und symbolischen als verbalen Zeichen.

3.2.2. Wie man durch Zeichen Objekte darstellt

Beim Ikon wird ein Objekt als Mittel zur Bezeichnung eines anderen Objekts verwendet, indem etwa ein Gegenstand als allgemeiner Typus für eine ganze Reihe konkreter Gegenstände stehen kann. Die Beziehung des Ikons zum bezeichneten Objekt besteht in der Ähnlichkeit. Dabei werden drei Arten von Ikons unterschieden: *Abbilder* geben einfach Wahrnehmungseigenschaften eines Objektes wieder, ganz gleich, ob ein solches Objekt nun in der Realität existiert oder nicht. Objekte von Abbildern können daher immer nur als Möglichkeiten aufgefasst werden, Möglichkeiten, die das Angebot der Identifikation, der Beziehung auf die eigene Situation beinhalten. In der Werbung gilt dies insbesondere für den Einsatz von Protagonisten, die die Zielgruppe ansprechen sollen. *Diagramme* reduzieren die Abbildung auf die Beziehung zwischen Teilen des Objekts, die in abstrakter Form wiedergegeben werden. Durch diese Zeichenform werden die Beziehungen als das wesentliche Objekt der Darstellung gekennzeichnet, dies gilt zum Beispiel für Pläne von Verkehrsverbindungen, Lageskizzen und ähnliche Anwendungen. *Metaphern* zeigen die wesentlich gemeinten Eigenschaften eines Objekts durch eine Parallelität in etwas anderem. Hier wird das ikonische Prinzip der Verwendung des Objektes als reines Mittel im Zeichenprozess besonders deutlich.

Im Gegensatz dazu verweist beim Index das Objekt auf sich selbst. Der Index ist damit ein Zeichen der realen Existenz seines Objekts. Man kann auch sagen, er ist durch das Objekt verursacht. Nach dieser Definition

littérature sémiotique. Néanmoins, la sémiotique a souvent été réduite à cet unique aspect. Aucun autre domaine de la théorie des signes n'a fait l'objet d'autant de malentendus fondamentaux. Il en va ainsi, par exemple, de la distinction souvent opérée entre les signes iconiques considérés comme figuratifs et les signes symboliques considérés comme verbaux.

3.2.2. La représentation d'objets par des signes

Dans l'icône, l'objet est utilisé comme moyen de désignation d'un autre objet dans la mesure où un objet donné, pris comme type général, peut représenter toute une série d'objets concrets. On distingue trois types d'icônes: les *images* proprement dites représentent simplement des caractéristiques de perception d'un objet, que cet objet existe ou non dans la réalité. Dès lors, les objets d'images ne peuvent jamais être pris que comme des possibilités, possibilités qui comprennent l'offre de l'identification, de la relation à la situation particulière. Dans la publicité, ceci s'applique notamment à la mise en jeu de protagonistes qui doivent s'adresser au groupe cible. Les *diagrammes* réduisent la représentation à la relation entre des parties de l'objet qui sont reproduites sous forme abstraite. Par cette forme de signe, les relations sont caractérisées comme l'objet essentiel de la représentation. Ceci s'applique, par exemple, aux plans de réseau des transports, aux plans d'orientation ou autres utilisations de ce type. Les *métaphores* représentent les caractéristiques essentiellement signifiées d'un objet en représentant un parallélisme dans quelque chose d'autre. Le principe iconique de l'utilisation d'un objet en tant que moyen pur dans le processus du signe apparaît ici de façon particulièrement claire.

Par opposition, dans l'indice, l'objet renvoie à lui-même. Ainsi, l'indice est un signe de l'existence réelle de son objet. L'on peut également dire qu'il est provoqué par l'objet. D'après cette

William Wondriska D 106
Jay Maisel Ph
Emil Schulthess D 107
Georg Gerster Ph

The two themes shown here are described as "likenesses" (Abbilder). It is the same, whether we visualize the informality of a town at night, a ski piste or the protagonists of advertising. This kind of sign is characterized by being interchangeable. Likenesses simulate conditions of perception, thereby signifying objects, whether these exist in reality or not. They are favoured for use in advertising campaigns because they generally contain an offer of identification.

Bei den beiden hier gezeigten Motiven handelt es sich um sogenannte Abbilder. Egal, ob wir uns die Unverbindlichkeit einer nächtlichen Stadt, einer Skipiste oder Protagonisten der Werbung vorstellen. Diese Zeichenart ist von Austauschbarkeit gekennzeichnet. Abbilder simulieren Wahrnehmungsbedingungen und bezeichnen dadurch Objekte, ganz gleich, ob diese in der Realität existieren oder nicht. Sie werden bei Werbestrategien gern eingesetzt, weil sie zumeist ein Identifikationsangebot enthalten.

Les motifs reproduits ici sont des images proprement dites. Il importe peu que nous nous représentions l'anonymat d'une ville la nuit, d'une piste de ski, ou des protagonistes de la publicité. Ce type de dessin est caractérisé par l'interchangeabilité. Les représentations simulent des conditions de perception et désignent ainsi des objets, qu'ils existent ou non en réalité. On les utilise volontiers dans les stratégies publicitaires car il comprennent le plus souvent une offre d'identification.

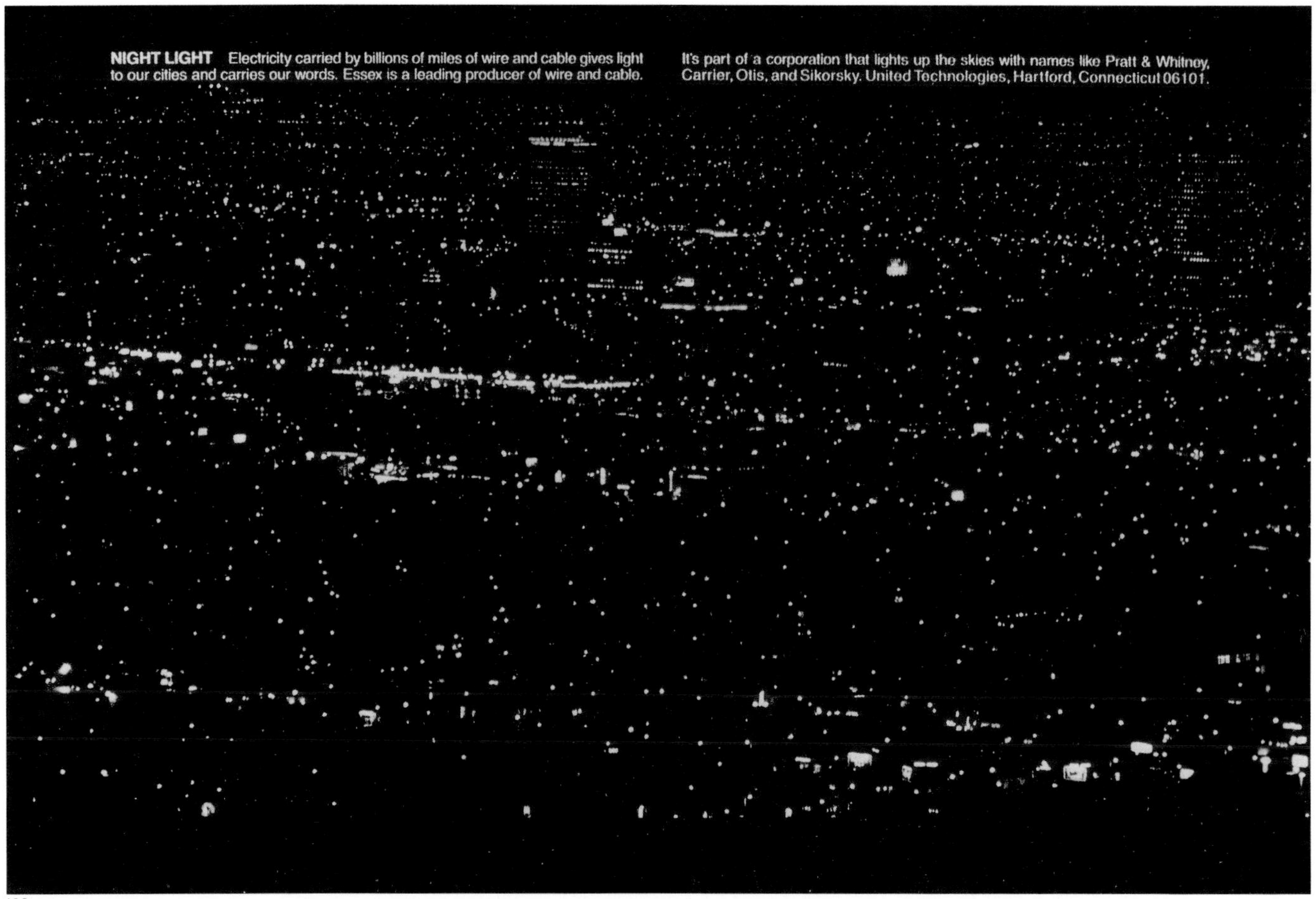

106

107

108

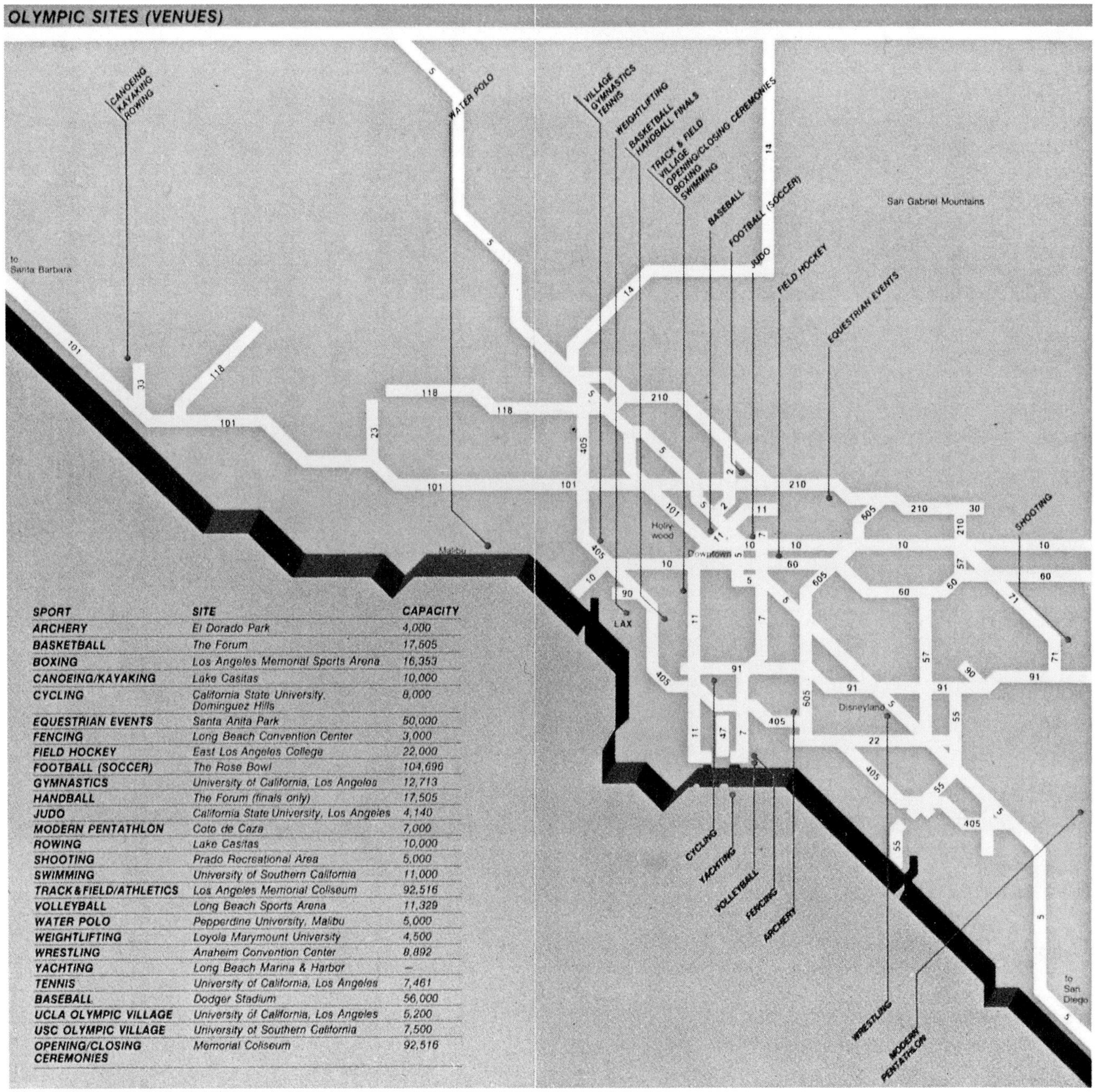

SPORT	SITE	CAPACITY
ARCHERY	El Dorado Park	4,000
BASKETBALL	The Forum	17,505
BOXING	Los Angeles Memorial Sports Arena	16,353
CANOEING/KAYAKING	Lake Casitas	10,000
CYCLING	California State University, Dominguez Hills	8,000
EQUESTRIAN EVENTS	Santa Anita Park	50,000
FENCING	Long Beach Convention Center	3,000
FIELD HOCKEY	East Los Angeles College	22,000
FOOTBALL (SOCCER)	The Rose Bowl	104,696
GYMNASTICS	University of California, Los Angeles	12,713
HANDBALL	The Forum (finals only)	17,505
JUDO	California State University, Los Angeles	4,140
MODERN PENTATHLON	Coto de Caza	7,000
ROWING	Lake Casitas	10,000
SHOOTING	Prado Recreational Area	5,000
SWIMMING	University of Southern California	11,000
TRACK&FIELD/ATHLETICS	Los Angeles Memorial Coliseum	92,516
VOLLEYBALL	Long Beach Sports Arena	11,329
WATER POLO	Pepperdine University, Malibu	5,000
WEIGHTLIFTING	Loyola Marymount University	4,500
WRESTLING	Anaheim Convention Center	8,892
YACHTING	Long Beach Marina & Harbor	—
TENNIS	University of California, Los Angeles	7,461
BASEBALL	Dodger Stadium	56,000
UCLA OLYMPIC VILLAGE	University of California, Los Angeles	5,200
USC OLYMPIC VILLAGE	University of Southern California	7,500
OPENING/CLOSING CEREMONIES	Memorial Coliseum	92,516

109

Odermatt & Tissi D 108
Richard Saul Wurman D 109

Diagrams in advertising provide reduced connexions between parts of their objects, by which means their similarity is reduced to their structure. Despite the precise power of statement of this sign system, it is hardly used at all for business communication.

Diagramme in der Werbung geben reduziert Beziehungen zwischen Teilen ihrer Objekte wieder, wobei sich die Ähnlichkeit auf die Struktur dieser Beziehungen beschränkt. Trotz der präzisen Aussagekraft dieses Zeichensystems wird es für wirtschaftliche Kommunikation kaum genutzt.

En publicité, les diagrammes reflètent, de manière réduite, les relations entre les parties de leurs objets; toutefois la ressemblance se limite à la structure de ces relations. Malgré la précision expressive de ce système de signes, il n'est guère utilisé pour la communication commerciale.

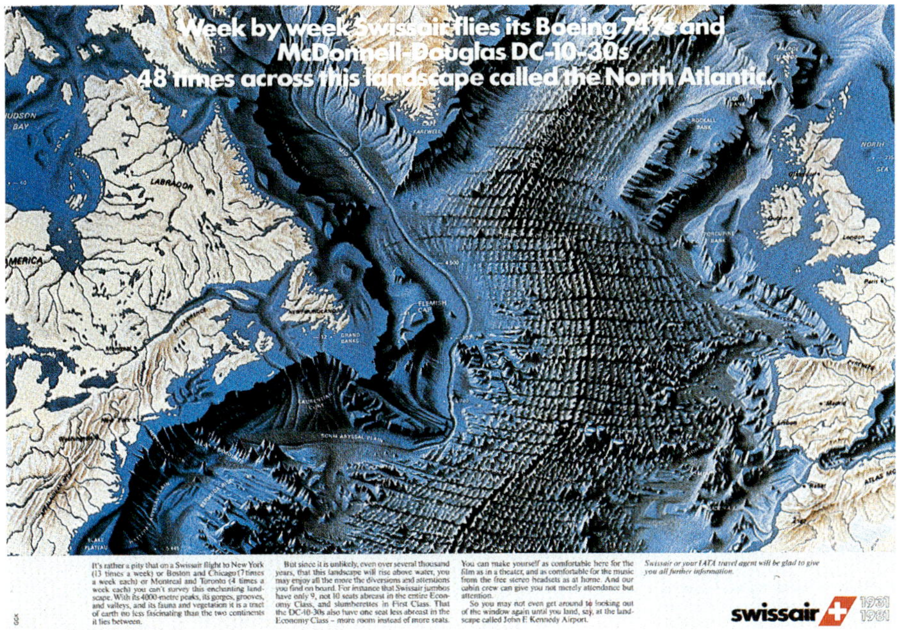

110

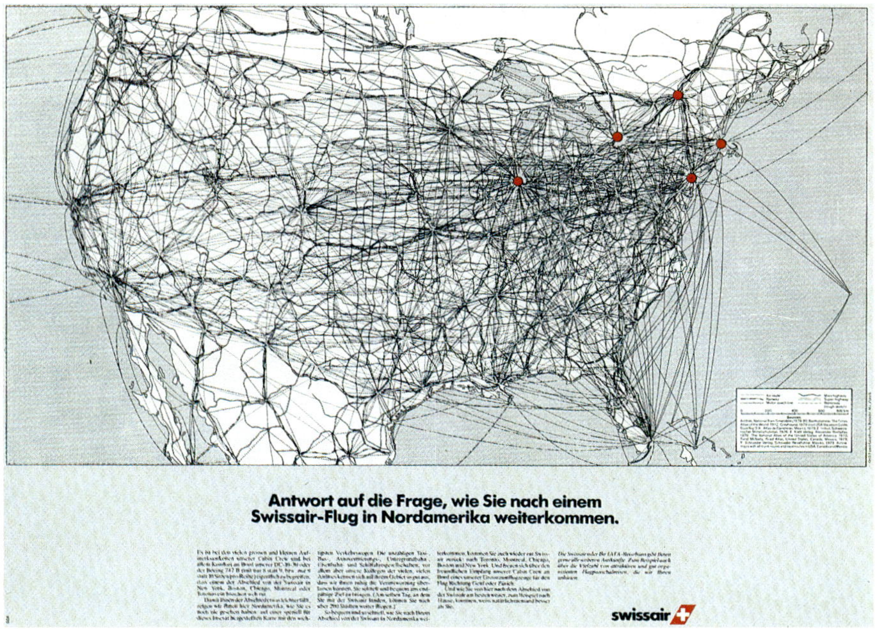

111

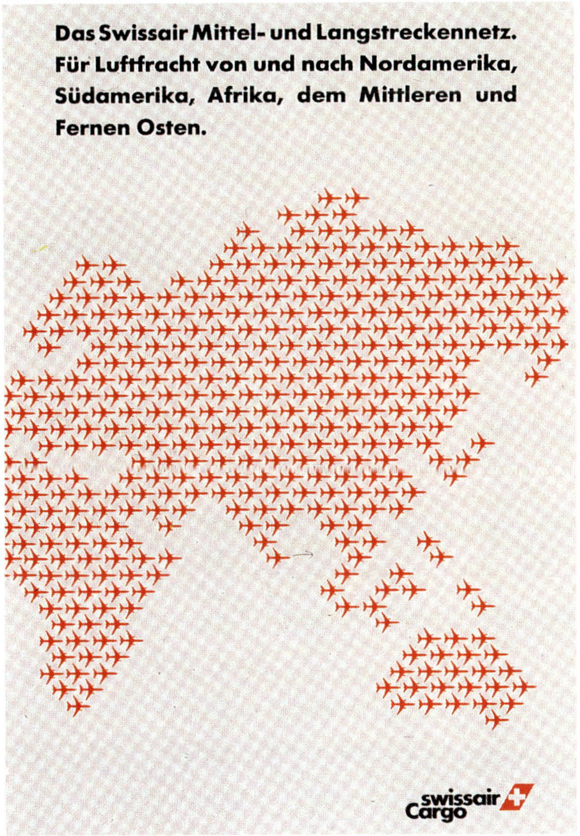

112

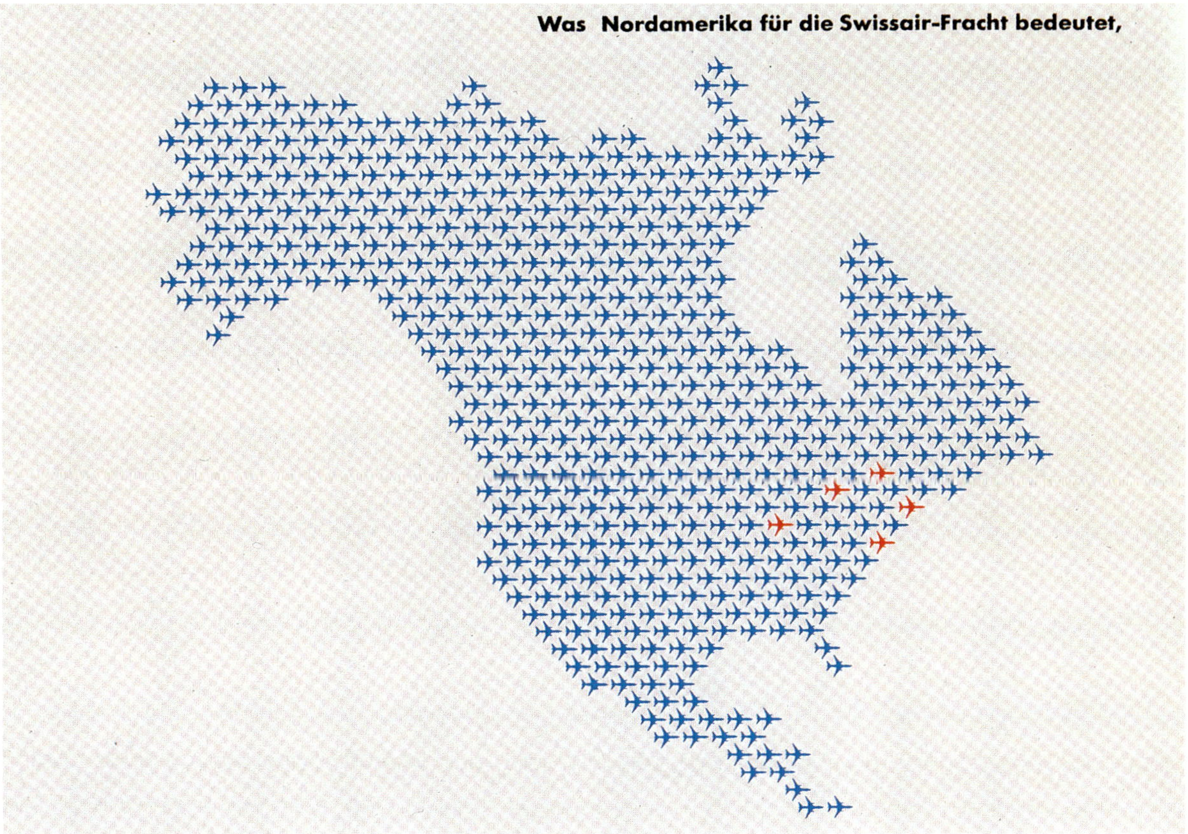

113

Ernst Bächtold AD 110
Tanguy de Rémur D
Manfred Willuweit AD 111
Orell Füssli D
Daniel Sulser AD 112, 113
GGK A

The variation of width in diagrams shown here provides an insight into the performance capacity of such systems.

Die hier vorgestellte Variationsbreite an Diagrammen vermittelt einen Einblick über die Leistungsfähigkeit solcher Systeme.

La marge de variation présentée ici pour les diagrammes donne une idée de l'efficacité de ces systèmes.

Hirokazu Hashimoto D 114
Richard Hess AD 115

Visual thinking manifests itself especially in the use of metaphors. They show the mainly intended characteristics of an object through a parallelism with something else. How great such a repertoire can be is here shown only by implication.

Visuelles Denken manifestiert sich besonders im Einsatz von Metaphern. Sie zeigen die wesentlich gemeinten Eigenschaften eines Objekts, durch eine Parallelität in etwas anderem. Wie gross ein solches Repertoire sein kann, wird hier nur andeutungsweise gezeigt.

La pensée visuelle se manifeste particulièrement dans l'utilisation de métaphores. Elles indiquent les qualités d'un objet que l'on veut exprimer par un parallélisme dans autre chose. Nous ne présentons ici qu'une infime partie de ce vaste répertoire.

114

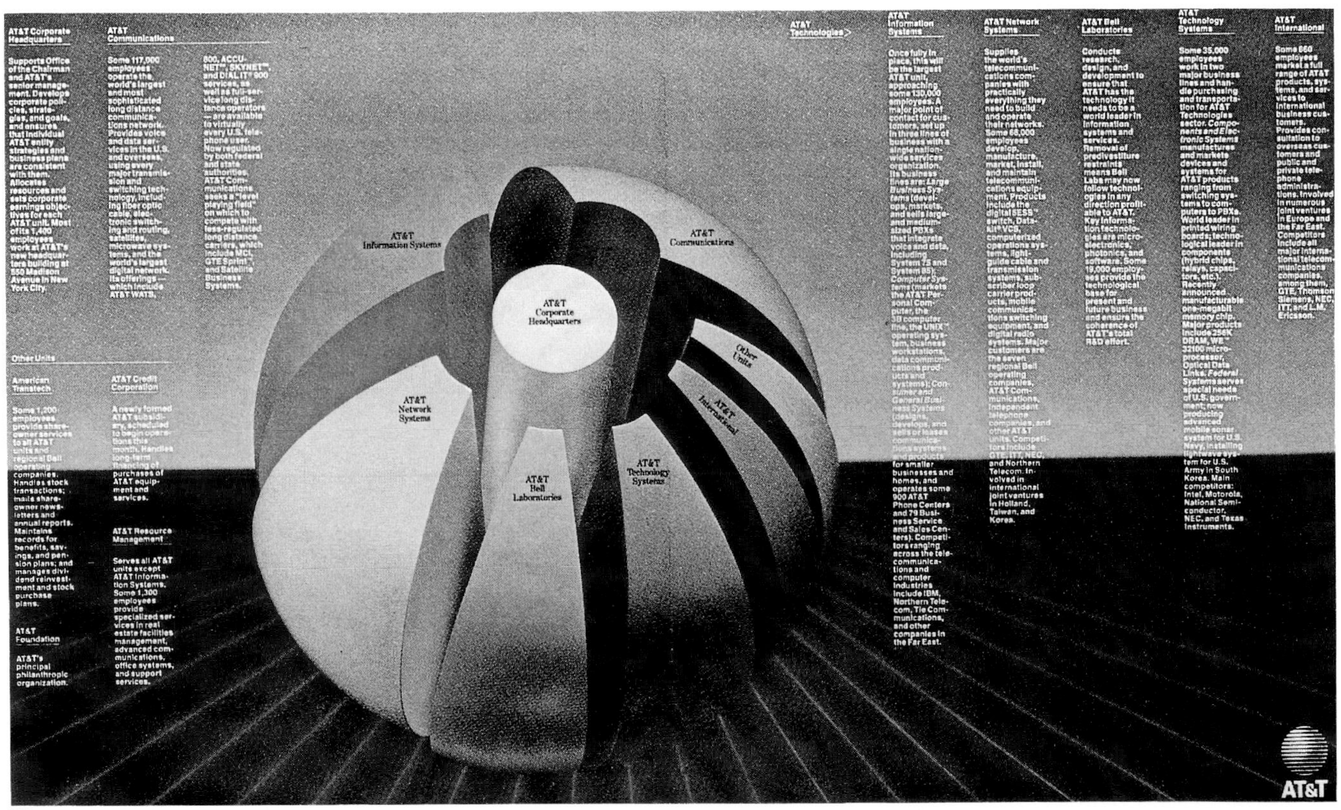

115

116

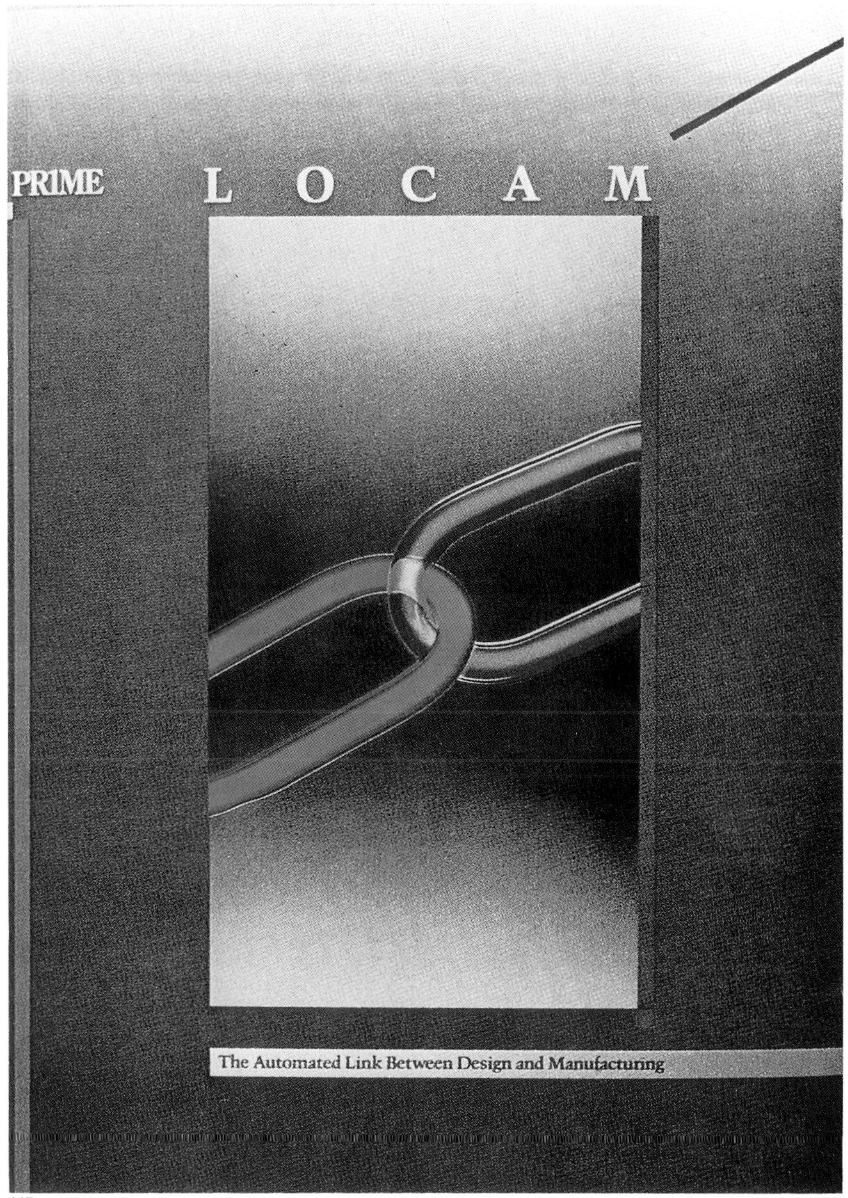

117

Nancy Skolos D 116, 117

Such impressive signs must always stand in a relationship of interaction to the enterprise concerned. They are able to express something about a company much more efficiently than can be done in speech.

Solche einprägsamen Zeichen müssen immer in einem Interaktionsbezug zum jeweiligen Unternehmen stehen. Sie sind in der Lage, viel effizienter etwas über ein Unternehmen auszusagen, als dies sprachlich geschehen kann.

Des signes aussi frappants doivent toujours se trouver en interaction avec l'entreprise correspondante. Il peuvent «parler» d'une entreprise avec beaucoup plus d'éloquence que la parole.

118

Makoto Nakamura	D	118
Kunio Hirajima	Ph	
Jeff Laramore	D	119
Pilippe Pollet Villard	AD	120
Jerry Oke	Ph	
Bruno Albertin	D	121
Young & Rubicam	A	

The kind of sign used here is described as an indication (Anzeichen). These indications are produced directly as traces, by the object itself. In advertising, such indices serve the relationship of a possible situation to a given product. In the whisky advertisement shown at the right, the designer even achieves the representation of the effect of a product with this kind of sign.

Die hier benutzte Zeichenart bezeichnet man als Anzeichen. Diese Anzeichen sind als Spuren unmittelbar vom Objekt verursacht. In der Werbung dienen solche Indices der Beziehung einer möglichen Situation auf ein bestimmtes Produkt. Bei der rechts abgebildeten Whisky-Anzeige gelingt dem Gestalter mit dieser Zeichenart sogar die Darstellung der Wirkung eines Produkts.

On nomme marque le type de signe utilisé ici. Ces marques sont des empreintes directement produites par l'objet. Dans la publicité, ces indices servent à établir le lien entre une situation possible et un produit déterminé. Dans l'annonce pour du whisky reproduite à droite, le concepteur a pu, en utilisant ce type de signe, représenter jusqu'à l'effet même d'un produit.

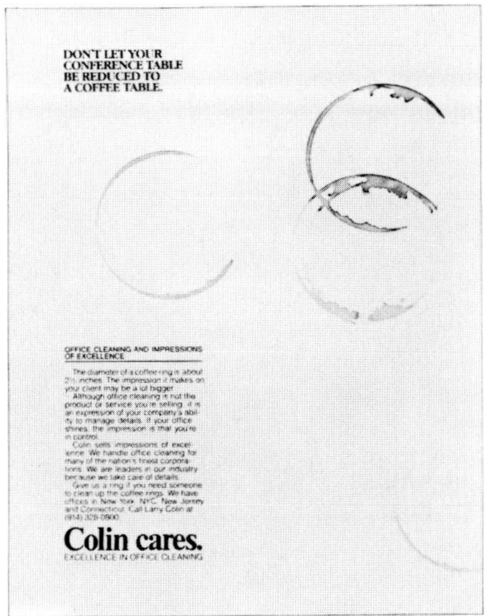

119

McRay Magleby D 122
Gisèle Freund F 123
David Johnson D 124
Vivienne Flesher D 125

Identifying likenesses, on the other hand, are based on the representation of the features characterizing the uniqueness of the object.

Identifizierende Abbilder hingegen beruhen auf der Darstellung der die Einmaligkeit des Objekts charakterisierenden Merkmale.

En revanche, les images d'identification se fondent sur la représentation des traits qui caractérisent l'unicité de l'objet.

120

121

To summarize: since the meaning of a sign is entirely determined by the establishment of its rules of use, the meaning of any sign can—at least in principle—be fully established by an objective investigation.

Charles William Morris

Zusammengefasst wäre zu sagen: Da die Bedeutung eines Zeichens durch die Feststellung seiner Gebrauchsregeln vollständig bestimmt ist, lässt sich die Bedeutung jedes Zeichens durch eine objektive Untersuchung – zumindest prinzipiell – vollständig feststellen.

Charles William Morris

En bref, on pourrait dire la chose suivante: le sens d'un signe étant complètement déterminé par l'établissement de ses règles d'utilisation, il est possible d'établir complètement – du moins en principe – le sens de chaque signe par un examen objectif.

Charles William Morris

the object. By this definition, two kinds of Indices can be distinguished:

Identifying images are based on the representation of the singularity of the object's characteristics. The clearest example of this function is the passport photo. Other examples are caricatures, in which certain identifying characteristics are made prominent, usually in an exaggerated form. Just as painted portraits can have an identifying character, photographs may have an iconic character in cases where a person is shown only as a type. *Indicators* may at first sight seem to have little in common with the identifying image but they go back to the same indexical principle. Indicators are produced directly by the object itself. This involves making a distinction once again between, for example, a footprint in the sand and an image of this footprint. To be perfectly precise, this distinction must be made. A lipstick impression on a love letter undoubtedly has a different effect from a mere painting of the same, although both are here interpreted as indicators.

The relationship of the third kind of sign, the Symbol, to its object is conventional. The association takes place only within a system formed by the interpretant. Thus the meaning of a symbol is strictly governed and the system is a necessary component of the sign. Even where the essence of the symbol consists in free association, this association is in most cases not purely arbitrary but follows certain principles. Thus one can distinguish between more iconically oriented and more indexically derived symbols, contrasting them with purely arbitrary symbols.

3.2.3. The best signs have something of everything

As has already been mentioned, one cannot allocate a sign to one particu-

kann man zwei Arten von Indices unterscheiden:

Identifizierende Abbilder beruhen auf der Darstellung der die Einmaligkeit des Objekts charakterisierenden Merkmale. Diese Funktion hat am deutlichsten das Passbild. Beispiele dafür sind aber auch Karikaturen, in denen bestimmte identifizierende Merkmale meist überspitzt hervorgehoben werden. Wie also gemalte Bilder auch identifizierenden Charakter haben können, so können Fotografien ikonischen Charakter haben, wenn etwa eine Person nur als Typ vorgestellt wird. *Anzeichen* haben zwar auf den ersten Blick wenig mit dem identifizierenden Abbild gemeinsam, gehen aber auf das gleiche indexikalische Prinzip zurück. Anzeichen sind als Spuren unmittelbar vom Objekt bewirkt. Es hiesse, die Sache unnötig zu komplizieren, wollte man im gegebenen Zusammenhang etwa zwischen Spur im Sand und der Abbildung dieser Spur noch einmal unterscheiden. Wollte man ganz exakt sein, so müsste man dies tun, denn ein auf einen Liebesbrief gehauchter Lippenabdruck hat zweifellos eine andere Wirkung als ein nur gemalter Kussmund, auch wenn hier beides gleichermassen als Anzeichen interpretiert wird.

Die Beziehung der dritten Zeichenart der Semantik, des Symbols, zu seinem Objekt ist konventionell. Die Zuordnung erfolgt nur innerhalb eines Systems, das den Interpretanten bildet. Die Bedeutung eines Symbols ist damit verbindlich geregelt, und das System ist notwendiger Bestandteil des Zeichens. Wenn auch das Wesen des Symbols in der freien Zuordnung besteht, so ist diese Zuordnung dennoch meist nicht rein willkürlich, sie folgt vielmehr gewissen Prinzipien. Man kann daher zwischen eher ikonisch orientierten und eher indexikalisch abgeleiteten Symbolen unterscheiden und diesen das rein willkürliche Symbol gegenüberstellen.

3.2.3. Die besten Zeichen haben von allem etwas

Es wurde bereits darauf aufmerksam gemacht, dass man ein Zeichen nicht

définition, il est possible de distinguer deux types d'indices:

Les *images d'identification* sont fondées sur la représentation des traits qui caractérisent l'unicité de l'objet. C'est la fonction de la photographie d'un passeport, pour prendre l'exemple le plus évident. On mentionnera également les caricatures, dans lesquelles certains traits d'identification sont généralement fortement exagérés. Tout comme des images peintes peuvent avoir un caractère d'identification, des photographies peuvent avoir un caractère iconique, quand, par exemple, une personne est présentée uniquement en tant que type. Au premier abord, les *marques* n'ont guère de points communs avec l'image d'identification; elles procèdent pourtant du même principe indiciaire. Les marques sont des traces directement produites par l'objet. Dans le présent contexte, il est inutile de compliquer les choses en opérant encore une distinction entre une trace dans le sable, par exemple, et la reproduction de cette trace. Néanmoins, si l'on voulait être tout à fait exact, il faudrait le faire, car une empreinte de lèvres sur une lettre d'amour a sans aucun doute un autre effet que les mêmes lèvres dessinées, même si nous les interprétons toutes les deux comme des marques.

Le symbole, troisième type de signe de la sémantique, a une relation conventionnelle avec son objet. L'attribution se fait uniquement dans un système qui constitue l'interprétant. La signification d'un symbole est ainsi soumise à une réglementation obligatoire, et le système est une partie constituante nécessaire du signe. Même si l'essence du symbole est celle de l'attribution libre, cette attribution, en règle générale, n'est pas purement arbitraire. Elle suit certains principes. Dès lors, on peut opérer une distinction entre les symboles à orientation plutôt iconique et ceux qui sont plutôt dérivés indiciairement, et leur opposer le symbole purement arbitraire.

3.2.3. Les meilleurs signes sont composites

Nous avons déjà souligné qu'il n'est

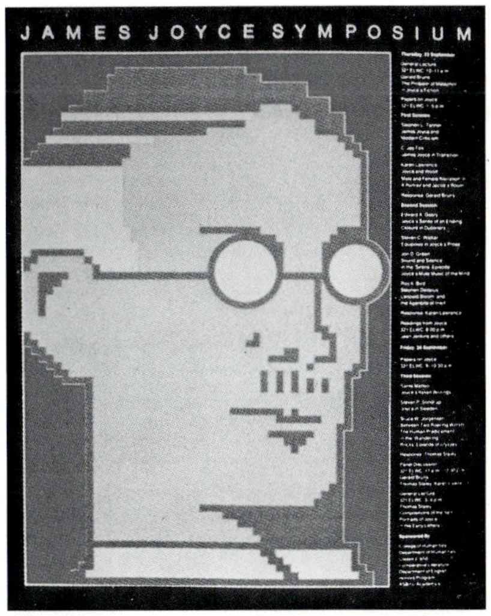

122

123

124

125

126

128

127

129

Will Hopkins / Ben Carucci	D	126
Michael O'Neill	Ph	
Rudolph de Harak	D	127
Franz Kliebhan	AD	128
Co Rentmeester	Ph	
Tom Smith	D	129
Andy Rossetti	Ph	

The relationship of the third kind of semantic sign, the symbol, to its object, is conventional. The classification is made only within a system formed by the interpretant. The use of such symbols, which in our example stand for work, printing, sport or cooperative store, shows how national symbols may be used.

Die Beziehung der dritten Zeichenart der Semantik, des Symbols zu seinem Objekt, ist konventionell. Die Zuordnung erfolgt nur innerhalb eines Systems, das den Interpretanten bildet. Die Benutzung solcher Symbole, die bei unserem Beispiel für Arbeit, Druck, Sport oder den Konsum stehen, belegt, wie nationale Symbole kommunikativ eingesetzt werden können.

Le symbole, troisième type de signe de la sémantique, a une relation conventionnelle avec son objet. L'attribution se fait uniquement dans un système qui constitue l'interprétant. L'utilisation de ces symboles, qui dans notre exemple représentent le travail, l'impression, le sport ou la consommation, illustre comment des symboles nationaux peuvent être utilisés à des fins de communication.

lar category on principle. It is much more the case that any sign contains the various component features with differing degrees of strength of expression, so that one can only establish points of emphasis. According to Peirce, the optimal sign for an object contains iconic, indexical and symbolic elements in a balanced relationship. Such a relationship should be striven for in the design of trademarks and logos in particular, as these signs should represent their objects in an all-inclusive way. In advertising statements, on the other hand, it is better to emphasize certain particular sign characteristics in order to make the communicative intention clear. The *continuum* of sign possibilities shows how the different kinds of sign, when they all relate to the same object, bring out different aspects of that object. The circular illustration is intended to show that the kinds of sign cannot always be clearly separated and that it is much more a question of continuous blending between them (see next page).

3.3. What is the meaning of pragmatics?

3.3.1. Signs and sign systems

It is often stated that pragmatics is concerned with the use of signs in concrete, real situations. In principle this is certainly not false, but it is not precise enough and allows many occasions for purely colloquial speculations which have little to do with the theoretical basis. In this connection, the term interpretant, in particular, is often incorrectly used. The interpretant should in no case be confused with the interpreter. The interpretant is the system within which the meaning of the sign is conveyed. This system is usually formed, or at least actualized, through the context, i.e. the concrete situation in which the sign is used. To this extent, the formula given at the head of this section is appropriate, but it does not provide very much further help for an analysis.

prinzipiell nur einer Zeichenart zuordnen kann, dass vielmehr ein Zeichen die verschiedenen Komponenten in unterschiedlich starker Ausprägung enthält und man nur Schwerpunkte feststellen kann. Nach Peirce enthält das optimale Zeichen für ein Objekt ikonische, indexikalische und symbolische Elemente in einem ausgewogenen Verhältnis. Ein solches ausgewogenes Verhältnis sollte man vor allem bei der Gestaltung von Markenzeichen und Signets anstreben, die ihre Objekte umfassend repräsentieren sollen. Bei werblichen Aussagen dagegen wird man eher bestimmte Zeichencharakteristiken betonen, um die kommunikative Absicht deutlich werden zu lassen. Wie die verschiedenen Zeichenarten, wenn sie sich alle auf das gleiche Objekt beziehen, unterschiedliche Aspekte dieses Objekts herausstellen, zeigt das *Kontinuum* der Bezeichnungsmöglichkeiten. Die Darstellung in Form eines Kreises soll darauf hinweisen, dass sich die Zeichenarten nicht immer deutlich voneinander abgrenzen lassen, dass es vielmehr kontinuierliche Übergänge zwischen ihnen gibt (nächste Seite).

3.3. Was verstehen wir unter Pragmatik?

3.3.1. Zeichen und Zeichensysteme

Es wird oft formuliert, die Pragmatik beschäftige sich mit der Anwendung von Zeichen in konkreten Situationen. Dies ist zwar vom Prinzip her nicht falsch, doch es ist nicht exakt genug und gibt vielfach Anlass zu rein umgangssprachlichen Spekulationen, die nur noch wenig mit der theoretischen Basis zu tun haben. In diesem Zusammenhang wird insbesondere der Begriff des Interpretanten oft falsch angewandt. Der Interpretant darf auf keinen Fall mit dem Interpreten verwechselt werden. Der Interpretant ist das System, in dem die Vermittlung der Bedeutung des Zeichens erfolgt. Gebildet oder zumindest aktualisiert wird dieses System meist durch den Kontext, die konkrete Situation der Zeichenverwendung. Insofern ist die eingangs genannte Formulierung zutreffend, doch hilft sie für eine Analyse nicht sehr viel weiter.

pas possible d'affirmer par principe qu'un signe appartient à une seule classe de signes. Au contraire, chaque signe comprend les différentes composantes à des degrés divers, et l'on ne peut que déceler des dominantes. Selon Peirce, le meilleur signe pour un objet comprend des éléments iconiques, indiciaires et symboliques en proportions équilibrées. Il faut surtout s'efforcer de trouver cet équilibre dans la création de marques de fabrique et de logos qui doivent représenter leur objet dans leur ensemble. En revanche, pour les annonces publicitaires, on soulignera plutôt certaines caractéristiques du signe pour exprimer clairement l'objectif de communication. Le continuum des possibilités de désignation montre comment les différents types de signes se rapportant tous au même objet mettent en évidence différents aspects de cet objet. La représentation sous forme de cercle souligne le fait que les différents types de signes ne peuvent pas toujours être clairement délimités: au contraire, on passe progressivement de l'un à l'autre (voir page suivante).

3.3. Que comprenons-nous par la pragmatique?

3.3.1. Signes et systèmes de signes

On affirme généralement que la pragmatique étudie l'utilisation des signes dans des situations concrètes. Sans être fausse, cette assertion n'est pas assez précise et donne bien souvent lieu à des spéculations relevant purement du parler d'usage et n'ayant pratiquement plus rien à voir avec la base théorique. Dans ce contexte, la notion d'interprétant est maintes fois utilisée de façon erronée. Il ne faut en aucun cas confondre l'interprétant avec l'interprète. L'interprétant est le système dans lequel se fait la transmission du sens du signe. Ce système est le plus souvent constitué, ou du moins actualisé, par le contexte, la situation concrète de l'utilisation du signe. Dans cette mesure, l'affirmation formulée au début de ce paragraphe est correcte, mais elle ne contribue guère à faire avancer l'analyse.

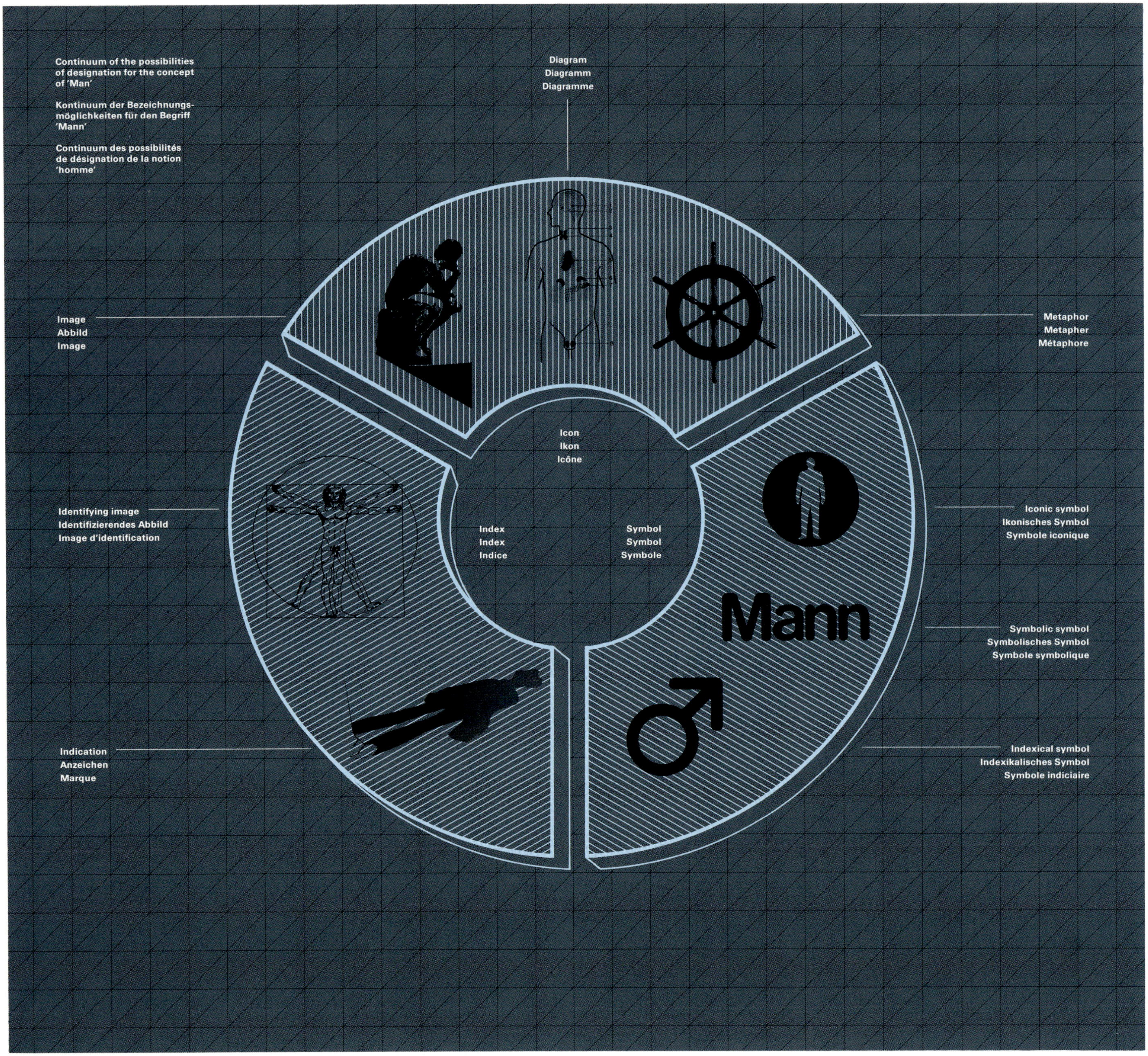
Continuum of the possibilities of designation for the concept of 'Man'
Kontinuum der Bezeichnungsmöglichkeiten für den Begriff 'Mann'
Continuum des possibilités de désignation de la notion 'homme'
Diagram
Diagramm
Diagramme
Image
Abbild
Image
Metaphor
Metapher
Métaphore
Icon
Ikon
Icône
Identifying image
Identifizierendes Abbild
Image d'identification
Index
Index
Indice
Symbol
Symbol
Symbole
Iconic symbol
Ikonisches Symbol
Symbole iconique
Mann
Symbolic symbol
Symbolisches Symbol
Symbole symbolique
Indication
Anzeichen
Marque
Indexical symbol
Indexikalisches Symbol
Symbole indiciaire

3.3.2. What has design to do with art?

The triadic sign relationship distinguishes between three different basic forms of conveyance of meaning, which are also derived from the relation with medium, object and interpretant. In the first case, the system of conveying meaning remains solely related to the medium. Here the meaning can only be fundamentally open, that is to say that there are no concrete objects which could thereby be clearly identified. Meanings of this kind are called *connotations:* these are resonances or associated meanings which can only be grasped emotionally. Connotations dominate in the field of art, but they also play an important part in advertising, which cannot manage without the emotional aspects of such an imparting of meaning. It may well be that the recipient of the sign is not usually conscious of its connotations, but their communicative effect can be empirically checked. Psychologists have developed a whole range of measuring methods for the associations through which meaning is often expressed. Recently there have been further developments of psychophysiological methods by which the strength of the emotional appeal can be determined. By these means we obtain not only the possibility of verifying hypotheses derived from semiotic theory, but also a way of monitoring the results of the creative process in this respect.

3.3.3. The mediation of concrete reality

In contrast to the emotional effect of connotation, *denotation* is related to communicative performance, the correct conveyance of information in practice. In denotative systems of imparting meaning, the relation to the object is central. Here, objects are treated as concrete reality, about which there is general agreement. Such a way of apprehending meaning

3.3.2. Was hat Design mit Kunst zu tun?

Die triadische Zeichenrelation unterscheidet zwischen drei verschiedenen Grundformen der Bedeutungsvermittlung, die ebenfalls wieder aus der Beziehung zu Mittel, Objekt und Interpretant abgeleitet werden. Im ersten Fall bleibt das System der Bedeutungsvermittlung rein auf die Mittel bezogen. Dabei kann die Bedeutung grundsätzlich nur offen sein, es gibt dann nämlich keine konkreten Objekte, die eindeutig identifiziert werden könnten. Bedeutungen dieser Art werden als *Konnotationen* bezeichnet; es sind mitschwingende Bedeutungen, Nebenbedeutungen, die lediglich gefühlsmässig erfasst werden können. Konnotationen dominieren im Bereich der Kunst, sie spielen aber auch für die Werbung eine grosse Rolle, da diese auf die emotionalen Aspekte einer solchen Bedeutungsvermittlung nicht verzichten kann. Konnotationen werden dem Zeichenempfänger zwar meistens nicht bewusst, dennoch ist die kommunikative Wirkung empirisch überprüfbar. Nebenbedeutungen äussern sich oft in Assoziationen, für die die Psychologie eine ganze Reihe von Messinstrumenten entwickelt hat. Gerade in der letzten Zeit wurden psychophysiologische Methoden weiterentwickelt, mit denen man die Stärke der emotionalen Ansprache bestimmen kann. Damit ist nicht nur die Möglichkeit gegeben, Hypothesen, die man aus der semiotischen Theorie ableiten kann, zu verifizieren, sondern darüber hinaus das Ergebnis des kreativen Prozesses auch in dieser Hinsicht empirisch zu überprüfen.

3.3.3. Die Vermittlung konkreter Realität

Im Gegensatz zur emotionalen Wirkung der Konnotation bezieht sich die *Denotation* auf die kommunikative Leistung, die sachlich richtige Vermittlung der Information. In denotativen Systemen der Bedeutungsvermittlung steht der Bezug auf das Objekt im Mittelpunkt. Objekte werden hier als konkrete Realität behandelt, über die allgemeine Übereinstimmung besteht. Eine solche Auffassung der

3.3.2. Le design et l'art: qu'ont-ils en commun?

La relation triadique du signe distingue trois formes fondamentales de la transmission du sens qui sont, elles aussi, dérivées de la relation au moyen, à l'objet et à l'interprétant. Dans le premier cas, le système de la transmission du sens reste purement rattaché aux moyens. Le sens ne peut alors qu'être ouvert, il n'existe en effet pas d'objets concrets qui pourraient être identifiés de façon univoque. Les sens de ce type sont appelés *connotations;* il s'agit de sens connexes qui ne peuvent être perçus qu'au niveau affectif. Les connotations dominent dans le domaine de l'art, mais elles jouent aussi un rôle dans la publicité, car cette dernière ne peut se passer des aspects affectifs d'une telle transmission du sens. Si le récepteur des signes n'est généralement pas conscient des connotations, il reste que le rôle qu'elles jouent dans la communication peut être démontré de façon empirique. Les connotations s'expriment souvent dans des associations pour l'étude desquelles la psychologie a développé un ensemble d'instruments de mesure. On a récemment perfectionné des méthodes psychophysiologiques qui permettent d'évaluer la force de la composante émotionnelle de la communication. On dispose ainsi non seulement de la possibilité de vérifier des hypothèses dérivées de la théorie sémiotique, mais aussi d'obtenir une confirmation empirique de l'impact du processus créatif à cet égard.

3.3.3. La transmission de la réalité concrète

A la différence de l'effet affectif de la connotation, la *dénotation* se rapporte à l'accomplissement de la communication, à la transmission neutre et correcte de l'information. Dans les systèmes dénotatifs de transmission du sens, la relation à l'objet constitue le point essentiel. Les objets sont traités ici comme la réalité concrète faisant l'unanimité générale. Cette conception du sens est caractéristique de

Ronald and Raul Shakespear	D	130, 132, 134
James Berte	D	131
Carlos A, Mendéz Mosquela, Gui Bonsiepe	D	133
Caritas		135
Rotes Kreuz		136
Schweizer Flagge		137
Karl Gerstner	D	138
Michael Schirner	D	139
GGK	A	
August Kehl	Ph	140

Precise conveyance of meaning is based on the definition of meanings within the framework of closed systems. The pictograms shown below represent 5 different systems, from hospitals to supermarkets. They apply to generality and must be self-explanatory. Symbolic meanings must be learned. This is shown by the simple cross-sign, which at the same time stands as Christian, humanitarian, mathematical and national sign and needs certain graphic constants in order to represent an airline.

Präzise Bedeutungsvermittlung beruht auf der Definition von Bedeutungen im Rahmen geschlossener Systeme. Die nachfolgend aufgeführten Piktogramme repräsentieren 5 verschiedene Systeme, das heisst, sie stehen für Krankenhäuser bis hin zu Supermärkten. Sie wenden sich an die Allgemeinheit und müssen das Merkmal der Selbsterklärung haben. Symbolische Bedeutungen müssen gelernt werden. Dies zeigt schon das einfache Kreuzzeichen, das einmal als christliches, humanitäres, mathematisches, nationales Zeichen steht und bestimmter grafischer Konstanten bedarf, um auch eine Fluggesellschaft zu repräsentieren.

Une transmission précise du sens se fonde sur la définition de significations dans le cadre de systèmes fermés. Les pictogrammes ci-après représentent 5 systèmes différents, c'est-à-dire que leur utilisation va d'hôpitaux à des supermarchés. Ils s'adressent à un public général et doivent avoir pour caractéristique une grande clarté. Les sens symboliques doivent être appris. C'est ce que montre déjà la simple croix, qui est signe chrétien, humanitaire, mathématique, national, et nécessite certaines constantes graphiques pour représenter aussi une compagnie aérienne.

130/131/132/133/134

135

136

137

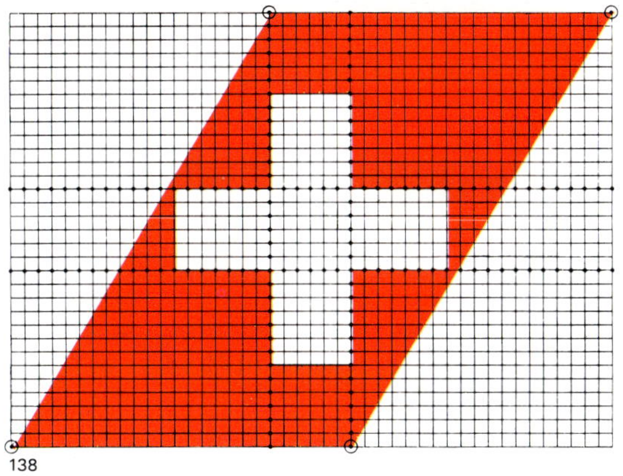

138

139

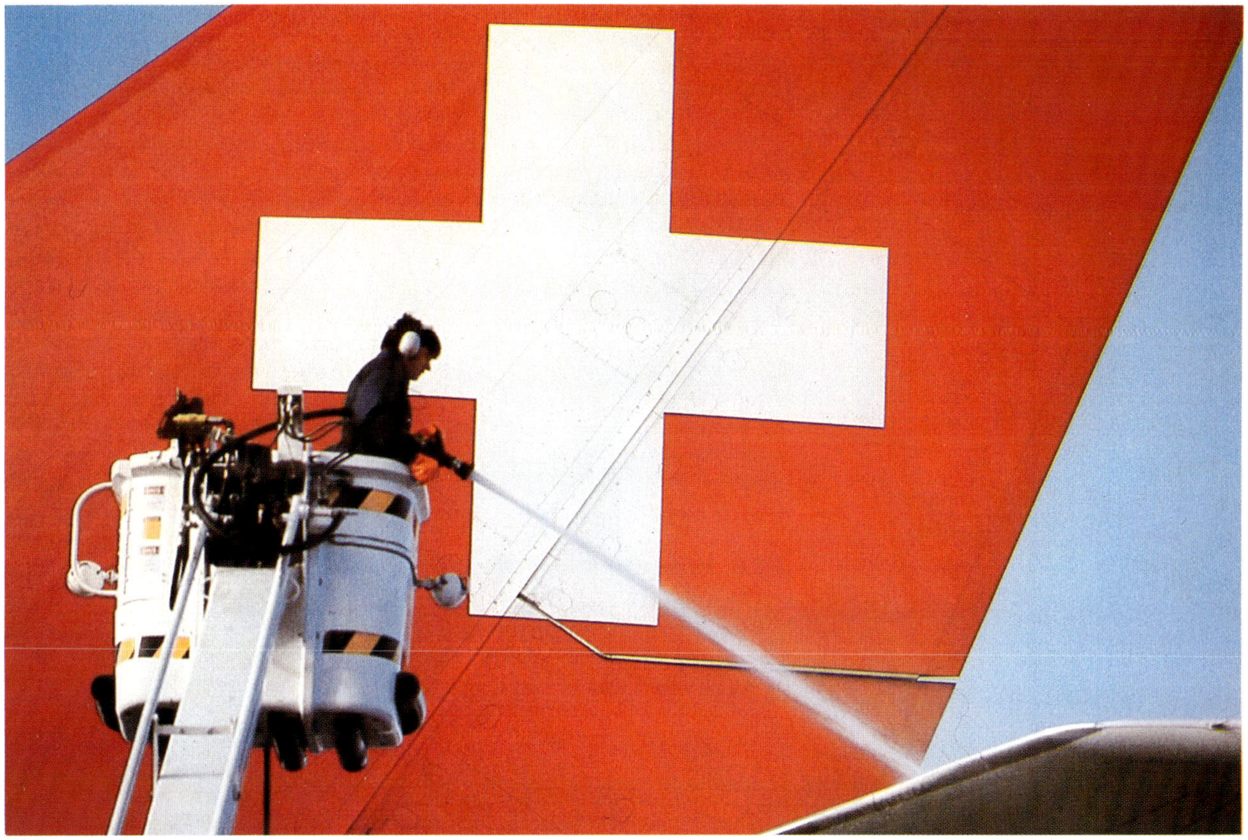

140

Masaru Katsumi	AD	141
Yusaku Kamekura	D	
Don Weller	D	142, 143
Robert Wages	AD	144
Mike Quon Design	D	145
Hirata Akira	AD	146
Mori Hiroshi / Hiroya Ryuji	D	
studios Eskind Waddell	D	147
Takenobu Igarashi	D	148
Pentagram	D	149, 150

The logos shown on the left document an increasing degree of abstraction within the development of the sign. Whereas in the past it was still possible to characterize a communicator and to give information about his products or functions, this is becoming more and more difficult today. The first row of the signs shown here begins with logos, whose purely iconic effect is associated in the rest of the series with symbolic characteristics. If the first logo in the second row can still designate an object, this aim is renounced in the rest of the series in favour of a greater originality. The existing tide of signs is supplemented by others which, in their symbolism, stand for other cultural areas. With a view to stronger differentiation, new ways must be sought for the development of signs.

Die rechts abgebildeten Signete dokumentieren einen zunehmenden Abstraktionsgrad innerhalb der Zeichenentwicklung. War es in der Vergangenheit noch möglich, einen Kommunikator zu kennzeichnen und über seine Produkte oder Aufgaben zu informieren, so wird das heute immer schwieriger. Die erste Reihe der hier abgebildeten Zeichen beginnt mit Signeten, deren rein ikonische Ausprägung im weiteren Verlauf mit symbolischen Eigenschaften verknüpft wird. Kann das erste Signet der zweiten Reihe zwar noch ein Objekt bezeichnen, so wird im weiteren Verlauf zugunsten einer grösseren Originalität darauf verzichtet. Zu der schon bestehenden Zeichenflut kommen Zeichen, die in ihrer Symbolik für andere Kulturkreise stehen. Angesichts erschwerter Differenzierungen muss nach neuen Wegen bei der Zeichenentwicklung gesucht werden.

Les logos reproduits à droite attestent d'un degré d'abstraction croissant dans le développement du signe. S'il était encore possible dans le passé de caractériser un communicateur et d'informer quant à ses produits ou ses fonctions, cela devient de plus en plus difficile aujourd'hui. La première rangée des signes présentés ici commence avec des logos dont l'expression purement iconique est ensuite combinée à des caractéristiques symboliques. Si le premier logo de la deuxième rangée peut encore désigner un objet, l'on y renonce par la suite au profit d'une plus grande originalité. Au déluge de signes que nous connaissons déjà viennent s'ajouter des signes dont la symbolique appartient à des cultures différentes. La différenciation devenant plus difficile, il est nécessaire de chercher de nouvelles voies dans le développement des signes.

is characteristic of all natural languages, which may be regarded as "half-open" systems. While they certainly have relatively fixed rules, which ensure understanding, they are also capable of extension from their own resources. Advertising, seen as a whole, is unequivocally a denotative system. In common with everyday language, its statements must be generally understood and its objects presented as having a real existence.

3.3.4. How can meaning be conveyed precisely?

The third kind of conveyance of meaning may be termed *precision.* The precise imparting of meaning is based on the definition of meanings within a closed system. In this case there must not be any contradictions in the relationship of the elements to one another. In consequence, these meanings are valid only within the system concerned and are entirely dependent on the interpretant. This principle has already been described as an essential precondition of science; but technology, too, must make use of this precision.

As already mentioned, a traffic sign, removed from its own system, can be understood in a denotative way within a new environment and may achieve a special effect through the resulting combination of familiarity and an unexpected appearance in a different context. Precise systems can, in fact, be used in a purely connotative way. If, for example, I make use of a complex technical drawing in an advertising statement, it is true that the drawing is not intrinsically understood, but simply owing to the medium in which it is used it connotes a scientific approach, exactness and high credibility.

3.3.5. How different kinds of sign operate

We have undertaken wide-ranging experiments to investigate the kinds of information that can be conveyed

Bedeutung ist charakteristisch für alle natürlichen Sprachen, die als halboffene Systeme anzusehen sind. Sie besitzen zwar relativ feste Regeln, die die Verständigung sichern, doch sie sind aus sich selbst heraus erweiterungsfähig. Werbung ist in ihrer Gesamtheit gesehen eindeutig ein denotatives System. Wie die Umgangssprache muss sie allgemeinverständliche Aussagen machen und ihre Objekte als real existent vorstellen.

3.3.4. Wie präzise lässt sich Bedeutung vermitteln?

Die dritte Art der Bedeutungsvermittlung kann als *Präzision* bezeichnet werden. Präzise Bedeutungsvermittlung beruht auf der Definition von Bedeutungen im Rahmen geschlossener Systeme; dabei dürfen in der Beziehung der Elemente untereinander keine Widersprüche auftreten. Konsequenterweise haben diese Bedeutungen auch nur innerhalb der Systeme Gültigkeit, sie sind also vollkommen vom Interpretanten abhängig. Dieses Prinzip wurde bereits als eine wesentliche Voraussetzung der Wissenschaft beschrieben; aber auch die Technik muss sich dieser Präzision bedienen.

Wie bereits erwähnt, kann ein Verkehrszeichen, herausgenommen aus diesem System, in einem neuen Umfeld denotativ verstanden werden und gerade durch die Kombination von Vertrautheit und unerwartetem Auftreten eine besondere Wirkung erzielen. Präzise Systeme können sogar rein konnotativ eingesetzt werden. Wenn ich zum Beispiel eine komplizierte technische Zeichnung in einer Werbeaussage verwende, so wird die Zeichnung zwar inhaltlich nicht verstanden, aber allein durch die verwendeten Mittel konnotiert sie Wissenschaftlichkeit, Exaktheit und hohe Glaubwürdigkeit.

3.3.5. Wie unterschiedliche Zeichenarten auf den Betrachter wirken

Am Beispiel von diversen Werbemitteln wurde von uns in umfangreichen Experimenten untersucht, welche Informationen durch die bildliche

toutes les langues naturelles, qui sont à considérer comme des systèmes à demi ouverts. Ils possèdent certes des règles relativement strictes qui assurent la compréhension, mais sont capables de s'élargir par eux-mêmes. Considérée dans son ensemble, la publicité est sans conteste un système dénotatif. Comme le parler d'usage, elle doit produire des énoncés accessibles à tous et présenter ses objets comme existant réellement.

3.3.4. Avec quelle précision le sens peut-il être transmis?

On nommera *précision* le troisième type de transmission du sens. Une transmission précise du sens est fondée sur la définition de sens dans le cadre de systèmes fermés. Il ne doit pas y avoir de contradictions dans la relation des éléments entre eux. En conséquence, ces sens ne sont valables que dans les systèmes: ils sont entièrement dépendants de l'interprétant. Nous avons déjà décrit ce principe comme étant une condition préalable essentielle à la science; la technique elle aussi doit faire usage de cette précision.

Comme nous l'avons déjà dit, un panneau de signalisation placé hors de son système peut être compris de façon dénotative dans un nouveau contexte et exercer un impact particulier par la combinaison même de son aspect familier et de son emplacement inattendu. On peut même utiliser de manière purement connotative des systèmes précis. Par exemple, si j'utilise un schéma technique compliqué dans une annonce publicitaire, son contenu ne sera pas compris, mais la connotation qu'il produira sera celle du caractère scientifique, de l'exactitude et d'une grande crédibilité – et ce uniquement en raison des moyens utilisés.

3.3.5. L'impact des différents types de signes

Nous avons mené des expériences approfondies sur différents supports publicitaires pour déterminer quelles informations peuvent être transmises

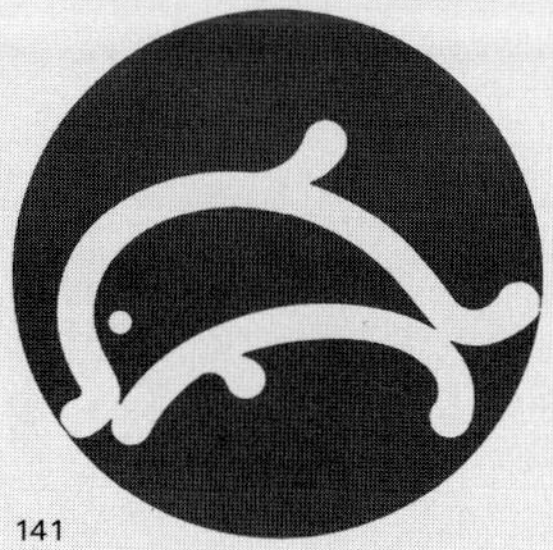
141

142

143

144

145

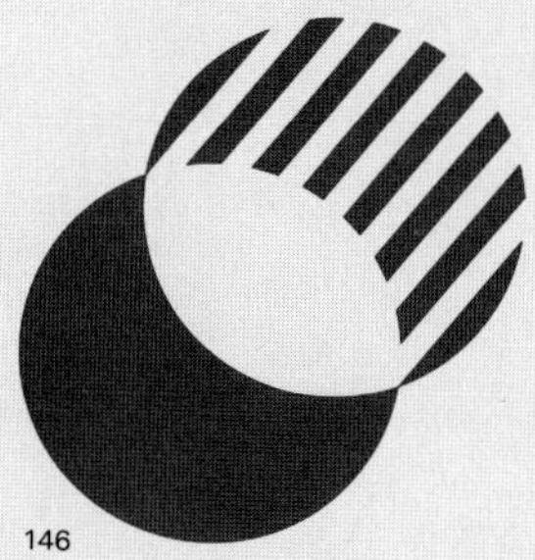
146

147

148

149

150

151

Stankowski / Duschek	D	151, 152
Walter Landor	D	153–155
GGK	A	156
Jan Michael / Ulrich Fuchs	Ph	

The development of logos must be thought out anew. The various future possibilities, which should be unlimited for a good logo, will make new demands in the future. The signs for the Frankfurt Fair or the Berchtesgaden Olympiad show perspectives of a differentiation, although they do not match the criteria of classical Gestalt theory.

Die Entwicklung von Signeten muss neu überdacht werden. Die verschiedenen zukünftigen Einsatzmöglichkeiten, die für ein gutes Signet unbegrenzt sein sollten, stellen in Zukunft neue Anforderungen. Die Zeichen für Messe Frankfurt oder Olympiade Berchtesgaden zeigen Perspektiven einer Differenzierung. Obwohl sie nicht den Kriterien der klassischen Gestalttheorie entsprechen.

Il convient de repenser le développement des logos. Les possibilités futures d'utilisation, qui devraient être illimitées pour un bon logo, vont poser de nouvelles exigences. Les signes pour la foire de Francfort ou les Jeux olympiques de Berchtesgaden montrent des perspectives de différenciation, même s'ils ne correspondent pas aux critères de la gestalttheorie classique.

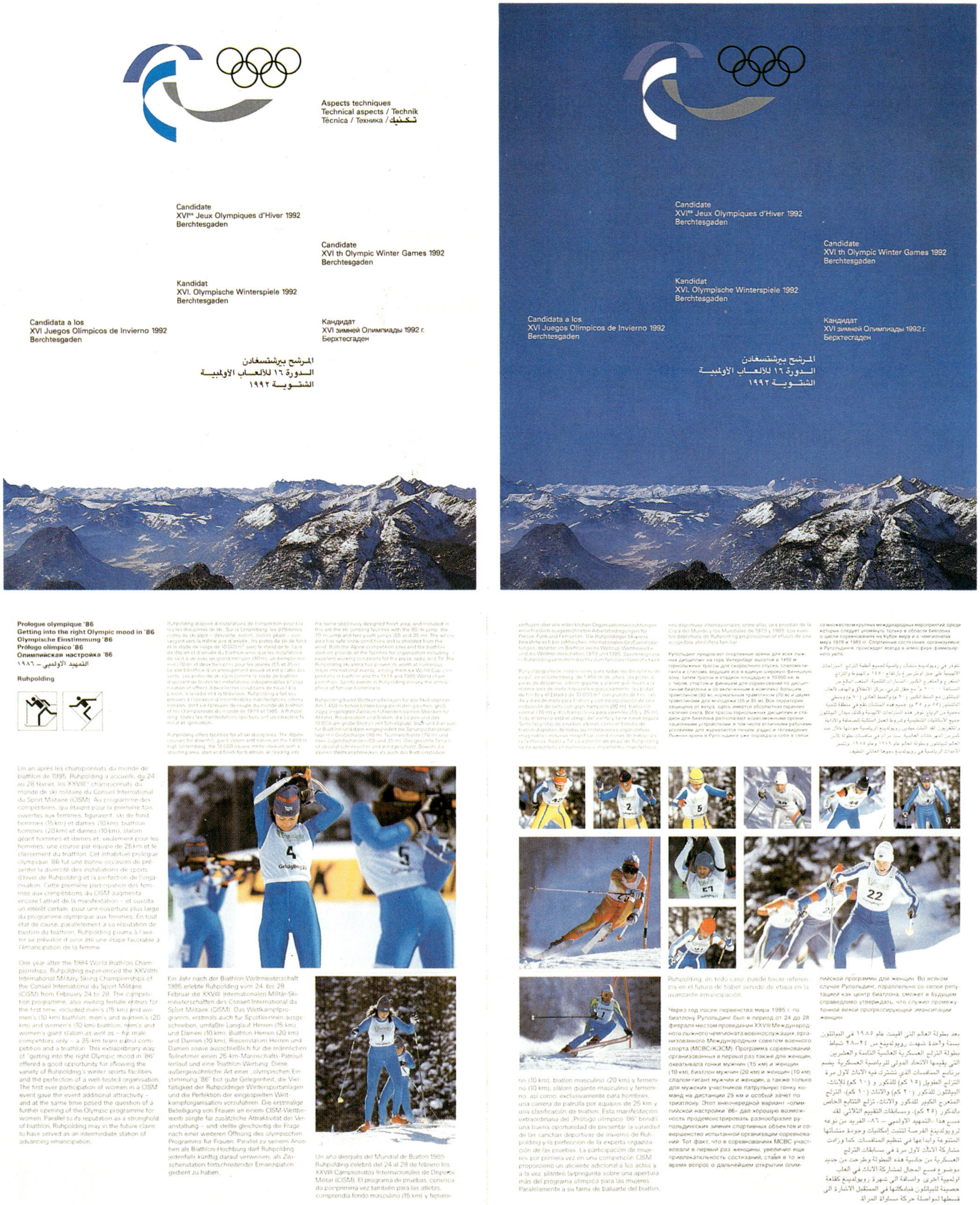

152

153

Dieter H. Hilbig	D	157
Craig Thompson	AD	158
Yves Simard	D	159
Aubertel Olinen	D	160
Andrew Nelson / Darrell Lomas	AD	161
Charles Coppock	D	
Pentagram	D	162
Woddy Pirtle	D	163

154

155

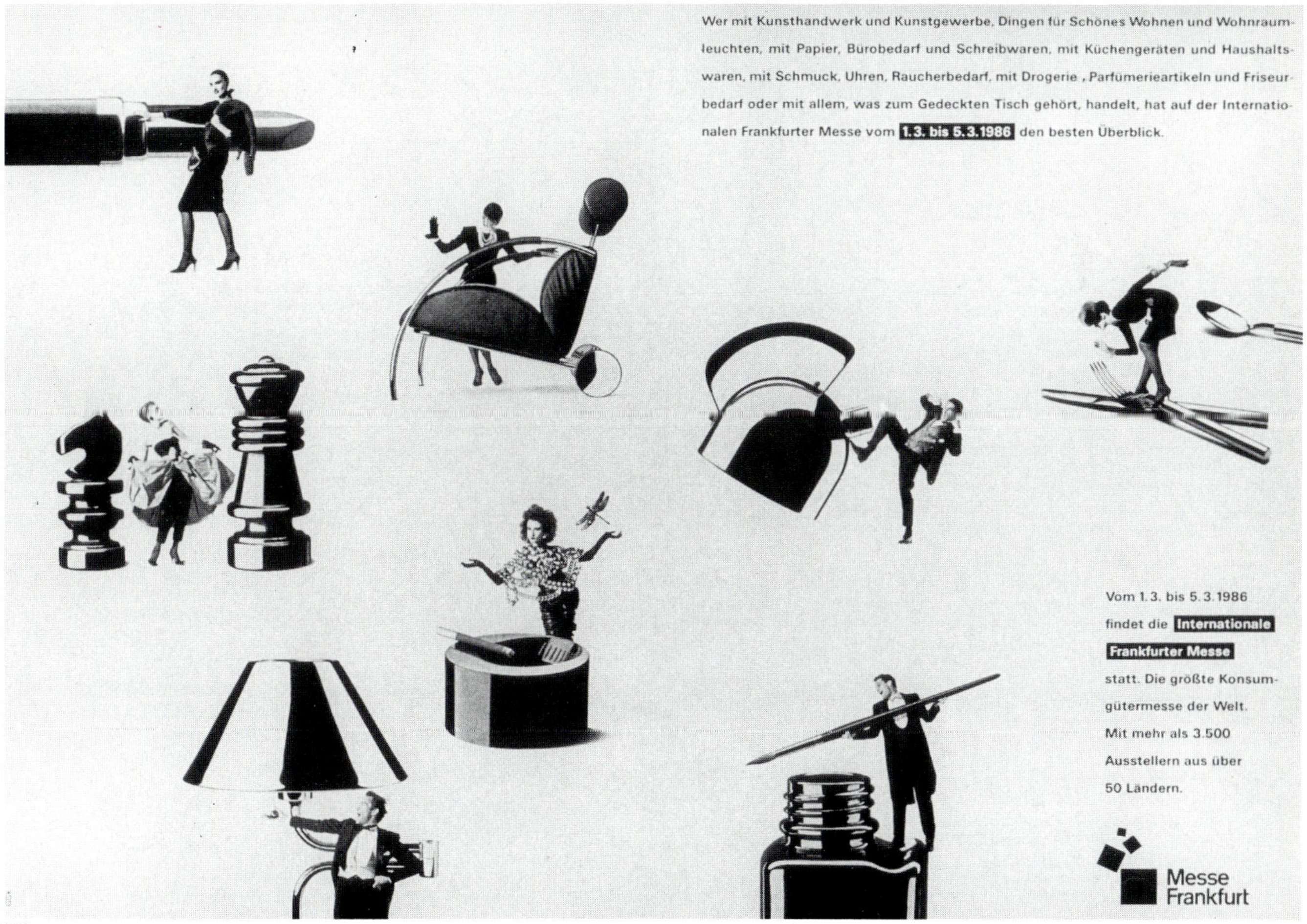

156

A closed system familiar to all is the organization of traffic signs. The form of these warning, request and instruction panels has been standardized. By now, the system has reached such a high degree of complexity that attempts are continually being made to reduce the number of signs. In the future our cars will be equipped with electronic piloting devices and new, simplified graphic information forms the basis of the "auto-pilot" scheme.
At the right we see how conventional signs, taken from the system, achieve special effectiveness.

Ein uns allen vertrautes geschlossenes System bildet die Strassenverkehrsordnung. Die Form dieser Verbots-, Gebots- und Hinweisschilder ist genormt. Dieses System hat in der Zwischenzeit einen so hohen Komplexitätsgrad erreicht, dass immer wieder Versuche gemacht werden, die Zeichen zu reduzieren. In Zukunft werden unsere Autos mit elektronischen Lotsen ausgestattet sein, und neue vereinfachte grafische Hinweise bilden die Grundlage des Travel-Pilots. Die rechte Seite zeigt, wie konventionelle Zeichen – herausgenommen aus dem System – eine besondere Wirkung erzielen.

Le code de la route est un système fermé connu de tous. La forme de ces panneaux d'indications, de prescriptions et d'interdictions est standardisée. Avec le temps, ce système a atteint un tel degré de complexité que l'on essaie fréquemment de réduire le nombre de signes. A l'avenir, nos voitures seront, équipées de pilotes automatiques, et des indications graphiques nouvelles, simplifiées, constitueront la base du fonctionnement du travel-pilot.
La page de droite montre comment des signes conventionnels – sortis de leur système – produisent un effet particulier.

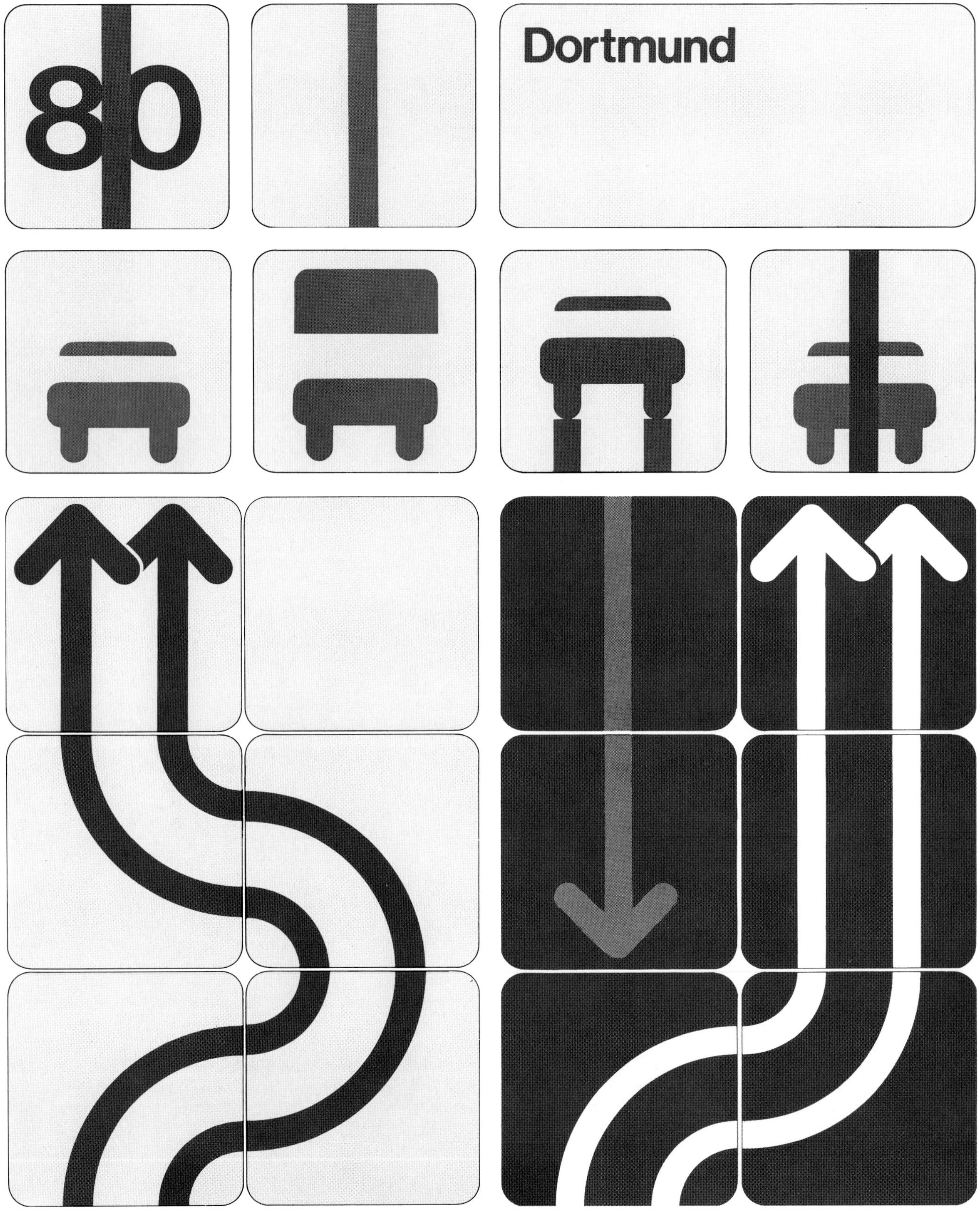

157

158

159

160

161

162

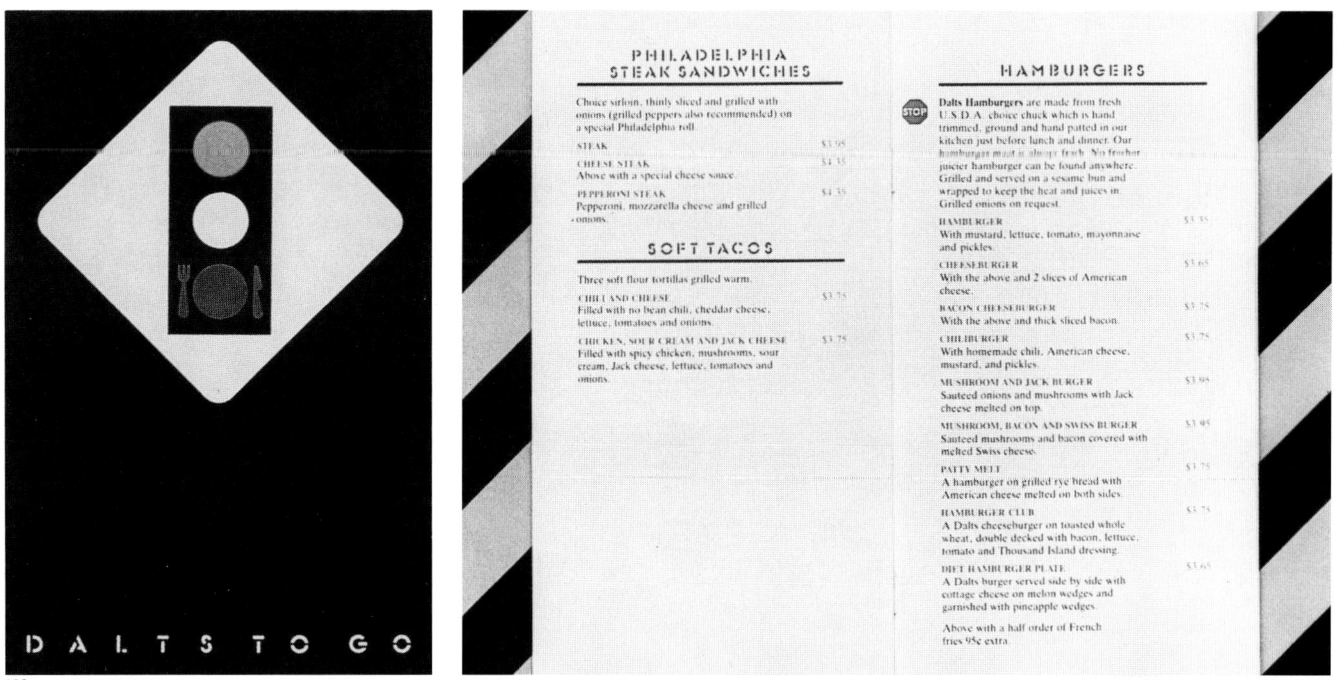

163

Following discussion of precise information, we are here concerned with another kind of information conveyance. Denotative information is characteristic of advertising. It must make generally understandable statements and present its objects as existing in reality. This kind of sign is generally used in a very naive way. It is taken for granted that a sign designates an object and that the target audience associates the same idea with it. The examples opposite, on the other hand, convey purely connotative information. They offer the greatest freedom of interpretation, comparably with abstract painting. In advertising, they appeal to our feelings.

Nach der Erörterung präziser Information handelt es sich hier um eine andere Art der Bedeutungsvermittlung. Denotative Information ist ein Kennzeichen der Werbung. Sie muss allgemein verständliche Aussagen machen und ihre Objekte als realexistent vorstellen. Der Gebrauch dieser Zeichenart erfolgt meist sehr naiv. Man nimmt als selbstverständlich an, dass ein Zeichen einen Gegenstand bezeichnet und dass die Zielgruppe die gleiche Vorstellung damit verbindet. Die gegenüberliegenden Beispiele hingegen vermitteln rein konnotative Informationen. Sie bieten die grösste Freiheit der Interpretation, die mit der abstrakten Malerei verglichen werden kann. In der Werbung appellieren sie an unsere Gefühle.

Après avoir abordé l'information précise, nous passons ici à un autre type de transmission du sens. L'information dénotative est une caractéristique de la publicité. Elle doit produire des énoncés compréhensibles de tous et doit présenter ses objets comme existant réellement. L'utilisation de ce type de signe est le plus souvent très naïve. L'on considère comme évident qu'un signe désigne un objet et que le groupe-cible y associe la même idée. Les exemples opposés, en revanche, transmettent des informations purement connotatives. Ils offrent la plus grande liberté d'interprétation, de façon comparable à la peinture abstraite. Dans la publicité, ils font appel à nos émotions.

164

165

166

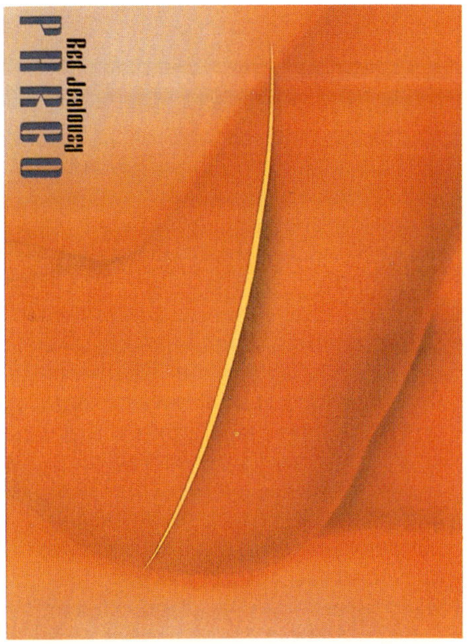

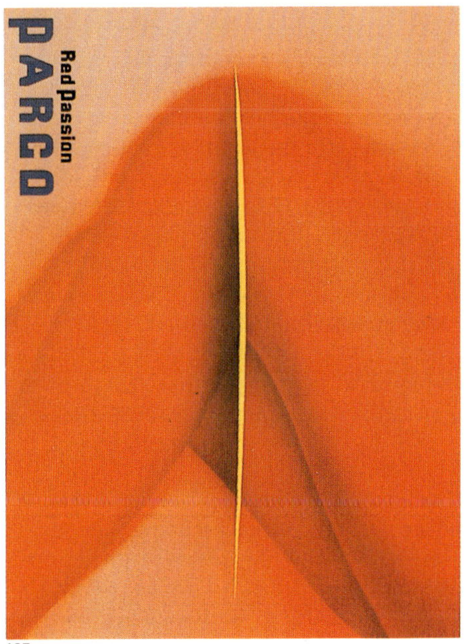

167

Peter Knaup	Ph	164
Bibiana Surma	AD	
Scholz & Friends	A	
GGK	D	165, 166
Masatoshi Toda	AD	167
Mamoru Suzuki	D	
Hans Hansen	Ph	168

168

Icon · Ikon · Icône

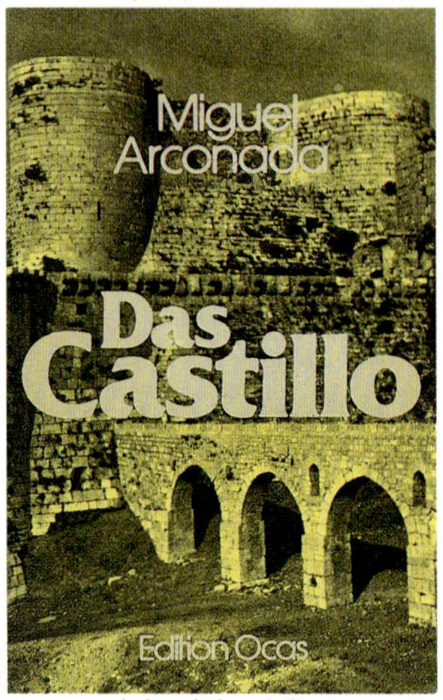

Index · Index · Indice

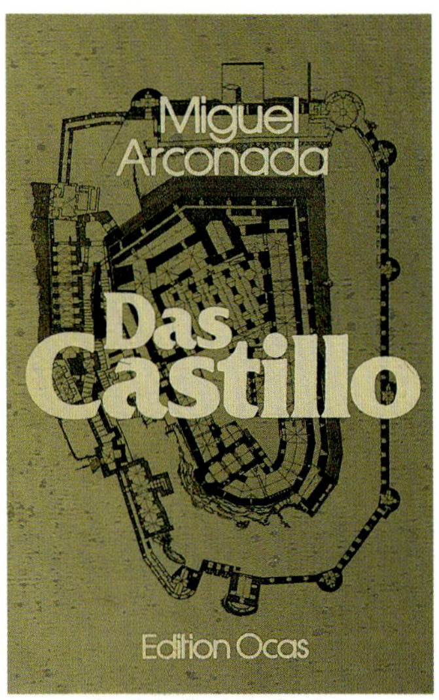

Symbol · Symbol · Symbole

through figurative or pictorial representation, using various forms of advertising as examples. We were not concerned with the specific content of the examples but with the ways in which they conveyed meaning. Different kinds of signs are found to convey different kinds of information, the latter depending mainly on the system of mediation used.

What does connotative information impart? Hypothetically speaking, connotative information represents only possibilities. The relation to real objects, persons or situations can, however, show widely differing degrees of freedom. The greatest freedom of interpretation is offered by abstract paintings, which give effect to feelings, resonances and associations. In contrast, the iconically designed figurative statements used in the experiment had relatively concrete relations to their objects, and yet they were clearly distinguishable from indexical statements. At its clearest, iconic design gives expression to the entertaining character of the content of a statement. Appraisal of imaginative or romantic contents is also associated solely with this design principle. Just like the concept of "personal feelings", these two qualities are excluded from both Index and Symbol. The iconic principle stands in the most divisive contrast with scientific method, and its rejection of objectivity also belongs in this connection.

These empirical results are in perfect harmony with the theoretical differentiation between connotation, denotation and precision. While connotation is predominantly emotional, producing an emotive relationship to the object signified, the relationship in denotation is primarily objective, though always emotionally modified to some extent through the accompanying connotations. Precision, on the other hand, is aimed directly at the exclusion of emotional elements from information. Scientific exactness can be achieved only through sober objectivity.

What does denotative information convey? Denotation is the typical way

Gestaltung vermittelt werden können. Dabei ging es nicht um konkrete Bildinhalte, sondern um die Art und Weise, wie Bilder Bedeutung vermitteln. Danach vermitteln verschiedene Zeichenarten unterschiedliche Arten der Information, wobei die Art der Information hauptsächlich vom System der Bedeutungsvermittlung abhängt.

Was vermittelt konnotative Information? Hypothetisch stellen konnotative Informationen lediglich Möglichkeiten dar. Der Bezug auf reale Objekte, Personen oder Situationen kann jedoch sehr unterschiedliche Grade der Freiheit aufweisen. Die grösste Freiheit der Interpretation bieten abstrakte Gemälde, die Gefühle, Klänge und Assoziationen wirken lassen. Demgegenüber hatten die für das Experiment ikonisch gestalteten Bildaussagen doch relativ konkrete Objektbezüge, dennoch hoben sie sich deutlich von den indexikalischen Aussagen ab. Am klarsten bringt die ikonische Gestaltung den unterhaltsamen Charakter eines Inhalts zum Ausdruck. Aber auch die Einschätzung als phantasievoll und romantisch wird nur mit diesem Gestaltungsprinzip verbunden. Ebenso wie der Begriff «gefühlvoll» werden diese beiden Eigenschaften sowohl für den Index wie für das Symbol abgelehnt. Im krassesten Widerspruch steht das ikonische Prinzip zur Wissenschaftlichkeit, wobei die Ablehnung der Sachlichkeit ebenfalls in diesen Zusammenhang hineingehört. Diese empirischen Ergebnisse stehen ganz im Einklang mit der theoretischen Differenzierung von Konnotation, Denotation und Präzision. Während die Konnotation dominant emotional ist, also einen gefühlsmässigen Bezug zum so bezeichneten Objekt herstellt, ist dieser Bezug in der Denotation primär sachlich, wird jedoch durch begleitende Konnotationen immer irgendwie emotional modifiziert. Präzision dagegen zielt gerade auf die Ausschaltung emotionaler Momente der Information, nur nüchterne Sachlichkeit kann wissenschaftliche Genauigkeit hervorbringen.

Was vermittelt die denotative Information? Denotation ist die typische

par la création visuelle. Il ne s'agissait pas d'étudier des contenus d'images concrets, mais la façon dont les images transmettent le sens. Nous sommes arrivés à la conclusion que différents types de signes transmettent différents types d'information. Notons que le type d'information dépend principalement du système de transmission du sens.

L'information connotative: que transmet-elle? Par hypothèse, les informations connotatives ne représentent que des possibilités. Cependant, le rapport aux objets, personnes ou situations réels peut présenter des degrés de liberté très variables. Les tableaux abstraits, qui font appel aux émotions, aux sons et aux associations, laissent la plus grande liberté d'interprétation. Par contre, les énoncés figuratifs conçus iconiquement pour l'expérience avaient des rapports relativement concrets aux objets, même s'ils se démarquaient clairement des énoncés indiciaires. C'est la création iconique qui exprime le plus clairement le caractère divertissant d'un contenu. En outre, l'appréciation «imaginatif et romantique» ne s'applique qu'à ce principe de création. Tout comme la notion «d'affectif», ces deux caractéristiques sont rejetées pour l'indice et le symbole. Le principe iconique est le plus nettement opposé au caractère scientifique. Il est aussi celui à propos duquel on rejette la notion d'objectivité.

Ces résultats empiriques sont en parfaite harmonie avec la différenciation théorique entre connotation, dénotation et précision. Alors que la connotation est avant tout affective, qu'elle crée une relation émotionnelle avec l'objet désigné, cette relation est principalement objective dans la dénotation, même si des connotations l'accompagnent toujours et la modifient de façon affective. En revanche, la précision vise à exclure les facteurs affectifs de l'information: seule l'objectivité peut engendrer la précision scientifique.

Que transmet l'information dénotative? La dénotation est le mode de

Icon · Ikon · Icône

Index · Index · Indice

Symbol · Symbol · Symbole

of imparting meaning in everyday language. Denotative signs are generally used in a very naive way, in that it is assumed as obvious that a term, or more generally speaking a sign, signifies a specific object, and that a partner in communication will associate the same idea with the same sign. The word "naive" should not be understood negatively in this context, but only as a description of the unreflective character of such a use of signs. One does not give any thought to the meaning of individual signs as their meanings appear to be inborn, even when they are, of course, the result of a process of education. It is precisely this attitude which governs the use of everyday language, and it is just in this way that indexical images are understood. It is taken for granted that they refer to a present reality. Why should one doubt this assumption in the case of a photograph, either, when it can come into being only if its object actually exists? The same applies, in fact, to painted indices such as portraits, and to drawings of objects of interest. Since indexical signs are related to reality, they are instructive and useful but have little to do with imagination or feelings. On the other hand, neither do they have anything intrinsically scientific about them, since they simply designate without analyzing.

Even though only the central tendencies are here described, and although photographs can also supply analyses and it is quite possible to take photographs in an imaginative way, it is never possible to eliminate the denotative character of this form of representation entirely.

Some of the photos used in our experiment also had strong iconic qualities, but the iconic content of their information hardly showed through. Particularly in view of the ever wider use of photography as an apparently easy design element to manipulate, credited with universal applicability, it would be advisable to return to the practice of giving more weight to

Art der Bedeutungsvermittlung für die Umgangssprache. Der Gebrauch denotativer Zeichen erfolgt meist sehr naiv, das heisst, man nimmt als selbstverständlich an, dass ein Begriff oder allgemeiner ein Zeichen einen bestimmten Gegenstand bezeichnet und dass ein Kommunikationspartner die gleiche Vorstellung damit verbindet. «Naiv» ist hier keineswegs als negativ wertend zu verstehen, sondern kennzeichnet nur den unreflektierten Charakter eines solchen Zeichengebrauchs. Man macht sich keine Gedanken über die Bedeutung einzelner Zeichen, diese erscheint wie angeboren, auch wenn sie natürlich das Ergebnis eines Erziehungsprozesses ist. Genau diese Haltung beherrscht die alltägliche Umgangssprache. Und genauso werden auch indexikalische Bilder verstanden. Man nimmt als selbstverständlich an, dass sie sich auf eine vorhandene Wirklichkeit beziehen. Warum sollte man dies auch bei einer Fotografie in Zweifel ziehen? – sie kann ja nur entstehen, wenn der Gegenstand tatsächlich existiert. Das gilt aber auch für gemalte Indices wie Porträts oder für gezeichnete Sehenswürdigkeiten. Da sich indexikalische Zeichen auf die Wirklichkeit beziehen, sind sie lehrreich und nützlich, haben aber wenig mit Phantasie und Gefühl zu tun. Anderseits haben sie aber auch nichts Wissenschaftliches an sich, sie analysieren nicht, sie zeigen einfach.

Auch wenn hier nur die zentrale Tendenz beschrieben wurde und wenn Fotografien auch Analysen liefern und wenn man auch phantasievoll fotografieren kann: man wird den denotativen Charakter dieser Darstellungsform niemals ganz eliminieren können.

Auch die in unserem Experiment verwendeten Fotografien hatten teilweise starke ikonische Qualitäten, dennoch schlug das ikonische Moment der Information kaum durch. Gerade angesichts der immer stärkeren Verbreitung der Fotografie als scheinbar leicht zu handhabendes Element der Gestaltung, dem man häufig eine universale Verwendbarkeit nachsagt, sollte man wieder mehr Gewicht auf

transmission du sens typique du parler d'usage. L'utilisation des signes dénotatifs est le plus souvent très naïve, à savoir que l'on considère comme évident qu'un concept, ou plus généralement un signe, désigne un objet donné, et qu'un interlocuteur y associe la même idée. «Naïf» ne doit pas être compris ici péjorativement: il caractérise simplement le caractère non réfléchi de ce type d'utilisation des signes. On ne pense pas au sens des différents signes: il semble inné, même s'il est naturellement le résultat d'un processus éducatif. C'est l'attitude prédominante dans le parler d'usage. Et c'est précisément ainsi que sont comprises les images indiciaires. On considère comme allant de soi qu'elles se réfèrent à une réalité existante. Pourquoi d'ailleurs émettre le moindre doute au sujet d'une photographie? Elle ne peut naître que si l'objet existe réellement. Néanmoins, ceci vaut également pour des indices peints, comme des portraits, ou pour des curiosités dessinées. Les signes indiciaires se référant à la réalité, ils sont pleins d'enseignements et fort utiles, mais ils n'ont pas grand-chose à voir avec l'imagination et le sentiment. D'autre part, ils n'ont rien de scientifique, ils n'analysent pas, ils montrent simplement.

Même si nous n'avons décrit ici que la tendance principale, et si les photographies apportent aussi des analyses, et même si l'on peut aussi photographier avec imagination, on ne pourra jamais éliminer complètement le caractère dénotatif de cette forme de représentation.

Certaines des photographies utilisées dans notre expérience avaient aussi des qualités iconiques marquées; pourtant le facteur iconique de l'information n'a guère percé. En raison de la diffusion croissante de la photographie, considérée comme un élément facile à utiliser pour la création et auquel on prête souvent un usage universel, il conviendrait de redonner de l'importance au dessin et à la

the techniques of drawing and painting, and also to graphics.

What does precise information convey? The precise imparting of information is the main characteristic of scientific systems. In such systems, the individual elements are defined and their meanings established through conventions or laws, which at the same time govern their relationships with other elements. The objective of such definitions is to exclude all ambiguities. Semiotically speaking, this means that all connotations and emotional associations, if not entirely excluded, are declared to be irrelevant. Precise information therefore has no emotional aspects: it is purely objective. The corresponding kind of sign is the Symbol. The fact that, in our experiment, both denotative and even connotative elements of information came into play, is due to the pictorial or figurative nature of the statements examined, despite their symbolic manner of design.

Iconically designed messages, in this case expressed through techniques of painting or drawing, convey emotive information, the content of which is classified as entertaining. Indexical design, in this case in the form of photographs, has the effect of making its content appear close to reality, comprehensible and useful. Design by the symbolic principle has associations of scientific method and objectivity.

In the manipulation of the experimental posters, book jackets and advertisements, the possible breadth of the various principles of design was by no means exhausted. On the contrary, very closely related examples were deliberately chosen in order to show that even slight nuances in the variation of design can be *informatically effective.* By using the science of semiotics as an underlying foundation, such nuances can be precisely controlled, so that the design of items of advertising *can be optimized* on this basis with regard to their effective performance in communication.

Zeichnung und Maltechnik einerseits und die Grafik andererseits legen.

Was vermittelt präzise Information? Präzise Informationsvermittlung ist das Kennzeichen wissenschaftlicher Systeme. In solchen Systemen sind die einzelnen Elemente definiert, ihre Bedeutungen sind durch Konventionen oder Gesetze festgelegt, die gleichzeitig ihre Beziehungen zu anderen Elementen regeln. Ziel solcher Definitionen ist die Ausschaltung aller Bedeutungsunsicherheiten. Semiotisch heisst, dass alle Konnotationen, alle gefühlsmässigen Nebenbedeutungen und Assoziationen wenn auch nicht ausgeschlossen, so doch für irrelevant erklärt werden. Präzise Information hat also keine emotionalen Aspekte, sie ist rein sachlich. Die entsprechende Zeichenart ist das Symbol. Dass jedoch im Experiment bei der symbolischen Gestaltung auch denotative und sogar konnotative Informationsmomente ins Spiel kommen, liegt zum einen daran, dass es sich trotz der symbolischen Gestaltung um Bildaussagen handelt.

Ikonisch gestaltete Botschaften – hier in Mal- und Zeichentechniken realisiert – vermitteln gefühlsmässige Information, der Inhalt wird als unterhaltsam eingestuft. Indexikalische Gestaltung – hier in Form von Fotografien – bewirkt, dass der Inhalt als wirklichkeitsnah, verständlich und nützlich eingeschätzt wird. Gestaltung nach dem symbolischen Prinzip assoziiert Wissenschaftlichkeit und Sachlichkeit.

Bei der Manipulation der experimentellen Plakate, Buchumschläge oder Anzeigen wurde die mögliche Breite der verschiedenen Gestaltungsprinzipien bei weitem nicht ausgeschöpft. Es wurden im Gegenteil bewusst sehr nahe beieinander liegende Beispiele gewählt, um zu zeigen, dass bereits Nuancen in der Variation der Gestaltung *informationswirksam* werden können. Auf der Grundlage der Semiotik sind solche Nuancen exakt steuerbar, so dass man die Gestaltung von Werbemitteln im Hinblick auf ihre Kommunikationsleistung auf dieser Grundlage *optimieren kann.*

technique picturale, d'une part, et à la graphique d'autre part.

Que transmet l'information précise? La transmission précise de l'information est caractéristique des systèmes scientifiques. Dans ces systèmes, les différents éléments sont définis, leurs sens sont fixés par des conventions ou des lois qui à leur tour réglementent leurs relations avec d'autres éléments. L'objectif de ces définitions est d'exclure toutes les incertitudes de sens. Sémiotiquement, cela signifie que toutes les connotations, tous les sens connexes et associations affectives, sans être exclus, sont toutefois considérés comme étant sans importance. Ainsi, l'information précise n'a pas d'aspects affectifs, elle est purement objective. Le type de signe qui lui correspond est le symbole. Si dans notre expérience des facteurs d'information dénotatifs et même connotatifs sont entrés en jeu avec la création symbolique, c'est en partie parce que malgré la création symbolique, il s'agissait d'énoncés sous forme d'images.

Les messages conçus iconiquement – réalisés ici par des techniques de peinture ou de dessin – transmettent une information affective dont le contenu est jugé distrayant. La création indiciaire – ici sous forme de photographies – est considérée comme ayant un contenu proche de la réalité, compréhensible et utile. La création selon le principe symbolique associe le caractère scientifique et l'objectivité.

Lors de la manipulation des affiches, couvertures de livres ou annonces expérimentales (ill.), nous n'avons pas épuisé – tant s'en faut – la palette des différents principes de création. Au contraire, nous avons sciemment choisi des exemples très proches les uns des autres pour montrer que même des variations minimes de la conception peuvent *influer sur l'information.* La sémiotique permet de maîtriser ces nuances avec précision, de sorte qu'il est possible d'*optimiser* la conception des supports publicitaires dans le souci d'une meilleure efficacité de la communication.

171

Kroehl Design D 169, 170
Takenobu Igarashi D 171, 174
Kroehl Design Ph 172
Kurth Wirth D 173

A pineapple is a pineapple . . . and can be firmly established only by an unreflective use of signs. With this simple object it becomes clear that even slight manipulations can be informatively effective. The effect on the viewer changes according to the kind of sign used, whether it be a symbolic design (171/174) in the form of a graphic interpretation, an indexical one (172) in the form of photographs or iconic (173) in the form of painting.

Eine Ananas ist eine Ananas . . . lässt sich nur bei einem unreflektierten Zeichengebrauch behaupten. An diesem einfachen Objekt wird deutlich, dass schon geringe Manipulationen informationswirksam werden können. Die Wirkung auf den Betrachter ist jeweils eine andere und wird von der Zeichenart bestimmt. Je nachdem, ob ich eine symbolische Gestaltung (171/174) in Form einer grafischen Interpretation, eine indexikalische Gestaltung (172) in Form von Fotografien oder eine ikonische Gestaltung (173) in Form einer Maltechnik wähle.

Un ananas est un ananas... à moins que l'on ne fasse une utilisation réfléchie du signe. Cet objet simple montre clairement que des manipulations mineures ont déjà un impact sur l'information. L'effet sur l'observateur change à chaque fois, et c'est le type de signe qui le détermine. Le résultat est différent selon que je choisis une conception symbolique (171/174) sous forme d'interprétation graphique, une conception indiciaire (172) sous forme de photographies, ou une conception iconique (173) sous forme de technique pictorale.

172

173

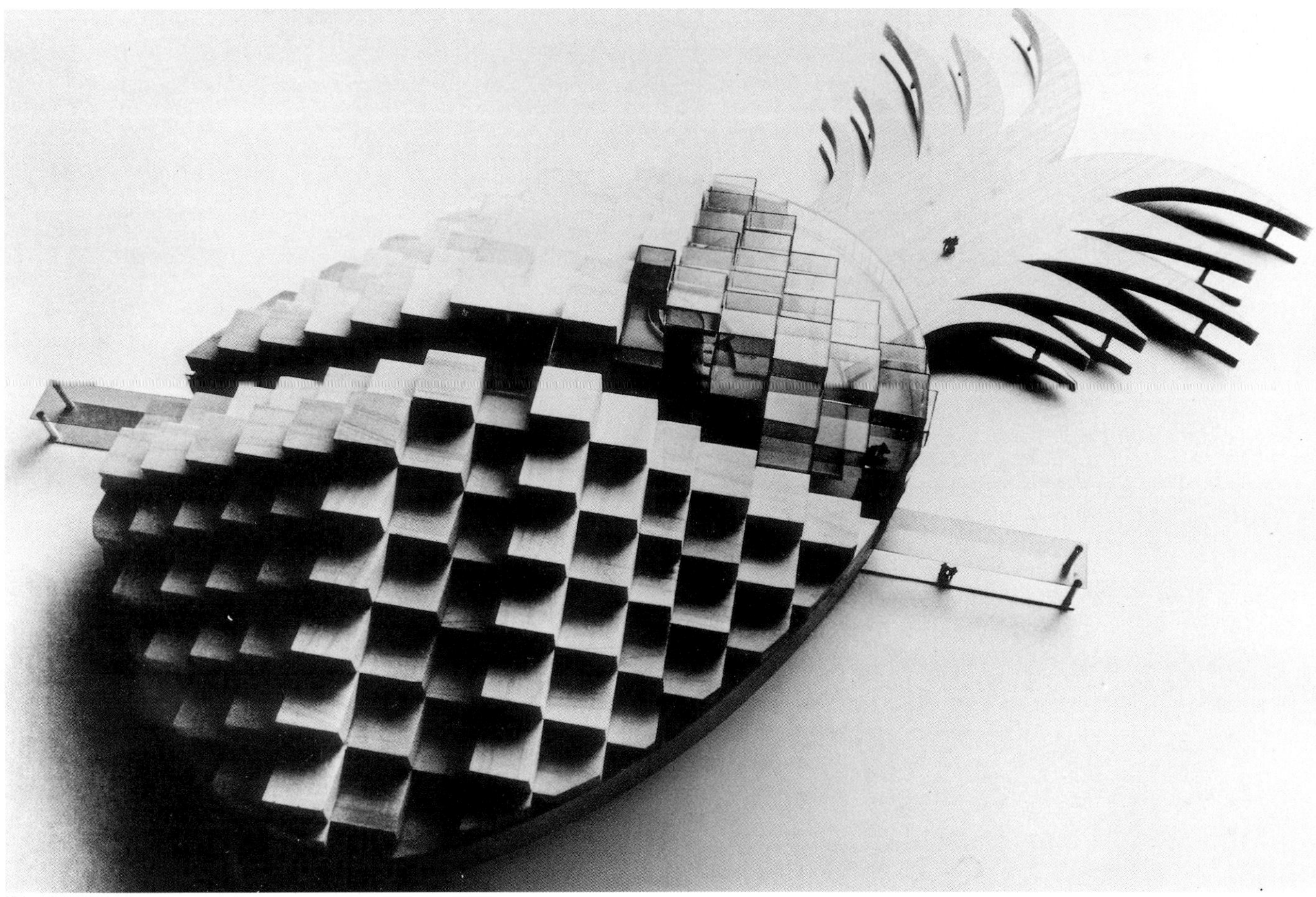
174

Takashi Kanome	D	175
Koji Mizuno	AD	176
Hideo Mukai / Nobuhiko Sugaya	D	
Keiko Hirohashi	D	177
Kroehl Design	D	178
Katsu Kimura	D	179, 180

One of the most important preconditions for the development of packaging is an aspect of the psychology of perception, namely the congruence between the packaging and the object packed, making a real association between the wrapping and the content. There must be more use made of research into the degree of freedom between functional and technical conditions, on the one hand, and aesthetic design possibilities, on the other, as a basis for experimentation. The criterion of sales appeal is visual attractiveness. The systematic manipulation of Qualisigns (colours and textures) and Sinsigns (purely formal aspects) can lead to attractive solutions.

Eine der wichtigsten Voraussetzungen für die Entwicklung von Verpackungen ist eine wahrnehmungspsychologische Komponente, nämlich die Kongruenz zwischen Verpackung und verpacktem Gegenstand – konkret von Hülle und Inhalt. Die Erforschung der Freiheitsgrade zwischen funktionalen und technischen Bedingungen und den ästhetischen Gestaltungsmöglichkeiten muss vermehrt die Grundlage von Experimenten sein. Kaufbeeinflussendes Kriterium ist die visuelle Attraktivität. Die systematische Manipulation von Quali-Zeichen (Farben und Texturen) sowie Sin-Zeichen (rein formale Aspekte) kann zu aufmerksamkeitswirksamen Lösungen führen.

L'une des conditions essentielles à remplir pour concevoir des emballages est une composante qui appartient à la psychologie de la perception, à savoir la congruence entre l'emballage et l'objet emballé – concrètement, entre l'enveloppe et le contenu. Il est nécessaire de mener davantage d'expériences pour étudier le degré de liberté entre les exigences fonctionnelles et techniques et les possibilités de conception esthétiques. L'attrait visuel est un critère qui influence l'achat. La manipulation systématique de qualisignes (couleurs et textures) et de sinsignes (aspects purement formels) peut conduire à des solutions efficaces pour attirer l'attention.

175

176

177

178

179

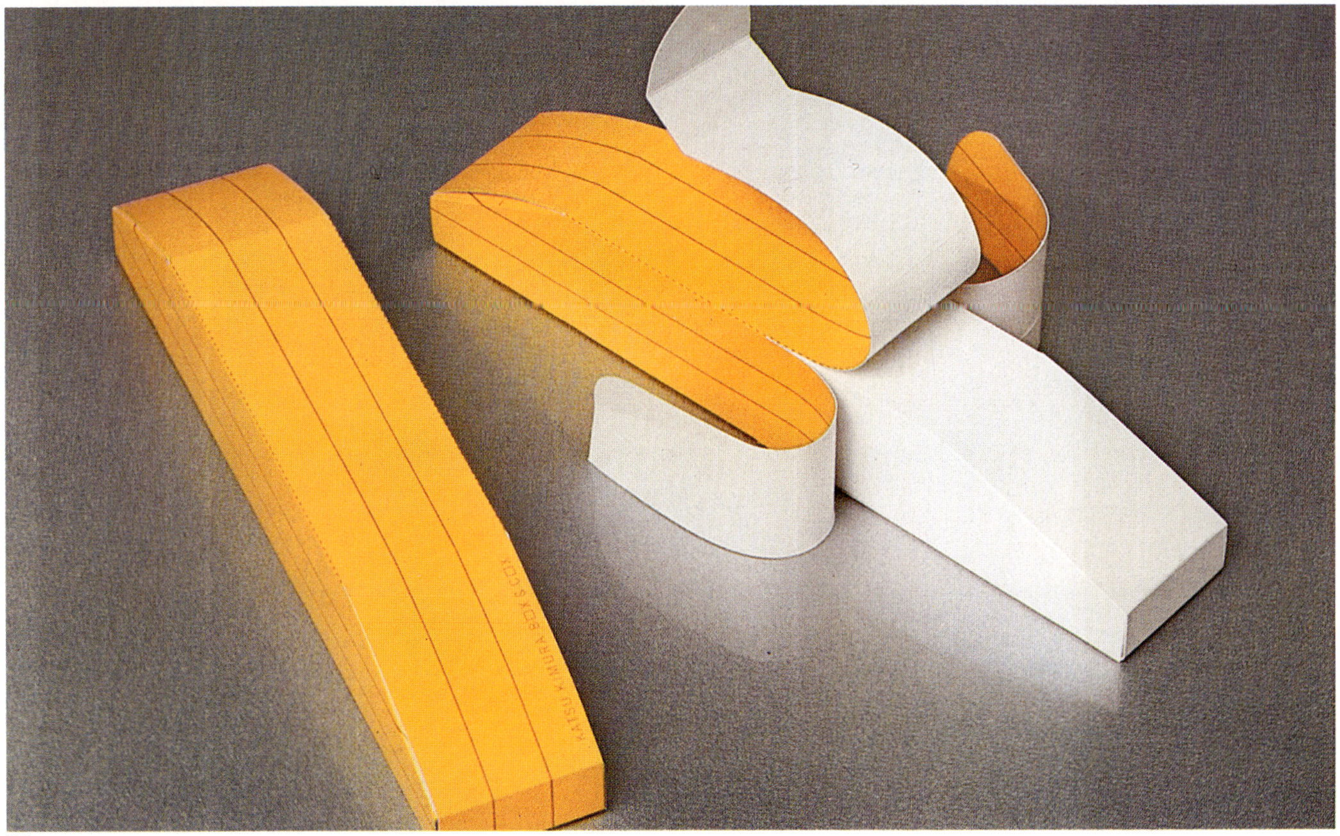

180

181

182

183

184

185

Kyllikki Salminen	D	181
Masao Saito	D	182, 184
Shin Matsunaga	D	183
Shigeo Okamoto	AD	185, 186
Michael Peters	AD	187, 188
Gail Sharp	D	

"In market psychology, it is not the objective character of a product that forms the reality, but only the consumer's idea of it", according to the psychologist Bernt Spiegel. Tests have shown that it is not the quantity and natural representation of tomatoes that give the strongest visualization of taste and quality, but a picture of one particularly luscious example. The pictures are positive examples of sales appeal, i.e. the appetizing nature of the product.

«Nicht die objektive Beschaffenheit einer Ware ist die Realität in der Marktpsychologie, sondern einzig die Verbrauchervorstellung», sagt der Psychologe Bernt Spiegel. So stellt sich bei Tests heraus, dass nicht möglichst viele und natürlich abgebildete Tomaten Geschmack und Qualität am stärksten visualisieren, sondern die überprägnant abgebildete Tomate. Die Bilder sind positive Beispiele für ein kaufbeeinflussendes Kriterium, nämlich die zu vermittelnde Appetitlichkeit einer Ware.

«En psychologie de marché, ce n'est pas la nature objective d'un produit qui est réalité, mais seulement l'idée que s'en fait le consommateur» affirme Bernt Spiegel, psychologue. Les tests montrent que l'expression visuelle la plus forte du goût et de la qualité des tomates n'est pas une illustration qui en montre le plus grand nombre possible avec le plus grand naturel, mais une représentation extrêmement dépouillée d'une seule tomate. Ces images sont de bons exemples d'un critère qui influence l'achat, à savoir le caractère appétissant d'un produit.

186

187

188

189

Yoichi Kato D 189
Koji Tabuchi AD 190

Recent research has shown that the consumer often experiences a misunderstanding between the content and the packaging. Designers will be expected to take into consideration simplicity and environmental factors in addition to novelty. The packs shown here have particularly high sympathy value, in the sequence of: paper, carton board, wood, aluminium foil, glass, plastics.

Wie neue Untersuchungen zeigen, stösst der Verbraucher oft auf ein Missverhältnis zwischen Inhalt und Verpackung. In Zukunft sind Designer aufgefordert, neben der Neuartigkeit von Verpackungen auch Schlichtheit und Umweltverträglichkeit zu berücksichtigen. Die hier abgebildeten Verpackungen haben besonders hohe Sympathiewerte, in der Rangfolge: Papier, Karton, Holz, Alufolie, Glas, Kunststoff.

Selon des études récentes, une inadéquation entre le contenu et l'emballage dérange souvent le consommateur. A l'avenir, les designers devront prendre en considération, outre la nouveauté des emballages, des éléments comme la simplicité et l'écologie. Les emballages représentés ici jouissent d'une grande sympathie auprès des consommateurs, selon le classement suivant: papier, carton, bois, feuille d'aluminium, verre, plastique.

190

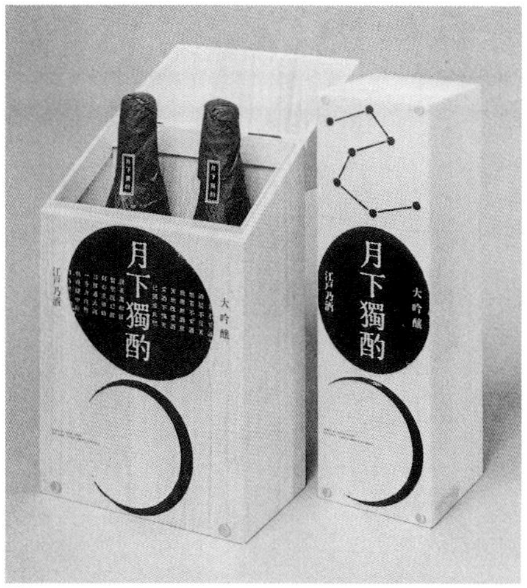

191

Shigeru Akizuki D 191
Keiko Hirohashi D 192
Kazuo Chiba AD 193

In addition to the conveyance of natural qualities, the visibility of the product is not to be underestimated as an element of sales appeal, as the following pages show.

Neben der Vermittlung natürlicher Qualitäten ist die Sichtbarkeit der Ware ein nicht zu unterschätzender Kaufanreiz, wie die nächsten Seiten zeigen.

Outre l'expression de qualités naturelles, la visibilité des produits est une incitation à l'achat à ne pas négliger, comme le montrent les pages suivantes.

192

193

194

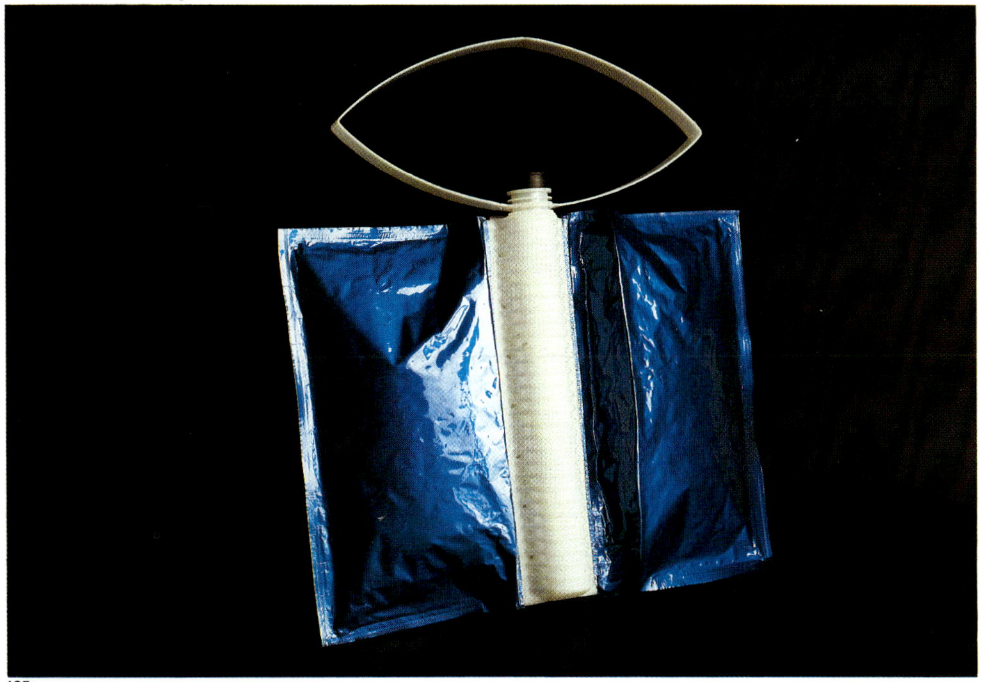

195

196

197

198

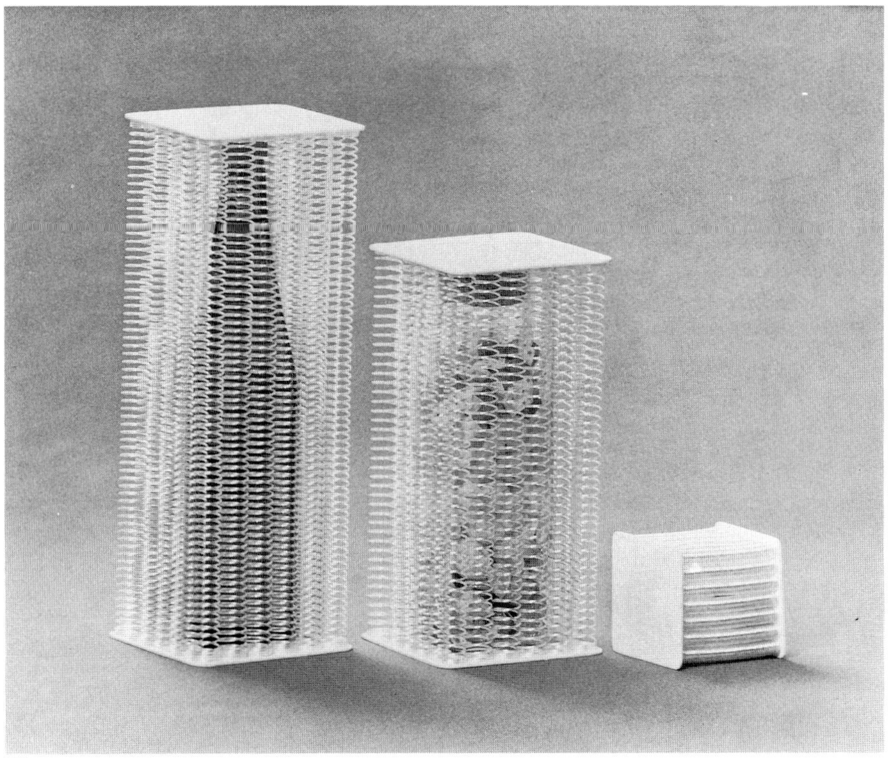

199

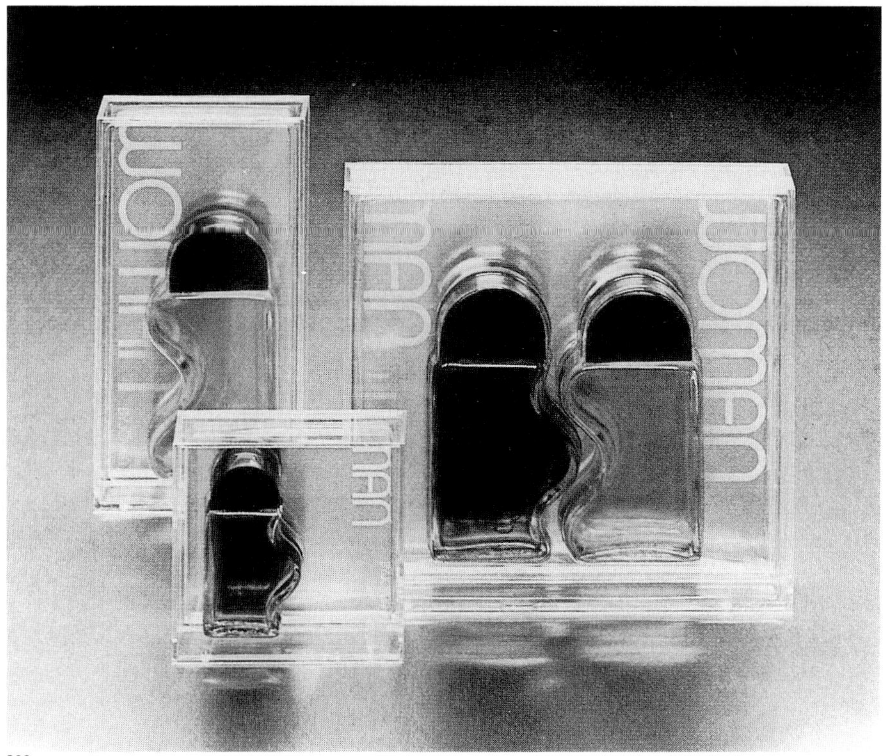

200

Motoko Naruse	AD	194, 196
Philippe Starck	D	195
Shunsaku Sugiura	AD	197
Takashi Kaneko / Tetsuo Togasawa	D	
Yakult Honsha Co.	D	198
Mitsuo Mihira	AD	199
Fred Podjasek	D	200
Alfred Lutz	D	201
Pinti Inox	D	202
Marc-Albert Passy / Marshall Harmon	D	203
John Boatright / Ed Baley / Jim Osborn	D	204
Peter Nikolits	D	205
Patty Lowry / Betty Chow	AD	206
Nicholas Bouyoukas	D	
Carl Selzer	AD	207
Milton Glaser	D	208
Jonson Pedersen Hinrichs & Shakery	A	209
Ivan Chermayeff	AD	210
Rogério Martins / Sergio Liuzzi	D	211

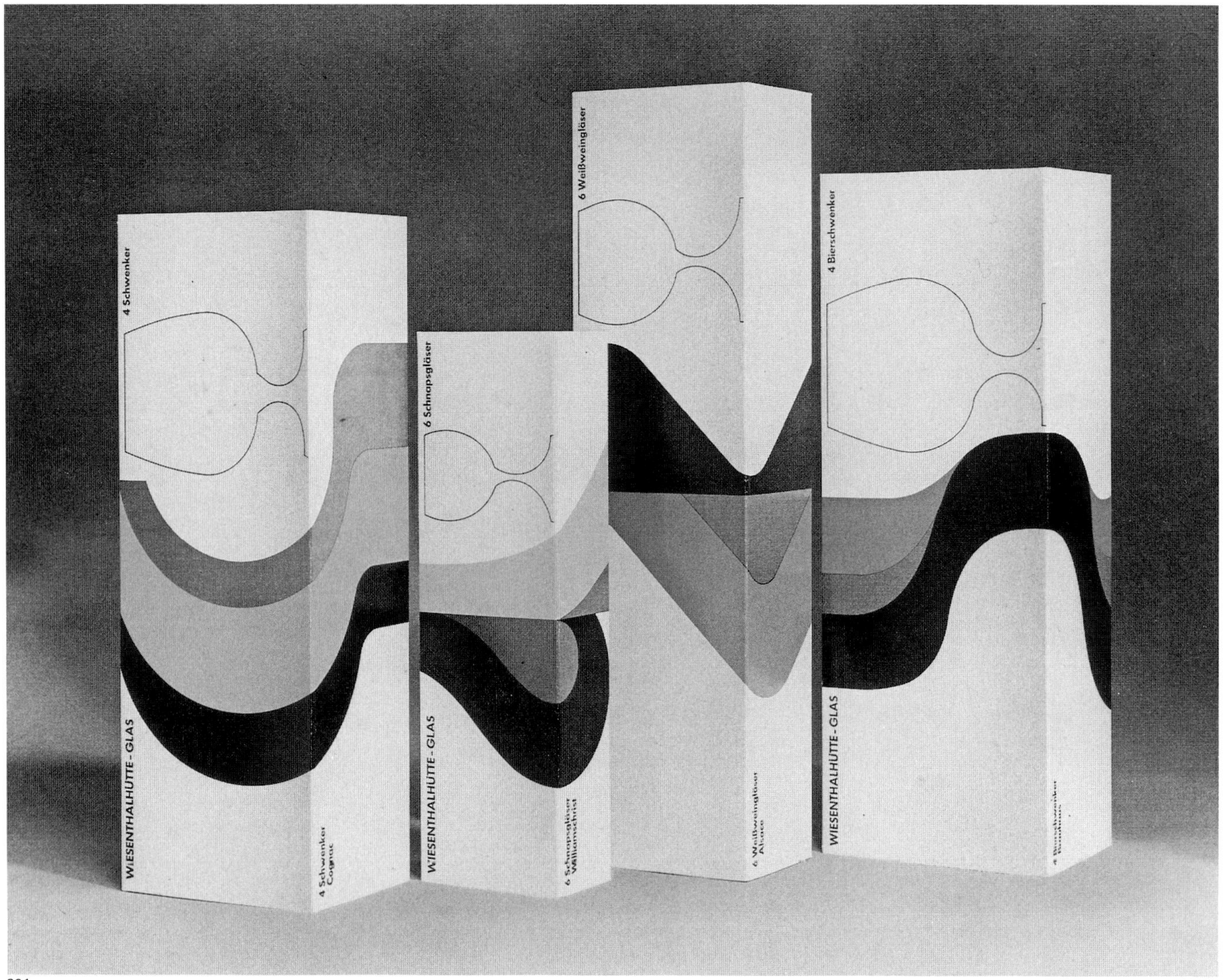

201

202

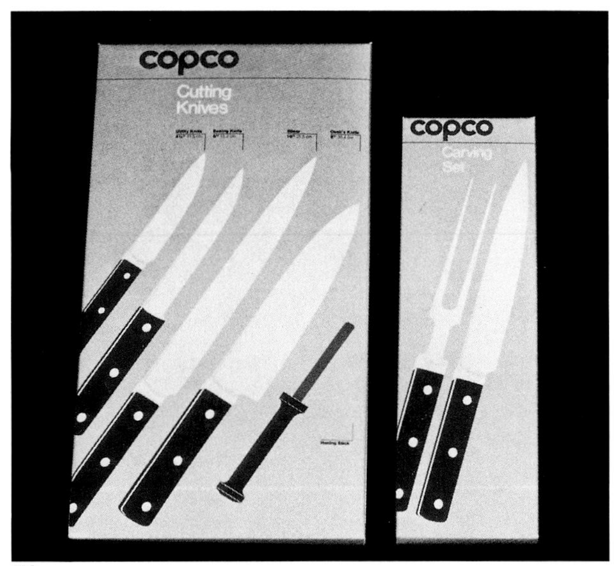

203

204

206

205

207

208

Miguel A. Zapata Garcia	AD	212
John Downs	D	213
Jerome Gould	D	214
Haruyo Tahira	AD	215
Keiko Uesawa / Mikio Kato	D	
Peter Eberle	D	216

While these examples are more representative of the Sinsign, so as to draw attention to the good form of details, those on the opposite page are more concerned with the use of Legisigns. Here an attempt is made to supply extra information. On the subsequent pages, on the other hand, there is both an attempt at a reduction to pure Qualisigns, and again an emphasis on the importance of formal components.

Während die Beispiele auf der gegenüberliegenden Seite mehr das Sinzeichen repräsentieren, um auf die gute Form von Details hinzuweisen, handelt es sich auf dieser Seite um den Einsatz von Legizeichen. Hier wird versucht, ein «Mehr» an Information zu liefern. Bei den nachfolgenden Seiten hingegen wird einerseits eine Reduktion auf reine Qualizeichen angestrebt, während wiederum andererseits die Wichtigkeit formaler Komponenten betont wird.

Alors que ces exemples représentent plutôt le sinsigne, pour faire observer la bonne forme des détails, il s'agit sur la page opposée de l'utilisation de légisignes. L'on essaie ici d'apporter un «plus» d'information. En revanche, sur les pages suivantes, on recherche d'une part une réduction aux qualisignes purs, alors que sur l'autre page on souligne de nouveau l'importance des composantes formelles.

Acrylic Matte Finish
Directions for use: Sand surfaces with fine sandpaper. Wipe with naphtha to remove dirt and grease. Thin 5 parts of enamel with 1 part toluol or xylol. Strain through cheesecloth into spray cup. Stir thoroughly before using and frequently during use.
Steelcase

209

Saks Fifth Avenue
Saks Fifth Avenue

210

HOT SHOES
HOT SHOES
HOT SHOES

211

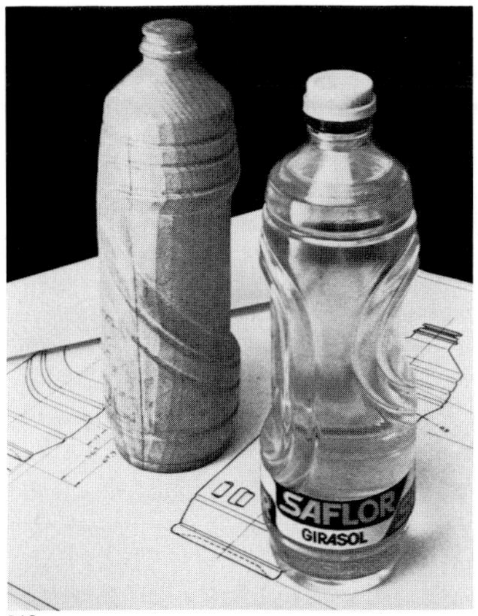

212

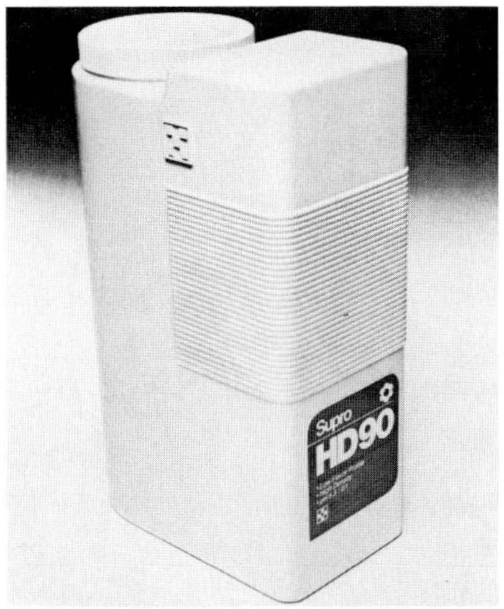

213

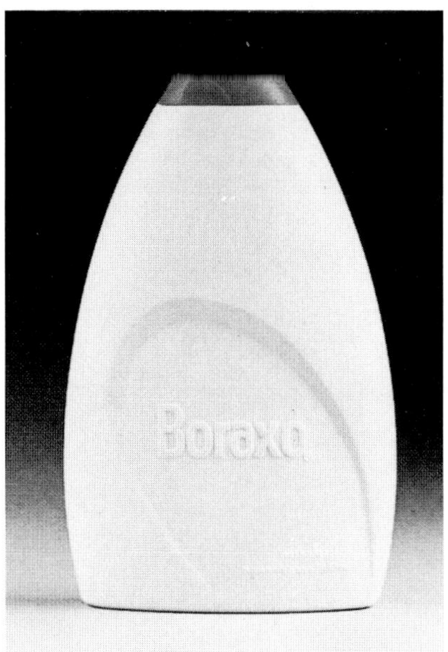

214

215

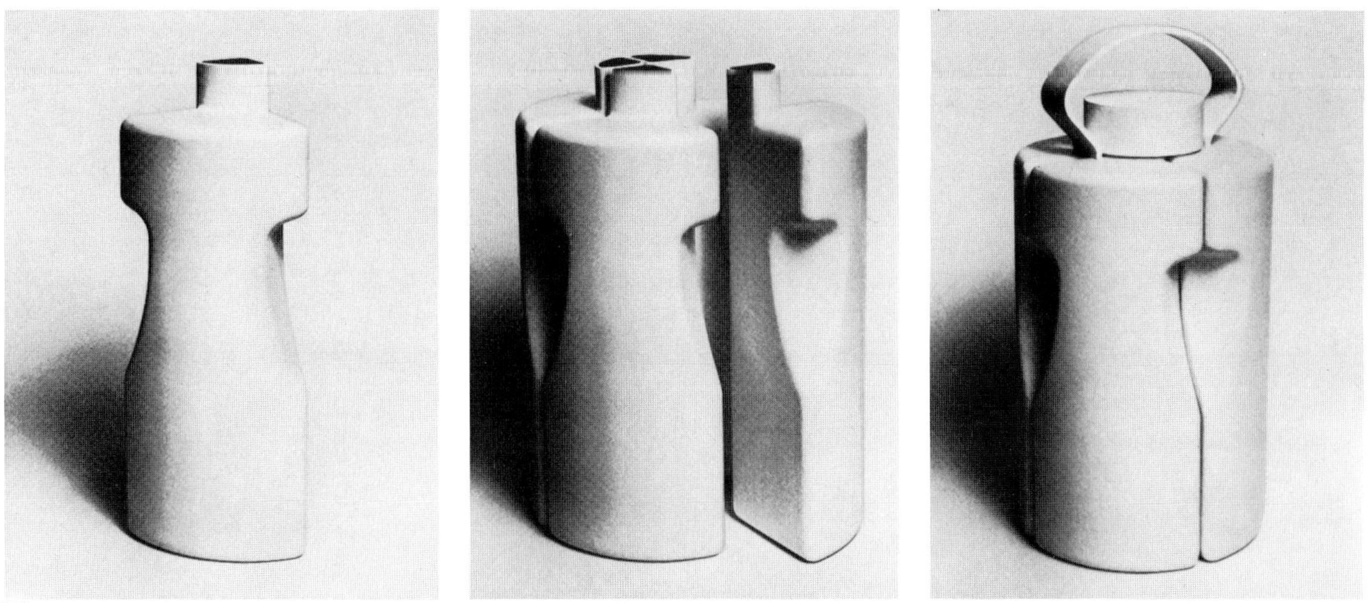
216

217

218

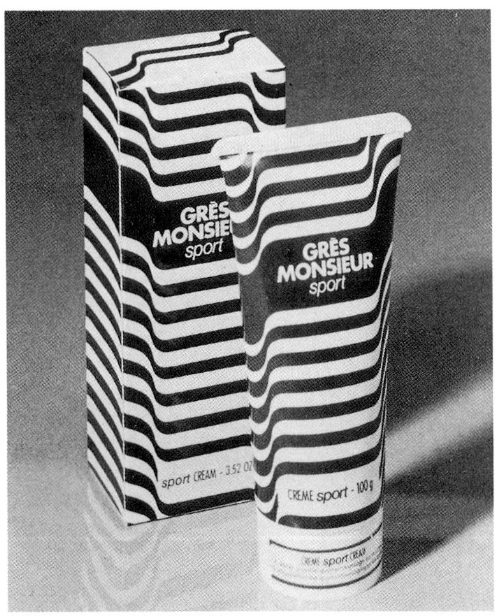

219

220

221

Pierre Dinand D 217
Pierre Vitou D 218
Alain de Mourgues D 219
Peter Schmidt D 220
Christoph Radl D 221

In these examples, optical refinement and convenience, taken together, play a dominant role. On the one hand, luxury goods such as high-quality cosmetics require a form of display to match their high prestige value. On the other hand it is evident that, to ensure unmistakeability, there is an increasing influence from the fields of modern sculpture and architecture.

Die optische Raffinesse und die Konvenienz der Verpackung als Ensemble spielt bei diesen Beispielen eine dominierende Rolle. Zum einen erfordern Luxusgüter, wie hochwertige Kosmetika, eine Aufmachung, die ihrem hohen Prestigewert entspricht. Zum anderen ist erkennbar, dass zur Sicherung der Unverwechselbarkeit zunehmend Anregungen aus Bereichen der modernen Skulptur und Architektur mit einfliessen.

Le raffinement optique et la commodité de l'emballage considérés comme un ensemble jouent un rôle primordial dans ces exemples. D'une part, les produits de luxe, comme les cosmétiques de haut de gamme, exigent une présentation correspondante à leur valeur. D'autre part, il apparaît que l'on s'inspire de la sculpture et de l'architecture modernes pour éviter tout risque d'interchangeabilité.

4. Modern communication design and practice

4.1. Observations on creativity and intuition

In questioning the principle of intuitive creativity in the foregoing, we referred not only to the proposed integration of science and creativity but also to the narrower field of design, i.e. the visual, audiovisual or purely auditive expression of the concept of communication. With reference to the above-mentioned basic principles of science, I wish to put forward the thesis that the creative process can be initiated on the basis of scientific theories. It can be controlled by systematization, and empirically checked. With this proposition, a more technical alternative is opposed to the concept of intuitive creativity. As can be demonstrated, a properly understood theoretical foundation and a systematization of the design process do not necessarily mean a narrowing of the scope of creativity, but, on the contrary, can systematically broaden that scope.

At the same time, the underlying closed system of sign theory gives the creative person the assurance of being able to work systematically on the solution of the task in hand without overlooking any of its important aspects. The degree of creativity — in the sense of originality and innovation — of the end product depends as ever on the ability to make creative use of the instrumentarium.

4.2. Systematics of the design process

Many roads lead to the same destination, and by presenting a systematic approach to the design process we do not imply that it is the only possible one. Everyone must find his own way, but in order to reach the destination,

4. Modernes Kommunikationsdesign und gestalterische Praxis

4.1. Bemerkungen zu Kreativität und Intuition

Wenn im vorangegangenen das Prinzip einer intuitiven Kreativität in Frage gestellt wurde, so bezog sich das nicht nur auf die skizzierte Integration von Wissenschaft und Kreativität, sondern schloss auch den engeren Bereich der Gestaltung, die visuelle, aber auch audiovisuelle und auditive Umsetzung von Kommunikationskonzepten mit ein. Ich will dies mit Bezug auf die bereits erwähnten Grundprinzipien der Wissenschaft in einer These präzisieren: Der kreative Prozess kann auf der Basis wissenschaftlicher Theorien initiiert werden.
Er kann durch Systematisierung gesteuert werden. Und er ist empirisch kontrollierbar. Mit dieser These wird dem intuitiven Kreativitätsbegriff eine mehr technische Alternative entgegengestellt. Wie gezeigt werden kann, bedeutet eine richtig verstandene theoretische Fundierung und Systematisierung des Gestaltungsprozesses nicht notwendigerweise eine Einengung des kreativen Spielraums, sondern kann diesen im Gegenteil systematisch erweitern.

Zugleich gibt das zugrunde liegende geschlossene System der Zeichentheorie dem Kreativen die Sicherheit, dass er sich systematisch an die Lösung der gestellten Aufgabe heranarbeiten kann, ohne wichtige Aspekte dabei zu übersehen. Wie kreativ – im Sinne von originell und innovativ – eine Lösung im Endeffekt ausfällt, hängt dabei nach wie vor von der Fähigkeit ab, mit seinem Instrumentarium kreativ umzugehen.

4.2. Eine Systematik des Gestaltungsprozesses

Viele Wege führen zum Ziel, und wenn im folgenden eine Systematik zum äusseren Ablauf des Gestaltungsprozesses vorgestellt wird, so kann das nicht bedeuten, dass es sich hier um den einzig möglichen handelte. Jeder muss hier seinen eigenen Weg finden. Man sollte den Weg aber konsequent

4. Le design de communication actuel et la pratique de la création

4.1. Remarques sur la créativité et l'intuition

Si nous avons plus haut mis en cause le principe d'une créativité intuitive, cela ne s'appliquait pas seulement à l'intégration esquissée de la science et de la créativité, mais comprenait également le domaine plus étroit de la création, de la transposition visuelle, mais aussi audiovisuelle et auditive de concepts de communication. Pour préciser, voici une thèse qui fait référence aux principes fondamentaux de la science que nous avons déjà mentionnés: le processus créatif peut être amorcé sur la base de théories scientifiques. Il peut être maîtrisé par la systématisation. Et on peut le contrôler empiriquement. Cette thèse oppose à la notion de créativité intuitive une solution plus technique. Il est possible de montrer qu'un fondement et une systématisation théoriques bien compris du processus de création n'entraînent pas nécessairement un rétrécissement de la marge de manœuvre créatrice, mais qu'ils peuvent au contraire l'élargir de façon systématique.

En outre, le système fermé de la théorie des signes permet au créateur d'être certain qu'il peut chercher systématiquement la solution au problème posé sans oublier d'aspects importants. Le degré de créativité – dans le sens d'originalité et de nouveauté – du résultat final dépend essentiellement de la capacité à se servir de ces instruments de manière créative.

4.2 Une systématisation du processus de création

Nombreuses sont les voies qui permettent d'atteindre un objectif, et si nous présentons ci-dessous une systématisation du déroulement extérieur du processus de création, nous ne prétendons pas qu'il s'agisse de la seule possible. Chacun doit ici trouver sa propre voie. Néanmoins, il est important de persévérer sur cette voie

It is unwise to circulate information simply because it is economically expedient without regard to the means, in order to emerge victorious in the image war. It is necessary for corporations to take into consideration the social effects of their own corporate image and to move towards adopting a design policy that is in keeping with the existing environment or that is edifying.

Takenobu Igarashi

Es wäre unüberlegt, heute Informationen zu verbreiten, nur weil es ökonomisch zweckmässig ist, ohne die Mittel zu beachten, die man einzusetzen hat, um aus dem Krieg der Bilder siegreich hervorzutreten. So ist es auch für Unternehmen wichtig, die gesellschaftlichen Auswirkungen eines Gesamterscheinungsbildes zu berücksichtigen und in eine Designpolitik einzubeziehen, die in einem direkten Kontakt zur Umwelt steht oder dieselbe prägt.

Takenobu Igarashi

Il serait irréfléchi de diffuser aujourd'hui des informations uniquement pour des raisons d'opportunité économique, sans prêter attention aux moyens à mettre en œuvre pour sortir victorieux de la guerre des images. Ainsi, pour les entreprises, il est important de tenir compte des répercussions sociales d'une image globale et de les inclure dans une politique du design qui se situe directement dans l'environnement ou qui y laisse son empreinte.

Takenobu Igarashi

the chosen way should be followed consistently. The following exposition should be understood as one example of such a way. The relatively abstract presentation of the process is subsequently illustrated by means of a concrete example.

The initiation of the creative process is based on semiotic theory, with differentiation of the various kinds of sign in each of the different dimensions. Since publicity and communication must use a generally understandable language, they are in principle denotative, so that the pragmatic dimension can be taken as given. The statements developed within the framework of the strategy are also given. Which of these statements are to be expressed verbally, and which figuratively or pictorially, must remain the decision of the creative person. Both forms of expression require a visual form, at least in the printed media. We are here concerned only with figurative or pictorial expression, but there is no intention to belittle the immense significance of typography.

4.2.1. Strategies of realization

In this instance, systematization is carried out with the aid of a flowchart, beginning with the terms of the strategy. It is assumed that the solution will be found by teamwork.

4.2.2. Conception and analysis

The terms of the strategy consist in general of relatively global statements, which must first be broken down into their components. This is done in a "brainstorming" session, where the components are also arranged into a sequence corresponding to their importance for the total concept. The first opportunity for monitoring arises when the results of the session, formulated as a "re-briefing", are checked with the client. In the next stage, all the components of the statements are tabulated with reference to the possible relationships to the object.

zu Ende gehen, wenn man das Ziel erreichen will. Als ein Beispiel dafür sind die folgenden Ausführungen zu verstehen. Die hier relativ abstrakt dargestellten Abläufe werden nachfolgend anhand eines konkreten Beispiels durchgespielt.

Die Initiierung des kreativen Prozesses beruht auf der semiotischen Theorie, mit der Differenzierung der verschiedenen Zeichenarten in den einzelnen Dimensionen. Da Werbung und Kommunikation sich einer allgemeinverständlichen Sprache bedienen müssen, sind sie vom Prinzip her denotativ, so dass man die pragmatische Dimension als vorgegeben ansehen kann. Vorgegeben sind ebenfalls die im Rahmen der Strategie entwickelten Aussagen. Welche dieser Aussagen bildlich und welche verbal umzusetzen sind, muss der Entscheidung des Kreativen überlassen bleiben. Beide Umsetzungen verlangen zumindest in den Printmedien eine visuelle Form. Wir wollen uns hier nur mit der bildlichen Umsetzung befassen, was aber die immense Bedeutung der Typografie in keiner Weise schmälern soll.

4.2.1. Strategien der Umsetzung

Die Systematisierung geschieht hier mit Hilfe eines Flussdiagramms, das bei den Vorgaben der Strategie einsetzt. Es wird davon ausgegangen, dass die Lösung der Aufgabe im Team erarbeitet wird.

4.2.2. Konzeption und Objektanalyse

Die Vorgaben der Strategie bestehen im allgemeinen aus relativ globalen Aussagen, die zunächst in ihre einzelnen Komponenten zu zerlegen sind. Dies geschieht im Rahmen eines Brainstormings, in dem die Komponenten zugleich in eine Rangfolge entsprechend ihrer Bedeutung für das Gesamtkonzept gebracht werden. Eine erste Möglichkeit der Kontrolle ergibt sich, wenn man das Ergebnis dieses Brainstormings in Form eines «Re-Briefings» noch einmal mit dem Auftraggeber abstimmt. Im nächsten Schritt erfolgt nun die Tabellierung aller Aussagenkomponenten im Hinblick auf die möglichen Objektbezüge.

si l'on veut atteindre son objectif. Les considérations suivantes sont apportées à titre d'exemple. Les déroulements présentés ici de façon assez abstraite seront plus loin concrétisés à l'aide d'exemples.

L'amorce du processus créatif est fondée sur la théorie sémiotique, avec la différenciation des différents types de signes dans les différentes dimensions. La publicité et la communication devant utiliser un langage accessible à tous, elles sont par principe dénotatives, de sorte que l'on peut considérer la dimension pragmatique comme donnée. De même, les énoncés élaborés dans le cadre de la stratégie sont données. Il appartient au créateur de décider quels sont les énoncés à transposer figurativement, et quels sont ceux qu'il convient de transposer verbalement. Les deux transpositions nécessitent, du moins dans les médias imprimés, une forme visuelle. Nous ne traiterons ici que de la transposition figurative, sans pour autant minimiser l'importance considérable de la typographie.

4.2.1. Stratégies de la transposition

La systématisation se fait ici à l'aide d'un organigramme qui intervient au niveau des données de la stratégie. On part du principe que la solution du problème est élaborée au sein d'une équipe.

4.2.2. Conception et analyse de l'objet

Les données de la stratégie consistent généralement en énoncés relativement globaux qui doivent d'abord être décomposés en leurs différentes composantes. Cette décomposition se fait dans le cadre d'un brainstorming au cours duquel les composantes sont classées selon leur importance, d'après leur signification pour la stratégie dans son ensemble. Il existe un première possibilité de contrôle si l'on organise un «re-briefing» avec le client afin de revoir avec lui le résultat du brainstorming. L'étape suivante consiste à mettre sous forme de tableau toutes les composantes d'énoncés en tenant compte des relations aux objets possibles.

	Object reference Objektbezug Référence à l'objet	Kiel Kiel Kiel	Week Woche Semaine	Sailing regattas Segelregatten Régates à la voile	Internationality Internationalität Caractère international	Meeting Begegnung Rencontre	Communication Verständigung Entente	Sea Meer Mer
Iconic Ikonisch Iconique	Image Abbild Image			• Regatta • Sailing boats • Sails, Cables, Masts • Keel • Pennants, Flags • Regatta • Segelboote • Segel, Taue, Masten Kiel Wimpel, Fahnen Régates Voiliers Voiles, Cables, Mâts Quille Flammes, Drapeaux		Meeting (e.g. of boats) (of people, of flags) Begegnung (z. B. von Booten) (von Personen, Flaggen) Rencontre (ex. bateaux) (personnes, fanions)	Speech situation Gesticulation, Codes Sprechsituation Gestik, Codes Situation d'énonciation Mimique, Codes	• Waves • Wellen • Vagues •
	Diagram Diagramm Diagramme	• Tom Kyle (on the bay) Tom kyle (an der Bucht) Tom kyle (la baie)				Diagram Diagramm Diagramme		•
	Metaphor Metapher Métaphore		Seven Sieben Sept	•				•
Indexical Indexikalisch Indiciaire	Identifying Identifizierend D'identification	Picture of town Typical buildings Bild der Stadt Typische Gebäude Image de la ville Bâtiments caractéristiques		• Sloping position of boats Wind-filled sails Relative positions of boats Starting flag Marker buoy Schräglage der Boote Geblähte Segel Stellung der Boote zueinander, Startfahne, Wendeboje	People of various nationalities Menschen verschiedener Nationalitäten Hommes et femmes de nationalité différente		Text Flag signal Text Flaggensignal Texte Signalisation par fanions	Water surface to horizon Wasserfläche bis zum Horizont Plan d'eau qui s'étend jusqu'à l'horizon
	Indication Anzeichen Marque	Street map Regional map Guide Stadtplan Landkarte Wegweiser Carte routière Carte géographique Panneau indicateur	Calendar sheet (sheets) Kalenderblatt (-blätter) Feuille(s) du calendrier	• Inclinaison des bateaux • Voiles gonflées Position des bateaux les uns par rapport aux autres Drapeau de départ Bouée de virage	Attributes of different countries Attribute verschiedener Länder Apports de différents pays	• e.g. Meeting of boats' wakes z. B. Zusammentreffen von Kielwassern ex. Mariage des sillages	Megaphone Hands as megaphone Megaphon Hände als Sprachrohr Mégaphone, Les mains en guise de porte-voix	Dunes, Sandbanks Lighthouse Sea-signs Dünen, Watt Leuchtturm Seezeichen Dunes, Lagune Phare Signal maritime
Symbolic Symbolisch Symbolique	Iconic Ikonisch Iconique				• Globe, World map Globus, Weltkarte Globe, Carte du monde			
	Indexical Indexikalisch Indiciaire		• Date Datum Date	•				
	Symbolic Symbolisch Symbolique	'Kiel' City arms City colours ‚Kiel' Stadtwappen Stadtfarben ‹Kiel› emblème et couleurs de la ville			• National flags Nationalflaggen Drapeaux		Signal system e.g. Flag code, Sea-signs Signal Systeme z. B. Flaggencode Seezeichen Systèmes de signalisation ex.: Bouée de mi-parcours Signal maritime	

222

223

224

225

226

227

228

229

Hans Hillmann	D	222
Georges Lacroix	D	223
Pierre Mendell	D	224
Ruedi Baur	D	225, 226
Asun Balzola	D	227
Hans Schweiss	D	228
Rudi Meyer	D	229

One of the oldest-established design competitions in the German Federal Republic has been in existence for 40 years. On the basis of semiotic theory, an exact definition can be made of the kinds of sign used up to now. Analysis shows that despite a high aesthetic level, a very one-sided use of signs has been made and the possible repertoire has hardly been used. This is shown explicitly by a chance selection of posters, where the first row has been limited to the representation of a sail, while the subjects of the second row again represent a sail, in association with waves.

Vierzig Jahre besteht einer der ältesten Design-Wettbewerbe der Bundesrepublik. Aufgrund der semiotischen Theorie lässt sich exakt definieren, welche Zeichenarten bis heute angewandt wurden. Die Analyse zeigt auf, dass trotz des hohen ästhetischen Niveaus eine recht einseitige Zeichenverwendung stattfindet, das Repertoire an Bezeichnungsmöglichkeiten hingegen bisher kaum genutzt wird.
Dies geht auch explizit aus der Zufallsauswahl von Plakaten hervor, bei der sich die erste Reihe auf die Wiedergabe eines Segels beschränkt, während die Sujets der zweiten Reihe wiederum ein Segel – verknüpft mit Wellen – repräsentieren.

L'un des plus anciens concours de design de la République Fédérale d'Allemagne existe depuis quarante ans. A l'aide de la théorie sémiotique, il est possible de définir exactement quels ont été les types de signes utilisés jusqu'à présent. L'analyse montre qu'en dépit d'un très bon niveau esthétique l'utilisation des signes est limitée et que le répertoire des possibilités de désignation n'a guère été exploité. Ces quelques affiches sélectionnées au hasard en témoignent: la première rangée se limite à la reproduction d'une voile, et la deuxième rangée reprend le thème de la voile – associé à des vagues.

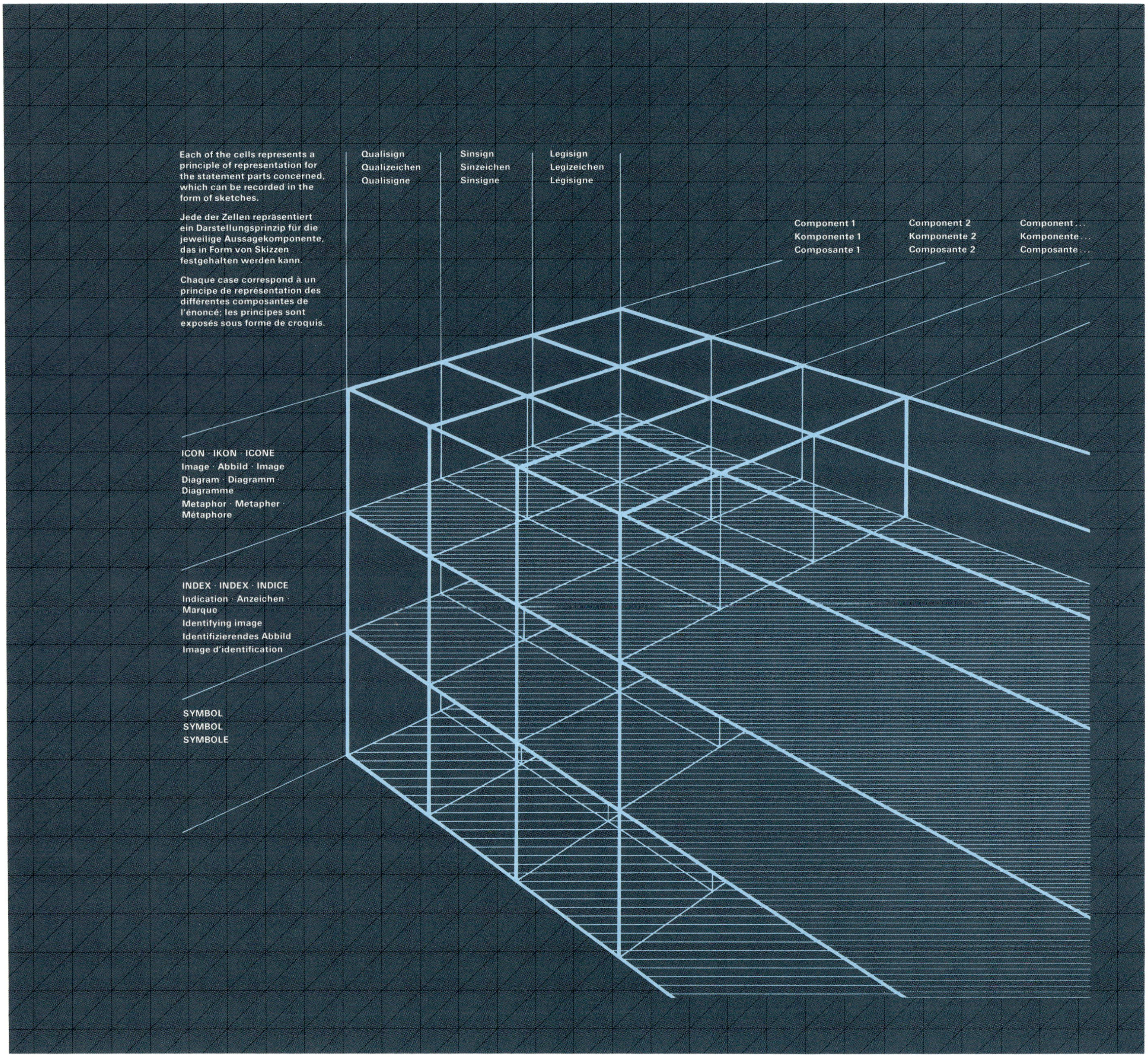
Each of the cells represents a principle of representation for the statement parts concerned, which can be recorded in the form of sketches.
Jede der Zellen repräsentiert ein Darstellungsprinzip für die jeweilige Aussagekomponente, das in Form von Skizzen festgehalten werden kann.
Chaque case correspond à un principe de représentation des différentes composantes de l'énoncé; les principes sont exposés sous forme de croquis.
Qualisign
Qualizeichen
Qualisigne
Sinsign
Sinzeichen
Sinsigne
Legisign
Legizeichen
Légisigne
Component 1
Komponente 1
Composante 1
Component 2
Komponente 2
Composante 2
Component...
Komponente...
Composante...
ICON · IKON · ICONE
Image · Abbild · Image
Diagram · Diagramm · Diagramme
Metaphor · Metapher · Métaphore
INDEX · INDEX · INDICE
Indication · Anzeichen · Marque
Identifying image
Identifizierendes Abbild
Image d'identification
SYMBOL
SYMBOL
SYMBOLE

The system diagram at left shows the interconnection of all components of a statement with regard to the possible relations to the object. The inclusion of the syntactic dimension is also made clear here. This may be called the phase of creative search and selection.

Die links abgebildete Systematik zeigt die Vernetzung aller Aussagekomponenten im Hinblick auf die möglichen Objektbezüge. Auch der Einbezug der syntaktischen Dimension wird hier deutlich. Man kann dies die Phase der kreativen Suche und Selektion nennen.

La systématique reproduite à gauche montre l'association de tous les composants d'énoncé par rapport aux références d'objet possibles. L'introduction de la dimension syntactique ressort clairement. L'on peut parler ici de la phase de la recherche créative.

Each cell represents a principle of representation for one of the components of a statement, which can be recorded in sketch form. In practice, the complete table is used only as an aid to planning, because, on the basis of the empirically verified hypotheses, there are clear connections between the nature and content of the statement and the appropriate kinds of sign. As early as the stage of analysis of the components of the statement, essential creative decisions are taken.

4.2.3. Systematic development of statements

These decisions should not place any limitations on the next stage, in which the table is extended to include the syntactical dimension. The output of this part of the process is controlled both by the preceding sketches and by the original tables.

Each item in the table is analyzed for its pictorial elements, i.e. broken down into Qualisigns, Sinsigns and Legisigns. It is not hard to see that the number of possible solutions is multipled at this stage, since every item is likely to be composed of a whole series of signs of the three types. The process of creative selection therefore becomes all the stronger at this point, but the decisive creative phase will begin with the production of associations between the connectible elements. In principle, the number of possible connections is infinite, for we are here dealing with a genuine grammar, which allows for the formulation of an infinite number of statements.

Most rough sketches are made at this stage of the design process, so the subsequent selection has a decisive function. The selection is best made at another "brainstorming" session, where the statements of each sketch are discussed. At such a discussion, ideas are mutually developed and initial approaches take on a more concrete form, from which full working out can begin. The resulting designs

Jede der Zellen repräsentiert ein Darstellungsprinzip für die jeweilige Aussagekomponente, das in Form von Skizzen festgehalten werden kann. In der Praxis wird die vollständige Tabelle nur als Denkhilfe benutzt, denn aufgrund der empirisch belegten Hypothesen gibt es klare Zusammenhänge zwischen Art und Inhalt der Aussage und geeigneten Zeichenarten. Schon in der Phase der Analyse der Aussagekomponenten fallen wesentliche kreative Entscheidungen.

4.2.3. Eine systematische Aussagenentwicklung

Diese Entscheidungen sollten jedoch nicht den nächsten Schritt bereits einengen, in dem die Tabelle um die syntaktische Dimension erweitert wird. Daher wird der Output dieses Teilprozesses sowohl von den vorangegangenen Skizzen als auch von der ursprünglichen Tabelle gesteuert.

Jedes Item der Tabelle wird dabei auf seine bildlichen Elemente hin analysiert, also in Quali-, Sin- und Legizeichen zerlegt. Es ist unschwer zu erkennen, dass sich hier die Zahl der möglichen Lösungen vervielfacht, da jedes Item meist aus einer ganzen Reihe von Zeichen der drei Typen zusammengesetzt ist. Um so stärker wird in dieser Phase die kreative Selektion. Die entscheidende kreative Phase beginnt aber erst jetzt mit der Herstellung von Verknüpfungen zwischen den verbindungsfähigen Elementen. Prinzipiell ist nämlich die Zahl der möglichen Verknüpfungen unendlich, denn wir haben es hier mit einer echten Grammatik zu tun, die die Formulierung einer unendlichen Zahl von Aussagen erlaubt.

In diesem Stadium des Gestaltungsprozesses entstehen die meisten Skizzen, so dass die anschliessende Selektion eine entscheidende Funktion hat. Diese Selektion erfolgt am besten wieder in einem Brainstorming, in dem über die Aussagen der einzelnen Skizzen diskutiert wird. In solch einer Diskussion ergänzen sich die Ideen gegenseitig, und erste Ansätze gewinnen konkretere Gestalt, so dass nun die Ausarbeitung begon-

Chaque case correspond à un principe de représentation pour la composante d'énoncé donnée. On peut noter ce principe sous forme d'esquisses. Dans la pratique, le tableau complet n'est utilisé que comme aide-mémoire, car en raison des hypothèses prouvées empiriquement, il existe des rapports clairs entre le type et le contenu de l'énoncé et les types de signes appropriés. Des décisions créatives importantes sont prises dans la phase d'analyse des composantes de l'énoncé.

4.2.3. Un développement systématique des énoncés

Toutefois, ces décisions ne doivent pas limiter l'étape suivante pendant laquelle on élargit le tableau grâce à la dimension syntactique. En conséquence, le résultat de ce processus partiel dépend à la fois des esquisses précédentes et du tableau d'origine.

Chaque unité du tableau est analysée selon ses éléments figuratifs, et ainsi décomposée en qualisignes, sinsignes et légisignes. A ce point, il va de soi que les solutions possibles se multiplient, car chaque unité est le plus souvent composée d'une série de signes des trois types. La sélection créative n'en est que plus intense pendant cette phase. Cependant, la phase créatrice décisive ne commence vraiment qu'avec la production de connexions entre les éléments qui peuvent être reliés. Le nombre de connexions possibles est en principe infini, car nous avons ici une grammaire véritable qui permet la formulation d'un nombre infini d'énoncés.

C'est à ce stade du processus de création que naissent les esquisses les plus nombreuses, de sorte que la sélection ultérieure a une fonction déterminante. On effectue de préférence cette sélection pendant un brainstorming qui permet un échange de vues sur les énoncés des différentes esquisses. Ce type de discussion permet de confronter et de parfaire les différentes idées, de concrétiser de simples approches, de sorte qu'il est alors possible de passer à l'élaboration. On peut soumettre les projets proposés à une vérification empirique à l'aide de

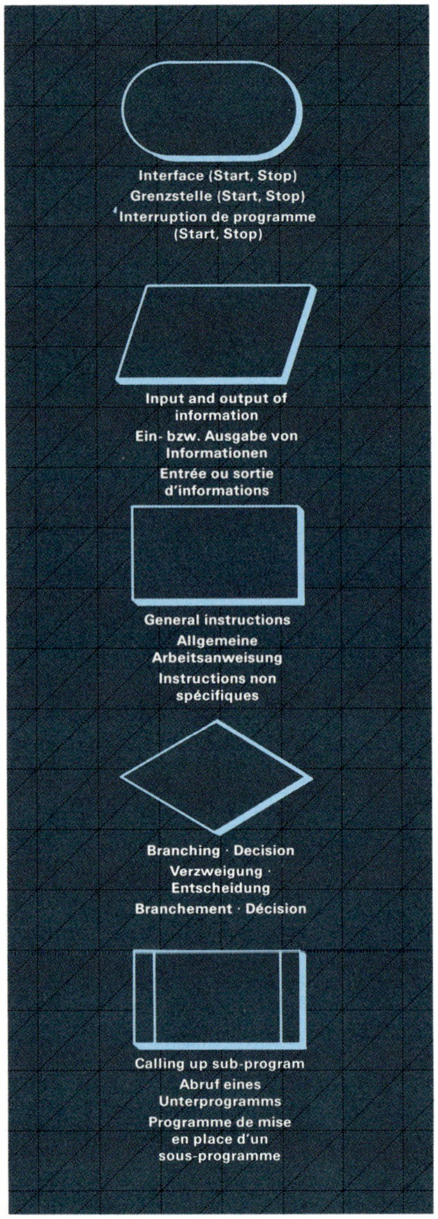

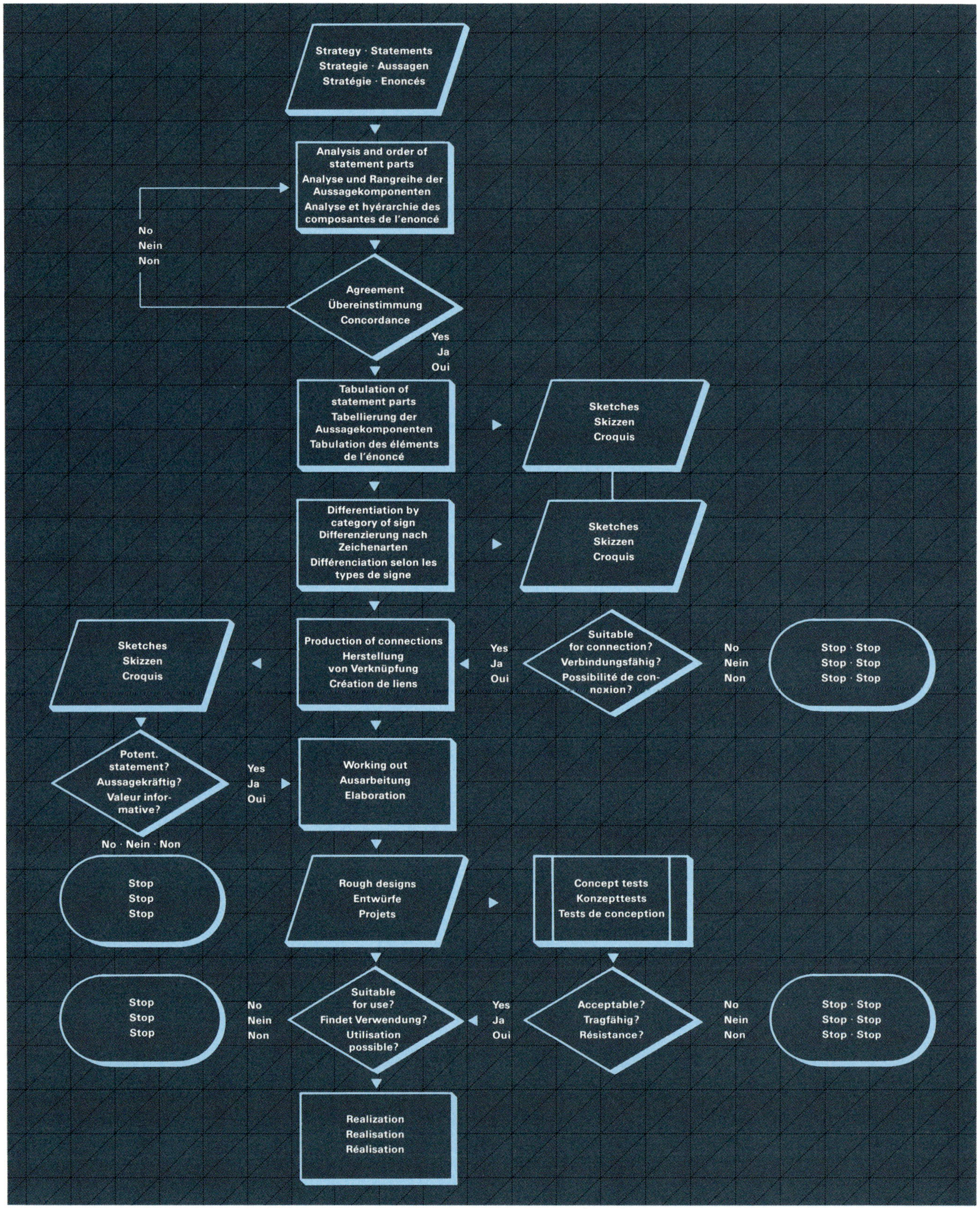

The illustration documents the systematization of the creative process. (The diagram corresponds to the flow-scheme of a computer program, whose elements are defined above.)

Die Darstellung dokumentiert die Systematisierung des kreativen Prozesses. (Das Diagramm entspricht dem Ablaufschema eines Computerprogramms, dessen Elemente oben definiert sind.)

Cette figure illustre la systématisation du processus créatif. (Le diagramme correspond au schéma de déroulement d'un programme informatique dont les éléments sont définis en haut.)

can be subjected to empirical checking by means of comparative tests of concepts. Since the statement of such tests is obtained only from comparison, the designs may be made in relatively rough form and without too much expense of time and cost. The final decision and realization of the project are then made on the basis of this final monitoring and selection.

If, up to this point, only a single project has been followed through, the benefits of the system can now be used for the working out of a whole campaign or for developments such as a corporate identity. Consistency, in such cases, exists not just in a superficial recurrence of constant factors but is the result of applying uniform design principles, which at the same time open up a broad scope for creativity. Such principles can consist, for example, in giving priority to the structural level instead of the "normal" level of statement in all figurative representations, in constantly repeating certain textures, maintaining an unusual perspective or continually using certain combinations of different kinds of signs.

Another point of view, which has attained a special significance in marketing today, is the maintenance of the closed nature of a communications campaign in a variety of media. The systematics presented here for the production of publicity statements have been explained only with regard to the pictorial sign system, but the same basic principles also apply to other kinds of sign system.

4.2.4. Example for use

A spa is a modern watering place, but the installation presented here goes far beyond that definition. It serves for the revitalization of people plagued by stress. For Baden-Baden, we developed a concept combining a luxury hotel, a clinic and a health farm under one roof in the most beautiful of European spas.

nen werden kann. Die dabei entstehenden Entwürfe können im Rahmen vergleichender Konzepttests einer empirischen Überprüfung unterzogen werden. Da die Aussage solcher Tests lediglich aus dem Vergleich gewonnen wird, können die Entwürfe bereits in einer relativ groben Fassung und damit ohne allzu grossen Aufwand getestet werden. Auf der Basis dieser letzten Kontrolle und Selektion erfolgt dann die Entscheidung und endgültige Realisation.

Wurde bisher lediglich eine einzelne Entwicklung verfolgt, so kann man nun den Nutzen der Systematik für eine ganze Kampagne oder für Massnahmen im Sinne einer Corporate Identity herausarbeiten. Einheitlichkeit in diesen Fällen liegt dann nicht nur in einer oberflächlichen Wiederkehr von Konstanten, sondern bildet das Ergebnis einheitlicher Gestaltungsprinzipien, die gleichzeitig einen breiten kreativen Spielraum eröffnen. Solche Prinzipien können etwa darin bestehen, dass man bei allen bildlichen Darstellungen statt der «normalen» Aussagenebene der Strukturebene einen besonderen Vorrang gibt, bestimmte Texturen immer wiederkehren lässt, eine ungewöhnliche Perspektive beibehält oder bestimmte Kombinationen von Zeichenarten kontinuierlich verwendet.

Ein weiterer Gesichtspunkt, dem heute im Marketing eine besondere Bedeutung zukommt, ist die Wahrung der Geschlossenheit einer Kommunikationskampagne beim Einsatz unterschiedlicher Medien. Die hier vorgestellte Systematik der Umsetzung von Werbeaussagen ist zwar nur für das bildliche Zeichensystem ausgeführt worden, doch gelten die gleichen Grundsätze auch in anderen Systemen.

4.2.4. Beispiel für die Anwendung

Ein Spa ist ein moderner Badeort. Die Einrichtung geht jedoch weit darüber hinaus. Sie dient der Revitalisierung stressgeplagter Menschen. Für Baden-Baden wurde von uns ein Konzept entwickelt, in dem ein Luxushotel, eine Klinik und eine Schönheitsfarm zum schönsten Spa Europas vereint sind.

tests de conception comparatifs. Le résultat de ces tests ne pouvant être obtenu que par comparaison, les projets peuvent y être soumis quand ils sont encore sous une forme assez grossière et sans entraîner de frais excessifs. La décision et la réalisation définitives sont fondées sur ce dernier contrôle et cette ultime sélection.

Si l'on a suivi un seul développement jusqu'à ce point, il est possible de dégager l'utilité de la systématisation pour une campagne complète ou pour des décisions dans le sens d'une corporate identity. Dans les cas présents, l'homogénéité ne réside pas seulement dans un retour superficiel de constantes, mais constitue le résultat de principes de création homogènes qui, en outre, ouvrent un large champ créatif. Ces principes peuvent consister, par exemple, en ce que pour toutes les représentations figuratives on donne la priorité au niveau structurel plutôt qu'au niveau «normal» de l'énoncé, on fasse revenir fréquemment certaines textures, on adopte une perspective inhabituelle ou l'on utilise continuellement certaines combinaisons de types de signes.

Dans le marketing, on attache aujourd'hui une grande importance à la préservation de l'unité d'une campagne de communication lorsque plusieurs médias sont utilisés. La systématique de transposition d'énoncés publicitaires présentée ici n'a été exposée que pour le système de signes figuratifs; néanmoins, les mêmes principes valent également dans d'autres systèmes de signes.

4.2.4. Exemple d'utilisation

Un spa, c'est une station thermale moderne. Cette installation dépasse toutefois la simple notion de ville d'eaux. Elle se propose en effet de rendre toute sa vigueur à l'homme, terrassé par le stress. Nous avons élaboré, pour la ville de Baden-Baden, un plan où cohabitent un hôtel de luxe, une clinique et un vaste institut de beauté, qui font de ce complexe le plus bel spa d'Europe.

1	**Spa**	**Spa**	**Spa**
2	**Health**	**Gesundheit**	**Santé**
3	**Beauty**	**Schönheit**	**Beauté**
4	**Exclusivity**	**Exklusivität**	**Exclusivité**
5	**Nature**	**Natur**	**Nature**
6	**Peace**	**Ruhe**	**Tranquillité**
7	**Activity**	**Aktivität**	**Activité**
8	**Culture**	**Kultur**	**Culture**

A precondition for the development of a corporate design, for example Brenner's Spa, is always an exact analysis. By this means the main object components are brought together and placed in order in accordance with their significance for the whole concept. The more abstract tables of various possibilities of signification, so far shown for an object, are now varied in sketch form for each of the components of the object.
Each of the sketches shown here stands as a representative of a large number of possible pictorial ideas, which form the repertoire and basis for further development.

Voraussetzung für die Entwicklung eines Corporate Design, so beispielsweise das Brenner's Spa, ist immer eine exakte Analyse. Dabei werden die wesentlichen Objektkomponenten zusammengetragen und nach ihrer Bedeutung für das Gesamtkonzept in eine Rangfolge gebracht. Die bisher mehr abstrakt dargestellten Tabellen verschiedener Bezeichnungsmöglichkeiten für ein Objekt werden nun für jede Objektkomponente in Form von Skizzen variiert.
Jede der Skizzen in dieser Darstellung steht stellvertretend für eine grosse Zahl möglicher Bildideen, die das Repertoire und die Basis für die weitere Entwicklung bilden.

Une analyse exacte est toujours la condition préalable à l'élaboration d'un Corporate Design, comme par exemple celui du Brenner's Spa. A cet effet, les composantes essentielles d'un objet sont rassemblées et classées selon leur importance dans le concept général. Les tableaux des différentes possibilités de désignation d'un objet, représentées plus abstraitement jusqu'à présent, vont servir de base à des esquisses pour chaque composante de l'objet.
Sous cette forme, chacune des esquisses représente un grand nombre d'idées d'images possibles qui constituent le répertoire et la base de l'élaboration ultérieure.

1 2 3

Icon
Image
Metaphor
Diagram

Ikon
Abbild
Metapher
Diagramm

Icône
Image
Métaphore
Diagramme

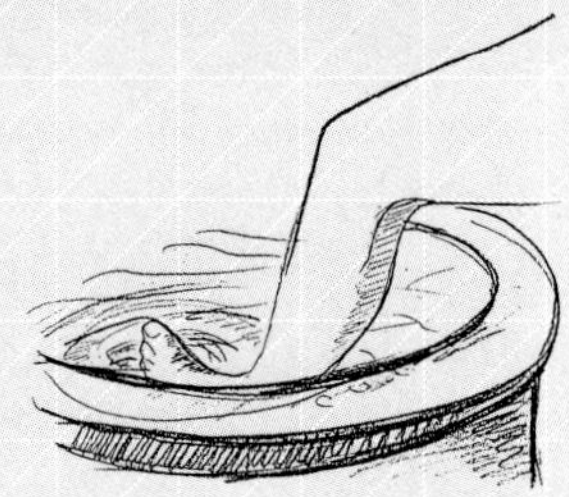

Index
Identifying image
Indication

Index
Identifizierendes Abbild
Anzeichen

Indice
Image identificatrice
Indication

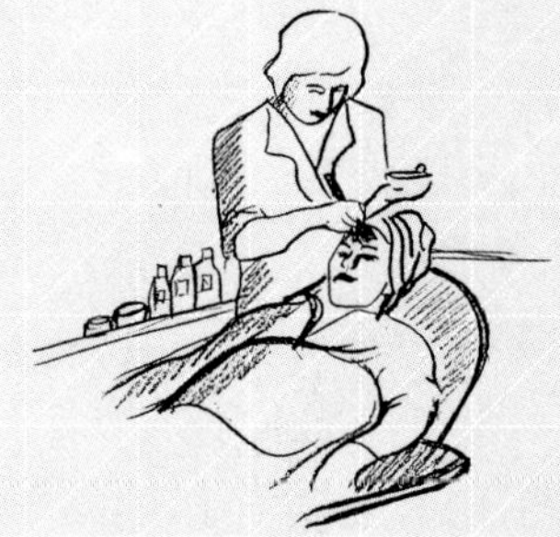

Symbol
Iconic symbol
Indexical symbol
Symbol in its proper sense

Symbol
Ikonisches Symbol
Indexikalisches Symbol
Symbol im eigentlichen Sinn

Symbole
Symbole iconique
Symbole indexical
Symbole au sens propre

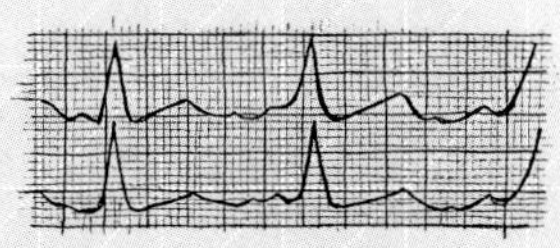

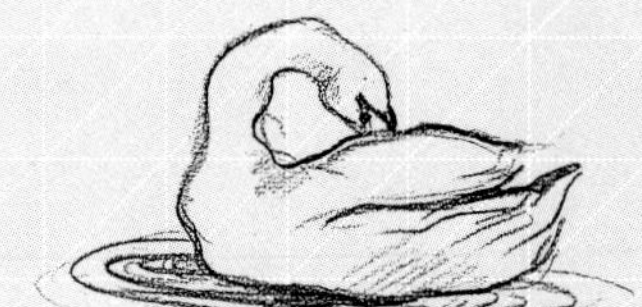

4

5

6

7

8

Kroehl Design D 230
Wolfgang Gassmann Ph

A development series as shown here is accompanied by a constant analysis of connotations. In designing the logo, the aim was to achieve a certain modernity while still admitting the influence of tradition.
The purely symbolic expression of the name Brenner's Spa needs no additional strengthening by means of a picture. The label — supported by the flowing and stimulating element of the textures — connotes all the relevant components of the subject.

Eine Entwicklungsreihe, wie hier dargestellt, ist von einer ständigen Analyse der Konnotationen begleitet. Bei der Gestaltung des Logos ging es darum, neben einer gewissen Modernität auch die Tradition mit einfliessen zu lassen.
Die rein symbolische Ausprägung des Namens Brenner's Spa bedarf keiner zusätzlichen Verankerung durch eine Bildmarke. Das Label – unterstützt durch das fliessende und belebende Element der Texturen – konnotiert alle relevanten Objektkomponenten.

Une série de développement, représentée ici, est accompagnée d'une analyse permanente des connotations. Il s'agissait, lors de la conception du logo, de faire ressortir, outre une certaine modernité, l'élément de la tradition.
Le caractère purement symbolique du nom Brenner's Spa ne nécessite nullement d'être renforcé par une image. Le label – appuyé par l'élément coulant et vivifiant des textures – connote toutes les composantes importantes de l'objet.

230

THE
BRENNERS
SPA®

231

Kroehl Design D 231
Peter Knapp / Wolfgang Gassmann Ph

Brenner's Spa consists of a clinic, a beauty farm and a hotel. Although united under one roof, these are completely independent establishments. The three-way division also determines the colour code: green for health, pink for beauty and blue for well-being.
In the design of the communication material and in the interior decoration, the policy maintained was that uniformity must not consist in the superficial repetition of constant elements but must be the result of uniform design principles.

Das Brenner's Spa besteht aus Klinik, Schönheitsfarm und Hotel. Obwohl unter einem Dach vereint, sind es aber durchweg eigenständige Einrichtungen. Diese Dreiteilung bestimmt auch den Farbcode, der sich in Grün (für Gesundheit), Rosé (für Schönheit) und Blau (für Wohlergehen) manifestiert.
Bei der Gestaltung der Kommunikationsmittel und des Interior Designs wurde davon ausgegangen, dass Einheitlichkeit nicht in der oberflächlichen Wiederkehr von Konstanten liegen muss, sondern das Ergebnis einheitlicher Gestaltungsprinzipien ist.

Le Brenner's Spa est constitué d'une clinique, d'un centre de beauté et d'un hôtel. Bien qu'elles soient réunies sous un seul toit, ces installations sont complètement indépendantes. Cette division en trois détermine le code de couleurs suivant: vert (pour la santé), rose (pour la beauté) et bleu (pour le bien-être).
Lors de la conception du moyen de communication et de l'interior design, on est parti de l'idée que l'unité ne devait pas résulter du retour superficiel de constantes, mais qu'il devait être le fruit de principes de réalisation homogènes.

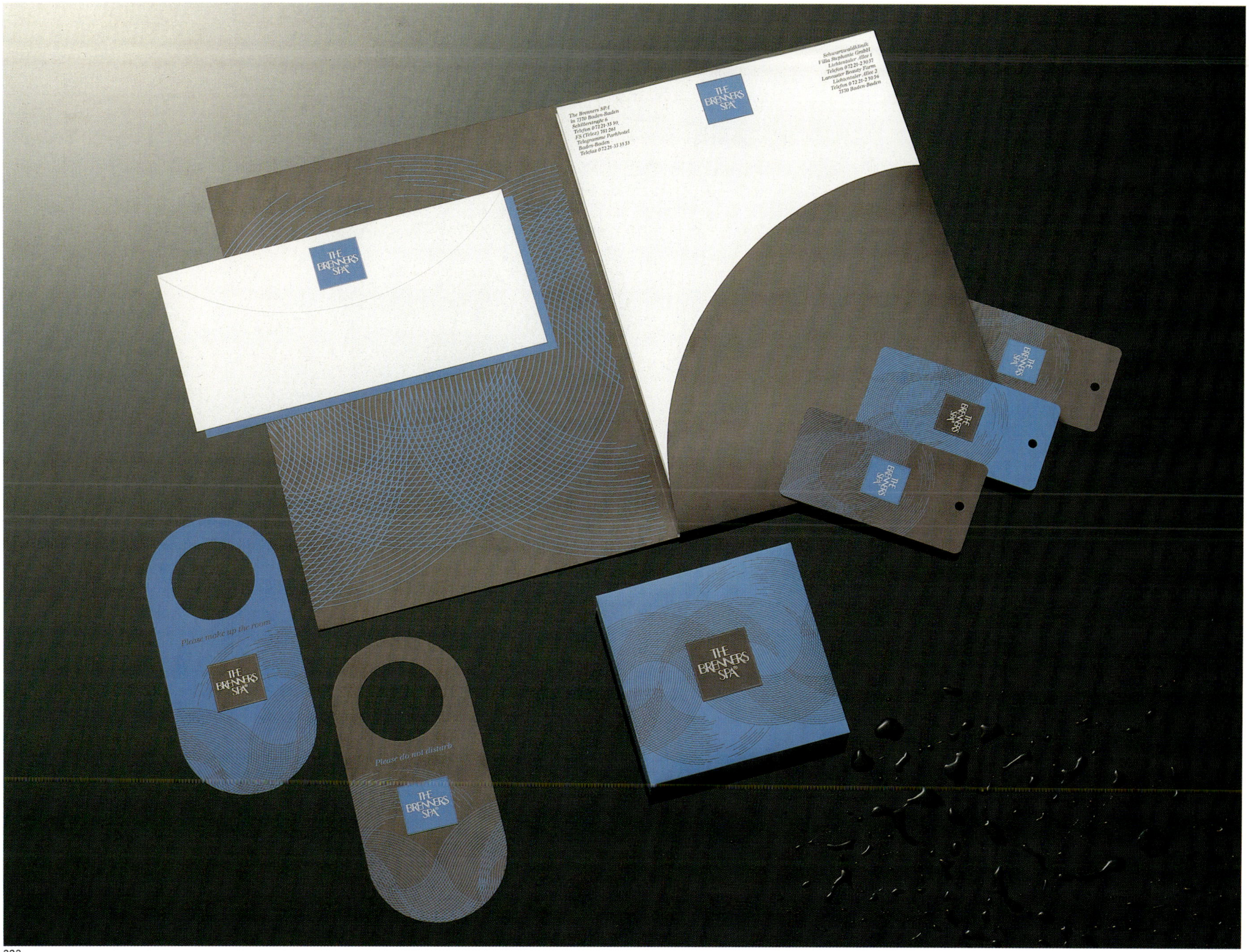

232

Kroehl Design D 232
Peter Knapp / Wolfgang Gassmann Ph

Reduction to the pure qualities of texture, structure and colours is here maintained, whereas photography provides pictures as signs of the real existence of that which is represented.

So ist einmal die Reduktion auf die reinen Qualitäten von Texturen, Strukturen und Farben vorgegeben, im Gegensatz dazu steht die Fotografie – Bilder als Zeichen der realen Existenz des Dargestellten.

La réduction aux qualités pures des textures, structures et couleurs est une donnée de départ. A l'opposé se trouve la photographie – les images sont le signe de l'existence réelle de ce qui est représenté.

233

Kroehl Design D 233
Peter Knapp / Wolfgang Gassmann Ph

Type and texture are so conceived as to be suitable for the many different forms of use, ranging from building decoration and other fittings and equipment to printed brochures and folders, together making up a whole palette.

Schriftmarke und Textur sind so konzipiert, dass sie den vielfältigen Anwendungsformen gerecht werden. Der Einsatz reicht vom Gebäudeschmuck und anderen Ausstattungselementen bis hin zu Broschüren und Prospekten, die zusammen eine Palette bilden.

La qualité de l'écriture et la texture sont conçues pour une grande variété d'utilisations. On les retrouve aussi bien dans l'ornementation des bâtiments et dans d'autres éléments de décoration que sur les brochures et les prospectus, ce qui permet d'obtenir une palette d'ensemble.

234

Kroehl Design D 234
Peter Knapp / Wolfgang Gassmann Ph

Going beyond the correlation of various means of design in house journal and business stationery, the whole ensemble in serial composition becomes an element of an overall structure, by means of which many other items including serviettes, fabrics, gift-wrappings, individual presents, etc. can all be designed.

Über die Symbiose verschiedener Gestaltungsmittel bei Hauszeitschrift und Geschäftspapieren hinausgehend, wird das Ensemble in der seriellen Komposition sogar zum Element einer Gesamtstruktur, mit der sich Servietten, Stoffe, Geschenkpapiere, individuelle Präsente und vieles andere mehr gestalten lassen.

Au-delà de la symbiose de différents moyens de réalisation dans le journal d'entreprise et les papiers d'affaires, l'ensemble devient même, dans la composition sérielle, l'élément d'une structure générale avec laquelle il est possible de réaliser des serviettes, des tissus, du papier-cadeau, des cadeaux individuels et bien d'autres choses encore.

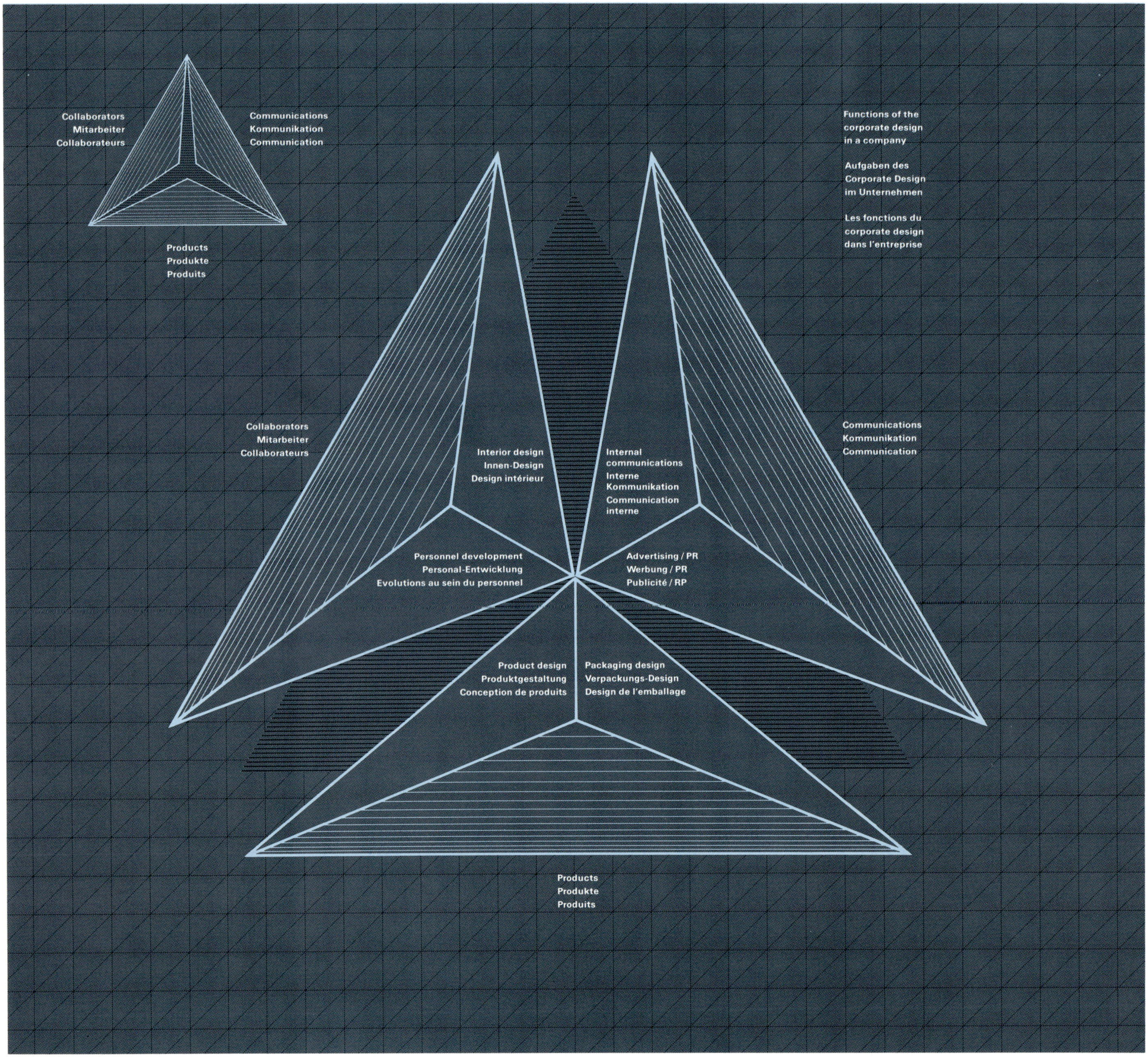
Collaborators
Mitarbeiter
Collaborateurs
Communications
Kommunikation
Communication
Products
Produkte
Produits
Functions of the corporate design in a company
Aufgaben des Corporate Design im Unternehmen
Les fonctions du corporate design dans l'entreprise
Collaborators
Mitarbeiter
Collaborateurs
Interior design
Innen-Design
Design intérieur
Internal communications
Interne Kommunikation
Communication interne
Communications
Kommunikation
Communication
Personnel development
Personal-Entwicklung
Evolutions au sein du personnel
Advertising / PR
Werbung / PR
Publicité / RP
Product design
Produktgestaltung
Conception de produits
Packaging design
Verpackungs-Design
Design de l'emballage
Products
Produkte
Produits

Corporate identity is the overall view of a company, in which three aspects work together:
Employees – Products – Communication.
Corporate identity can exist only when corporate design has created the necessary conditions. Consequently, the model of a three-sided pyramid (at left) is a necessary basis for the understanding of corporate design. The inner walls of the pyramid are the areas of contact between the sectors and involve thoroughgoing design tasks. *Product design* is mainly determined by the company staff. *Packaging design* flows in the direction of communication. *Advertising* is communication about products. *Internal communication* is addressed to the employees. *Personnel development* is an aspect of communication. *Interior design* has an influence on the products (also design of the production process).

Corporate Identity ist die ganzheitliche Betrachtung eines Unternehmens, bei der drei Aspekte zusammenwirken:
Mitarbeiter – Produkte – Kommunikation.
CI kann aber nur entstehen, wenn das Corporate Design die notwendigen Voraussetzungen schafft. Deswegen ist das links abgebildete Modell einer dreiseitigen Pyramide für das Verständnis von CD eine notwendige Grundlage. Die Innenwände der Pyramide sind die Berührungsflächen zwischen den Bereichen und beinhalten durchgehend Designaufgaben. *Produktgestaltung* wird wesentlich von den Mitarbeitern bestimmt. *Verpackungsdesign* fliesst in Richtung Kommunikation. *Werbung* ist Kommunikation über Produkte. *Interne Kommunikation* wendet sich an Mitarbeiter. *Personalentwicklung* ist ein Kommunikationsaspekt. *Interior Design* hat Einfluss auf Produkte (auch Gestaltung des Produktionsprozesses).

La Corporate Identity est la considération d'une entreprise dans son ensemble, où trois aspects agissent de concert:
Collaborateurs – Produits – Communication.
Toutefois, la CI ne peut exister que si le Corporate Design crée les conditions préalables indispensables. En conséquence, le modèle présenté à gauche, une pyramide à trois côtés, est nécessaire pour comprendre le CD. Les parois internes de la pyramide sont les surfaces de contact entre les différents domaines et comprennent toujours des missions de design. *La conception du produit* est largement déterminée par les collaborateurs. Le *design de l'emballage* va en direction de la communication. La *publicité* est de la communication sur les produits. La *communication interne* s'adresse aux collaborateurs. Le *développement du personnel* est un aspect de la communication. L'*Interior Design* influence le produits (conception du processus de production également).

5. Communication design and the media environment

5.1. Developments in environmental design

Product design, like media design, relates to the environment. It is only in recent times that researchers have recognized the significance of company and institutional images for public perception and memory. For both of these, it is a matter of visual presentation of products, colours and shapes and their effects on the attitude of the recipient. A "reception image" means one in which the representation of the object is materially perceived by the individual. For this purpose, we need signs. A trademark with a clear and attractive configuration of signs is preferred to others. This fact has important consequences for marketing thinking. When one bears in mind how sensitively mankind has always reacted to signs and signals, the value of visualization for corporate identity and positioning becomes apparent. The translation of a company philosophy into a visual language is the central problem of establishing an identity. Many companies fall down on this visual language transmission because they have not mastered the necessary instrumentarium. The extent to which images communicate, or convey meaning, has been shown in the foregoing part of this book.

The pictorial examples which follow do not only cover the social, cultural and economic dimensions of design but also document the establishment of an identity which becomes visually readable in direct and clear language. Design, in fact, begins with the consumer, not in production or development. Unfortunately, the marketing profession is still blinded by classical thinking about products and conventional communications strategies. Working out a corporate design places heavy demands on planning

5. Kommunikationsdesign und mediales Umfeld

5.1. Entwicklungen im Umweltdesign

Genauso wie Mediendesign ist Produktdesign ein Teil der Umweltgestaltung. Erst jetzt entdeckt die Forschung die Bedeutung von Wahrnehmungs- und Gedächtnisbildern für Unternehmen und Institutionen. In beiden Fällen handelt es sich um visuelle Vorstellungen von Produkten, Farben und Formen und ihre Auswirkungen auf das Verhalten des Rezipienten. Von einem Wahrnehmungsbild wird dann gesprochen, wenn der Gegenstand oder eine Abbildung des Objekts vom Individuum sinnlich wahrgenommen wird. Dazu benötigen wir Zeichen. Eine Marke, die mit klaren und anziehenden Zeichenfigurationen arbeitet, wird gegenüber anderen Marken bevorzugt. Daraus werden sich erhebliche Konsequenzen für das Marketingdenken ergeben. Zieht man ausserdem in Betracht, wie sensibel die Menschen seit jeher auf Zeichen und Signale reagieren, wird verständlich, welchen Stellenwert die Visualisierung für die Positionierung und Corporate Identity hat. Die Übersetzung einer Firmenphilosophie in eine visuelle Sprache ist das eigentliche Kernproblem einer Identität. An der visuellen Sprachübermittlung scheitern viele Unternehmen, weil sie das hierfür notwendige Instrumentarium nicht beherrschen. Wie weit nun Bilder kommunizieren – also Bedeutung vermitteln – wurde im vorhergehenden Teil des Buches aufgezeigt.

Die nachfolgenden Bildbeispiele belegen also nicht nur die sozialen, kulturellen oder ökonomischen Dimensionen der Gestaltung, sie dokumentieren auch, wie eine Identität entstehen kann, die visuell lesbar wird in direkter und klarer Sprache. Denn Design beginnt beim Verbraucher und nicht in der Produktion oder Entwicklung. Leider ist das Marketing immer noch vom klassischen Produktdenken und konventionellen Kommunikationsstrategien geblendet. Ein zu erarbeitendes Corporate Design stellt hohe

5. Le design de communication et l'environnement médiatique

5.1. Tendances du design pour l'environnement

Tout comme le design des médias, le design des produits appartient à l'aménagement de l'environnement. La recherche ne découvre que maintenant l'importance des images de perception et de mémoire pour les entreprises et les institutions. Dans les deux cas, il s'agit de présentations visuelles de produits, de couleurs et de formes, et des effets qu'ils exercent sur le comportement du destinataire. On parle d'image de perception quand l'objet ou une représentation de l'objet est perçu sensoriellement par l'individu. A cet effet, il nous faut des signes. Une marque qui travaille avec des figurations de signes claires et séduisantes est préférée aux autres. Il va s'ensuivre des répercussions considérables pour la conception du marketing. Si l'on considère en outre à quel point l'homme est sensible depuis toujours aux signes et aux signaux, on comprend l'importance de la visualisation pour le positionnement et la corporate identity. La traduction de la philosophie d'une entreprise en un langage visuel constitue le problème-clé d'une identité. Bien des entreprises échouent dans ce domaine parce qu'elles ne maîtrisent pas les instruments appropriés. Nous avons montré dans la partie précédente de cet ouvrage à quel point les images communiquent, c'est-à-dire transmettent du sens.

Les exemples illustrés qui suivent prouvent non seulement les dimensions sociales, culturelles ou économiques de la création, mais montrent aussi comment peut naître une identité lisible visuellement et exprimée dans un langage clair et direct. En effet, le design commence au niveau du consommateur, et non à celui de la production ou du développement. Malheureusement, le marketing reste aveuglé par la conception classique du produit et les stratégies de communication traditionnelles. Un corporate design, qui reste à élaborer, pose

At this point the question arises, since we once again acknowledge the sign language of architecture, what is to be done with it? Symbolism extends the domain of architecture to include meaning and expression and to develop a clear connection of both a denotative and a connotative kind.

Robert Venturi

An dieser Stelle erhebt sich jetzt, da wir die Zeichensprache in der Architektur wieder anerkennen, die Frage, was mit ihr zu tun ist. So dehnt die Symbolik die Reichweite der Architektur aus, um Bedeutung und Ausdruck einzubeziehen und einen klaren Zusammenhang zu fördern, sowohl denotativer als auch konnotativer Art.

Robert Venturi

L'architecture reconnaissant de nouveau le langage des signes, la question se pose ici de savoir ce que l'on doit en faire. Ainsi, la symbolique élargit la portée de l'architecture pour inclure le sens et l'expression, pour favoriser une cohésion claire, aussi bien de nature dénotative que connotative.

Robert Venturi

and objective analysis. As explained in the preceding chapters, there is a need for clearly directed strategy. When design is seen as a thought process, one of its elements must be science, which introduces system and enables basic assumptions to be questioned. Science can provide essential stimuli and suggestions but can never replace creativity. For creative tasks, there is never a single solution, and hardly any that can be worked out by sheer logic. To this extent, creativity, spontaneous ideas and aesthetic categories will always play a leading part. Corporate design is a new venture, combining inwardly and outwardly directed design policies.

This extended concept of design includes all visually appearing elements, together with location, architecture and vehicles. Not only the means of communication and product design but also the equipment and presentation of buildings, rooms and workplaces are signs with a content of meaning in which the identity of the manufacturing or service organization is mirrored. The attraction of products and services and the consequent preferences are strongly marked by the effects of experience. The selection which follows provides a vivid documentation of varied and purposeful design.

Because the meaning and effect of architecture and interior design have hardly been investigated, and because corporate design for companies and associations also includes these items, the areas of activity concerned are briefly presented. In emphasizing their semiotic interpretability, reference is here made to a neglected theme of marketing, the possibilities at the point of sale. Here, where the customer is directly confronted by the goods or services, there is hardly any deliberate use of the elements of activating design.

Anforderungen an Planung und Objektanalyse. Also Ziel- und Strategienotwendigkeit, wie sie in den vorhergehenden Kapiteln dargelegt wurden. Wenn man Design als Denkprozess begreift, dann ist Wissenschaft ein Element dieses Prozesses, ein Element, das es erlaubt, den Designprozess zu systematisieren und dabei zugrunde gelegte Annahmen zu überprüfen. Wissenschaft kann wesentliche Anstösse und Anregungen geben, sie kann aber Kreativität nie ersetzen. Für kreative Aufgaben gibt es niemals nur eine Lösung und schon gar keine, die rein logisch erarbeitet werden könnte. Insofern wird Kreativität, werden spontane Ideen und ästhetische Kategorien immer eine zentrale Rolle spielen. Corporate Design ist ein neuer Ansatz durch die Symbiose von nach aussen und nach innen gerichtetem Design.

Dieser erweiterte Designbegriff schliesst neben Standort, Architektur, Fahrzeugen – kurz, alle visuell in Erscheinung tretenden Elemente mit ein. Nicht nur Kommunikationsmittel und Produktgestaltung, sondern auch Ausstattung und Präsentation von Gebäuden, Räumen und Plätzen sind Zeichen mit Bedeutungsinhalten, in denen sich die Identität von Produktions- oder Dienstleistungsunternehmen widerspiegelt. Die Anziehungskraft von Produkten und Dienstleistungen und die damit verbundenen Präferenzen werden stark von Erlebniswirkungen geprägt. Ein anschauliches Beispiel für abwechslungsreiches und zielgruppenspezifisches Design dokumentiert die nachfolgende Auswahl.

Gerade weil die Bedeutung und Wirkung von Architektur und Interiordesign kaum untersucht ist und andererseits das Corporate Design für Unternehmen und Kommunen auch diese Bereiche mit einschliesst, werden diese Aufgabenfelder kurz aufgeführt. In der Betonung ihrer semiotischen Interpretierbarkeit soll hier auf ein vernachlässigtes Thema des Marketings verwiesen werden. Dort, wo der Kunde mit den Waren oder Dienstleistungen direkt konfrontiert wird, fehlen häufig die Elemente aktivierender Gestaltung.

des exigences élevées quant à la planification et à l'analyse de l'objet. Il y a donc une nécessité d'objectif et de stratégie, comme nous l'avons décrite dans les chapitres précédents. Si l'on comprend le design comme un processus de la pensée, la science est un élément de ce processus, un élément qui permet de systématiser le processus du design et de vérifier les hypothèses sous-jacentes. La science peut donner des impulsions, apporter des suggestions, mais elle ne remplace jamais la créativité. Les problèmes de création n'ont jamais une seule solution, et encore moins une solution qui pourrait être élaborée par la logique seule. C'est pourquoi la créativité, les idées spontanées et les catégories esthétiques joueront toujours un rôle central. Le corporate design est une nouvelle approche née de la symbiose entre un design orienté vers l'extérieur et un design dirigé vers l'intérieur.

Cette notion élargie du design englobe le site, l'architecture, les véhicules, en un mot tous les éléments qui se manifestent visuellement. Ce ne sont pas seulement les moyens de communication et la conception du produit, mais aussi le mobilier et la présentation des bâtiments, des pièces et des espaces qui sont des signes porteurs de signification dans lesquels se reflète l'identité des entreprises de production ou de services. L'attrait des produits et des services et les préférences qu'ils suscitent sont fortement marqués par la façon dont ils sont perçus. La sélection présentée ci-après apporte un exemple éloquent de design varié et destiné à un groupe-cible.

C'est parce que l'on n'a guère étudié l'importance de l'architecture et de l'interior design et parce que le corporate design pour communes et entreprises englobe aussi ces domaines qu'il faut les mentionner. Insister sur la possibilité d'une interprétation sémiotique permet d'évoquer un thème négligé en marketing. Là où le client entre en contact avec les biens et services, les éléments d'une utilisation consciente de la création active font souvent défaut.

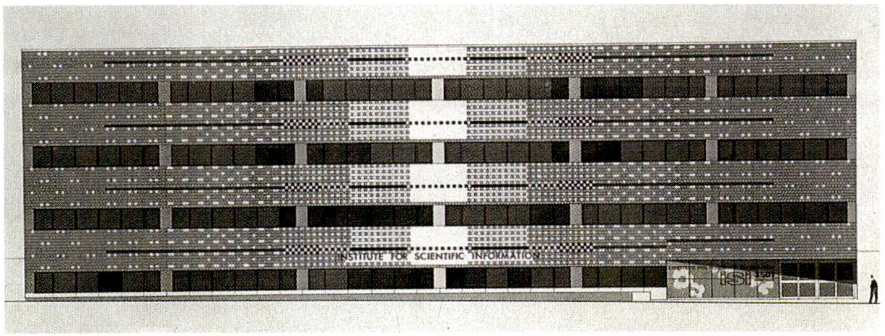

235

236

237

238

239

Robert Venturi	Ar	235
Venturi / Rauch / Scott Brown	Ar	236, 238, 239
Tom Bernard	Ph	
Hans Hollein	D	237

In these examples, the iconic signs — which in themselves contain statements such as colourfulness and happiness — are also carriers of communicative meaning. It is not only symbols and house colours but also the simplest Qualisigns that can characterize a building.

Auch die ikonischen Zeichen dieser Beispiele – die für sich genommen schon Aussagen, wie Buntheit und Fröhlichkeit, enthalten – sind Träger kommunikativer Bedeutung. Nicht nur Symbole oder Kennfarben, sondern auch einfachste Qualizeichen können ein Bauwerk bezeichnen.

Les signes iconiques de ces exemples – qui comprennent déjà en eux-mêmes des énoncés comme la couleur et la gaieté – sont aussi des vecteurs de sens. Les symboles ou les couleurs distinctives ne sont pas le seul moyen de représenter un édifice: il peut aussi s'agir de qualisignes extrêmement simples.

240

241

242

243

Norman Foster	Ar	240
Ian Lambot	Ph	
Helmut Jahn	Ar	241
James R Steinkamp	Ph	
Mario Botta	Ar	242
Antonio Martinelli	Ph	
Arquitectonia	Ar	243
Dorothea Schwarzhaupt	Ph	

As can be clearly seen here, each of these forms of architecture is overlaid by semiotic codes. These pictures, in particular, show the development from earlier functional buildings to an emphasis on formal qualities. The principles of transparency, veiling, mirroring, breaking out and penetration can be analysed in terms of sign theory.

Wie hier deutlich zu sehen, ist jede dieser Architekturen von semiotischen Codes überlagert. Besonders diese Bilder zeigen die Entwicklung von früheren Zweckbauten hin zur formbetonten Architektur. Das Prinzip der Transparenz, des Verhüllens und Verspiegelns, des Aufbrechens, des Durchdringens ist zeichentheoretisch analysierbar.

L'on voit clairement ici que chacune de ces architectures est chargée de codes sémiotiques. Ces images, en particulier, montrent l'évolution d'anciens bâtiments fonctionnels vers une architecture qui privilégie la forme. Le principe de la transparence, du voile et des reflets, de l'ouverture, de la pénétration, peut être analysé à l'aide de la théorie des signes.

SITE Ar 244
Robert Venturi Ar 245
Tom Bernard Ph

244

Today, the designer can make use of the results of behavioural research. Modern hypermarkets, like supermarkets, must not be dreary or boring. An important element of decision, particularly among the younger customers, is that they must "have fun" while shopping. Optical holding points, the strategic selection of points of vision, making allowance for natural curiosity: these form the background for means of design which will arouse attention. The sign-process documented here runs dynamically with the direction of reading. Through being placed in series, symbols obtain an iconic character and become decorative patterns.

Der Designer kann sich heute Erkenntnisse der Verhaltensforschung zunutze machen. Moderne Einkaufsstätten, wie Supermärkte, müssen nicht öde und langweilig sein. Ein wichtiges Entscheidungskriterium, gerade bei jüngeren Verbrauchern, ist, dass sie «Spass beim Einkaufen» haben wollen. Optische Anker, die strategische Auswahl von Blickpunkten, die Berücksichtigung des Neugier-Verhaltens bilden den Hintergrund für aufmerksamkeitserregende Gestaltungsmittel. Der hier dokumentierte Zeichenprozess verläuft dynamisch mit der Leserichtung. Symbole erhalten durch Seriation einen ikonischen Charakter und werden zu dekorativen Mustern.

Aujourd'hui, le designer peut mettre à profit les enseignements de l'étude du comportement. Les lieux d'achat actuels, comme les supermarchés, ne doivent pas être monotones et ennuyeux. Pour les jeunes consommateurs notamment, le «plaisir de faire des achats» est un élément de décision important. Des élémens qui accrochent le regard, le choix stratégique des points de vue, la prise en considération de la curiosité forment la base des moyens de conception destinés à attirer l'attention. Le processus de signe présenté ici progresse dynamiquement avec le sens de lecture. Par la sériation, les symboles reçoivent un caractère iconique et deviennent des motifs décoratifs.

245

246

248

247

249

SITE Ar 246–251

An example of surprise and difference in a firm's philosophy. The turnover of these department stores was quadrupled with the new image. Commercial gain was accompanied by cultural success through highly regarded museum presentations for "Buildings for best products".

Überraschung und Andersartigkeit als Firmenphilosophie. So konnte der Umsatz dieser Warenhäuser durch das neue Erscheinungsbild vervierfacht werden. Neben den kommerziellen Gewinn trat der kulturelle Erfolg, durch vielbeachtete Museumspräsentationen «Buildings for best products».

Surprise et différence, une philosophie d'entreprise. La nouvelle image de marque de ces grands magasins leur a permis de quadrupler leur chiffre d'affaires. Réussite commerciale, certes, mais aussi culturelle, comme le montre l'excellent accueil fait aux présentations comme dans les musées de «Buildings for best products».

250

251

Chermayeff and Geismar	D	252, 256
Carbone Smolan Associates	D	253
Venturi / Rauch / Scott Brown	Ar	254, 255
Tom Bernard	Ph	
Chermayeff and Geismar	D	257
Thomas Leighton	Ph	

With these examples, too, it is a matter of the characterization of buildings, except that these "supersigns", as environments, are dissociated from architecture. The heightening effect can make a substantial contribution to communication through the bringing together of individual segments, whether lined up or merged.
The striking effect of such configurations of signs is increased not only through the contrast between large and small but also and above all through colour, better still a sequence of colour.

Auch bei diesen Beispielen geht es um die Kennzeichnung von Gebäuden, nur sind diese Superzeichen als Environments losgelöst von der Architektur. Die Superierung kann durch Aneinanderreihung von Einzelsegmenten, aber auch durch deren Verschmelzung zu grösseren Gebilden eine beachtliche Kommunikationswirkung entfalten.
Die Merkfähigkeit solcher Zeichenfigurationen wird nicht nur durch den Gross/Klein-Kontrast, sondern vor allem durch Farbe – besser sogar durch eine Farbsequenz – gesteigert.

Ici encore, il s'agit de l'identification de bâtiments, mais ces supersignes sont détachés de l'architecture. Par l'alignement de segments isolés ou par leur fusion en formes plus grandes, ces dimensions peuvent produire un effet de communication considérable.
L'effet frappant de ces configurations de signes est accru non seulement par le contraste dimensionnel, mais surtout par la couleur – ou mieux encore par une séquence de couleurs.

252

253

The intelligibility of the supersign in its wider connection is called its communicative information value.
The unusual character of the association of five individual signs, its improbability as an event, is called the technical information value. One can also say that precisely because supersigns, through their unexpected occurrence, activate or even irritate the viewer, they are sure to receive the greatest attention.

Die Verständlichkeit des im grösseren Zusammenhang gebildeten Superzeichens nennt man den kommunikativen Informationswert.
Die Ungewöhnlichkeit der Verknüpfung von fünf Einzelzeichen, ihre geringe Ereigniswahrscheinlichkeit, nennt man den technischen Informationswert. Man kann auch sagen, gerade weil Superzeichen durch ihr unerwartetes Auftreten den Betrachter aktivieren oder sogar irritieren ist ihnen höchste Aufmerksamkeit gewiss.

L'intelligibilité des supersignes formés dans un vaste contexte s'appelle la valeur informative de communication.
Le caractère inhabituel de l'association de cinq signes différents, leur faible probabilité d'incidence est appelée valeur informative technique. L'on peut aussi affirmer que le supersigne, étant donné qu'il stimule, voire irrite le spectateur en apparaissant de manière inattendue, est très efficace pour attirer l'attention.

254

255

256

257

Hans Hollein	Ar	258, 259
Hans Hollein /Jerzy Surwillo	Ph	
SITE	Ar	260, 261
Andreas Sterzing	Ph	

The arrangement of public spaces is also a design problem. There are plenty of occasions to promote culture in towns: simply expressed, a feeling of togetherness, a variety of experience and communication. The example from Munich shown here — fascinating in its changing day and night aspects — is an interesting contribution to the design of public areas, which frequently offer no more than mediocre art, decoration or modish ornamentation.

Auch die Gestaltung öffentlicher Räume ist ein Design-Problem. Es gibt genügend Anlässe, Kultur in der Stadt, vereinfacht ausgedrückt ein Wir-Gefühl, Erlebnisvielfalt und Kommunikation, zu fördern. Das hier vorgestellte - und in wechselnden Tag- und Nachtsituationen faszinierende - Münchener Modell ist ein interessanter Beitrag zur Gestaltung öffentlicher Zonen, die häufig nur Durchschnittskunst, Dekoration oder modische Verzierung bieten.

La conception de locaux publics est aussi un problème de design. Il existe bien des possibilités de promouvoir la culture dans la ville, ce que l'on pourrait appeler pour simplifier un sentiment de communauté, une diversité d'expériences, et la communication. Le fascinant modèle munichois présenté ici - de nuit et de jour - est une contribution intéressante à la conception de zones publiques, qui n'offrent souvent que des réalisations artistiques moyennes, de la décoration ou des ornements à la mode.

258

259

Municipal officials, town-planners and architects are hopelessly out of their depth when they act as animators in a given sector. The results are often apparently legitimate in terms of aesthetics and education but they leave the basic needs of the citizen out of consideration. This example from Canada shows what a stimulating visual adventure can be. The uncompromising concept touches on fears and love of live, but also on the joy of discovery through ironical "quotations".

Kommunale Beamte, Stadtplaner, aber auch Architekten sind hoffnungslos überfordert, wenn sie in einem bestimmten Bereich als Animateure auftreten. Oft sind es Lösungen von scheinbar legitimierter Ästhetik und Pädagogik, die die Grundbedürfnisse der Bürger ausser acht lassen. Dieses Modell in Kanada demonstriert, was ein stimulierendes Augenabenteuer sein kann. Die kompromisslose Konzeption berührt Ängste und Lebenslust, aber auch Entdeckerfreude durch ironische Zitate.

Les fonctionnaires communaux, les urbanistes et même les architectes sont dépassés quand ils doivent exercer une fonction d'animateur dans un domaine précis. Leurs solutions s'inspirent généralement d'une esthétique et d'une pédagogie apparemment légitimées qui ne tiennent pas compte des besoins fondamentaux des citoyens. Ce modèle canadien illustre ce que peut être une aventure stimulante pour les yeux. Cette conception sans compromis touche les angoisses et la joie de vivre, mais aussi le plaisir de la découverte par des citations ironiques.

260

261

262

263

Otto Herbert Hajek D 262–264
Horst Rellecke Ar 265–267
Gerda Jucho Ph

This colourful garden of sculpture is situated on a site of more than 15 acres (6 ha) in the city centre of Adelaide.

Mitten im Stadtzentrum von Adelaide befindet sich dieser farbige Skulpturengarten auf einem über 6 ha grossen Gelände.

En plein centre d'Adelaide, on trouve ce jardin de sculptures coloré sur un terrain de plus de 6 ha.

264

265

266

Modern architecture has displaced a tradition which used to combine painting, sculpture and graphic elements. The visual language of architecture is expressed in these wrought-iron figures, whose forms seize on the imaginative iconography of American examples.

Die moderne Architektur hat eine Tradition verdrängt, die einstmals Malerei, Plastik und grafische Elemente miteinander verbunden hatte. Die neue Sprache der Architektur kommt im Hammer-Elefanten zum Ausdruck, dessen Gestalter wiederum die phantasievolle Ikonografie amerikanischer Vorbilder aufgreift.

L'architecture moderne a chassé une tradition qui associait la peinture, la plastique et les éléments graphiques. Le nouveau langage de l'architecture s'exprime dans l'éléphant-marteau dont le concepteur reprend l'iconographie pleine d'imagination des modèles américains.

267

268

269

270

Sunny Side, Central Kogei D 268–270
G. Yasuhiro Goto Ph

Increasing fashion-consciousness is leading to greatly increasing demands on shop design and equipment. The popularity of "looking around the shops" is growing all the time. Research has shown that nearly 50 per cent of women prefer to obtain their fashion information by visiting boutiques and similar establishments.
The retail trade as a whole has not yet recognized this fact, as is evident from the lack of ideas and the uniform appearance of most shops.

Zunehmendes Modebewusstsein führt zu enorm steigenden Ansprüchen an Design und Ladenausstattungen. Die Beliebtheit des Einkaufsbummels nimmt kontinuierlich zu. Untersuchungen belegen, dass fast 50 Prozent der Frauen ihre Modeinformationen am liebsten durch Besuche in Boutiquen o. ä. holen.
Nur der Handel hat diesen Trend noch nicht erkannt, wie die Einfallslosigkeit und Uniformität der meisten Geschäfte belegen.

Un sens de la mode de plus en plus aigu engendre des exigences croissantes en matière de design et d'aménagement des magasins. La popularité du shopping ne cesse de se développer. Des études montrent que presque 50% des femmes préfèrent s'informer de la mode en fréquentant des boutiques ou établissements similaires.
Seul le commerce n'a pas encore compris cette tendance, comme le montrent le manque d'imagination et l'uniformité de presque tous les magasins.

271

272

273

Junji Nanno D 271–273
G. Yasuhiro Goto Ph

The new kind of interior design is determined by semiotic rules of arrangement. One could describe this interior as a "multi-sensual design", since it comprises all categories of sensual perception through forms, colours, odours and sounds. Here the act of walking over an arrangement of pebblestones or an imitation of a classical mosaic floor becomes a sensual experience. Starting with the elegantly conceived entrance, everything is laid out to bring relaxation and emotional well-being to the customer.

Die neue Art von Interior Design wird bestimmt von semiotischen Gestaltungsregeln. Man kann dieses Interior auch als multisensuales Design bezeichnen, denn es umfasst die gesamte sinnlich wahrnehmbare Gestaltung durch Formen, Farben, Geruch und Geräusche. Hier wird das Begehen eines Arrangements von Kieselsteinen oder eines nachempfundenen klassischen Mosaikbodens zum sinnlichen Erleben. Beginnend mit dem raffiniert konzipierten Eingang ist alles darauf angelegt, dem Kunden Entspannung und emotionales Wohlbefinden zu vermitteln.

Les règles de conception sémiotiques déterminent le nouveau style d'Interior Design. On peut définir cet Interior comme un Design multisensuel, car il inclut l'ensemble de la conception perceptible par les sens en faisant appel aux couleurs, aux formes, aux odeurs et aux bruits. Ici, le passage sur un arrangement de galets ou sur un sol imitant une mosaïque classique devient une expérience sensuelle. Dès l'entrée, conçue avec raffinement, tout est prévu pour la détente et le bien-être du client.

Hans Hollein Ar 274–279
Franz Hubmann / Jerzy Surwillo Ph

These three examples also show how a visual identity can be created through a congruence of outside appearance and interior fittings. Visual formulations of shops are here put into practice. It is exactly because they can be held in the memory as inner images, owing to their clarity, that they are preferred by customers. This is also proven by increases in turnover up to three times.

Auch diese drei Beispiele zeigen, wie aufgrund einer Kongruenz von Aussenbild und Innenausstattung eine visuelle Identität entstehen kann. Hier werden Konzeptionen von Geschäften visuell ausformuliert. Gerade weil sie sich wegen ihrer Klarheit als innere Bilder speichern lassen, werden sie von Käufern präferiert. Dies belegen auch Umsatzsteigerungen bis zur dreifachen Höhe.

Ces trois exemples montrent comment une identité visuelle peut naître de la congruence de l'image extérieure avec l'aménagement intérieur. Les conceptions des magasins sont formulées visuellement. En raison de leur clarté, elles peuvent être enregistrées comme images internes et suscitent ainsi la préférence des acheteurs. L'augmentation du chiffre d'affaire – qui peut être multiplié par trois – en apporte la preuve.

274

275

276

277

278

279

280

Kim Design Office D 280
T. Nacása & Partners Ph

These two "future shops" also show a change of trend in modern shopfitting. From a semiotic point of view, the dominant signs here are Qualisigns, such as wood, steel and stone. The archaic and simple element is the basis for a bizzarre "stage setting", aimed at youthful target groups.

Auch diese beiden «Future Shops» belegen eine Trendwende in der modernen Ladengestaltung. Semiotisch gesehen dominieren hier Qualizeichen, wie Holz, Stahl oder Stein. Das Archaische und Einfache ist Grundlage einer bizarren Inszenierung, die auf jugendliche Zielgruppen zugeschnitten ist.

Ces deux «Future Shops» illustrent aussi un changement de tendance dans l'aménagement moderne des boutiques. Du point de vue sémiotique, les qualisignes dominent: bois, acier ou pierre. Le caractère archaïque et la simplicité constituent la base d'une mise en scène bizarre conçue pour les groupes-cibles jeunes.

281

Shiro Kuramata . D 281
Mitsumasa Fujitsuka Ph

In future, the retail trade must offer more innovations, starting from the point of sale, where the goods and attractive prices no longer occupy the foreground. Instead, competent advice and modern communication centres must be the model for development.

Der Handel muss zukünftig mehr Innovationen bieten. Ausgehend vom point of sale, wo nicht mehr Ware und günstiger Preis im Vordergrund stehen, sondern neben kompetenter Beratung moderne Kommunikationszentren als Vorbild dienen müssen.

A l'avenir, le commerce doit offrir davantage d'innovations. A commencer par le point de vente, où l'accent n'est plus mis sur le produit et le prix, mais sur la qualité du conseil et de la communication.

282

283

Kazumi Fujimoto	D	282
Ryo Komatsu, Masatoshi Watanabe	D	283
Mami Kawasaki	D	284
Tamiko Tanaka	Ph	
Toshio Yamagata	D	285
Yoshiaki Murakami	Ph	
Sekiharu Suenaga, Michio Yamazaki	D	286
Harutoshi Kada, Hiroaki Nagai	D	287
Kunihiro Shinohara	Ph	
Kanji Tanaka	D	288

The classical style of window-dressing has served its turn and within a few years will belong to the past. Displays must become a medium for emotional experience. Experiments have shown that physically intensive attractions — the formation of supersigns or interesting combinations of colours (Fig. 282–284), emotional attractions (Fig. 285–286) or intellectually surprising attractions (Fig. 287–288) capture the viewer's interest and can therefore be used.

Die klassische Schaufenstergestaltung hat ausgedient und wird in wenigen Jahren der Vergangenheit angehören. Die Auslagen müssen zu einem Medium für emotionales Erleben werden. Experimentelle Untersuchungen belegen, dass besonders physikalisch intensive Reize – die Bildung von Superzeichen oder interessante Farbkombinationen also (Abbildung 282–284), emotionale Reize (Abbildung 285–286) oder gedanklich überraschende Reize (Abbildung 287–288) – das Interesse des Betrachters fesseln und somit genutzt werden können.

L'aménagement classique des vitrines est dépassé et aura disparu dans quelques années. Les étalages doivent devenir un moyen de susciter une réaction affective. Des études expérimentales prouvent que des stimuli physiques intenses – comme la formation de supersignes ou des combinaisons intéressantes de couleurs (figures 282–284), des stimuli émotionnels (figures 285–286) ou des stimuli surprenants pour l'esprit (figures 287–288) – captent l'intérêt du spectateur et peuvent ainsi être utilisés.

284

285

286

287

288

Displays in shop windows and salerooms, properly used, are never a wasted investment. The presentation must be tailored to the goods, according to the value of the product. These showpieces, which carry an aura of meaning through the use of refined metaphor, likeness and indication, can be placed in the correct light through the use of modern spotlights and electrical circuits.
For this purpose, large-scale and often cost-intensive development work is necessary, so as to obtain freedom from standard and system thinking, which has everywhere led to uniformity.

Displays in Schaufenstern und Verkaufsräumen richtig eingesetzt sind niemals Fehlinvestitionen. Die Präsentation muss der Ware angemessen sein, je nach Wertigkeit des Produktes. Diese Schaustücke, die durch verfeinerte Metaphern, Abbilder und Anzeichen eine Aura von Bedeutung mit sich herumtragen, lassen sich durch modernste elektrische Spotanlagen und Schaltungen ins rechte Licht rücken.
Hierzu ist eine aufwendige und manchmal kostenintensive Entwicklungsarbeit notwendig, um sich vom Standard- und Systemdenken zu befreien, das allerorten zu einer Uniformität geführt hat.

Bien utilisés dans les vitrines et les locaux de vente, les displays ne sont jamais de mauvais investissements. La présentation doit être adaptée au produit: elle dépendra de sa valeur. Des circuits électriques et des spots ultra-modernes permettent de donner la lumière qu'elles méritent à ces pièces magnifiques, entourées d'une aura de signification faite de métaphores, d'images et de marques raffinées.
Ce résultat exige un travail d'élaboration long et parfois coûteux, indispensable pour s'écarter des idées toutes faites qui ont mené partout à l'uniformité.

289

290

291

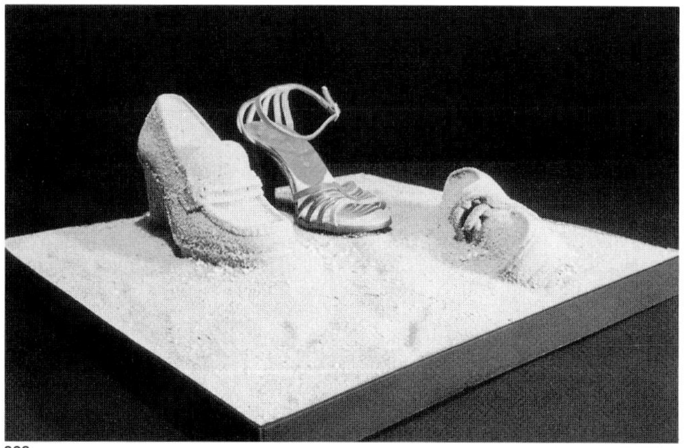

292

293

SITE	D	289, 291, 292
Satoshi Kamo, Shigeo Toya	D	290
Takumi Wataya	Ph	
Edward Hopper		293
Sekiharu Suenaga, Michio Yamazaki	D	294
Setsuo Kitaoka	D	295
Yoshio Shiratori	Ph	

Boldly conceived arrangements of trading premises are rarely to be seen. They reflect little of the spirit of the times, as is the case with these examples, where the products have apparently been given a subsidiary role.
Inspired by themes of Edward Hopper (see small picture) and other artists, the objects of such a pictorial statement cannot simply be equated with the items illustrated. Too much evaluation and feeling become involved, in this case mainly unrelatedness and emptiness. In the other subject, on the other hand, indolence and individualism are present as the expression of a life style.

Kühne Arrangements für Verkaufsräume sind selten. Sie spiegeln auch wenig den Zeitgeist wider, wie es bei diesen Beispielen der Fall ist, wo Produkte scheinbar nebensächlich werden.
Inspiriert von Themen Edward Hoppers (siehe kleines Bild) oder anderen Künstlern können die Objekte einer solchen bildlichen Aussage nicht einfach mit den abgebildeten Gegenständen gleichgesetzt werden. Zu sehr fliessen Wertungen und Gefühle mit ein, in diesem Fall vor allem Beziehungslosigkeit und Leere. Beim anderen Motiv sind es hingegen Lässigkeit und Individualismus, als Ausdruck von Life-Style.

Rares sont les locaux de vente aux aménagements hardis. Bien souvent, ils ne reflètent guère l'esprit du temps, à la différence de ces exemples où les produits semblent devenir accessoires.
Inspirés de thèmes d'Edward Hoppers (cf. petite photo) ou d'autres artistes, les objets de cet énoncé figuratif ne peuvent être simplement assimilés aux objets représentés. La charge subjective et émotionnelle est trop importante, dans ce cas principalement l'incohérence et le vide. L'autre motif, en revanche, évoque la nonchalance et l'individualisme, expressions du mode de vie.

294

295

In comparison with other instruments of communication and sources of information, trade fairs have a high value as events. The exhibition of products and wares, and the demonstration of product innovations, can produce a considerable effect on the public, which cannot be achieved by the usual means of picture and text communication.
Empirical findings have shown that the stand with the best information facilities is the one that also promises the best success, whereas system construction and lack of innovation often make one stand indistinguishable from another.

Im Vergleich zu anderen Kommunikationsinstrumenten und Informationsquellen haben Messen einen hohen Ereigniswert. Die Ausstellung von Produkten und Waren, aber auch Vorstellung von Produktinnovationen können einen beachtlichen Öffentlichkeitseffekt auslösen, der mit den üblichen Mitteln der Bild- und Textkommunikation nicht zu erreichen ist.
Nach empirischen Befunden ist der informationsfreundlichste Stand die Konzeption, die auch den grössten Messeerfolg verspricht. Durch Systembauweise und Mangel an Innovation gleicht aber oft ein Stand dem anderen.

Comparées à d'autres instruments de communication et sources d'information, les foires ont une grande valeur d'événement. L'exposition de produits, mais aussi la présentation de nouveautés, peuvent avoir sur le public un impact bien supérieur à celui des moyens habituels de communication par l'image et le texte.
Selon des constatations empiriques, c'est le stand où l'information circule le mieux qui offre le plus de chance de succès à une foire. Toutefois, la construction par unités de montages et le manque d'innovation donne souvent à tous les stands le même aspect.

296

297

298

299

Hirofumi Hirabayashi	D	296
Yuji Hirata	D	297
Satoshi Bando	Ph	
Endo Lighting, Design Associates	D	298
Terutoshi Hirasawa	D	299
Yukiyo Yoshida	Ph	

How is an atmosphere favourable to communication created? Answering a questionnaire, a large percentage of buyers and visitors expressed a desire for undisturbed information. Like islands, information and presentation desks arise here from an atmospheric environment, signalizing an invitation to communication.

Wie schafft man eine kommunikationsfreundiche Atmosphäre? Ein hoher Anteil an Käufern und Besuchern äussert in Befragungen den Wunsch nach unbehelligter Information. Gleich Inseln tauchen hier Präsentationstische aus einem atmosphärischen Umfeld auf und signalisieren somit eine Einladung zur Kommunikation.

Comment créer une atmosphère favorable à la communication? Selon les sondages, un pourcentage élevé d'acheteurs et de visiteurs souhaite être informé sans être importuné. Ici, les tables d'information apparaissent comme des îles dans un environnement agréable. Elles invitent à la communication.

300

301

Kazushi Nakamura, Tomoyoshi Ohashi, Hiroshi Hattori	D	300
Joji Ito	D	301
Yoshinori Sekine	Ph	
Kazuhide Kataoka, Noboru Muroi, Yuichi Kunisada	D	302
Emilio Ambasz	D	303
Hiroshi Inagaki	AD	304
Masami Daito	Ph	

302

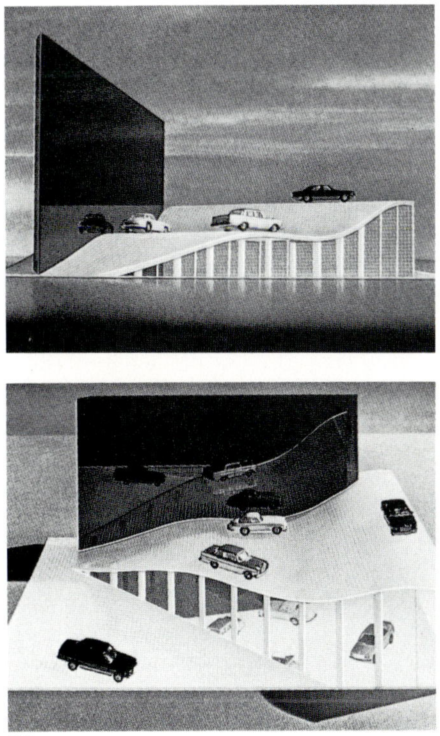

303

New information techniques and exhibition ideas are becoming necessary in order to make the complex procedures of high technology clearly understandable to interested parties. Not only trade fairs but also new concepts for product display, such as the design for a Mercedes showroom, are expressions of a new design concept.

Neue Informationstechniken und Ausstellungskonzeptionen werden notwendig, um dem Interessenten komplizierte Vorgänge der Hochtechnologie transparent zu machen. Aber nicht nur Messen, sondern auch neue Konzepte für die Ausstellung von Produkten, wie der Entwurf für einen Mercedes-Show-Room, sind Ausdruck einer neuen Designauffassung.

Des techniques d'information et des conceptions d'exposition nouvelles sont nécessaires pour faire comprendre aux personnes intéressées les procédés compliqués de la haute technologie. La nouvelle approche du design s'exprime non seulement dans les foires, mais aussi dans de nouveaux concepts d'exposition des produits, comme l'illustre ce projet de salle d'exposition Mercedes.

304

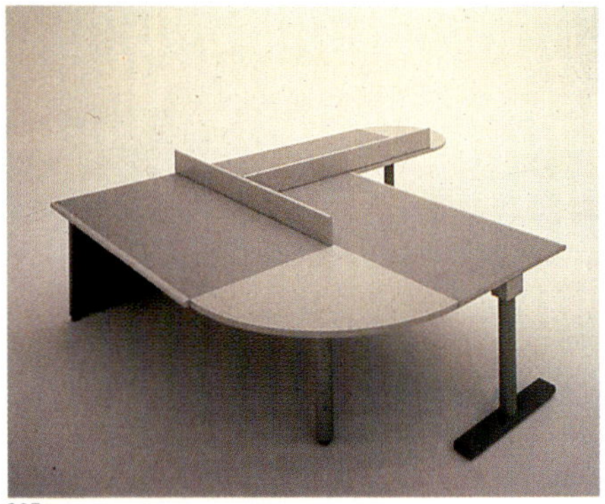

305

306

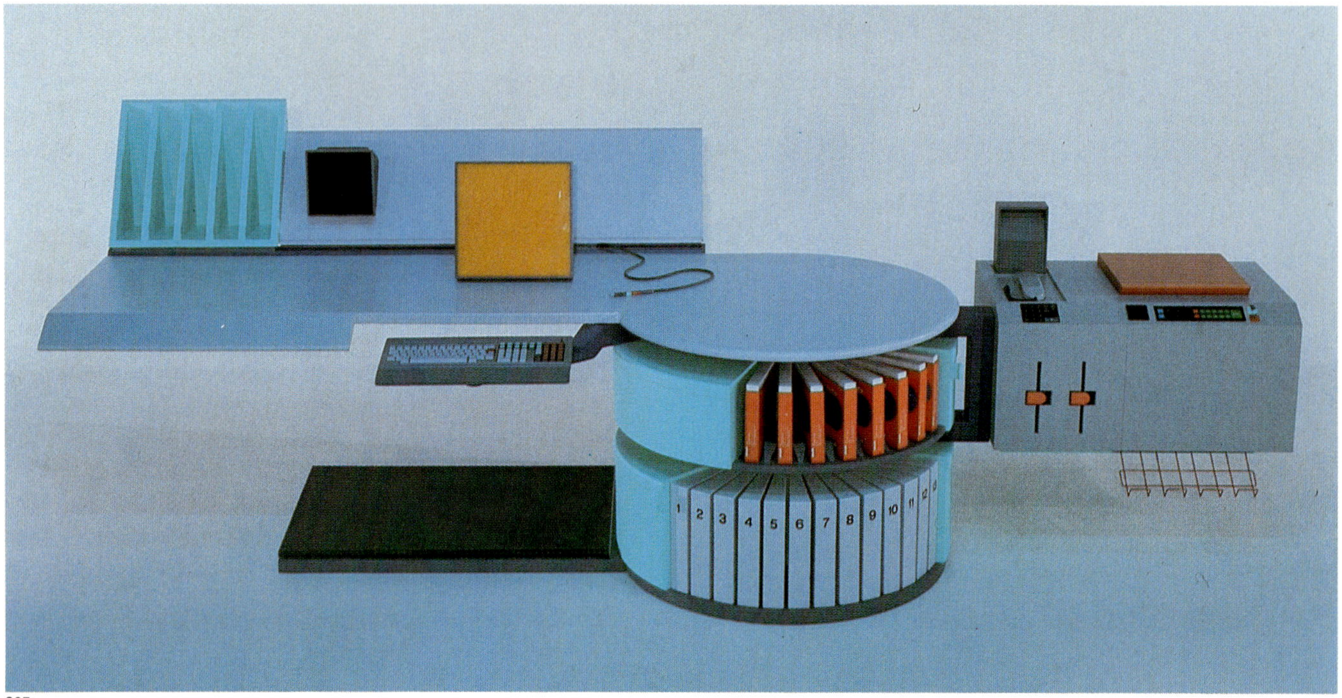

307

308

Michele de Lucchi D 305, 306, 308
Hans von Klier D 307
Massimo Vignelli D 309–311
Ettore Sottsass D 312, 313

An important individual aspect of the total "company project" is the office of the future. The functional variability and compatibility of the systems shown here are enough to indicate a completely new approach to this field of activity. The last two examples, in particular, can be described as the real discovery of an office landscape of the future.

Ein wichtiger Einzelaspekt zu dem Gesamtprojekt «Unternehmen» ist das Büro der Zukunft. Allein die funktionale Variabilität und Kompatibilität der hier vorgestellten Systeme weist auf eine völlig neue Betrachtungsweise dieses Aufgabenfeldes hin. Besonders die letzten beiden Beispiele kann man als die eigentliche Entdeckung einer Bürolandschaft von Morgen bezeichnen.

Le bureau de demain est un aspect important du projet d'ensemble "entreprise". La variabilité et la compatibilité fonctionnelles des systèmes présentés ici suffisent à illustrer l'approche radicalement nouvelle de ce champ d'action. Les deux derniers exemples, en particulier, peuvent être considérés comme la découverte véritable de l'espace bureau de demain.

309

310

311

312

313

For the designer, four sectors of electronic communication are of prime importance; they overlap in many ways, as shown in the diagram.

Für den Designer sind vier Bereiche der elektronischen Kommunikation von zentraler Bedeutung; sie überschneiden sich in vielfältiger Weise, wie die Grafik veranschaulichen soll.

Parmi les procédés électroniques de communication, le designer distingue quatre domaines essentiels; comme l'indique ce graphique, les chevauchements sont nombreux.

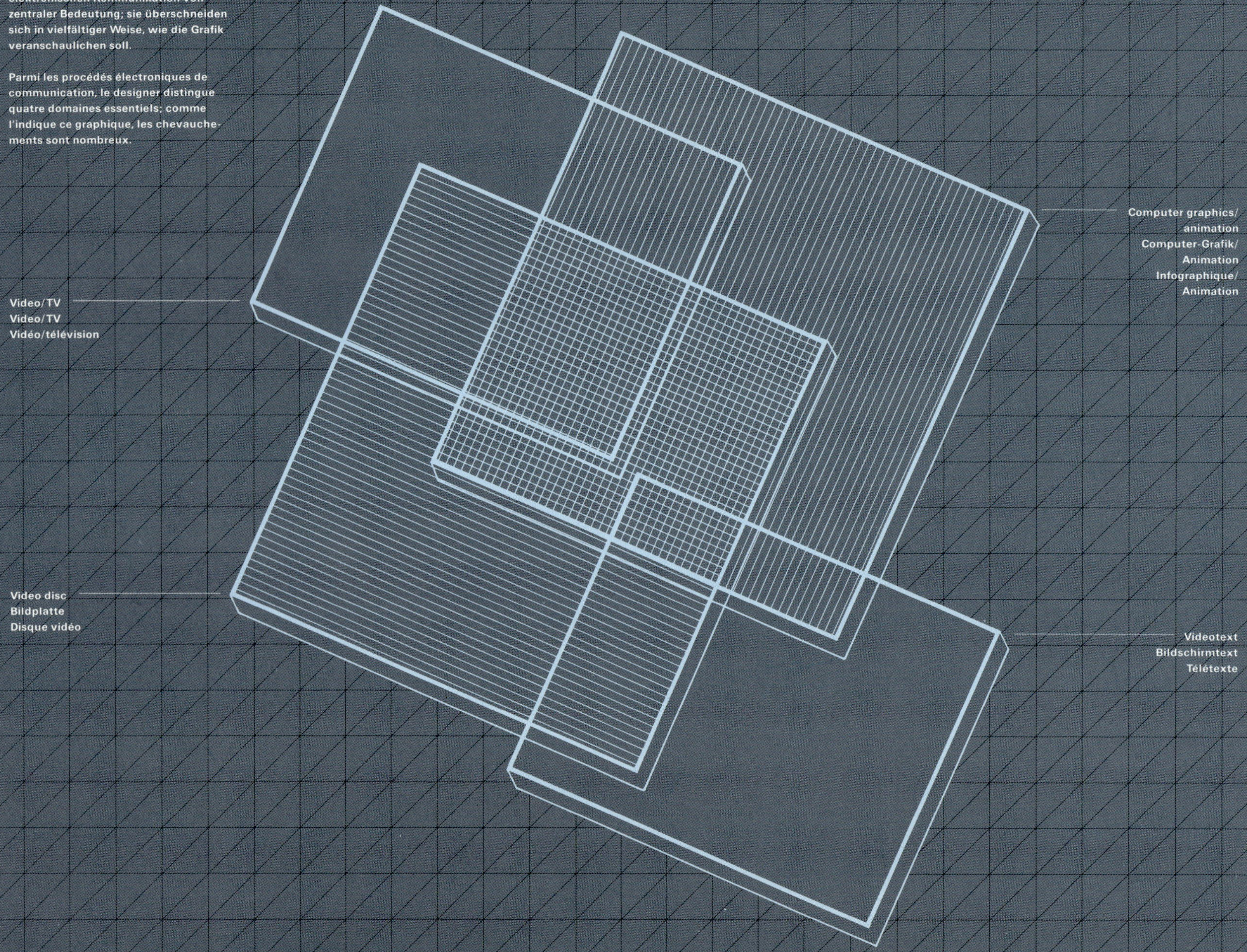

5.2. The influence of the new communication techniques

For several hundred years printing and paper were the only widespread media techniques, on the basis of which an extensive media supply was developed. Film and television brought a differentiation of the media, which has undergone an almost unimaginable acceleration since the emergence of microelectronics. Video, the microcomputer, videotext, video disc, computer graphics and CD-ROM are not new media but new media technologies, each of which produces a multitude of media supplies, which will hardly be less than those of the print sector. This estimate is particularly apt when one also considers the possibilities of mixed media.

The catchphrase "new media" signifies, in a general way, a development in which the most varied forms of electronic communication are gaining more and more importance. On closer examination it can be seen that, in this development, new techniques are mixed with new forms of communication and both aspects with new fields of application, where purely quantitative factors play a part which is not to be underestimated. Thus the use of video is not new, but the rapid growth in the number of applications of video techniques compels designers to pay more attention to the possibilities of this medium. Cable TV and satellite TV are no more than new channels of distribution, but one must nevertheless pay more attention to the design of the TV medium in the competition between publicly-owned and private networks. Computer graphics and computer animation are already profiting from this development. By contrast, new techniques such as videotext and disc bring a new quality of interactivity to electronic communication, creating a completely new field of activity for the designer.

5.2. Der Einfluss der neuen Kommunikationstechniken

Über einige hundert Jahre waren Druck und Papier die einzige verbreitete Medientechnik, auf deren Basis sich ein breites Medienangebot entwickelte. Mit Film und Fernsehen begann eine Ausdifferenzierung der Medien, die seit dem Auftauchen der Mikroelektronik eine fast unvorstellbare Beschleunigung erfahren hat: Video, Mikrocomputer, Bildschirmtext, Bildplatte, Computergrafik und CD-ROM sind nicht neue Medien, sondern neue Medientechnologien, von denen jede eine Vielfalt von Medienangeboten hervorbringt, die der Vielfalt im Printbereich kaum nachstehen wird. Dies insbesondere auch, wenn man die möglichen Medienkombinationen mit einbezieht.

Das Schlagwort von den «neuen Medien» bezeichnet etwas undifferenziert eine Entwicklung, in der die verschiedensten Formen der elektronischen Kommunikation immer mehr an Bedeutung gewinnen. Bei genauerem Hinsehen vermischen sich in dieser Entwicklung neue Techniken mit neuen Formen der Kommunikation und beide Aspekte wiederum mit neuen Anwendungsbereichen, wobei vielfach schlicht quantitative Gesichtspunkte eine nicht zu unterschätzende Rolle spielen. So ist der Einsatz von Video nichts Neues, doch zwingt die sprunghaft gestiegene Zahl der Videoanwendungen die Gestalter zu einer verstärkten Auseinandersetzung mit den Möglichkeiten dieses Mediums. Kabel- und Satellitenfernsehen sind nichts weiter als neue Verteilwege, dennoch wird man der Gestaltung des Mediums Fernsehen in der Konkurrenz zwischen öffentlich-rechtlichen Anstalten und privaten Anbietern vermehrt Aufmerksamkeit widmen müssen. Schon heute profitieren Computergrafik und Computeranimation von dieser Entwicklung. Demgegenüber bringen neue Techniken, wie Bildschirmtext und Bildplatte, mit der Interaktivität eine neue Qualität in die elektronische Kommunikation, die für den Gestalter ein völlig neues Aufgabenfeld mit sich bringt.

5.2. L'influence des nouvelles techniques de communication

Pendant quelques siècles, l'impression sur papier a constitué la seule technique de communication largement diffusée et sur la base de laquelle s'est développée une large offre médiatique. Le cinéma et la télévision ont marqué une première diversification des médias qui s'accélère à une vitesse extraordinaire depuis l'apparition de la microélectronique: vidéo, micro-ordinateur, télétexte, vidéodisque, infographie et CD-ROM ne sont pas de nouveaux médias, mais de nouvelles techniques médiatiques. Chacune d'entre elles apporte une variété d'offres médiatiques qui n'est guère en deçà de la diversité apportée par l'imprimerie. C'est d'autant plus vrai si l'on prend en considération les différentes combinaisons de médias possibles.

L'expression «nouveaux médias» désigne de manière assez peu nuancée une évolution qui fait une part toujours plus belle aux formes les plus variées de la communication électronique. Une analyse plus poussée de ce développement révèle que de nouvelles techniques s'y mèlent avec de nouvelles formes de communication et que ces deux composantes se combinent à leur tour avec de nouveaux domaines d'application, les aspects purement quantitatifs jouant un rôle non négligeable. Ainsi, l'utilisation de la vidéo ne représente rien de nouveau, mais la croissance extraordinaire de ses applications oblige les créateurs à approfondir leur réflexion sur les possibilités de ce média. La télévision par câble et par satellite n'offre en fait que de nouveaux canaux de diffusion: cependant, il sera nécessaire de prêter une attention redoublée à la conception du média télévision dans la concurrence entre les entreprises du secteur public et les compagnies privées. L'infographie et l'animation par ordinateur bénéficient déjà de ce développement. D'autre part, de nouvelles techniques comme le télétexte et le vidéodisque apportent, grâce à l'interactivité, une nouvelle qualité à la communication électronique.

For the training of designers, four areas of electronic communication are of central importance. They overlap one another in many ways, as shown by the graphic illustration.

While video and videotext have nothing in common, the video disc combines elements of both media and computer graphics finds applications in all three, although its biggest field is still outside them, namely in the printing sector. With regard to the video disc, it is evident that it has a need for computer graphics or animation which goes well beyond the sector conditioned by video or videotext. The source of this need will become clear when the individual subjects are discussed. At this point, in order to clarify the importance of these techniques for design practice, we give a brief summary of the various fields of application.

It is hard to say whether the video boom at the *point of sale* is not already in a state of decline. If so, this is mainly due to problems of equipment maintenance and wear and tear of tapes. Both these problems are largely overcome by the use of the video disc, giving a new stimulus to video in terms of usage. This tendency is supported by the interactivity of the video disc, leading to active use of information by the consumer, who is so to speak watered with useful facts.

This trend can also be observed in the use of video at *exhibitions and trade fairs.* Here the video disc also penetrates the area of traditional multivision; but the possibilities of this area are not yet exhausted, if one considers, for example, the possible uses of computer graphics.

Also on the way in is video in the *customer service* sector, but for reasons of cost the video disc is hardly a contender in this sector. Despite a relatively slow start, it can be assumed that videotext will become an impor-

Für die Ausbildung von Gestaltern sind vier Bereiche der elektronischen Kommunikation von zentraler Bedeutung; sie überschneiden sich in vielfältiger Weise, wie die vorangestellte Grafik veranschaulichen soll.

Während Video und Btx keine Gemeinsamkeiten haben, verbindet die Bildplatte Elemente beider Medien miteinander. Die Computergrafik findet in allen drei Medien ihre Anwendung, hat ihr grösstes Anwendungsfeld aber immer noch ausserhalb, nämlich im Printsektor. Im Hinblick auf die Bildplatte fällt auf, dass sie einen Bedarf an Computergrafik bzw. -animation hat, der über den Video- oder Btx-bedingten Teil deutlich hinausgeht. Woher das kommt, wird bei der Behandlung der einzelnen Themen deutlich. Um jedoch die Bedeutung dieser Techniken für die Praxis des Gestalters erkennbar werden zu lassen, sei zunächst kurz auf die Anwendungsbereiche hingewiesen.

Es ist schwer zu sagen, ob der Videoboom am *Point-of-Sale* nicht schon wieder am Abklingen ist. Wenn, so liegt dies vor allem an Problemen mit der Wartung der Geräte und dem Verschleiss der Bänder. Beide Probleme werden durch den Einsatz der Bildplatte weitgehend ausgeschlossen, so dass Video am Einsatz gemessen wieder Auftrieb erhält. Unterstützt wird diese Tendenz durch die Interaktivität der Bildplatte, die von der passiven Berieselung des Konsumenten zur aktiven Informationsnutzung führt.

Dieser Trend ist auch beim Videoeinsatz auf *Messen und Ausstellungen* zu beobachten. Hier dringt die Bildplatte auch in den Bereich der traditionellen Multivision ein. Aber auch die Möglichkeiten der Multivision sind heute noch nicht ausgeschöpft, wenn man beispielsweise an den Einsatz der Computergrafik in diesem Feld denkt.

Weiterhin im Kommen ist Video im Bereich der *Kundenberatung,* dabei ist aus Kostengründen kaum an den Einsatz der Bildplatte zu denken. Trotz des relativ langsamen Starts kann man davon ausgehen, dass Bild-

Quatre domaines de la communication électronique revêtent une importance capitale pour la formation des créateurs; ces secteurs se chevauchent sur bien des points, comme l'illustre la figure.

Si la vidéo et le télétexte n'ont rien en commun, le vidéodisque relie certains éléments des deux premiers. L'infographie trouve son application dans ces trois médias. Néanmoins, son champ d'application principal se situe ailleurs: dans le secteur de l'impression. L'on remarque que le vidéodisque a besoin de l'infographie ou de l'animation élaborée par ordinateur dans une mesure qui dépasse largement celle que réclame la composante vidéo ou télétexte. L'examen des différents médias permettra d'expliquer ce phénomène. Parlons tout d'abord des champs d'application de ces différentes techniques afin d'en montrer l'importance pratique pour le créateur.

Il est difficile de déterminer si l'essor fulgurant de la vidéo sur les *points de vente* n'est pas déjà sur le déclin. Si tel est le cas, les raisons en sont principalement les difficultés d'entretien et l'usure des bandes. Ces deux problèmes sont quasiment exclus si l'on a recours au vidéodisque, de sorte que l'utilisation de la vidéo s'intensifie de nouveau. Cette tendance est soutenue par l'interactivité du vidéodisque, qui permet de passer de l'arrosage passif du consommateur à une exploitation active de l'information.

On observe la même évolution dans l'utilisation de la vidéo sur les *foires* et dans les *expositions.* Le vidéodisque y fait irruption dans le champ de la multivision traditionnelle. Toutefois, l'on n'a pas encore épuisé les possibilités de la multivision: que l'on pense, par exemple, à l'utilisation de l'infographie dans ce secteur.

La vidéo se développe dans le domaine du *conseil à la clientèle.* Il n'est ici guère envisageable d'utiliser le vidéodisque en raison de son coût. Malgré un début assez lent, tout porte à penser que le télétexte jouera un rôle considérable pour le premier

tant medium in this sector for first contacts and planned initial advice, particularly in the field of capital goods.

The association of teletext with video disc will have a lasting influence, particularly in the *technical service* sector. In view of the increasing rate of change of products and machine models, the video disc offers the ideal medium for on-site training of service technicians. In this case, savings in time and cost, together with improved quality of service, will quickly pay for the relatively high costs of video disc production. Videotext allows spare parts to be promptly ordered and the video disc supplies the instructions for fitting.

Here, as everywhere in the *education and training* sector, the need to illustrate technical procedures and connections gives the designer some interesting tasks, using computer graphics and animation as suitable tools.

5.2.1. Design contributions of electronic communication

Computer graphics and animation
The rapid development of computer technology has given the graphic artist a new instrument. A computer graphics system can best be compared with a synthesizer in music. Just as the synthesizer simulates musical instruments, the graphic system simulates instruments such as the pencil, ruler and compasses, paintbrush, airbrush and eraser. What makes the graphic system superior to these instruments, apart from its speed in producing lines and shapes, is the ability to revise the results, so that alternative designs can be considered without much expenditure of time or cost. Especially with 3D systems, the objects that have been constructed can be manipulated in their three dimensions. The recording of such manipulations in time sequence produces computer animation (see illustration on the next page).

schirmtext in diesem Bereich ein wichtiges Medium für den ersten Kontakt und die gezielte Anfangsberatung werden wird. Dies wird vor allem im Investitionsgütersektor gelten.

Die Verbindung von Btx und Bildplatte wird insbesondere den *Servicebereich* auf längere Sicht nachhaltig beeinflussen. Angesichts der immer schneller werdenden Produkt- oder Modellwechsel stellt die Bildplatte das ideale Medium für die Schulung von Servicetechnikern vor Ort dar. Zeit- und Kostenersparnis sowie die Qualität des Service machen hier die relativ hohen Kosten einer Bildplattenproduktion schnell bezahlt. Über Btx ist ein Ersatzteil schnell bestellt, die Bildplatte liefert die Montageanleitung.

Hier wie überhaupt im Bereich *Schulung und Ausbildung* stellt die Notwendigkeit der Veranschaulichung technischer Vorgänge und Zusammenhänge dem Gestalter hochinteressante Aufgaben, wobei Computergrafik und -animation die passenden Werkzeuge liefern.

5.2.1. Gestaltungsbeiträge elektronischer Kommunikation

Computergrafik und -animation
Die rasante Entwicklung der Computertechnologie hat dem Grafiker ein neues Werkzeug in die Hand gegeben. Am ehesten kann man ein Computergrafiksystem mit einem Synthesizer in der Musik vergleichen. Wie der Synthesizer Musikinstrumente simuliert, so simuliert das Grafiksystem Werkzeuge wie Bleistift, Lineal und Zirkel, Pinsel, Sprühpistole oder Radiernadel. Was das Grafiksystem diesen Werkzeugen überlegen macht, ist neben der Schnelligkeit, mit der sich Linien und Figuren konstruieren lassen, die Revidierbarkeit der Arbeitsergebnisse, so dass sich Gestaltungsalternativen ohne grossen Aufwand abprüfen lassen. Besonders bei 3D-Systemen können einmal konstruierte Gegenstände im Raum manipuliert werden. Aus der Aufzeichnung solcher Manipulationen im Zeitablauf ergibt sich die Computeranimation (siehe Abbildung nächste Seite).

contact et l'apport de conseils initiaux spécifiques, notamment dans le secteur des biens d'équipement.

C'est principalement sur le *service après-vente* que la combinaison du télétexte et du vidéodisque va exercer une influence durable. Comme les produits ou les modèles changent de plus en plus rapidement, le vidéodisque constitue le média idéal pour la formation sur place des techniciens du service après-vente. Les économies de temps et d'argent ainsi que la qualité du service permettent d'amortir rapidement les frais relativement élevés de la production de vidéodisques. Le télétexte permet de commander rapidement une pièce de rechange, et le vidéodisque fournit les instructions de montage.
Ce domaine, comme celui de la *formation* en général, offre au créateur des missions fort intéressantes en raison de la nécessité d'illustrer des procédés techniques. L'infographie et l'animation élaborée par ordinateur sont ici des instruments appropriés.

5.2.1. Les contributions de la communication électronique à la création

Infographie et animation élaborée par ordinateur
L'évolution fulgurante de l'informatique a donné un nouvel instrument au graphiste. Un système graphique informatisé est comparable à un synthétiseur dans le domaine musical. Tout comme le synthétiseur simule des instruments de musique, le système graphique simule des instruments comme le crayon, la règle et le compas, le pinceau, le pistolet pulvérisateur ou le burin. Le système graphique surpasse ces instruments: d'une part, il permet de créer des lignes et des figures avec une grande rapidité, d'autre part, et surtout, il permet de réviser les résultats obtenus, de sorte que plusieurs solutions peuvent être évaluées sans que cela entraîne de dépenses excessives. Les systèmes en relief permettent de manipuler dans l'espace des objets réalisés. L'animation élaborée par ordinateur naît de l'enregistrement périodique de ces manipulations (voir illustration à la page suivante).

Bibo TV D 314, 315
R. Scott Miller D 316
ECG TV-Studio D 317–322

Today it can be established that colour photography, despite its versatility and exactness, is a static affair in comparison with a computer system.
The camera can record only what it sees; but a future demand will be to make the invisible visible.
Television has a great need for graphics, as is made clear by the logos of various TV stations reproduced here.
The true field of activity of computer animation in the future, however, will be found in the scientific and technical sector.
Here is the field of activity, for example in explaining the functioning of a braking system or demonstrating the qualities of a motor oil.

Heute kann man feststellen, dass die Farbfotografie trotz ihrer Vielseitigkeit und Exaktheit im Vergleich zu einem Computersystem eine statische Angelegenheit ist.
Die Kamera kann nur das aufnehmen, was sie sieht. Zukünftig geht es aber um die Forderung: Unsichtbares sichtbar zu machen.
Das Fernsehen hat einen grossen Bedarf an TV-Grafik, wie die hier vorgestellten Logos verschiedener Fernsehanstalten verdeutlichen.
Das eigentliche Aufgabenfeld der Computeranimation ist aber zukünftig im Bereich von Wissenschaft und Technik zu sehen.
Hier liegt das Feld, um beispielsweise die Funktionsweise eines Bremssystems zu erklären oder Qualitäten eines Motorenöls zu verdeutlichen.

L'on constate aujourd'hui que la photographie en couleurs, malgré sa polyvalence et sa précision, est un support statique comparé à un système informatique.
L'appareil photo ne peut enregistrer que ce qu'il voit. A l'avenir, on exigera que l'invisible devienne visible.
La télévision a un grand besoin graphique, comme le montrent ces logos de différentes chaînes.
A l'avenir, toutefois, le véritable champ d'application de l'animation élaborée par ordinateur sera la science et la technique.
C'est dans ce domaine qu'il faudra, par exemple, expliquer le fonctionnement d'un système de freinage ou illustrer les qualités d'une huile pour moteurs.

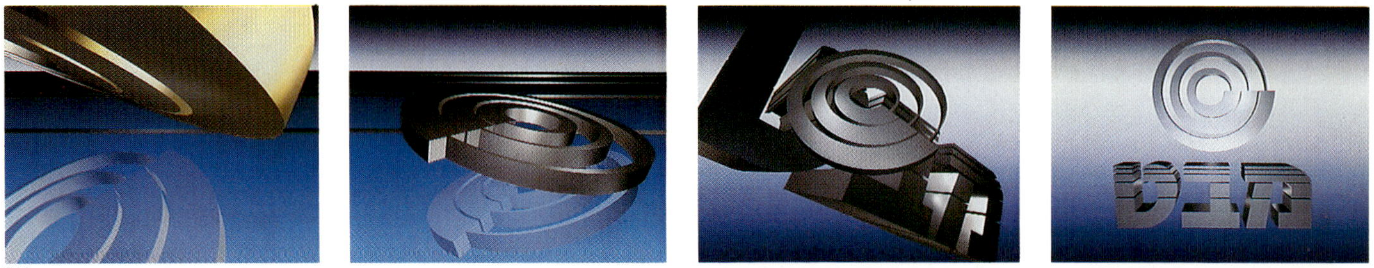
314

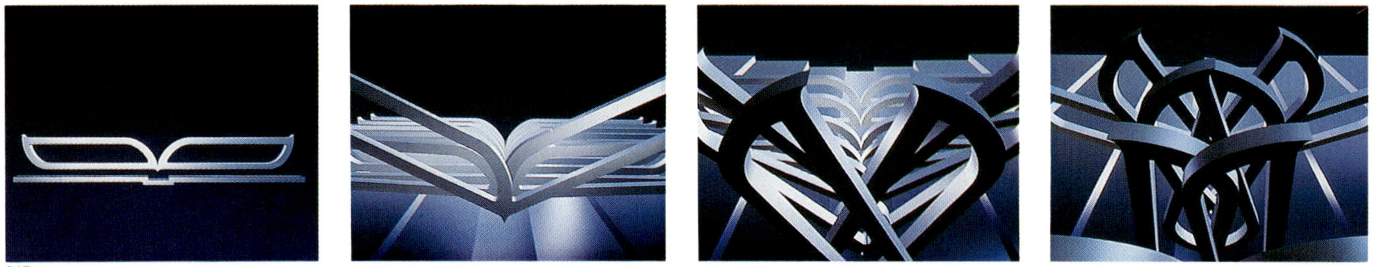
315

316

317

318

319

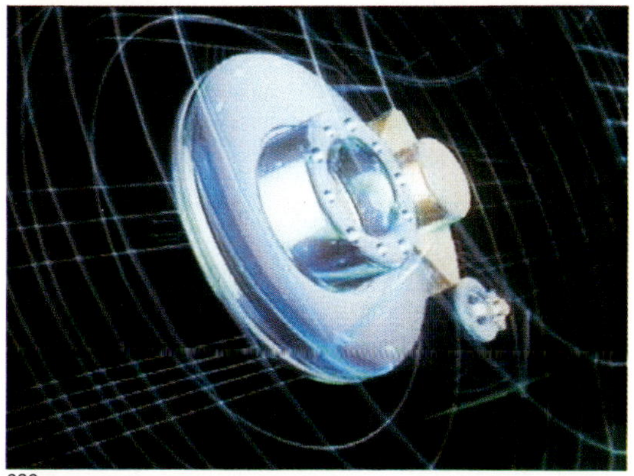
320

321

322

It is clear that the system cannot replace creativity but may offer it new possibilities of development. Surprising at first sight, but on closer inspection only logical, there is a parallel between the semiotic theory of visual communication and the working methods of graphics computers. The facility for manipulating visual patterns in the computer depends on their exact mathematical description. For this purpose, the smallest elements must be defined and the rules described, by which they can be assembled into larger units. This corresponds to the semiotic definition of codes. Textures, outlines and perspectives are only theoretical constructs in the field of semiotics, where they are intended to make the conveyance of visual information comprehensible. In the computer, these elements can be immediately converted into the generation of visual signs and complexes. Thus semiotics provides the understanding of that which happens in construction at the graphic computer, and is therefore an essential precondition for the professional use of such computers.

Videotext
As with graphics computers, the purely technical mastery of the equipment is here to be left out of consideration; nor can the palette of design possibilities be our subject. These factors are simply regarded as essential prerequisites.

Videotext is first and foremost a text medium. For the designer, therefore, its use in the first place is a typographical job, which must meet the conditions of readability on the screen. Graphic elements such as colours, solids and lines fall in with this function. Full graphics require a relatively long production process and may involve substantial waiting times when called up by the user, so their use must be based on their function in the process of information conveyance. The cen-

Aus dieser Darstellung wird deutlich, dass diese Systeme Kreativität nicht ersetzen können, ihr aber neue Entfaltungsmöglichkeiten bieten. Auf den ersten Blick überraschend, bei näherem Hinsehen aber nur logisch, ist die Parallele zwischen der semiotischen Theorie der visuellen Kommunikation und der Arbeitsweise von Grafikcomputern. Die Manipulierbarkeit visueller Muster im Computer setzt deren exakte mathematische Beschreibung voraus. Dazu müssen die kleinsten Elemente definiert und die Regeln beschrieben werden, nach denen sie sich zu grösseren Einheiten zusammenfügen lassen. Dies entspricht der semiotischen Definition der Codes. Texturen, Umrisslinien, Texturgradienten und Perspektive sind im Rahmen der Semiotik nur theoretische Konstrukte, die den Prozess der Vermittlung visueller Information fassbar machen sollen. Im Computer lassen sich diese Elemente unmittelbar in die Generierung visueller Zeichen und Komplexe umsetzen. Die Semiotik vermittelt daher das Verständnis dessen, was bei der Konstruktion am Grafikcomputer vorgeht, und ist damit eine wesentliche Voraussetzung für seine professionelle Handhabung.

Bildschirmtext
Wie beim Grafikcomputer soll auch hier die rein technische Beherrschung der Geräte bei der Betrachtung ausser acht bleiben. Auch die Palette der Gestaltungsmöglichkeiten kann hier nicht Gegenstand sein. Sie werden als unabdingbare Voraussetzungen betrachtet.

Btx ist in erster Linie ein Textmedium. Für den Gestalter stellt es sich damit zunächst einmal als typografische Aufgabe, die den Bedingungen des Lesens am Bildschirm gerecht werden muss. Grafische Elemente, wie Farben, Flächen und Linien, ordnen sich in diese Funktion ein. Ausgesprochene Grafiken erfordern einen relativ grossen Aufwand bei der Erstellung und können beim Abruf durch den Nutzer erhebliche Wartezeiten in Anspruch nehmen, ihr Einsatz muss daher durch ihre Funktion im Prozess der Informationsvermittlung begrün-

La description que nous venons de faire montre clairement que ces systèmes ne peuvent remplacer la créativité. En revanche, ils lui donnent de nouvelles possibilités de s'épanouir. S'il surprend à première vue, le parallélisme entre la théorie sémiotique de la communication visuelle et le fonctionnement des ordinateurs graphiques semble très logique après réflexion. En effet, la possibilité de manipuler des motifs visuels dans l'ordinateur nécessite qu'ils soient au préalable décrits avec une exactitude mathématique. Il est donc nécessaire de définir les plus petits éléments et d'établir les règles qui gouvernent leur assemblage en unités plus grandes. Ceci correspond à la définition sémiotique des codes. En sémiotique, les textures, les lignes de contour, les gradients de texture et les perspectives ne sont que des constructions théoriques qui doivent cependant permettre de comprendre le processus de la transmission de l'information visuelle. Dans l'ordinateur, ces éléments sont transposés directement dans la production de signes et complexes visuels. Ainsi, la sémiotique permet de saisir le processus de la construction à l'aide de l'ordinateur graphique et constitue par là une condition essentielle à son utilisation professionnelle.

Télétexte
Comme pour l'ordinateur graphique, nous ne parlerons pas ici de la maîtrise purement technique des installations. Nous ne pouvons pas non plus étudier ici la palette des possibilités de création. Ces deux éléments sont considérés comme des conditions préalables indispensables.

Le télétexte est avant tout un média «texte». Ainsi, le créateur se trouve d'abord confronté à une tâche typographique qui doit répondre aux conditions de la lecture à l'écran. Les éléments graphiques comme les couleurs, les surfaces et les lignes relèvent de cette fonction. Les réalisations graphiques proprement dites exigent une préparation relativement longue et imposent parfois à l'utilisateur qui les appelle une attente considérable. En conséquence, leur utilisa-

The conditions for the effectiveness of communication are subject to major changes: competition is increasing in communications, new media are being used, the consumer's impressionability is altering, and so on. Advertising must adapt itself to these changed conditions, or its effects will be adversely affected to a high degree.

Dankwart Rost

Die Bedingungen für die Wirksamkeit der Kommunikation sind starken Änderungen unterworfen: Die Informationskonkurrenz nimmt zu, neue Medien werden benutzt, die Beeinflussbarkeit der Konsumenten ändert sich usw. Die Werbung muss sich diesen veränderten Bedingungen anpassen. Andernfalls werden ihre Wirkungen erheblich beeinträchtigt.

Dankwart Rost

Les conditions de l'efficacité de la communication connaissent des bouleversements: la concurrence augmente dans le domaine de l'information, on utilise de nouveaux médias, le caractère influençable des consommateurs varie, etc. La publicité doit s'adapter à ces nouvelles considérations. Sinon, son impact sera gravement compromis.

Dankwart Rost

tral task in the design of videotext information is, however, the meaningful structuring of all the information from the point of view of command by the user. Videotext, as an interactive medium, continually offers the user the possibility of determining the sequence of the information process and choosing the next step in accordance with his needs. The corresponding formal structure of a videotext program is a "search tree", which incorporates all these possible choices and systematically links the components of the information, one with another.

Video disc
Similar requirements with regard to interactivity are encountered in video disc design work. In principle, one could treat the 54,000 single images of one side of a disc as a videotext data bank, with a greatly increased range of possibilities of representation through the use of video stills and film sequences. New requirements arise where the film sequences are neither arranged in a linear fashion nor regarded in isolation, but can be variably assembled on call-up. For this purpose, an interactive scenario has to be produced. In this case, in addition to the structuring of information as a "search tree", there must be formal description by means of flow diagrams, which have to be converted into appropriate programming of the information flow.

The possible use of "trick film" techniques on the video disc makes it particularly appropriate for the representation of technical connections. In this case computer graphics and animation provide the corresponding design medium.

The kinds of possibilities available for video disc control depend very largely on the hardware used. The configurations on the market range from simple section control up to connection with mainframe computers.

det sein. Die zentrale Aufgabe bei der Gestaltung von Btx-Informationsangeboten liegt jedoch in der sinnvollen Strukturierung der Gesamtinformation unter Gesichtspunkten der Nutzerführung. Btx als interaktives Medium bietet dem Nutzer immer wieder die Möglichkeit, den Fortgang des Informationsprozesses selbst zu bestimmen, den nächsten Informationsschritt nach seinen Bedürfnissen auszuwählen. Der entsprechende formale Aufbau eines Btx-Programmes besteht aus einem Suchbaum, der alle diese Wahlmöglichkeiten realisiert und die verschiedenen Informationsbestandteile systematisch miteinander verbindet.

Bildplatte
Im Hinblick auf solche Interaktivität stellen sich bei der Gestaltung einer Bildplatte vergleichbare Anforderungen. Prinzipiell könnte man die 54 000 Einzelbilder einer Bildplattenseite als Btx-Datenbank behandeln, deren Darstellungsmöglichkeiten durch Videostandbilder und Filmsequenzen wesentlich erweitert sind. Neue Anforderungen entstehen jedoch, wenn Filmsequenzen weder linear aneinandergereiht noch isoliert betrachtet werden, sondern beim Abruf variabel zusammengesetzt werden können. Hierfür ist ein interaktives Drehbuch zu erstellen. Neben die Strukturierung der Information in Form von Suchbäumen tritt in diesem Fall die formale Beschreibung durch Flussdiagramme, die dann in entsprechende Programmierungen des Informationsablaufs umgesetzt werden.

Durch die besonderen Tricktechniken, die die Bildplatte bietet, eignet sie sich besonders gut für die Darstellung technischer Zusammenhänge, wobei Computergrafik und -animation die äquivalenten Gestaltungsmittel zur Verfügung stellen.

Welche Möglichkeiten für die Bildplattensteuerung gegeben sind, hängt sehr stark von der jeweils eingesetzten Hardware ab. Die im Markt befindlichen Konfigurationen reichen von der einfachen Kapitelsteuerung bis hin zur Verbindung mit Grossrechnern.

tion doit être justifiée par leur fonction dans le processus de la transmission de l'information. Lors de la conception d'offres informatives destinées au télétexte, la préoccupation centrale doit être de structurer judicieusement l'ensemble des informations en tenant compte du guidage de l'utilisateur. Le télétexte, média interactif, permet à l'utilisateur de déterminer lui-même le déroulement du processus informatif, de choisir l'étape suivante selon ses propres besoins. La structure formelle correspondante d'un programme de télétexte est un schéma d'accès qui réalise toutes ces possibilités de choix et relie systématiquement les différentes composantes de l'information.

Vidéodisque
En raison de l'interactivité, des conditions comparables doivent être remplies lors de la conception d'un vidéodisque. On pourrait en principe utiliser les 54 000 images individuelles d'un vidéodisque comme une banque de données de télétexte, dont les possibilités de représentation sont considérablement élargies par les images vidéo fixes et les séquences filmées. Toutefois, de nouvelles exigences apparaissent si les séquences filmées ne sont pas prises ordonnées linéairement ni isolées mais si l'on veut pouvoir les assembler de manière variable lors de l'interrogation. A cet effet, il est nécessaire de réaliser un scénario interactif. Outre la structuration de l'information sous forme de schémas d'accès, la description formelle se présente ici sous forme d'organigrammes qui sont ensuite transposés en programmations correspondantes du déroulement de l'information.

Les effets spéciaux que permet le vidéodisque sont particulièrement bien adaptés à la représentation de systèmes techniques. L'infographie et l'animation élaborée par ordinateur offrent des moyens de conception.

Les possibilités de commande du vidéodisque dépendent du matériel utilisé. Les configurations que l'on trouve sur le marché vont de la simple commande de section jusqu'à la connexion à des ordinateurs géants.

TEAM / BBDO A 323
M. Eisenbeis D 324

The need for interactivity, i. e. the combination of text, pictures and film sequences, cannot be confined to the possibilities of design. It is a question of creating processes of communication, including the production of interactive scenarios. Our graphics, which visualize the multi-media of the future, show that in addition to the print medium, an effective preparation of information requires video, videotext, video disc and computer animation.
The pictures shown here give evidence that the main concern is the presentation of a homogeneous unity of product and communication.

Die Notwendigkeit der Interaktivität, also die Kombination von Text, Bild und Filmsequenzen, kann sich nicht auf die Möglichkeit des Designs beschränken. Es geht darum, Kommunikationsprozesse zu gestalten, dazu gehört die Erstellung interaktiver Drehbücher. Unsere Grafik, die den zukünftigen Medienverbund visualisiert, zeigt, dass es neben dem Printbereich Video, Bildschirmtext, Bildplatte und Computeranimation sind, die eine mediengerechte Aufbereitung der Information verlangen.
Die hier gezeigten Bilder belegen, dass es vor allem um die Darstellung einer homogenen Einheit von Produkt und Kommunikation geht.

La nécessité de l'interactivité, c'est-à-dire de la combinaison du texte, de l'image et des séquences filmées, ne peut se limiter à la possibilité du design. Il s'agit de concevoir des processus de communication, ce qui inclut la création de scénarios interactifs. Notre illustration représente l'association future des médias. Elle montre qu'un traitement de l'information approprié aux médias est nécessaire non seulement dans le domaine de l'impression, mais aussi pour la vidéo, le télétexte, le vidéodisque et l'animation élaborée par ordinateur.
Ces images montrent qu'il est important de présenter une unité homogène du produit et de la communication.

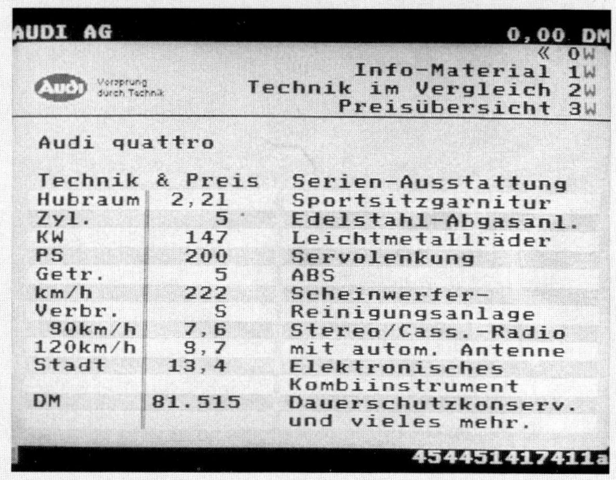

Videotext is in fact a text medium and, through graphic configurations such as diagrams, it offers the possibility of conveying pictorial information as well.
An optimization of such representations is possible through a great number of variables:
for example, underlinings and changes of size. Different modifications of "blink" for the emphasizing of sign elements.
Dynamic page build-up, also making it possible to represent flow movements.

BTX ist eigentlich ein Textmedium und bietet durch grafische Konfigurationen, wie Diagramme, eine Möglichkeit, auch bildliche Informationen zu vermitteln.
Eine Optimierung solcher Darstellungen ist durch zahlreiche Variablen möglich:
wie beispielsweise Unterstreichungen und Grössenveränderungen. Unterschiedliche Blinkmodi zur Hervorhebung von Zeichenelementen.
Dynamischer Seitenaufbau, womit es möglich ist, auch Bewegungsabläufe darzustellen.

Le télétexte est en fait un média «texte», mais il offre aussi la possibilité de transmettre des informations figuratives à l'aide de configurations graphiques, comme les diagrammes.
Ces présentations peuvent être optimisées à l'aide de nombreuses variables:
soulignage, modifications de taille, par exemple.
Modes de clignotement variables pour faire ressortir certains éléments de signe.
Mise en page dynamique permettant de représenter le déroulement de mouvements.

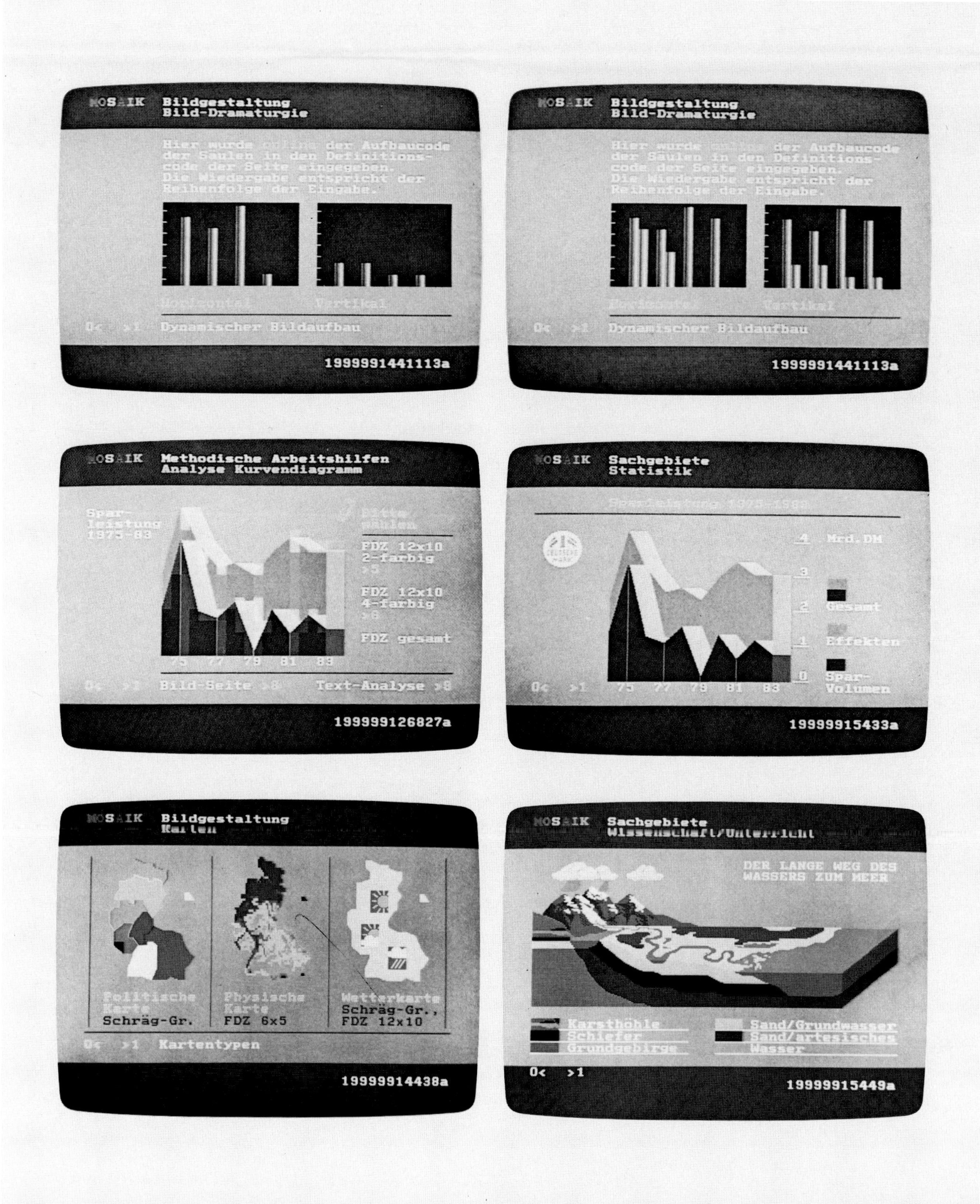

Video, TV
There is no doubt that the increased number of applications of video technology in a great variety of fields gives rise to requirements which have not been sufficiently considered in training or in practice up to now. As in the other sectors mentioned, the problem relates less to the physical manipulation of the equipment, which must naturally form part of the training process, and more to the understanding of these media from the communicative point of view, where the circumstances of reception by the user play a decisive role.

In this connection, an overview and some general comments must suffice. One thing is clear: that we are faced with an overwhelming wave of innovation in communications technology which will directly affect our professional activities.

5.2.2. Qualities of the communications designer

The future is what we make of it. For this reason, those who play such a decisive role in the design of our environment cannot afford to be self-satisfied or indifferent towards the intellectual developments and key subjects of our times. Everything is in a state of flux: new technologies, new materials, new methods of manufacture. We must observe and include these trends in our considerations. At the same time, we must always bear the human element in mind, studying and identifying the great variety of human needs. For this purpose we need better transfer of knowledge and improved collaboration between international associations and organizations. There is also a need for more effective education at all stages.

The perspectives of such a scenario are of interest only when the necessary driving forces are present to put a further development of design into

Video, TV
Es ist keine Frage, dass die vermehrte Zahl von Videoanwendungen in den unterschiedlichsten Bereichen Anforderungen mit sich bringt, denen man in der bisherigen Ausbildung und Praxis nur unzureichend Rechnung getragen hat. Wie in den anderen dargestellten Bereichen auch, bezieht sich dies weniger auf die handwerkliche Handhabung, die selbstverständlich zu den Ausbildungsinhalten gehören muss. Es geht vielmehr darüber hinaus um die Konzeption dieser Medien unter kommunikativen Aspekten, bei denen das jeweilige Umfeld der Rezeptionssituation eine entscheidende Rolle spielt.

Im gegebenen Zusammenhang kann es deshalb bei einem Überblick und mehr allgemeinen Hinweisen bleiben. Eines wird klar – wir stehen an einer ausschlaggebenden Innovationsschwelle der kommunikationstechnischen Entwicklung, die unseren Beruf unmittelbar tangieren wird.

5.2.2. Zum Selbstverständnis des Kommunikationsdesigners

Die Zukunft ist, was wir aus ihr machen. Deshalb ist davon auszugehen, dass sich im Grunde niemand, der an der Gestaltung unserer Umwelt so entscheidend mitarbeitet, selbstzufriedene Gleichgültigkeit gegenüber den geistigen Entwicklungen, den Auseinandersetzungen unserer Zeit leisten kann. Alles ist im Fluss, neue Technologien, neue Materialien, neue Fertigungsmethoden. Wir müssen sie prüfen und in unsere Überlegungen einbeziehen. Wir müssen anderseits dem Menschen gerecht werden und dessen grosse Vielfalt von Bedürfnissen erforschen und erkennen. Dazu brauchen wir einen verstärkten Wissenstransfer, eine verbesserte Zusammenarbeit nationaler und internationaler Verbände und Organisationen. Aber auch eine verstärkte Berücksichtigung der Aus- und Weiterbildung.

Die Perspektiven eines solchen Szenariums sind nur interessant, wenn die notwendigen Antriebskräfte vorhanden sind, die eine Weiterentwicklung

Vidéo, télévision
Sans aucun doute, la multiplication des applications de la vidéo dans les domaines les plus variés impose des exigences auxquelles la formation et la pratique n'ont pas suffisamment prêté attention jusqu'à présent. Comme pour les autres domaines décrits, ce problème ne touche guère l'utilisation purement technique, qui doit bien entendu faire partie de la formation. Il s'agit bien plus de la conception de ces médias du point de vue de la communication, où la situation de réception joue un rôle décisif.

Il est donc possible, dans le contexte présent, d'en rester à une vue d'ensemble et à des indications plus générales. Une chose est certaine: nous nous trouvons à un seuil d'innovation décisif du développement des techniques de communication, et cette évolution va toucher directement notre profession.

5.2.2. De l'image que le designer de communication a de lui-même

L'avenir est ce que nous en faisons. Il faut dès lors considérer qu'aucune personne qui participe de façon aussi décisive à la conception de notre environnement ne peut se permettre d'adopter une attitude d'indifférence suffisante vis-à-vis de la vie intellectuelle et des débats de notre époque. Les nouvelles technologies, les nouveaux matériaux et les nouvelles méthodes de production se succèdent. Nous devons les examiner et les inclure dans notre champ de réflexion. D'autre part, nous devons tenir compte de l'homme, étudier et reconnaître ses multiples besoins. Pour cela, nous avons besoin d'un meilleur transfert des connaissances, d'une meilleure collaboration des associations et organisations internationales. Il faut également renforcer et améliorer la formation et le perfectionnement.

Les perspectives de ce scénario sont intéressantes à condition qu'existent les forces de progrès nécessaires à un développement plus poussé du

It is therefore important to cease regarding the traditional form of design as an isolated object: such things as the design of a desk-lamp, a typewriter, a potato ricer or a piece of furniture, which up to now have been the classic tasks of the designer and have formed the programmes of design schools. We are much more concerned with a global design of the environment and a comprehensive programme, based on environmental psychology, concerned with the influence of the physical environment on human behaviour.

Abraham A. Moles

Es ist daher wichtig, nicht mehr die traditionelle Form des Designs als alleinigen Gegenstand der Betrachtung zu sehen: die Entwürfe von Bürolampen und Schreibmaschinen, von Kartoffelpressen und Möbeln, die bis jetzt die klassische Aufgabenstellung des Designers dargestellt haben – und die das Programm der Schulen bestimmten. Es handelt sich vielmehr um ein globales Design der Umgebung, des Environments und der umfassenden Programme, abgeleitet von der Umweltpsychologie, die sich mit dem Einfluss der physischen Umwelt auf das menschliche Verhalten beschäftigt.

Abraham A. Moles

En conséquence, il est important de ne plus considérer la forme traditionnelle du design comme seul objet d'observation: les projets de lampes de bureau et de machines à écrire, de presse-purée et de meubles qui jusqu'à présent constituaient la mission classique du designer – et qui déterminaient le programme des écoles. Il s'agit bien plus d'un design global de l'environnement et des programmes d'ensemble, dérivé de la psychologie de l'environnement et qui tient compte de l'influence de l'environnement sur le comportement humain.

Abraham A. Moles

effect. Above all, we must thoroughly prepare the next generation of designers for their task, for without creative power there are no "new media", only new techniques with old contents.

The development of the means of communication has always been accompanied by doubts and questions, above all with regard to the communicative relationships of people with one another and with their communications environment. This is not a matter of the anthropologically determined question as to whether we wish to realize everything that is technically possible. The absolutely decisive points for us are the structural changes both in society as a whole and in the labour market, and the need to adapt design education to this development. In the centre of all these considerations stands the greatly increased significance of the information factor in production, as an aspect of political economy, and its relevance for the designer.

5.2.3. Consequences for education

In conclusion, there remains one question to be answered. Do we need such a specialized education? First there was the classical academy, still highly valued today because of its artistic freedom. For many pioneers of advertising art, graphics and design, this was the one and only kind of educational institution, associated as it was with a philosophy of education reaching back well into the 19th century. Secondly, the Bauhaus regarded itself as the modern opposite of this idea and its methods of teaching set standards for the industrial age which reach forward into the present time. The conditions which we can expect for the communications society of the year 2000 are quite different. Seen from this viewpoint, the world is one vast network of communications. For these conditions we need new concepts, so that education will not be exclusively based on short-term considerations. It is only a lack of perspective that can account for the fact that there are now no more "schools"

im Design bewirken können. Vor allem, wenn wir den kreativen Nachwuchs gründlich darauf vorbereiten. Denn ohne die kreativen Kräfte gibt es keine «neuen Medien», sondern allenfalls neue Techniken mit alten Inhalten.

Schon immer haben auch Zweifel und Fragen die Entwicklung der Kommunikationsmittel begleitet. Vor allem im Hinblick auf die kommunikativen Beziehungen der Menschen zueinander und zu ihrer Kommunikationsumwelt. Hier geht es nicht um die anthropologisch gestellte Frage, ob wir alles realisieren wollen, was technisch möglich wäre. Die absolut entscheidenden Gesichtspunkte für uns sind die strukturellen Veränderungen sowohl der Gesellschaft als auch des Arbeitsmarktes und die Notwendigkeit, die Designausbildung dieser Entwicklung anzupassen. Im Mittelpunkt aller Überlegungen steht die gewaltig gewachsene volkswirtschaftliche Bedeutung des Produktionsfaktors Information und seiner Relevanz für den Gestalter.

5.2.3. Konsequenzen für die Ausbildung

Zum Schluss ist noch die Frage zu stellen: Brauchen wir eine so spezialisierte Ausbildung? Denn war die klassische Akademie – gerade weil sie auch heute noch wegen ihres künstlerischen Freiraums geschätzt wird – für viele Pioniere der Werbung, der Grafik und des Designs die Ausbildungsstätte schlechthin, verbunden mit einem Bildungsideal, das weit ins 19. Jahrhundert reichte, so betrachtete sich das Bauhaus als modernen Antipoden dieser Idee und setzte durch die Bauhaus-Pädagogik im industriellen Zeitalter Massstäbe, die bis in die Gegenwart reichen. Nur sind die Bedingungen der Kommunikationsgesellschaft im Jahr 2000 gänzlich anders. Aus dieser Perspektive betrachtet ist die Welt ein riesiges Kommunikationsnetz. Hierzu braucht man neue Konzepte, damit die Ausbildung nicht nur auf kurzfristigen Überlegungen basiert. Nur durch den Mangel an Perspektiven ist es zu erklären, dass es für die Designausbildung keine

design. Il faut dès lors préparer une relève créative qualifiée. En effet, sans forces créatives, il n'y a pas de «nouveaux médias», mais tout au plus de nouvelles techniques avec des contenus anciens.

L'évolution des moyens de communication a toujours été accompagnée de doutes et de questions, notamment au sujet des relations des hommes entre eux et vis-à-vis de leur environnement. Il ne s'agit pas ici de la question anthropologique de savoir si nous voulons réaliser tout ce qui est techniquement possible. Pour nous, les aspects décisifs sont les suivants: les modifications structurelles de la société et du marché du travail, et la nécessité d'adapter la formation des designers à cette évolution. Au centre de toute réflexion se trouve le poids considérablement accru du facteur de production information et son importance pour le créateur.

5.2.3. Conséquences pour la formation

Pour conclure, il reste à poser la question suivante: une formation aussi spécialisée est-elle nécessaire? En effet, si l'académie classique – qui reste appréciée aujourd'hui en raison de sa liberté artistique – a été le seul établissement de formation de nombreux pionniers de la publicité, de la graphique et du design, institution liée à un idéal d'éducation encore en vigueur au XIXe siècle, le Bauhaus s'est considéré comme l'antipode moderne de cette idée et, à l'ère industrielle, a imposé par sa pédagogie des critères qui restent en vigueur à notre époque. Cependant, les réalités de la société de communication de l'an 2000 sont complètement différentes. Vu de cette perspective, le monde est un immense réseau de communication. Ainsi, de nouveaux concepts sont nécessaires, pour que la formation ne soit pas basée sur des considérations à court terme. Seul le manque de perspectives explique qu'il n'existe plus pour la formation en design «d'écoles», dont les spécialistes, les

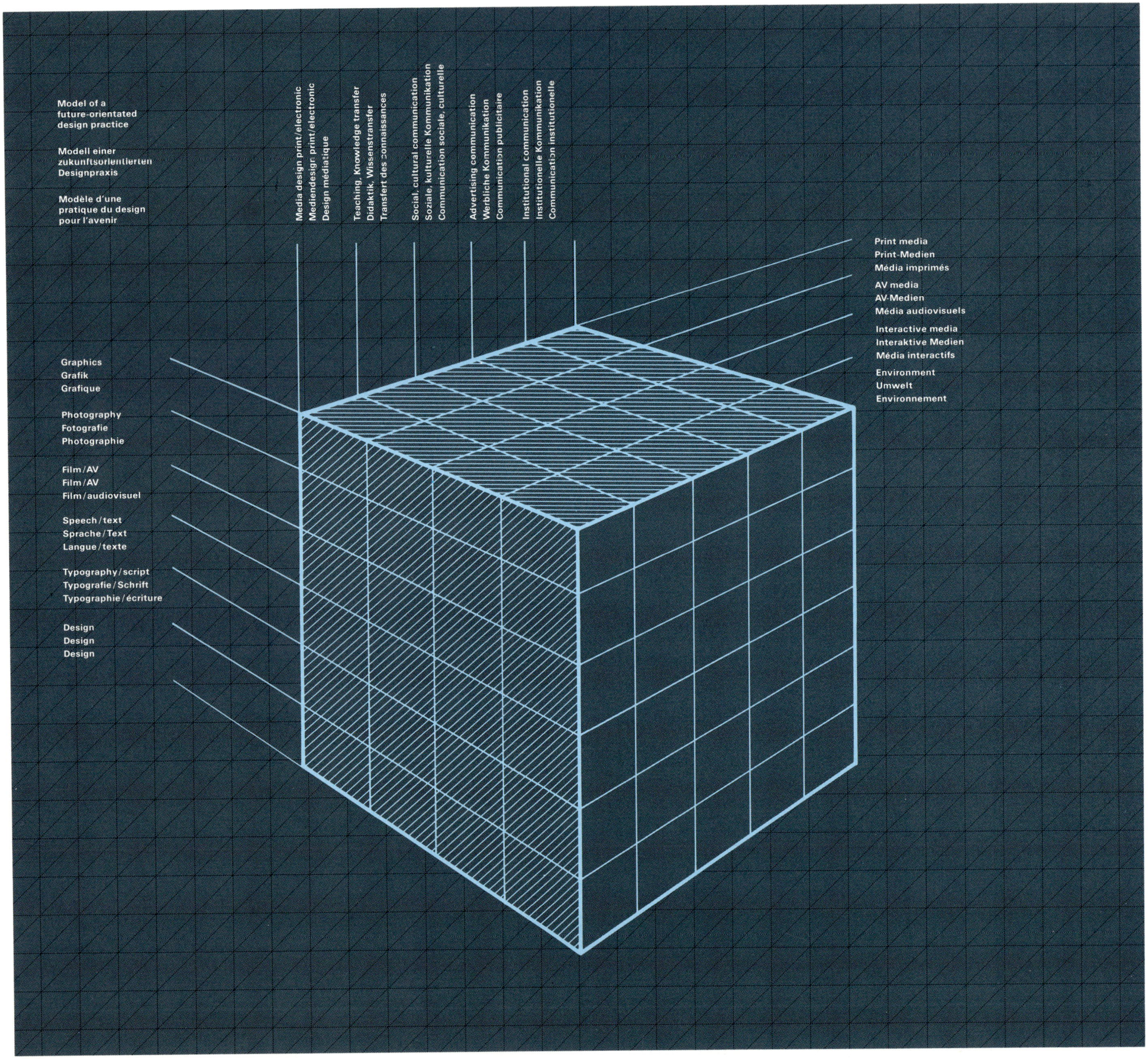
Model of a
future-orientated
design practice
Modell einer
zukunftsorientierten
Designpraxis
Modèle d'une
pratique du design
pour l'avenir
Media design print/electronic
Mediendesign print/electronic
Design médiatique
Teaching, Knowledge transfer
Didaktik, Wissenstransfer
Transfert des connaissances
Social, cultural communication
Soziale, kulturelle Kommunikation
Communication sociale, culturelle
Advertising communication
Werbliche Kommunikation
Communication publicitaire
Institutional communication
Institutionelle Kommunikation
Communication institutionelle
Print media
Print-Medien
Média imprimés
AV media
AV-Medien
Média audiovisuels
Interactive media
Interaktive Medien
Média interactifs
Environment
Umwelt
Environnement
Graphics
Grafik
Grafique
Photography
Fotografie
Photographie
Film/AV
Film/AV
Film/audiovisuel
Speech/text
Sprache/Text
Langue/texte
Typography/script
Typografie/Schrift
Typographie/écriture
Design
Design
Design

of design education with an influential character fully recognized by practitioners, educators and politicians. From this point of view it is only natural that freedom of communication in a human environment must be one of the systems of values to be mediated. This sociopolitical aspect tells us much about the risks, and also the opportunities, of the future.

In this respect, the designer is directly involved in the process of economic and social change, and in the future he will need to take on a new social role. This is primarily a matter of communicating company images, products and advertising messages, but at the same time the designer must make their meaning more open to examination for future development. The question is how he is to fulfil this new role as communicator. Finally, mention must be made of one more perspective that is traced out by development and, through research, is applied to the designer. It is well known how strongly the material conditions of the environment influence human behaviour, with the consequence that every manipulation of the environment entails a changing effect on the individual. It must be emphasized that those who make a substantial contribution to the design of our environment obtain a social position which is now recognizable only in its early stages. This position can no longer be only that of an "auxiliary" of production or a mediator between producer and consumer. The extension of the design function outlined here is fundamentally new and can be reduced to a brief common denominator: the designer is becoming one who creates and interprets values.

As documented in this book, modern design practice exists in a state of tension between the unavoidable specialization of the jobs in hand and the wide use of means often necessary for their solution. This network of fields of activity, media and communication techniques is shown in the accompanying matrix diagram.

«Schulen» gibt, deren prägender Charakter von Fachleuten, Erziehern und Politikern immer wieder betont wird. Aus dieser Sicht ist es nur natürlich, dass die Freiheit von Kommunikation in einer humanen Umwelt zu dem zu vermittelnden Wertesystem gehören muss. Dieser gesellschaftspolitische Aspekt hat eine nicht zu unterschätzende Aussagekraft über die Risiken, aber auch die Chancen der Zukunft.

Somit ist der Designer direkt am Prozess des wirtschaftlichen und sozialen Wandels beteiligt. Nur wird er in Zukunft eine neue soziale Rolle übernehmen müssen. So geht es zwar primär um die Vermittlung von Unternehmensbildern, Produkten oder Werbebotschaften, aber er muss auch verstärkt deren Bedeutung für die zukünftige Entwicklung einsehbar machen. Die Frage ist, wie er diese neue Kommunikatorenrolle ausfüllt. Zuletzt wäre noch eine Perspektive zu erwähnen, die von der Entwicklung vorgezeichnet und durch die Forschung an den Designer herangetragen wird. Man weiss, wie sehr die materiellen Gegebenheiten der Umgebung das Verhalten der Menschen beeinflussen und infolgedessen jede Manipulation der Umgebung eine Veränderung des Individuums nach sich zieht. Damit soll unterstrichen werden, dass derjenige, der in so erheblichem Masse zur Gestaltung unserer Umwelt beiträgt, eine gesellschaftliche Position erhält, die erst in den Ansätzen erkennbar wird. Dies wäre dann nicht mehr das Bild einer Hilfskraft der Produktion oder eines Vermittlers zwischen Produzent und Konsument. Die hiermit angesprochene Funktionserweiterung ist grundsätzlich neu, sie lässt sich auf einen kurzen Nenner bringen: Der Designer wird selbst einer, der erschafft; er interpretiert die Werte.

Wie in diesem Buch dokumentiert, bewegt sich die Designpraxis in einem Spannungsfeld von unvermeidlicher Spezialisierung der Aufgaben und dem oft für die Lösung notwendigen breiten Einsatz von Mitteln. Diese Vernetzung von Aufgabenfeldern, Medien und Kommunikationstechniken wird durch die abgebildete Matrix deutlich.

enseignants et les hommes politiques soulignent constamment le caractère essentiel. De ce point de vue, il est naturel que la liberté de communiquer dans un environnement humain doive figurer parmi les systèmes de valeurs à transmettre. N'oublions pas que cet aspect social exprime à la fois les risques que nous réserve l'avenir et les chances qu'il nous offre.

Ainsi, le designer participe directement au processus de changement social et économique. A l'avenir, il devra assumer un nouveau rôle social. Bien entendu, il s'agit avant tout de la transmission d'images d'entreprises, de produits ou de messages publicitaires, mais il doit également montrer plus clairement leur importance pour le développement futur. La question est de savoir comment il va remplir ce nouveau rôle de communicateur. Mentionnons encore une perspective ébauchée par l'évolution et soumise au designer par la recherche. L'on sait à quel point les caractéristiques matérielles de l'environnement influencent le comportement de l'homme, et par conséquent comment chaque manipulation de cet environnement provoque une modification de l'individu. Nous voulons souligner par là que quiconque contribue de façon décisive à l'aménagement de notre cadre de vie occupe une position sociale que l'on commence seulement à percevoir. Il ne s'agirait plus de l'image d'un «auxiliaire» de la production ou d'un intermédiaire entre le producteur et le consommateur. Cet élargissement de la fonction est fondamentalement nouveau et peut être résumé comme suit: le designer devient lui-même quelqu'un qui crée, il interprète les valeurs.

Cet ouvrage illustre la tension existant pour la pratique du design moderne, entre l'inévitable spécialisation des tâches, et l'utilisation pourtant indispensable de moyens nécessairement trop répandus. L'enchevêtrement entre les domaines spécialisés, les média et les techniques de communication est représenté sur cette figure.

Impressum
Impressum

Auteur et conception graphique
Heinz Kroehl

Traductions
Andrew Bluhm, anglais
Benoît Willaume, français

Couverture du livre
Kazumasa Nagai
Heinz Kroehl

Photolithographies
Cliché+Litho AG, Zurich

Production générale
Offset+Buchdruck AG, Zurich

Autor und grafische Gestaltung
Heinz Kroehl

Übersetzungen
Andrew Bluhm, Englisch
Benoît Willaume, Französisch

Schutzumschlag
Kazumasa Nagai
Heinz Kroehl

Fotolithos
Cliché+Litho AG, Zürich

Gesamtherstellung
Offset+Buchdruck AG, Zürich

Author and graphic design
Heinz Kroehl

Translations
Andrew Bluhm, English
Benoît Willaume, French

Book-jacket
Kazumasa Nagai
Heinz Kroehl

Color separations
Cliché+Litho AG, Zurich

Total production
Offset+Buchdruck AG, Zurich

ISBN 3-85504-106-7
Printed in Switzerland